The Poetry Teacher's Book of Lists

Sylvia M. Vardell

Pomelo Books
4580 Province Line Road
Princeton, NJ 08540
www.pomelobooks.com
info@pomelobooks.com

ISBN-13: 978-1475100747
ISBN-10: 1475100744

Of Making Lists

Imagine all the books to recommend
If hours were limitless as drops of rain.
Of making lists in life there is no end.

Bestsellers to the classics, deftly-penned
Short stories, novels—it can be a strain
Imagining the books to recommend.

Take poetry, for instance, you could lend
The obvious or go against the grain—
Remaking lists in life? There is no end.

Present this book, especially to a friend
Of poetry for the young, and then explain
Imagine all the books to recommend….

Well, this one does it for you, it's a blend
Of old and new that's sure to entertain.
Of making lists in life there is no end.

And with the book, you get a dividend:
A one-way ticket on a nonstop train
Imagining the books you'd recommend!
Of making lists in life there is no end.

J. Patrick Lewis
Children's Poet Laureate

Introduction

Dear Reader,

Are you a lover of lists like I am? I'm guessing you are and I hope you find this book helpful in providing a rich variety of bibliographies, tips, and strategies for selecting and sharing poetry with the young people in your life. This book is intended for teachers, librarians, and parents who are looking for input on selecting poetry for young people ages 0-18. It contains 155 different lists and cites nearly 1500 poetry books—in a variety of categories:

1. Poetry Awards and "Best" Lists (27)
2. Seasonal and Holiday Poetry Booklists (19)
3. Multicultural and International Poetry Booklists (7)
4. Thematic or Topical Poetry Booklists (6)
5. Poetry Booklists Across the Curriculum (21)
6. Booklists Highlighting the Form of Poetry (20)
7. Creating a Poetry-Friendly Environment (19)
8. Sharing and Responding to Poetry Out Loud (12)
9. Teaching Poetry Writing (15)
10. General Poetry Teaching Resources (9)

If you are looking for poetry books for Mother's Day or for a unit on insects and bugs, for example, or you want to be sure you have all the major poetry award winners, look no further. You'll find lists for each of those. I've scoured the best and most popular poetry books published for young people and corralled them for you in multiple lists here. The focus is largely on books published since 1990, although there are many wonderful poetry books published before this date and unfortunately many titles cited that are already out of print, but all may still be available on library shelves or for purchase as "used." All the poetry books are put in topical categories, but many books can serve more than one category, of course. The topics are admittedly ethnocentric in terms of the (North American) holidays, seasons, and books that are cited, but with international connections made wherever possible. New poetry books are being published all the time and I am sure I've missed some older favorites too, so I welcome suggestions for additions to the lists on the supplemental blog: **PoetryTeachersBookofLists.Blogspot.com**.

I'd like to thank Children's Poet Laureate J. Patrick Lewis for his generosity in sharing his clever villanelle, "Of Making Lists" to open this book and poet and friend Janet Wong for all her guidance. Thanks also to my graduate students (especially Christina Russ Winckler and Catherine Allicia Saldana) for their help with various parts of this project. My blog readers and commenters, professional friends and colleagues, and the children's poet community at large have also been so wonderfully kind and enthusiastic. Thank you, all. But the longest list of thanks (how do I count the ways?) goes to my ever-patient spouse, Russell Vardell, for his seemingly unending patience and support.

Sylvia Vardell

Table of Contents

POETRY AWARDS AND "BEST" LISTS

In this area you will find lists of the winners of the major poetry awards in literature for young people, as well as a round up of established lists that feature the best books of the year in various categories. In addition, there are several lists of recommended poems, poets, anthologies, and poetry collections by age level. Finally, I offer my own annotated list of favorite poetry books for young people by year since 2004. Annual updates of my "favorites" list are available on PoetryforChildren.Blogspot.com

    The NCTE Award for Excellence in Poetry for Children
    Children's Poet Laureate
    Lee Bennett Hopkins Award for Poetry for Children
    The Claudia Lewis Award for Poetry
    The Lion and the Unicorn Award
    Lee Bennett Hopkins Promising Poet Award
    Cybils Award for Poetry
    NCTE Poetry Notables
    Children's Choices Poetry Picks
    Poetry and the Notable Social Studies Trade Books
    Poetry and the Outstanding Science Trade Books
    Joseph Thomas's Canon of U.S. Children's Poetry
    Poetry for the Common Core
    A Canon of Classic Poems for Young People
    Best Multi-Poet Anthologies for Young People
    Most Anthologized Poets for Young People
    50 Poetry Books for the Very Young Child (Ages 0-5)
    100 Poetry Books for Children (Ages 6-12)
    100 Poetry Books for Young Adults (Ages 13-18)
    Favorite Poetry for Young People 2011
    Favorite Poetry for Young People 2010
    Favorite Poetry for Young People 2009
    Favorite Poetry for Young People 2008
    Favorite Poetry for Young People 2007
    Favorite Poetry for Young People 2006
    Favorite Poetry for Young People 2005
    Favorite Poetry for Young People 2004

The NCTE Award for Excellence in Poetry for Children

The National Council of Teachers of English established its Award for Excellence in Poetry for Children in 1977 to honor a living American poet for his or her lifetime achievement in works for children ages 3–13. The award was given annually until 1982, at which time it was decided that the award would be given every three years. In 2008 the Poetry Committee updated the criteria and changed the time frame to every other year. For award updates: http://www.ncte.org/awards/poetry

Recipients

2013	Joyce Sidman
2011	J. Patrick Lewis
2009	Lee Bennett Hopkins
2006	Nikki Grimes
2003	Mary Ann Hoberman
2000	X. J. Kennedy
1997	Eloise Greenfield
1994	Barbara Esbensen
1991	Valerie Worth
1988	Arnold Adoff
1985	Lilian Moore
1982	John Ciardi
1981	Eve Merriam
1980	Myra Cohn Livingston
1979	Karla Kuskin
1978	Aileen Fisher
1977	David McCord

Children's Poet Laureate

The Children's Poet Laureate was established by the Poetry Foundation in 2006 to raise awareness of the fact that children have a natural receptivity to poetry and are its most appreciative audience, especially when poems are written specifically for them. The Children's Poet Laureate receives a $25,000 cash prize and a medallion that includes the inscription "Permit a child to join," taken from an Emily Dickinson poem. The Children's Poet Laureate serves as a consultant to the Foundation for a two-year period and gives at least two major public readings for children and their families, teachers, and librarians during his/her term. He/She will also serve as an advisor to the Poetry Foundation on children's literature, and may engage in a variety of projects and events to help instill a love of poetry among the nation's youngest readers. For award updates:
http://www.poetryfoundation.org/children/poet-laureate

Recipients

2011 J. Patrick Lewis

2008 Mary Ann Hoberman

2006 Jack Prelutsky

Lee Bennett Hopkins Award for Poetry for Children

The Lee Bennett Hopkins award established in 1993 is presented annually to an American poet or anthologist for the most outstanding new book of children's poetry published in the previous calendar year. Web site: http://www.pabook.libraries.psu.edu/activities/hopkins/index.html
For activities and ideas for promoting award and honor books, go to the Lee B. Hopkins Poetry Award Teaching Toolbox here:
http://leebennetthopkinsaward.blogspot.com/

2012   WINNER
Wardlaw, Lee. 2011. *Won Ton: A Cat Tale Told in Haiku.* Ill. by Eugene Yelchin. New York: Henry Holt.

2012   HONOR BOOK
Frost, Helen. 2011. *Hidden.* New York: Farrar, Straus & Giroux.

2011   WINNER
Millen, C. M. 2010. *The Ink Garden of Brother Theophane.* Ill. by Andrea Wisnewski. Watertown, MA: Charlesbridge.

2011   HONOR BOOK
Sidman, Joyce. 2010. *Dark Emperor and Other Poems of the Night.* Ill. by Rick Allen. Boston: Houghton Mifflin Harcourt.

2010   WINNER
Schertle, Alice. 2009. *Button Up.* New York: Houghton Mifflin.

2010   HONOR BOOKS
Franco, Betsy. 2009. *A Curious Collection of Cat*s. San Francisco: Tricycle Press.
Frost, Helen. 2009. *Crossing Stones.* New York: Farrar, Straus & Giroux.
Hoberman, Mary Ann and Winston, Linda. 2009. *The Tree that Time Built; A Celebration of Nature, Science, and Imagination.* Naperville, IL: Sourcebooks.

2009   WINNER
Frost, Helen. 2008. *Diamond Willow.* New York: Farrar, Straus & Giroux.

2009   HONOR BOOKS
McKissack, Patricia. 2008. *Stitchin' and Pullin' a Gee's Bend Quilt.* New York: Random House.
Engle, Margarita. 2008. *The Surrender Tree; Poems of Cuba's Struggle for Freedom.* New York: Henry Holt.

2008   WINNER
Weatherford, Carole Boston. 2007. *Birmingham, 1963.* Honesdale, PA: Wordsong/Boyds Mills Press.

2008   HONOR BOOKS
Grandits, John. 2007. *Blue Lipstick: Concrete Poems.* New York: Clarion.
Sidman, Joyce. 2007. *This is Just to Say; Poems of Apology and Forgiveness.* Boston: Houghton Mifflin.

2007   WINNER
Myers, Walter Dean. 2006. *Jazz.* Ill. by Christopher Myers. New York: Holiday House.

2007   HONOR BOOKS
Prelutsky, Jack. 2006. *Behold the Bold Umbrellaphant* . New York: Greenwillow.
Frost, Helen. 2006. *The Braid.* New York: Farrar, Straus & Giroux.
Siebert, Diane. 2006. *Tour America: A Journey through Poems and Art.* San Francisco, CA: Chronicle.

2006   WINNER
Sidman, Joyce. 2005. *Song of the Water Boatman and Other Pond Poems.* Boston: Houghton Mifflin.

2006   HONOR BOOKS
Nelson, Marilyn. 2005. *A Wreath for Emmett Till.* Boston: Houghton Mifflin.
Nye, Naomi Shihab. 2005. *A Maze Me: Poems for Girls.* New York: Greenwillow.

2005   WINNER
Myers, Walter Dean. 2004. *Here in Harlem: Poems in Many Voices.* New York: Holiday House.

2005   HONOR BOOKS
Nye, Naomi Shihab, ed. 2004. *Is This Forever, or What? Poems and Paintings from Texas.* New York: Greenwillow.
Singer, Marilyn. 2004. *Creature Carnival.* New York: Hyperion.

2004   WINNER
Mitchell, Stephen. 2003. *The Wishing Bone and Other Poems.* Cambridge, MA: Candlewick.

2004   HONOR BOOKS
Ackerman, Diane. 2003. *Animal Sense.* New York: Knopf.
Keyser, Samuel Jay. 2003. *The Pond God and Other Stories.* Asheville, NC: Front Street.
Myers, Walter Dean. 2003. *Blues Journey.* New York: Holiday House.
Smith, Hope Anita. 2003. *The Way a Door Closes.* New York: Henry Holt.

2003   WINNER
Levy, Constance. 2002. *Splash! Poems of Our Watery World.* New York: Orchard.

2003   HONOR BOOKS
Adoff, Jaime. 2002. *The Song Shoots Out of My Mouth.* New York: Dutton.
Testa, Maria. 2002. *Becoming Joe DiMaggio.* Cambridge, MA: Candlewick.
Wayland, April Halprin. 2002. *Girl Coming in for a Landing: A Novel in Poems.* New York: Knopf.

2002   WINNER
Hines, Anna Grossnickle. 2001. *Pieces: A Year in Poems and Quilts.* New York: Greenwillow.

2002   HONOR BOOKS
High, Linda Oatman. 2001. *A Humble Life: Plain Poems.* New York: Eerdmans.
Janeczko, Paul B, comp. 2001. *A Poke in the I: A Collection of Concrete Poems.* Cambridge, MA: Candlewick.
Smith, Charles R., Jr. 2001. *Short Takes: Fast-Break Basketball Poetry.* New York: Dutton.

2001   WINNER
Rosenberg, Liz, ed. 2001. *Light-gathering Poems.* New York: Henry Holt.

2001   HONOR BOOK
Janeczko, Paul B, comp. 2000. *Stone Bench in an Empty Park.* New York: Orchard.

2000   WINNER
Nye, Naomi Shihab, comp. 1999. *What Have You Lost?* New York: Greenwillow.

2000   HONOR BOOKS
Johnston, Tony. 1999. *An Old Shell: Poems of the Galapagos.* New York: Farrar, Straus & Giroux.
Wong, Janet. 1999. *The Rainbow Hand: Poems about Mothers and Children.* New York: Margaret McElderry.

1999   WINNER
Johnson, Angela. 1998. *The Other Side: Shorter Poems.* New York: Orchard.

1998   WINNER
George, Kristine O'Connell. 1997. *The Great Frog Race and Other Poems.* New York: Clarion.

1997   WINNER
Bouchard, Dave. 1996. *Voices from the Wild.* San Francisco: Chronicle Books.

1996   WINNER
Esbensen, Barbara Juster. 1995. *Dance with Me.* New York: HarperCollins.

1995   WINNER

Florian, Douglas. 1994. *Beast Feast: Poems and Paintings.* San Diego, CA: Harcourt Brace.

1994   WINNER

Wood, Nancy. 1993. *Spirit Walker.* New York: Doubleday.

1993   WINNER

Bryan, Ashley. 1992. *Sing to the Sun.* New York: HarperCollins.

The Claudia Lewis Award for Poetry

The Claudia Lewis Award is given by Bank Street College in New York and was established in 1998. The award is given annually for the best poetry book of the year in honor of the late Claudia Lewis, a distinguished children's book expert and longtime member of the Bank Street College faculty and Children's Book Committee. For award updates:
http://www.bnkst.edu/cbc/awards/ and for a toolbox with teaching ideas:
http://claudialewispoetryaward.blogspot.com/

Recipients

2012   *Emma Dilemma: Big Sister Poems* by Kristine O'Connell George (Clarion, 2011) and *The Watch That Ends the Night: Voices from the Titanic* by Allan Wolf (Candlewick, 2011)

2011   *Guyku: A Year of Haiku for Boys* by Bob Raczka (Houghton Mifflin, 2010)

2010   *Red Sings From Treetops; A Year in Colors* by Joyce Sidman (Houghton Mifflin, 2009)

2009   *The Surrender Tree* by Margarita Engle (Henry Holt, 2008)

2008   *Here's a Little Poem; A Very First Book of Poetry* compiled by Jane Yolen and Andrew Fusek Peters (Candlewick, 2007)

2007   none awarded

2006   *A Kick In The Head An Everyday Guide to Poetic Forms* compiled by Paul B. Janeczko (Candlewick, 2005)

2005   *Here in Harlem: Poems in Many Voices* by Walter Dean Myers (Holiday House, 2004)

2004   *The Way a Door Closes* by Hope Anita Smith (Henry Holt, 2003)

2003   *Little Dog and Duncan* by Kristine O'Connell George (Clarion, 2002)

2002   *Love that Dog* by Sharon Creech (HarperCollins, 2001)
and   *Amber was Brave, Essie was Smart* by Vera B. Williams (Greenwillow, 2001)

2001   *Mammalabilia* by Douglas Florian (Harcourt, 2000)

2000   *Stop Pretending; What Happened When My Big Sister Went Crazy* by Sonya Sones (HarperCollins, 1999)

1999   *I, Too, Sing America; Three Centuries of African American Poetry* compiled by Catherine Clinton (Houghton Mifflin, 1998)

1998   *The Invisible Ladder; An Anthology of Contemporary American Poems for Young Readers* compiled by Liz Rosenberg (Henry Holt, 1996)

The Lion and the Unicorn Award for Excellence in North American Poetry

The Lion and the Unicorn Award for Excellence in North American Poetry focuses on North American poetry for young people and carries on the prior tradition begun by the British journal, Signal, to "instigate, provoke, and sustain a conversation about poetry published for children." Recipients are now from both the U.S. and Canada. In addition, the Lion and the Unicorn Award includes an essay which discusses the award winners as well as speculates on issues unique to writing and publishing poetry for children, "painting a picture of that year in children's poetry." The essays can be found here: http://www-rohan.sdsu.edu/~jtthomas/LandUAward.html and for a toolbox with teaching ideas: http://lionandunicornpoetryaward.blogspot.com/

2011 WINNER
Susan Blackaby. *Nest, Nook & Cranny.* Ill. by Jamie Hogan. Watertown, MA: Charlesbridge, 2010.

2011 HONOR BOOKS
Rob Jackson. *Weekend Mischief.* Ill. by Mark Beech. Honesdale, PA: Wordsong/Boyds Mills Press, 2010.
X.J. Kennedy. *City Kids: Street & Skyscraper Rhymes.* Ill. by Philippe Béha. Vancouver: Tradewind Books, 2010.

2010
No award given

2009 WINNER
JonArno Lawson. *A Voweller's Bestiary, from Aardvark to Guineafowl (and H).* Erin, Ontario: Porcupine's Quill, 2008.

2009 HONOR BOOKS
Helen Frost. *Diamond Willow.* New York: Farrar, Straus & Giroux, 2008.
William H. New. *The Year I Was Grounded.* Vancouver: Tradewind Books, 2008.

2008 WINNER
Linda Sue Park. *Tap Dancing on the Roof: Sijo (Poems).* Ill. by Istvan Banyai. New York: Clarion, 2007.

2008 HONOR BOOKS
Jay M. Harris. *The Moon Is La Luna: Silly Rhymes in English & Spanish.* Ill. by Matthew Cordell. Boston: Houghton Mifflin, 2007.
Carole Boston Weatherford. *Birmingham, 1963.* Honesdale, PA: Wordsong/Boyds Mills Press, 2007.

2007 WINNER
JonArno Lawson. *Black Stars in a White Night Sky.* Ill. by Sherwin Tjia. Toronto: Pedlar Press, 2006.

2007 HONOR BOOKS

Jorge Argueta. *Talking with Mother Earth/Hablando con Madre Tierra.* Ill. by Lucía Angela Pérez. Toronto: Groundwood/House of Anansi, 2006.

Helen Frost. *The Braid.* New York: Frances Foster/Farrar Straus & Giroux, 2006.

Walter Dean Myers. *Jazz.* Ill. by Christopher Myers. New York: Holiday House, 2006.

Walter Dean Myers. *Street Love.* New York: Amistad/HarperTempest, 2006.

2006 WINNER

Wynton Marsalis. *Jazz A·B·Z: An A to Z Collection of Jazz Portraits.* Ill. by Paul Rogers. Somerville, MA: Candlewick, 2005.

2006 HONOR BOOKS

Marilyn Nelson. *A Wreath for Emmett Till.* Ill. by Philippe Lardy. Boston: Houghton Mifflin, 2005.

Naomi Shihab Nye. *A Maze Me: Poems for Girls.* Ill. by Terre Maher. New York: Greenwillow, 2005.

Shel Silverstein. *Runny Babbit: A Billy Sook.* New York: HarperCollins, 2005.

2005 WINNER

Marilyn Nelson. *Fortune's Bones: The Manumission Requiem.* Asheville, NC: Front Street Books, 2004.

2005 HONOR BOOKS

Helen Frost. *Spinning Through the Universe: A Novel in Poems from Room 214.* New York: Farrar, Straus & Giroux, 2004.

JonArno Lawson. *The Man in the Moon-Fixer's Mask.* Toronto: Pedlar Press, 2004.

Walter Dean Myers. *Here in Harlem: Poems in Many Voices.* New York: Holiday House, 2004.

Allan Wolf. *New Found Land: Lewis and Clark's Voyage of Discovery.* Somerville, MA: Candlewick, 2004.

Lee Bennett Hopkins Promising Poet Award

The Lee Bennett Hopkins Promising Poet Award was established by Hopkins along with the International Reading Association in 1995 to encourage new poets in their writing. These poets have only published two books (to qualify for the award), but their work has already been judged to be of high quality. The award is given every three years.

2010 Gregory Neri
Neri, Gregory. 2009. *Chess Rumble.* New York: Lee & Low Books.

2007 Joyce Lee Wong
Wong, Joyce Lee. 2006. *Seeing Emily.* New York: Abrams.

2004 Lindsay Lee Johnson
Johnson, Lindsay Lee. 2002. *Soul Moon Soup.* Asheville, NC: Front Street.

2001 Craig Crist-Evans
Crist-Evans, Craig. 1999. *Moon Over Tennessee: A Boy's Civil War Journal.* Boston: Houghton Mifflin.

1998 Kristine O'Connell George
George, Kristine O'Connell. 1997. *The Great Frog Race and Other Poems.* New York: Clarion.

1995 Deborah Chandra
Chandra, Deborah. 1993. *Rich Lizard and Other Poems.* New York: Farrar, Straus & Giroux.

Cybils Award for Poetry

The "Cybils" award was established in 2006 to recognize the role of bloggers in the "kidlitosphere," the online children's literature world. "Cybils," an acronym for the "Children's and Young Adult Bloggers' Literary Awards," are given in a variety of genre and format categories, including poetry. For more information go to: http://www.cybils.com/

2011
Requiem: Poems of the Terezin Ghetto
by Paul B. Janeczko
Candlewick Press
"'I am a watcher/sitting with those about to die.' These are the words of Elisha Schorr/25565 as imagined by poet Paul Janeczko. In *Requiem: Poems of the Terezin Ghetto*, we all become watchers, viewing snapshots of the Holocaust, one after the other, each one deepening the grief and raising questions to which there are no answers. We watch, but we also hear the story of Terezin, voice by voice, insistent and haunting, so that the effect by the end of the collection is almost choral. For each song of despair, there is a concordant and essential song of anger, tenderness or resignation; like a recurring melodic theme, the voice of one child appears and fades and appears again. We hear the violin of one victim playing 'as only the heartbroken can play.'"

2010
Mirror, Mirror: A Book of Reversible Verse
by Marilyn Singer, illustrated by Josée Masse
Penguin
"The poems in this collection are called reversos because they're written as two different versions of the same story. In the case of *Mirror Mirror*, the stories are fairy tales. It was the determination of the poetry judges that the form - the style, the poems themselves - inspire creativity, as evidenced by the number of readers inspired to create their own (inevitably discovering that a true reverso is difficult to achieve indeed).

That one can tell a single story from two different points of view by reversing a poem is quite impressive. Every word in a reverso has to be chosen properly; the placement of the words affects the meaning of the poem, since placement dictates how it is read upwards as well as down. As one of our judges noted, 'For some poems, the reverso form actually gave me *aha!* moments, causing me to look at a familiar story in a fresh way.'"

2009
Red Sings from Treetops: A Year in Colors
by Joyce Sidman; illustrated by Pamela Zagarenski
Houghton Mifflin Harcourt
"Observation, discovery, connection . . . *Red Sings From the Treetops* embodies everything poetry is meant to be. The vivid words of poet Joyce Sidman -- which are fresh even when writing about the oldest of concepts, color -- and the gloriously hue-soaked pictures of illustrator Pamela

Zagarenski combine to create a poetry book that is both thoughtful and exuberant. Readers can hunt for small details in the sweep of larger images and thrill to a-ha! moments of discovery. They can read the book as one full, circular story or as a series of individual, eye-opening poems. Either way, the beauty of this book will leave them feeling connected to something larger than themselves."

2008
Honeybee
by Naomi Shihab Nye
HarperCollins
"*Honeybee* is a hybrid of delicious poetry and lyrical prose poems on wide-ranging themes blending science and observation alongside personal memoir and political challenge. There are ideas buzzing here that young people have probably felt in their gut, but may not have verbalized. Isn't this what poetry is supposed to do?"

2007
This Is Just to Say: Poems of Apology and Forgiveness
by Joyce Sidman, illustrated by Pamela Zagarenski
Houghton Mifflin
"Everyone messes up. The characters in Sidman's original, funny, and heart-wrenching book certainly do. But in individual poems spoken in utterly believable and age-appropriate voices, by turns hilarious and piercing, this collection offers poems of apology and response that build to an overarching story that will knock your emotional socks off. Kids can read this book straight through like a short story, flip back and forth between the poems of apology and response, study the form and style of a favorite poem, follow one of the appealing, diverse characters, or lose themselves in the expressive and clever illustrations. And if they are suddenly overcome by the urge to write their own imperfect, but perfectly honest, poems after reading this book, it will be with the blessing of poets like Sidman, who understands that poetry is for everyone, and especially for those who mess up."

2006
Butterfly Eyes and Other Secrets of the Meadow
by Joyce Sidman, illustrated by Beth Krommes
Houghton Mifflin
"Three cheers for *Butterfly Eyes and Other Secrets of the Meadow*! Each poem is a nature riddle--guessing the answers will keep children hopping. Joyce Sidman's rich, rhythmic language and Beth Krommes' intricate scratchboard illustrations make the Cybils poetry winner a book to return to again and again."

NCTE Poetry Notables

The National Council of Teachers of English Committee on Excellence in Poetry Award selects the recipient of the award for the most outstanding children's poet and is also charged with "exploring ways to acquaint teachers and children with poetry" including establishing an issuing a regular list of "poetry notables" for young people. What follows is the first list compiled in 2003-2006 and featuring the 10 best poetry books published during each of those three years, based on the criteria for excellence for the award itself: literary merit, imagination, authenticity of voice, evidence of a strong persona, universality and timelessness, and appeal to children. The committee included Sylvia M. Vardell, Peggy Oxley, Georgia Heard, Jan Kristo, Gail Wesson Spivey, Janet Wong, Poet, and Dan Woolsey. Check the NCTE.org site for current "poetry notables" lists.

2004

Dotlich, Rebecca Kai. 2004. *Over in the Pink House: New Jump Rope Rhymes.* Honesdale, PA: Wordsong/Boyds Mills.

Frost, Helen. 2004. *Spinning through the Universe.* New York: Farrar, Straus & Giroux.

George, Kristine O'Connell. 2004. *Hummingbird Nest: A Journal of Poems.* New York: Harcourt.

Grimes, Nikki. 2004. *Tai Chi morning: Snapshots of China.* Chicago: Cricket Books.

Grimes, Nikki. 2004. *What is Goodbye?* New York: Jump at the Sun/Hyperion.

Hopkins, Lee Bennett. 2004. *Wonderful Words: Poems about Reading, Writing, Speaking and Listening.* New York: Simon & Schuster.

Lyne, Sandford. Ed. 2004. *Soft Hay Will Catch You: Poems by Young People.* New York: Simon & Schuster.

Myers, Walter Dean. 2004. *Here in Harlem: Poems in Many Voices.* New York: Holiday House.

Prelutsky, Jack. 2004. *If Not for the Cat: Haiku.* New York: Greenwillow.

Singer, Marilyn. 2004. *Creature Carnival.* New York: Hyperion.

2005

Alarcón, Francisco X. 2005. *Poems to Dream Together/ Poemas para Sonar Juntos.* New York: Lee & Low.

George, Kristine O'Connell. 2005. *Fold Me a Poem.* San Diego, CA: Harcourt Brace.

Hopkins, Lee Bennett. Ed. 2005. *Days to Celebrate: A Full Year of Poetry, People, Holidays, History, Fascinating Facts, and More.* New York: Greenwillow.

Janeczko, Paul B. Ed. 2005. *A Kick in the Head: An Everyday Guide to Poetic Forms.* Somerville, MA: Candlewick.

Lewis, J. Patrick. 2005. *Please Bury Me In The Library.* Orlando, FL: Gulliver Books/Harcourt.

Lewis, J. Patrick. 2005. *Vherses: A Celebration of Outstanding Women.* Mankato, MN: Creative Editions.

Moore, Lilian. 2004. *Mural on Second Avenue, and Other City Poems.* Somerville, MA: Candlewick.

Nelson, Marilyn. 2005. *A Wreath for Emmett Till.* Boston: Houghton Mifflin.

Nye, Naomi Shihab. 2005. *A Maze Me: Poems for Girls.* New York: Greenwillow.

Sidman, Joyce. 2005. *Song of the Water Boatman and Other Pond Poems.* Ill. by Beckie Prange. Boston: Houghton Mifflin.

2006

Brown, Calef. 2006. *Flamingos on the Roof.* Boston: Houghton Mifflin.

Florian, Douglas. 2006. *Handsprings.* New York: Greenwillow.

Frost, Helen. 2006. *The Braid.* New York: Farrar, Straus & Giroux.

Greenfield, Eloise. 2006. *The Friendly Four.* Ill. by Jan Spivey Gilchrist. New York: HarperCollins.

Heard, Georgia. 2006 (reissued). *This Place I Know: Poems of Comfort.* Somerville, MA: Candlewick.

Lewis, J. Patrick and Janeczko, Paul B. 2006. *Wing Nuts: Screwy Haiku.* New York: Little, Brown.

Lewis, J. Patrick and Rebecca Kai Dotlich. 2006. *Castles: Old Stone Poems.* Honesdale, PA: Wordsong/Boyds Mills.

Lewis, J. Patrick. 2006. *Once Upon a Tomb: Gravely Humorous Verses.* Candlewick.

Sidman, Joyce. 2006. *Butterfly Eyes and Other Secrets of the Meadow.* Ill. by Beth Krommes. Boston: Houghton Mifflin.

Siebert, Diane. 2006. *Tour America: A Journey through Poems and Art.* San Francisco: Chronicle.

Based on: Vardell, S.M., Oxley, P., Heard, G., Kristo, J., Spivey, G.W., Wong, J., and Woolsey, D. (2007). Best poetry books for children 2003-2006. *Language Arts.* 84, (6), 552-557.

Children's Choices Poetry Picks

Here you'll find recommendations of books that children themselves have chosen as some of their favorites based on the nation-wide Children's Choices project cosponsored annually by the International Reading Association and the Children's Book Council. Each year, approximately 10,000 children ages 5 to 13 from different regions of the United States choose 100 favorites. Here are the POETRY titles children chose as their favorites for 2001-2011 (in the age/grade categories that appear on the lists). For more information on Children's Choices:
http://www.reading.org/resources/booklists/childrenschoices.aspx

2011
Advanced Readers (Grades 5-6)
Seibold, J. Otto. 2010. *Other Goose: Re-Nurseried!! and Re-Rhymed!! Children's Classics.* San Francisco: Chronicle.

2010
Young Readers (Grades 3-4)
Shange, Ntozake, 2009. *Coretta Scott.* Ill. by Kadir Nelson. New York: HarperCollins.

2009
Advanced Readers (Grades 5-6)
Dickinson, Emily. 2008. *My Letter to the World and Other Poems.* Ill. Isabelle Arsenault. Toronto, ON: Kids Can Press.
Weston, Robert Paul. 2008. *Zorgamazoo.* New York: Razorbill.

2008
Beginning Readers (Grades K-2)
Bateman, Donna. 2007. *Deep in the Swamp.* Watertown, MA: Charlesbridge.

Advanced Readers (Grades 5-6)
Evans, John D. 2007. *Diary of a Renaissance Man: Axioms, Aphorisms, Art, and Poetry.* Bloomington, IN: iUniverse.
Grandits, John. 2007. *Blue Lipstick: Concrete Poems.* New York: Clarion.
Spinelli, Eileen. 2007. *Summerhouse Time.* New York: Knopf.

2007
Beginning and Young Readers (Grades K-4)
MacLachlan, Patricia & Emily MacLachlan Charest. 2006. *Once I Ate A Pie.* New York: HarperCollins.

2006
Beginning Readers (Grades K-2)
Hopkins, Lee Bennett. 2005. *Oh, No! Where Are My Pants? And Other Disasters: Poems.* New York: HarperCollins.
Gottfried, Maya. 2005. *Good Dog.* New York: Random House.

Young Readers (Grades 3-4)
Rowden, Justine. 2005. *Paint Me a Poem: Poems Inspired by Masterpieces of Art*. Honesdale, PA: Boyds Mills.
Silverstein, Shel. 2005. *Runny Babbit: A Billy Sook*. New York: HarperCollins.

2005
Young Readers (Grades 3-4)
Krensky, Stephen. 2004. *The Once Was a Very Odd School and Other Lunch-Box Limericks*. New York: Dutton.
Smith, Charles R., Jr. 2004. *Hoop Kings*. Cambridge, MA: Candlewick.

Advanced Readers (Grades 5-6)
Bosak, Susan V. 2004. *Dream: A Tale of Wonder, Wisdom, & Wishes*. Toronto: KCP Press.

2004
Intermediate Readers (Grades 3-4)
Florian, Douglas. 2003. *Bow Wow Meow Meow*. San Diego: Harcourt.
Hollyer, Brenda, ed. 2003. *The Kingfisher Book of Family Poems*. New York: Kingfisher.
Longfellow, Henry Wadsworth. 2003. *Paul Revere's Ride: The Landlord's Tale*. New York: HarperCollins.
Smith, Charles R., Jr. 2003. *Hoop Queens*. Cambridge, MA: Candlewick.

Advanced Readers (Grades 5-6)
Woodson, Jacqueline. 2003. *Locomotion*. New York: Putnam.

2003
Beginning Readers (Grades K-2)
Shields, Carol Diggory. 2002. *The Bugliest Bug*. Cambridge, Massachusetts: Candlewick.

Intermediate Readers (Grades 3-4)
Demarest, Chris. 2002. *I Invited a Dragon to Dinner: And Other Poems to Make You Laugh Out Loud*. New York: Philomel.
Hopkinson, Deborah. 2002. *Under the Quilt of Night*. New York: Atheneum.

Advanced Readers (Grades 5-6)
George, Kristine O'Connell. 2002. *Swimming Upstream: Middle School Poems*. New York: Clarion.
Testa, Maria. 2002. *Becoming Joe DiMaggio*. Cambridge, MA: Candlewick.

2002
Intermediate Readers (Grades 3-4)
Creech, Sharon. 2001. *Love That Dog*. New York: Joanna Cotler Books.
Whitehead, Jenny. 2001. *Lunch Box Mail: And Other Poems*. New York: Henry Holt.

2001

Beginning Readers (Grades K-2)

Freymann, Saxton & Joost Elffers. 2000. *Dr. Pompo's Nose*. New York: Scholastic.

Kraus, Robert. 2000. *Mouse in Love*. New York: Orchard.

Peters, Lisa Westberg. 2000. *Cold Little Duck, Duck, Duck*. New York: Greenwillow.

Trapani, Iza. 2000. *Shoo Fly!* Watertown, MA: Charlesbridge.

Waber, Bernard. 2000. *The Mouse That Snored*. Boston: Houghton Mifflin.

Intermediate Readers (Grades 3-4)

Florian, Douglas. 2000. *Mammalabilia*. San Diego: Harcourt.

Prelutsky, Jack. 2000. *It's Raining Pigs & Noodles*. New York: Greenwillow.

Wilbur, Richard. 2000. *The Pig in the Spigot*. San Diego: Harcourt.

Poetry and the Notable Social Studies Trade Books for Young People

Since 1972, each year the National Council for the Social Studies in cooperation with the Children's Book Council selects a list of "Notable" children's books (K-12) looking for books that emphasize human relations, represent a diversity of groups and are sensitive to a broad range of cultural experiences, present an original theme or a fresh slant on a traditional topic, are easily readable and of high literary quality, have a pleasing format, and, where appropriate, include illustrations that enrich the text. Here is a list of the poetry books that have been included in each year's list since 2001 with a total of 55 works of poetry on the combined lists and an average of 5 poetry titles per year. (Complete annotated bibliographies are available on the NCSS and CBC web sites.)

2011 (books published in 2010)
Richards, Jame. 2010. *Three Rivers Rising*. New York: Knopf.
Hill, Laban Carrick. 2010. *Dave the Potter: Artist, Poet, Slave*. Ill. by Bryan Collier. New York: Little, Brown.
Adoff, Arnold. 2010. *Roots and Blues, A Celebration*. New York: Houghton Mifflin Harcourt.
Engle, Margarita. 2010. *The Firefly Letters; A Suffragette's Journey to Cuba*. New York: Henry Holt.

2010
Nelson, Marilyn. 2009. *Sweethearts of Rhythm; The Story of the Greatest All-Girl Swing Band in the World*. Ill. by Jerry Pinkney. NY: Dial.
Engle, Margarita. 2009. *Tropical Secrets: Holocaust Refugees in Cuba*. New York: Holt.

2009
Winters, Kay. 2008. *Colonial Voices, Hear Them Speak*. New York: Dutton.
Hopkins, Lee Bennett. 2008. *America at War*. New York: McElderry.
Rappaport, Doreen. 2008. *Lady Liberty*. Somerville, MA: Candlewick.
Bryant, Jen. 2008. *Ringside 1925; Views From the Scopes Trial*. New York: Knopf.
Engle, Margarita. 2008. *The Surrender Tree*. New York: Holt.
LeZotte, Ann Clare. 2008. *T4*. Boston: Houghton Mifflin.

2008
Bernier-Grand, Carmen T. 2007. *Frida: ¡Viva la vida! Long Live Life!* New York: Marshall Cavendish.
Smith, Charles R. Jr. 2007. *Twelve Rounds to Glory: The Story of Muhammad Ali*. Somerville, MA: Candlewick.
Zimmer, Tracie Vaughn. 2007. *Reaching for Sun*. New York: Bloomsbury.
Lewis, J. Patrick. 2007. *The Brothers' War: Civil War Voices in Verse*. Washington, DC: National Geographic.
Applegate, Katherine. 2007. *Home of the Brave*. New York: Square Fish.
Schlitz, Laura Amy. 2007. *Good Masters! Sweet Ladies!: Voices from a Medieval Village*. Somerville, MA: Candlewick.

2007

McCormick, Patricia. 2006. *Sold*. New York: Hyperion.

Siebert, Diane. 2006. *Tour America: A Journey through Poems and Art*. San Francisco: Chronicle.

Weatherford, Carole Boston. 2006. *Dear Mr. Rosenwald*. Ill. by R. Gregory Christie. New York: Scholastic.

Bryant, Jen. 2006. *Pieces of Georgia*. New York: Knopf.

Sandell, Lisa Ann. 2006. *The Weight of the Sky*. Viking.

Frost, Helen. 2006. *The Braid*. New York: Farrar, Straus & Giroux.

2006

Marsalis, Wynton. 2005. *Jazz ABZ: An A to Z Collection of Jazz Portraits*. Somerville, MA: Candlewick.

Lewis, J. Patrick. 2005. *Heroes and She-Roes: Poems of Amazing and Everyday Heroes*. New York: Dial.

Carlson, Lori M. Ed. 2005. *Red Hot Salsa; Bilingual Poems on Being Young and Latino in the United States*. New York: Henry Holt.

Carvell, Marlene. 2005. *Sweetgrass Basket*. New York: Dutton.

Nelson, Marilyn. 2005. *A Wreath for Emmett Till*. Boston: Houghton Mifflin.

2005

Bernier-Grand, Carmen T. 2004. *César; ¡Sí, Se Puede! Yes, We can!* New York: Marshall Cavendish.

Kerley, Barbara. 2004. *Walt Whitman: Words For America*. Ill. by Brian Selznick. New York: Scholastic.

High, Linda Oatman. 2004. *City of Snow: The Great Blizzard of 1888*. New York: Walker.

2004

Niven, Penelope. 2003. Carl Sandburg: Adventures of a Poet. San Diego, CA: Harcourt.

Ochoa, Annette Piña, Betsy Franco, and Traci L. Gourdine, Eds. 2003. Night is Gone, Day is Still Coming; Stories and Poems by American Indian Teens and Young Adults. Somerville, MA: Candlewick.

Bates, Katharine Lee. 2003. *America the Beautiful*. Ill. by Wendell Minor. New York: Putnam.

Hesse, Karen. 2003. *Aleutian Sparrow*. Simon & Schuster.

Myers, Walter Dean. 2003. *Blues Journey*. New York: Holiday House.

Meltzer, Milton. Ed. 2003. *Hour of Freedom: American History in Poetry*. Honesdale, PA: Wordsong/Boyds Mills.

Longfellow, Henry Wadsworth. 2003. *Paul Revere's Ride: The Landlord's Tale*. Ill. by Charles Santore. New York: HarperCollins.

2003

Grimes, Nikki. 2002. *Talkin' About Bessie: The Story of Aviator Elizabeth Coleman*. Ill. by E.B. Lewis. New York: Orchard.

Fields, Terri. 2002. *After the Death of Anna Gonzales*. New York: Holt.

Heard, Georgia. 2002. *This Place I Know: Poems of Comfort*. Somerville, MA: Candlewick.

Mak, Kam. 2001. *My Chinatown: One Year in Poems*. New York: HarperCollins.

Mannis, Celeste Davidson. *One Leaf Rides the Wind: Counting in a Japanese Garden*. Ill. by Susan K. Hartung. New York: Viking.

Weatherford, Carole Boston. 2002. *Remember the Bridge: Poems of a People*. New York: Philomel.

2002

Nelson, Marilyn. 2001. *Carver: A Life in Poems*. Asheville, NC: Front Street.

Clifton, Lucille. 2001. *One of the Problems of Everett Anderson*. Ill. by Ann Grifalconi. New York: Henry Holt.

Siebert, Diane. 2001. *Mississippi*. Ill. by Greg Harlin. New York: HarperCollins.

High, Linda Oatman. 2001. *A Humble Life: Plain Poems*. New York: Eerdmans.

Rochelle, Belinda. Ed. 2001. *Words with Wings: A Treasury of African-American Poetry and Art*. New York: HarperCollins.

Mora, Pat. 2001. Ed. *Love to Mamá: A Tribute to Mothers*. New York: Lee & Low.

Grimes, Nikki. 2000. *Stepping out with Grandma Mac*. New York: Simon & Schuster.

2001

Kurtz, Jane. 2000. *River Friendly, River Wild*. New York: Simon & Schuster.

Beaton, Clare. 2000. *Mother Goose Remembers*. New York: Barefoot Books.

Weatherford, Carole Boston. 2000. *The Sound that Jazz Makes*. New York: Walker.

Based on: Vardell, Sylvia M. (2011). Everyday Poetry: Social Studies Poetry "Notables." *Book Links*. September.

Poetry and the Outstanding Science Trade Books for Young People

Since 1973, the Children's Book Council has collaborated with the National Science Teachers Association (NSTA) to produce an annual list of "Outstanding Science Trade Books for Students K-12" with an eye for books that "convey the thrill of science" and provide the "the perfect way for students to build literacy skills while learning science content." Here is a list of the poetry books that have been included in each year's list since 2001 with a total of 24 works of poetry on the combined lists and an average of 2 poetry titles per year. (Complete annotated bibliographies are available on the NSTA and CBC web sites.)

2012 (books published in 2011)
Bulion, Leslie. 2011. *At the Sea Floor Café; Odd Ocean Critter Poems.* Ill. by Leslie Evans. Peachtree.

Arnosky, Jim. 2011. *At This Very Moment.* New York: Dutton.

Hauth, Katherine. 2011. *What's for Dinner? Quirky, Squirmy Poems from the Animal World.* Charlesbridge.

2011
Verstraete, Larry. 2010. *S is for Scientists: A Discovery Alphabet.* Farmington Hills, MI: Sleeping Bear Press.

Wolf, Sallie. 2010. *The Robin Makes a Laughing Sound.* Charlesbridge.

Sidman, Joyce. 2010. *Dark Emperor and Other Poems of the Night.* Ill. by Rick Allen. Boston: Houghton Mifflin.

Florian, Douglas. 2010. *Poetrees.* New York: Simon & Schuster.

Sidman, Joyce. 2010. *Ubiquitous: Celebrating Nature's Survivors.* Ill. by Becky Prange. Boston: Houghton Mifflin.

Schwartz, David M. and Schy, Yael. 2010. *What in the Wild? Mysteries of Nature Concealed… and Revealed.* Berkeley, CA: Tricycle.

2010
Bardhan-Quallen, Sudipta, 2009. *Flying Eagle.* Watertown, MA: Charlesbridge.

Mortensen, Lori. 2009. *In the Trees, Honey Bees!* Nevada City, CA: Dawn Publishing.

Schwartz, David M. and Schy, Yael. 2009. *Where Else in the Wild? MORE Camouflaged Creatures Concealed… and Revealed.* Berkeley, CA: Tricycle.

2009
Gerber, Carole. 2008. *Winter Trees.* Ill. by Leslie Evans. Watertown, MA: Charlesbridge.

2008
Dowson, Nick. 2007. *Tracks of a Panda.* Somerville, MA: Candlewick.

Schwartz, David M. and Schy, Yael. 2007. *Where in the Wild? Camouflaged Creatures Concealed… and Revealed.* Berkeley, CA: Tricycle.

Posada, Mia. 2007. *Guess What is Growing Inside This Egg.* Brookfield, CT: Millbrook.

2007
Sidman, Joyce. 2006. *Butterfly Eyes and Other Secrets of the Meadow*. Ill. by Beth Krommes. Boston: Houghton Mifflin.

2006
Sidman, Joyce. 2005. *Song of the Water Boatman and Other Pond Poems*. Ill. By Beckie Prange. Boston: Houghton Mifflin.
Schoenberg, Jane. 2005. *My Bodyworks: Songs About Your Bones, Muscles, Heart, and More!* Crocodile Books/Interlink Publishing

2005
NONE SELECTED

2004
Burleigh, Robert. 2004. *Into the Woods: John James Audubon Lives His Dream*. New York: Atheneum.

2003
Posada, Mia. 2002. *Ladybugs: Red, Fiery, and Bright*. Minneapolis, MN: Carolrhoda.

2002
Yolen, Jane. 2001. *Welcome to the River of Grass*. New York: Putnam.

2001
Glaser, Linda. 2000. *Our Big Home: An Earth Poem*. Brookfield, CT: Millbrook
Moss, Miriam. 2000. *This Is the Tree*. San Diego, CA: Kane/Miller.

Based on: Vardell, Sylvia M. 2012. Everyday Poetry: Outstanding Science Poetry. *Book Links.* July.

Joseph Thomas's Canon of U.S. Children's Poetry

In his seminal work, Poetry's Playground: The Culture of Contemporary American Children's Poetry *(Wayne State University Press, 2007, p. 109), Joseph Thomas identifies eight key anthologies he suggests are children's poetry essentials. He notes he chose anthologies with editors from "differing ideological standpoints" and from a variety of "historical moments," hoping to be "descriptive, not prescriptive" and lay the groundwork for "future inquiry." They are listed here in chronological order.*

Untermeyer, Louis, comp. 1959. *The Golden Treasury of Poetry.* New York: Golden Press.

Dunning, Stephen, Luders, Edward, and Smith, Hugh, comp. 1966. *Reflections on a Gift of Watermelon Pickle.* New York: Scholastic.

Kennedy, X.J. and Kennedy, Dorothy, comp. 1982. *Knock at a Star: A Child's Introduction to Poetry.* Boston: Little, Brown.

Prelutsky, Jack, comp. 1983. *The Random House Book of Poetry for Children.* New York: Random House.

Koch, Kenneth, and Farrell, Kate, comp. 1985. *Talking to the Sun; An Illustrated Anthology of Poems for Young People.* New York: Henry Holt.

Sword, Elizabeth Hauge and McCarthy, Victoria, comp. 1995. *A Child's Anthology of Poetry.* New York: Franklin Watts.

Kennedy, X.J. and Kennedy, Dorothy, comp. 1999 (revised edition). *Knock at a Star: A Child's Introduction to Poetry.* Boston: Little, Brown.

Hall, Donald, comp. 1999. *The Oxford Illustrated Book of American Children's Poems.* New York: Oxford University Press.

Poetry for the Common Core

The newly developed Common Core State Standards Initiative offers English Language Arts standards that include a substantial poetry component. Individual poems are identified as study source material across the grade levels in terms of "complexity, quality, and range." Most are from the public domain and thus are largely classic poems by poets of the past. But a sprinkling of contemporary and even multicultural poems is also included. It's an interesting list to consider, but by no means exclusive—indeed the Standards home page (corestandards.org) notes, "They expressly do not represent a partial or complete reading list." Here is a list of the suggested poems for your consideration.

K–1 Poetry Text Exemplars
Anonymous. "As I Was Going to St. Ives"
Rossetti, Christina. "Mix a Pancake"
Fyleman, Rose. "Singing-Time"
Milne, A. A. "Halfway Down"
Chute, Marchette. "Drinking Fountain"
Hughes, Langston. "Poem"
Ciardi, John. "Wouldn't You?"
Wright, Richard. "Laughing Boy"
Greenfield, Eloise. "By Myself"
Giovanni, Nikki. "Covers"
Merriam, Eve. "It Fell in the City"
Lopez, Alonzo. "Celebration"
Agee, Jon. "Two Tree Toads"

K-1 Read-Aloud Poetry
Anonymous. "The Fox's Foray"
Langstaff, John. *Over in the Meadow*
Lear, Edward. "The Owl and the Pussycat"
Hughes, Langston. "April Rain Song"
Moss, Lloyd. *Zin! Zin! Zin! A Violin*

Grades 2–3 Poetry Text Exemplars
Dickinson, Emily. "Autumn"
Rossetti, Christina. "Who Has Seen the Wind?"
Millay, Edna St. Vincent. "Afternoon on a Hill"
Frost, Robert. "Stopping by Woods on a Snowy Evening"
Field, Rachel. "Something Told the Wild Geese"
Hughes, Langston. "Grandpa's Stories"
Jarrell, Randall. "A Bat Is Born"
Giovanni, Nikki. "Knoxville, Tennessee"
Merriam, Eve. "Weather"
Soto, Gary. "Eating While Reading"

Grades 2-3 Read-Aloud Poetry
Lear, Edward. "The Jumblies"
Browning, Robert. *The Pied Piper of Hamelin*

Johnson, Georgia Douglas. "Your World"
Eliot, T. S. "The Song of the Jellicles"
Fleischman, Paul. "Fireflies"

Grades 4–5 Poetry Text Exemplars
Blake, William. "The Echoing Green"
Lazarus, Emma. "The New Colossus"
Thayer, Ernest Lawrence. "Casey at the Bat"
Dickinson, Emily. "A Bird Came Down the Walk"
Sandburg, Carl. "Fog"
Frost, Robert. "Dust of Snow"
Dahl, Roald. "Little Red Riding Hood and the Wolf"
Nichols, Grace. "They Were My People"
Mora, Pat. "Words Free As Confetti"

Grades 6–8 Poetry Text Exemplars
Longfellow, Henry Wadsworth. "Paul Revere's Ride"
Whitman, Walt. "O Captain! My Captain!"
Carroll, Lewis. "Jabberwocky"
Navajo tradition. "Twelfth Song of Thunder"
Dickinson, Emily. "The Railway Train"
Yeats, William Butler. "The Song of Wandering Aengus"
Frost, Robert. "The Road Not Taken"
Sandburg, Carl. "Chicago"
Hughes, Langston. "I, Too, Sing America"
Neruda, Pablo. "The Book of Questions."
Soto, Gary. "Oranges"
Giovanni, Nikki. "A Poem for My Librarian, Mrs. Long"

Grades 9–10 Poetry Text Exemplars
Shakespeare, William. "Sonnet 73"
Donne, John. "Song"
Shelley, Percy Bysshe. "Ozymandias"
Poe, Edgar Allan. "The Raven"
Dickinson, Emily. "We Grow Accustomed to the Dark"
Houseman, A. E. "Loveliest of Trees"
Johnson, James Weldon. "Lift Every Voice and Sing"
Cullen, Countee. "Yet Do I Marvel"
Auden, Wystan Hugh. "Musee des Beaux Arts"
Walker, Alice. "Women"
Baca, Jimmy Santiago. "I Am Offering This Poem to You"

Grades 11–CCR Poetry Text Exemplars
Li Po. "A Poem of Changgan"
Donne, John. "A Valediction Forbidding Mourning"
Wheatley, Phyllis. "On Being Brought From Africa to America"
Keats, John. "Ode on a Grecian Urn"
Whitman, Walt. "Song of Myself"
Dickinson, Emily. "Because I Could Not Stop for Death"
Tagore, Rabindranath. "Song VII"

Eliot, T. S. "The Love Song of J. Alfred Prufrock"
Pound, Ezra. "The River Merchant's Wife: A Letter"
Frost, Robert. "Mending Wall"
Neruda, Pablo. "Ode to My Suit"
Bishop, Elizabeth. "Sestina"
Ortiz Cofer, Judith. "The Latin Deli: An Ars Poetica"
Dove, Rita. "Demeter's Prayer to Hades"
Collins, Billy. "Man Listening to Disc"

A Canon of Classic Poems for Young People

Here is a list of classic poems still popular with young people. The subject matter, language, rhythm, and imagery of these poems are still inviting for today's readers and listeners. Most of these selections continue to be included in current anthologies of popular children's poetry and many are available online as well.

Hilaire Belloc, "The Vulture"
William Blake, "The Tyger"
Gwendolyn Brooks, "We Real Cool"
Lewis Carroll, "Jabberwocky"
Samuel Taylor Coleridge, "The Rime of the Ancient Mariner"
Emily Dickinson, Poem: 288, "I'm Nobody! Who are You?"
T.S. Eliot, "The Naming of Cats"
Eugene Field, "Wynken, Blynken, and Nod"
Robert Frost, "Stopping by Woods"
Mary Howitt, "The Spider and the Fly"
Langston Hughes, "Dreams"
Rudyard Kipling, "If"
Joyce Kilmer, "Trees"
Edward Lear, "The Owl and the Pussycat"
Henry Wadsworth Longfellow, "Paul Revere's Ride"
John Masefield, "Sea Fever"
A.A. Milne, "If I Were King"
Clement Moore, "A Visit from St. Nicholas"
Ogden Nash, "The Tale of Custard the Dragon"
Edgar Allen Poe, "The Raven"
Jack Prelutsky, "Homework, Oh, Homework"
Laura E. Richards, "Eletelephony"
Christina Rossetti, "The Wind"
Carl Sandburg, "Fog"
Robert Louis Stevenson, "My Shadow"
Edna St. Vincent Millay, "Afternoon on a Hill"
Ernest Thayer, "Casey at the Bat"
Walt Whitman, "O Captain! My Captain!"
William Wordsworth, "I Wandered Lonely as a Cloud"

Best Multi-Poet Anthologies for Young People

There are many, many wonderful poetry anthologies published for children, full of poems by different poets. In addition, new poets often appear FIRST in anthologies before publishing their own individual collections of poetry. Here is a beginning list of some of the most popular and acclaimed poetry anthologies that include quality works by a variety of poets gathered around many interesting themes and topics.

Brenner, Barbara. Ed. 1994. *The Earth is Painted Green: A Garden of Poems about Our Planet.* New York: Scholastic.

Brenner, Barbara. Ed. 2000. *Voices: Poetry and Art from Around the World.* Washington, DC: National Geographic Society.

Clinton, Catherine. Ed. 1993/1998. *I, Too, Sing America: Three Centuries of African American Poetry.* Boston: Houghton Mifflin.

Cohn, Amy L. Ed. 1993. *From Sea to Shining Sea: A Treasury of American Folklore and Folk Songs.* New York: Scholastic.

Cullinan, Bernice and Wooten, Deborah. Eds. 2009. *Another Jar of Tiny Stars*; *Poems by NCTE Award-winning Poets.* Honesdale, PA: Wordsong/Boyds Mills.

Dunning, Stephen, Edward Luders, and Hugh Smith. Eds. 1966. *Reflections on a Gift of Watermelon Pickle.* New York: Scholastic.

Greenberg, Jan. 2001. Ed. *Heart to Heart: New Poems Inspired by Twentieth-Century American Art.* New York: Abrams.

Greenberg, Jan. 2008. Ed. *Side by Side: New Poems Inspired by Art from Around the World.* New York: Abrams.

Hall, Donald. Ed. 1999. Ed. *The Oxford Illustrated Book of American Children's Poems.* New York: Oxford University Press.

Heard, Georgia. 2002. Ed. *This Place I Know: Poems of Comfort.* Somerville, MA: Candlewick.

Hoberman, Mary Ann and Wilson, Linda. Eds. 2009. *The Tree That Time Built: A Celebration of Nature, Science, and Imagination.* Naperville, IL: Sourcebooks.

Hopkins, Lee Bennett. Ed. 1990. *Good Books, Good Times.* New York: Trumpet. Reprinted, New York: HarperTrophy, 2000.

Hopkins, Lee Bennett. Ed. 2005. *Days to Celebrate: A Full Year of Poetry, People, Holidays, History, Fascinating Facts, and More.* New York: Greenwillow.

Hopkins, Lee Bennett. Ed. 2010. *Amazing Faces.* New York: Lee and Low.

Hopkins, Lee Bennett. Ed. 2008. *America at War.* New York: McElderry.

Hopkins, Lee. Bennett. Ed. 2010. *Sharing the Seasons.* New York: McElderry.

Hudson, Wade. Ed. 1993. *Pass It On: African American Poetry for Children.* New York: Scholastic.

Janeczko, Paul B. Ed. 2005. *A Kick in the Head: An Everyday Guide to Poetic Forms.* Somerville, MA: Candlewick.

Janeczko, Paul. Ed. 2002. *Seeing the Blue Between: Advice and Inspiration for Young Poets.* Somerville, MA: Candlewick.

Katz, Bobbi. Ed. 2004. *Pocket Poems.* New York: Dutton.

Katz, Bobbi. Ed. 2009. *More Pocket Poems.* New York: Dutton.

Kennedy, Caroline. Ed. 2005. *A Family of Poems: My Favorite Poetry for Children*. New York: Hyperion.

Kennedy, X.J and Dorothy Kennedy. Eds. 1999. *Knock at a Star: A Child's Introduction to Poetry* (Revised edition). New York: Little Brown.

Koch, Kenneth, and Kate Farrell. Eds. 1985. *Talking to the Sun*. New York: Henry Holt.

Lansky, Bruce. Ed. 1994. *A Bad Case of the Giggles: Kid's Favorite Funny Poems*. Deephaven, MN: Meadowbrook Press.

Martin, Bill, Jr. and Sampson, Michael. Eds. 2008. *The Bill Martin Jr. Big Book of Poetry*. New York: Simon & Schuster.

Nye, Naomi Shihab. Ed. 1992. *This Same Sky: A Collection of Poems from Around the World*. New York: Four Winds Press.

Panzer, Nora. Ed. 1994. *Celebrate America in Poetry and Art*. New York: Hyperion.

Paschen, Elise and Raccah, Dominique. Eds. 2005. *Poetry Speaks to Children*. Naperville, IL: Sourcebooks.

Paschen, Elise and Raccah, Dominique. Eds. 2010. *Poetry Speaks; Who I Am*. Naperville, IL: Sourcebooks.

Philip, Neil. Ed. 1996. *The New Oxford Book of Children's Verse*. Oxford, NY: Oxford University Press.

Prelutsky, Jack Ed. 1997. *The Beauty of the Beast*. New York: Knopf.

Prelutsky, Jack. Ed. 1983. *The Random House Book of Poetry for Children*. New York: Random House.

Prelutsky, Jack. Ed. 1999. *The 20th Century Children's Poetry Treasury*. New York: Knopf.

Rochelle, Belinda. Ed. 2001. *Words with Wings: A Treasury of African-American Poetry and Art*. New York: HarperCollins.

Rosen, Michael and Graham, Bob. Eds. 2004. *Poems for the Very Young*. New York: Kingfisher.

Rosenberg, Liz. Ed. 2001. *Light-gathering Poems*. New York: Henry Holt.

Sullivan, Charles. Ed. 1994. *Here is My Kingdom: Hispanic-American Literature and Art for Young People*. New York: Abrams.

Sword, Elizabeth Hauge and Victoria Flournoy McCarthy. Eds. 1995. *A Child's Anthology of Poetry*. New York: Franklin Watts.

Untermeyer, Louis. Ed. 1959. *The Golden Treasury of Poetry*. New York: Golden Press.

Whipple, Laura. Ed. 1989. *Eric Carle's Animals, Animals*. New York: Scholastic.

Whipple, Laura. Ed. 1994. *Celebrating America: A Collection of Poems and Images of the American Spirit*. New York: Philomel.

Willard, Nancy. Ed. 1998. *Step Lightly: Poems for the Journey*. San Diego: Harcourt.

Most Anthologized Poets for Young People

In his seminal work, Poetry's Playground: The Culture of Contemporary American Children's Poetry *(Wayne State University Press, 2007, p. 117-119), Joseph Thomas identifies the poets listed below as the most frequently anthologized within a selection of these key anthologies he suggests are children's poetry essentials.*

- Untermeyer, Louis. *The Golden Treasury of Poetry* (1959)
- Dunning, Stephen, Luders, Edward, and Smith, Hugh. *Reflections on a Gift of Watermelon Pickle* (1966)
- Prelutsky, Jack. *The Random House Book of Poetry for Children* (1983)
- Koch, Kenneth, and Farrell, Kate. *Talking to the Sun; An Illustrated Anthology of Poems for Young People* (1985)
- Sword, Elizabeth Hauge and McCarthy, Victoria. *A Child's Anthology of Poetry* (1995)
- Kennedy, X.J. and Kennedy, Dorothy. *Knock at a Star: A Child's Introduction to Poetry* (both the 1982 and 1999 editions)
- Hall, Donald. *The Oxford Illustrated Book of American Children's Poems* (1999)

The following poets appeared in at least half of these "canon" anthologies and are listed in descending order of frequency.

Frost, Robert
Sandburg, Carl
cummings, e e
Roethke, Theodore
Coatsworth, Elizabeth
Dickinson, Emily
Hughes, Langston
Carroll, Lewis
De la Mare, Walter
Lear, Edward
Merriam, Eve
Smith, William Jay
Williams, William Carlos
Blake, William
Brooks, Gwendolyn
Ciardi, John
Field, Rachel
Frances, Robert
Herford, Oliver
Kennedy, X. J.
McCord, David
McGinley, Phyllis
Millay, Edna St. Vincent
Nash, Ogden

Rossetti, Christina
Stevenson, Robert Louis
Tennyson, Lord Alfred
Whitman, Walt
Field, Eugene
Guiterman, Arthur
Housman, A. E.
Kuskin, Karla
Lawrence, D. H.
Longfellow, Henry W.
Prelutsky, Jack
Roberts, Elizabeth Madox
Silverstein, Shel
Yeats, William Butler

50 Poetry Books for the Very Young Child (Ages 0-5)

From birth—if not before—children respond to the rhythm and rhyme of poetry. Indeed, children's book author and literacy expert Mem Fox claims, "Rhymers will be readers; it's that simple. Experts in literacy and child development have discovered that if children know eight nursery rhymes by heart by the time they're four years old, they're usually among the best readers by the time they're eight" (Reading Magic; Why Reading Aloud to Our Children Will Change Their Lives Forever, *2001, p. 85). Here are 50 recommended titles of poetry written with our youngest listeners in mind.*

1. Ada, Alma Flor and Campoy, Isabel, comp. 2010. *Muu, Moo! Rimas de animales/Animal Nursery Rhymes*. Rayo/HarperCollins.
2. Ada, Alma Flor, and Isabel Campoy, comp. 2003. *Pio Peep! Traditional Spanish Nursery Rhymes*. New York: HarperCollins.
3. Ahlberg, Allan and Ingram, Bruce. 2010. *Everybody Was a Baby Once*. Candlewick.
4. Anholt, Catherine and Laurence Anholt. 1998. *Big Book of Families*. Cambridge: Candlewick.
5. Archer, Peggy. 2007. *From Dawn to Dreams; Poems for Busy Babies*. Ill. by Hanako Wakiyama. Cambridge, MA: Candlewick.
6. Bagert, Brod. 2007. *Shout! Little Poems that Roar*. New York: Dial.
7. Calmenson, Stephanie. 2002. *Welcome, Baby! Baby Rhymes for Baby Times*. New York: HarperCollins.
8. Calmenson, Stephanie. 2005. *Kindergarten Kids: Riddles, Rebuses, Wiggles, Giggles, and More*! New York: HarperCollins Publishers.
9. Crews, Nina. 2004. *The Neighborhood Mother Goose*. New York: Greenwillow.
10. Crews, Nina. 2011. *Neighborhood Sing Along*. HarperCollins.
11. Delacre, Lulu, comp. 1992. *Arroz con Leche: Popular Songs and Rhymes from Latin America*. New York: Scholastic.
12. Delacre, Lulu. 2004. *Arrorró Mi Niño: Latino Lullabies and Gentle Games*. New York: Scholastic.
13. Dotlich, Rebecca Kai. 2004. *Over in the Pink House: New Jump Rope Rhymes*. Honesdale: Wordsong/Boyds Mills Press.
14. Ehlert, Lois. 2008. *Oodles Of Animals*. Harcourt.
15. Ehlert, Lois. 2010. *Lots of Spots*. Beach Lane Books.
16. Elliott, David. 2010. *In the Wild*. Cambridge, MA: Candlewick.
17. Elliott, David. 2008. *On the Farm*. Cambridge, MA: Candlewick.
18. Foreman, Michael. 2002. *Michael Foreman's Playtime Rhymes*. Cambridge: Candlewick.
19. Fox, Dan, ed. 2003. *A Treasury of Children's Songs: Forty Favorites to Sing and Play*.
20. Franco, Betsy. 2004. *Counting Our Way to the 100th Day*. New York: Margaret K. McElderry Books.
21. George, Kristine O'Connell. 1999. *Little Dog Poems*. New York: Clarion.
22. Grimes, Nikki. 2000. *Shoe Magic*. New York: Orchard.

23. Hague, Michael. 1997. *Teddy Bear, Teddy Bear: A Classic Action Rhyme*. New York: Morrow.
24. Hale, Glorya, ed. 1997. *Read-aloud Poems for Young People: An Introduction to the Magic and Excitement of Poetry*. New York: Black Dog & Leventhal.
25. Henderson, Kathy. 2011. *Hush, Baby, Hush! Lullabies from Around the World*. Ill. by Pam Smy. Seattle: Frances Lincoln.
26. Hoberman, Mary Ann. 2001. *Very Short Stories to Read Together*. Boston: Little, Brown.
27. Hoberman, Mary Ann. 2005. *You Read to Me, I'll Read to You; Very Short Mother Goose Tales to Read Together*. Ill. by Michael Emberley. Boston: Little, Brown.
28. Hopkins, Lee Bennett, comp. 1998. *Climb Into My Lap: First Poems To Read Together*. New York: Simon & Schuster.
29. Hubbell, Patricia. 2010. *Snow Happy!* Tricycle Press.
30. Katz, Bobbi. 2001. *A Rumpus of Rhymes: A Book of Noisy Poems*. New York: Dutton.
31. Lewis, J. Patrick. 2007. *Big is Big (and Little, Little)*. Holiday House.
32. Mayo, Margaret. 2002. *Wiggle Waggle Fun: Stories and Rhymes for the Very Very Young*. New York: Knopf.
33. Moore, Lilian. 2001. *I'm Small and Other Verses*. Cambridge: Candlewick.
34. Mora, Pat. 1996. *Uno Dos Tres*. New York: Clarion.
35. Newcome, Zita. 2000. *Head, Shoulders, Knees, and Toes and Other Action Rhymes*. Cambridge: Candlewick.
36. Opie, Iona 1999. *Here Comes Mother Goose*. Ill. by Rosemary Wells. Cambridge: Candlewick.
37. Orozco, José Luis. 2002. *Diez Deditos: Ten Little Fingers and Other Play Rhymes and Action Songs from Latin America*. New York: Dutton.
38. Prelutsky, Jack. Comp. 1986. *Read-aloud Rhymes for the Very Young*. New York: Knopf.
39. Prelutsky, Jack. 1986. *Ride a Purple Pelican*. New York: Greenwillow.
40. Prelutsky, Jack. 1990. *Beneath a Bule Umbrella*. New York: Greenwillow.
41. Rylant, Cynthia. 2008. *Baby Face: A Book of Love for Baby*. Illus. by Diane Goode. New York: Simon & Schuster.
42. Sanderson, Ruth. 2008. *Mother Goose and Friends*. New York: Little, Brown.
43. Scheffler, Axel. 2007. *Mother Goose's Storytime Nursery Rhymes*. New York: Scholastic.
44. Schertle, Alice. 2003. *Teddy Bear, Teddy Bear*. New York: HarperCollins.
45. Schertle, Alice. 2009. *Button Up! Wrinkled Rhymes*. Ill. by Petra Mathers. New York: Harcourt.
46. Sierra, Judy. 2005. *Schoolyard Rhymes: Kids' Own Rhymes for Rope Skipping, Hand Clapping, Ball Bouncing, and Just Plain Fun*. New York: Knopf.
47. Singer, Marilyn. 2008. *Shoe Bop!* New York: Dutton.

48. Wright, Danielle (Ed). 2008. *My Village; Rhymes from Around the World.* Wellington, NZ: Gecko Press.
49. Yolen, Jane and Peters, Andrew Fusek. Comp. 2007. *Here's a Little Poem' A Very First Book of Poetry.* Cambridge, MA: Candlewick.
50. Yolen, Jane and Peters, Andrew Fusek. Comp. 2010. *Switching on the Moon; A Very First Book of Bedtime Poems.* Cambridge, MA: Candlewick.

100 Poetry Books for Children (Ages 6-12)

Sharing poetry during these pivotal years of childhood is an important component in developing their literacy skills, as well as broadening their appreciation of literature in all forms. In fact, research commissioned by the Poetry Foundation found that "most poetry readers (80 percent) first encounter poetry as children, at home or in school." Fortunately, there are many, many excellent works available for sharing with this age group. Here are 100 exemplary titles to get you started.

1. Adoff, Arnold. 2010. *Roots and Blues, A Celebration.* Houghton Mifflin Harcourt.
2. Agee, Jon. 2009. *Orangutan Tongs; Poems to Tangle Your Tongue.* New York: Disney-Hyperion.
3. Alarcón, Francisco X. 2005. *Poems to Dream Together/ Poemas para Sonar Juntos.* New York: Lee & Low.
4. Andrews, Julie and Hamilton, Emma Watson. 2009. *Julie Andrews' Collection of Poems, Songs, and Lullabies. Ill. by James McMullan.* New York: Little, Brown.
5. Argueta, Jorge. 2001. *A Movie in My Pillow/Una película en mi almohada.* San Francisco, CA: Children's Book Press.
6. Ashman, Linda. 2008. *Stella, Unleashed.* New York: Sterling.
7. Bagert, Brod. 2000. *Giant Children.* Honesdale, PA: Wordsong/Boyds Mills Press.
8. Brenner, Barbara. 1994. *The Earth is Painted Green: A Garden of Poems about Our Planet.* New York: Scholastic.
9. Brenner, Barbara. 2000. *Voices Poetry and Art from Around the World.* Washington, DC: National Geographic Society.
10. Brown, Calef. 2006. *Flamingos on the Roof.* Boston: Houghton Mifflin.
11. Bruchac, Joseph. 1992. *Thirteen Moons on Turtle's Back: A Native American Year of Moons.* New York: Philomel Books.
12. Bulion, Leslie. 2006. *Hey There, Stink Bug!* Watertown, MA: Charlesbridge.
13. Clinton, Catherine. 1998. *I, Too, Sing America: Three Centuries of African American Poetry.* Boston: Houghton Mifflin.
14. Creech, Sharon. 2001. *Love That Dog.* New York: HarperCollins.
15. Cullinan, Bernice and Wooten, Deborah, eds. 2009. *Another Jar of Tiny Stars.; Poems by NCTE Award-winning Poets.* Honesdale, PA: Wordsong/Boyds Mills.
16. Dakos, Kalli. 1990. *If You're Not Here, Please Raise Your Hand.* New York: Four Winds.
17. Engle, Margarita. 2008. *The Surrender Tree.* New York: Holt.
18. Fleishman, Paul. 1988. *Joyful Noise: Poems for Two Voices.* New York: Harper & Row.
19. Florian, Douglas. 1994. *Bing Bang Boing.* New York: Harcourt Brace.
20. Florian, Douglas. 2009. *Dinothesaurus.* New York: Simon & Schuster.

21. Franco, Betsy. 2009. *Curious Collection of Cats*. Ill. by Michael Wertz. San Francisco, CA: Tricycle Press.
22. Frost, Helen. 2008. *Diamond Willow*. New York: Farrar, Straus & Giroux.
23. George, Kristine O'Connell. 2004. *Hummingbird Nest: A Journal of Poems*. New York: Harcourt.
24. Giovanni, Nikki. Coll. 2008. *Hip Hop Speaks to Children*. Naperville, IL: Sourcebooks.
25. Graham, Joan Bransfield. 1999. *Flicker Flash*. Boston: Houghton Mifflin.
26. Grandits, John. 2004. *Technically, It's Not My Fault: Concrete Poems*. New York: Clarion.
27. Greenfield, Eloise. 1999. *Night on Neighborhood Street*. Bound to Stay Bound.
28. Grimes, Nikki. 1994. *Meet Danitra Brown*. New York: Lothrop, Lee & Shepard.
29. Grimes, Nikki. 1998. *Jazmin's Notebook*. New York: Dial.
30. Gunning, Monica. 2004. *America, My New Home*. San Francisco, CA: Children's Book Press.
31. Harley, Avis. 2000. *Fly with Poetry; An ABC of Poetry*. Honesdale, PA: Wordsong/Boyds Mills.
32. Harrison, David L. 1993. *Somebody Catch my Homework*. Honesdale, PA: Wordsong/Boyds Mills Press.
33. Heard, Georgia. Ed. 2002. *This Place I Know: Poems of Comfort*. Cambridge, MA: Candlewick.
34. Hesse, Karen. 1997. *Out of the Dust*. New York: Scholastic.
35. Hines, Anna Grossnickle. 2011. *Peaceful Pieces: A Year in Poems and Quilts*. New York: Greenwillow.
36. Ho, Minfong. 1996. *Maples in the Mist: Poems for Children from the Tang Dynasty*. New York: Lothrop, Lee, & Shepard.
37. Hoberman, Mary Ann and Wilson, Linda. Eds. 2009. *The Tree That Time Built: A Celebration of Nature, Science, and Imagination*. Naperville, IL: Sourcebooks.
38. Hoberman, Mary Ann. 1998. *The Llama Who Had No Pajama: 100 Favorite Poems*. San Diego: Harcourt.
39. Hopkins, Lee Bennett. Ed. 2000. *Good Books, Good Times*. Bound to Stay Bound.
40. Hopkins, Lee. Bennett. Ed. 2010. *Sharing the Seasons*. Margaret McElderry.
41. Hughes, Langston. (75th anniversary edition) 2007. *The Dream Keeper* (and seven additional poems). New York: Knopf.
42. Janeczko, Paul B. Ed. 2002. *Seeing the Blue Between: Advice and Inspiration for Young Poets*. Cambridge, MA: Candlewick.
43. Janeczko, Paul B. Ed. 2005. *A Kick in the Head: An Everyday Guide to Poetic Forms*. Cambridge, MA: Candlewick.
44. Katz, Bobbi. 2004. *Pocket Poems*. Ill. by Deborah Zemke. New York: Dutton.
45. Kennedy, Caroline. Ed. 2005. *A Family of Poems: My Favorite Poetry for Children*. Ill. by Jon J. Muth. New York: Hyperion.

46. Kuskin, Karla. 2003. *Moon, Have You Met My Mother? The Collected Poems of Karla Kuskin.* New York: HarperCollins.

47. Lai, Thanhha. 2011. *Inside Out and Back Again.* HarperCollins.

48. Lansky, Bruce. Ed. 1998. *Miles of Smiles: Kids Pick the Funnies Poems, Book #3.* New York: Scholastic.

49. Larios, Julie. 2006. *Yellow Elephant: A Bright Bestiary.* Ill. by Julie Paschkis. San Diego, CA: Harcourt.

50. Lawson, JonArno. 2008. *Black Stars in a White Night Sky.* Honesdale, PA: Boyds Mills/Wordsong.

51. Lewis, J. Patrick. 2005. *Please Bury Me In The Library.* Orlando, FL: Gulliver Books/Harcourt.

52. Lewis, J. Patrick. 2009. *Countdown to Summer: A Poem for Every Day of the School Year.* Ill. by Ethan Long. New York: Little, Brown.

53. Martin, Bill, Jr. and Sampson, Michael. Eds. 2008. *The Bill Martin Jr. Big Book of Poetry.* New York: Simon & Schuster.

54. McCord, David. 1999. *Every Time I Climb a Tree.* New York: Little, Brown.

55. Merriam, Eve. 1995. *Halloween ABC.* New York: Aladdin.

56. Moore, Lilian. 2004. *Mural on Second Avenue, and Other City Poems.* Cambridge, MA: Candlewick.

57. Mora, Pat. 1996. *Confetti: Poems for Children.* New York: Lee & Low.

58. Mora, Pat. 2007. *Yum! Mmmm! Que Rico!: America's Sproutings.* New York: Lee & Low.

59. Mordhorst, Heidi. 2009. *Pumpkin Butterfly; Poems from the Other Side of Nature.* Honesdale PA: Wordsong/Boyds Mills Press.

60. Myers, Walter Dean. 2006. *Jazz.* Ill. by Christopher Myers. New York: Holiday House.

61. Nesbitt, Kenn. 2009. *My Hippo Has the Hiccups with CD: And Other Poems I Totally Made Up.* Naperville, IL: Sourcebooks.

62. Nicholls, Judith. 2003. *The Sun in Me: Poems about the Planet.* Cambridge, MA: Barefoot Books.

63. Nye, Naomi Shihab. 2005. *A Maze Me: Poems for Girls.* New York: Greenwillow.

64. O'Neill, Mary. 1989. *Hailstones and Halibut Bones: Adventures in Color.* New York: Doubleday.

65. Paschen, Elise and Raccah, Dominique. Eds. 2005. *Poetry Speaks to Children.* Naperville, IL: Sourcebooks.

66. Paul, Ann. Whitford. 1996. *Eight Hands Round: A Patchwork Alphabet.* New York: HarperTrophy.

67. Prelutsky, Jack. Ed. 1983. *The Random House Book of Poetry for Children.* New York: Random House.

68. Prelutsky, Jack. Ed. 1999. *The 20th Century Children's Poetry Treasury.* New York: Knopf.

69. Prelutsky, Jack. 1984. *The New Kid on the Block.* New York: Greenwillow.

70. Prelutsky, Jack. 2006. *Behold the Bold Umbrellaphant: And Other Poems.* New York: Greenwillow.

71. Raczka, Bob. 2010. *Guyku: A Year of Haiku for Boys.* Ill. by Peter Reynolds. Boston: Houghton Mifflin.

72. Rex, Adam. 2005. *Frankenstein Makes a Sandwich*. San Diego: Harcourt.
73. Rosenthal, Betsy R. 2004. *My House is Singing*. New York: Harcourt.
74. Ruddell, Deborah. 2009. *A Whiff of Pine, A Hint of Skunk*. New York: Simon & Schuster.
75. Salas, Laura. 2009. *Stampede! Poems to Celebrate the Wild Side of School!* New York: Clarion.
76. Schertle, Alice. 1996. *Keepers*. New York: Lothrop, Lee & Shepard.
77. Schlitz, Laura Amy. 2007. *Good Masters! Sweet Ladies!: Voices from a Medieval Village*. Cambridge, MA: Candlewick.
78. Schwartz, Alvin. 1992. *And the Green Grass Grew All Around: Folk Poetry from Everyone*. New York: HarperCollins.
79. Shields, Carol Diggory. 1995. *Lunch Money and Other Poems about School*. New York: Dutton.
80. Sidman, Joyce. 2009. *Red Sings From Treetops; A Year in Colors*. Ill. by Pamela Zagarenski. Boston: Houghton Mifflin.
81. Sidman, Joyce. 2010. *Dark Emperor and Other Poems of the Night*. Ill. by Rick Allen. Boston: Houghton Mifflin.
82. Silverstein, Shel. 1974. *Where the Sidewalk Ends*. New York: Harper and Row. New York: HarperCollins.
83. Silverstein, Shel. 1981. *A Light in the Attic*. New York: Harper & Row.
84. Silverstein, Shel. 1996. *Falling Up: Poems and Drawings*. New York: HarperCollins.
85. Singer, Marilyn. 1989. *Turtle in July*. New York: Macmillan.
86. Singer, Marilyn. 2010. *Mirror, Mirror*. Dutton.
87. Steptoe, Javaka. Ed. 1997. *In Daddy's Arms I Am Tall: African Americans Celebrating Fathers*. New York: Lee & Low.
88. Thomas, Joyce Carol. 2008. *The Blacker the Berry*. Illus. by Floyd Cooper. New York: Amistad.
89. Viorst, Judith. 1981. *If I Were in Charge of the World and Other Worries: Poems for Children and Their Parents*. New York: Atheneum.
90. Viorst, Judith. 1995. *Sad Underwear: And Other Complications More Poems for Children and Their Parents*. New York: Atheneum.
91. Weatherford, Carole Boston. 2002. *Remember the Bridge: Poems of a People*. New York: Philomel.
92. Weinstock, Robert. 2009. *Food Hates You, Too*. New York: Disney-Hyperion.
93. Weston, Robert Paul. 2008. *Zorgamazoo*. New York: Razorbill/Penguin.
94. Willard, Nancy. 1981. *A Visit to William Blake's Inn: Poems for Innocent and Experienced Travelers*. San Diego, CA: Harcourt.
95. Williams, Vera B. 2001. *Amber Was Brave, Essie Was Smart*. New York: Greenwillow.
96. Wolf, Allan. 2003. *The Blood-Hungry Spleen and Other Poems about Our Parts*. Cambridge, MA: Candlewick.
97. Wong, Janet S. 1996/2008. *A Suitcase of Seaweed, and Other Poems*. New York: McElderry.
98. Wong, Janet S. 2000. *Night Garden: Poems from the World of Dreams*. New York: Margaret K. McElderry.

99. Worth, Valerie. 2007. *Animal Poems*. Ill. by Steve Jenkins. New York: Farrar, Straus & Giroux.
100. Yolen, Jane. 2000. *Color Me a Rhyme: Nature Poems for Young People*. Honesdale, PA: Wordsong/Boyds Mills Press.

100 Poetry Books for Young Adults (Ages 13-18)

As young adults move toward reading and responding to classic poetry for adults, let's not forget there are many rich collections of poetry published just for them. 'Tweens and teens will find many fascinating options here in poetry about young love, culturally rich poems, absorbing novels in verse, and even poetic works written by other young people. This list is only a beginning.

1. Adoff, Arnold. 2010. *Roots and Blues, A Celebration*. Boston: Houghton Mifflin Harcourt.
2. Aguado, Bill. Ed. 2003. *Paint Me Like I Am: Teen Poems from WritersCorps*. New York: HarperTeen.
3. Appelt, Kathi. 2004. *My Father's Summers*. New York: Henry Holt.
4. Atkins, Jeannine. 2010. *Borrowed Names; Poems About Laura Ingalls Wilder, Madam C. J. Walker, Marie Curie, and Their Daughters*. Henry Holt.
5. Begay, Shonto. 1995. *Navajo: Visions and Voices Across the Mesa*. New York: Scholastic.
6. Bernier-Grand, Carmen T. 2007. *Frida: ¡Viva la vida! Long Live Life!* New York: Marshall Cavendish.
7. Block, Francesca Lia. 2008. *How to (Un)Cage a Girl*. New York: Joanna Cotler.
8. Brenner, Barbara. Ed. 2000. *Voices Poetry and Art from Around the World*. Washington, DC: National Geographic Society.
9. Bryant, Jen. 2009. *Kaleidoscope Eyes*. Knopf.
10. Burg, Ann. 2009. *All the Broken Pieces*. Scholastic.
11. Carlson, Lori M. Ed. 2005. *Red Hot Salsa; Bilingual Poems on Being Young and Latino in the United States*. New York: Henry Holt.
12. Chaltas, Thalia. 2009. *Because I Am Furniture*. Viking.
13. Clinton, Catherine. Ed. 1998. *I, Too, Sing America: Three Centuries of African American Poetry*. Boston: Houghton Mifflin.
14. Clinton, Catherine. Ed. 2003. *A Poem of Her Own; Voices of American Women Yesterday and Today*. New York: Abrams.
15. Crisler, Curtis. 2007. *Tough Boy Sonatas*. Honesdale, PA: Wordsong/Boyds Mills Press.
16. Dunning, Stephen, et. al. 1967. *Reflections on a Gift Watermelon Pickle*. New
17. Engle, Margaret. 2006. *The Poet Slave of Cuba: A Biography of Juan Francisco Manzano*. New York: Holt.
18. Engle, Margarita. 2010. *The Firefly Letters; A Suffragette's Journey to Cuba*. Henry Holt.
19. Fields, Terri. 2002. *After the Death of Anna Gonzales*. New York: Henry Holt.
20. Fletcher, Ralph. 1994. *I Am Wings; Poems About Love*. New York: Atheneum.
21. Fletcher, Ralph. 1997. *Ordinary Things: Poems from a Walk in Early Spring*. New
22. Franco, Betsy. Ed. 2008. *Falling Hard: Teenagers on Love*. Cambridge, MA: Candlewick.

23. Franco, Betsy. Ed. 2001. *Things I Have to Tell You: Poems And Writing by Teenage Girls.* Cambridge, MA: Candlewick.
24. Franco, Betsy. Ed. 2001. *You Hear Me? Poems and Writing by Teenage Boys.* Cambridge, MA: Candlewick.
25. Frost, Helen. 2003. *Keesha's House.* New York: Farrar, Straus, and Giroux.
26. Frost, Helen. 2009. *Crossing Stones.* New York: Farrar, Straus & Giroux.
27. George, Kristine O'Connell. 2002. *Swimming Upstream: Middle School Poems.* New York: Clarion.
28. Glenn, Mel. 1996. *Who Killed Mr. Chippendale?* New York: Lodestar.
29. Glenn, Mel. 1997. *The Taking of Room 114: A Hostage Drama in Poems.* New York:
30. Glenn, Mel. 2000. *Split Image: A Story in Poems.* New York: HarperCollins.
31. Gordon, Ruth. Ed. 1995. *Pierced by a Ray of Sun: Poems about the Times We Feel Alone.* New York: HarperCollins.
32. Grandits, John. 2007. *Blue Lipstick: Concrete Poems.* New York: Clarion.
33. Greenberg, Jan. Ed. 2001. *Heart to Heart: New Poems Inspired by Twentieth-Century American Art.* New York: Abrams.
34. Greenberg, Jan, ed. 2008. *Side by Side: New Poems Inspired by Art from Around the World.* Abrams.
35. Grimes, Nikki. 2002. *Bronx Masquerade.* Carmel: Hampton-Brown.
36. Grover, Lorrie Ann. 2002. *Loose Threads.* New York: McElderry Books.
37. Havill, Juanita. 2008. *Grow.* Atlanta: Peachtree.
38. Heard, Georgia. Ed. 2002. *This Place I Know: Poems of Comfort.* Cambridge: Candlewick.
39. Hemphill, Stephanie. 2007. *Your Own, Sylvia.* Knopf.
40. Hemphill, Stephanie. 2010. *Wicked Girls; A Novel of the Salem Witch Trials.* HarperCollins.
41. Herrera, Juan Felipe. 2011. *Skate Fate.* HarperCollins.
42. Herrick, Steven. 2004. *The Simple Gift.* New York: Simon & Schuster.
43. Holbrook, Sara. 1996. *The Dog Ate My Homework.* Honesdale, PA: Boyds Mills Press.
44. Holbrook, Sara & Wolf, Allan. 2008. *More Than Friends; Poems from Him and Her.* Boyds Mills Press.
45. Hopkins, Lee Bennett. Ed. 2008. *America at War.* McElderry.
46. Hopkins, Ellen. 2008. *Identical.* McElderry.
47. Hughes, Langston. (75th anniversary edition) 2007. *The Dream Keeper* (and seven additional poems). New York: Knopf.
48. Janeczko, Paul. Ed. 2004. *Blushing: Expressions of Love.* New York: Scholastic.
49. Johanson, Paula. Ed. 2010. *Poetry Rocks: World Poetry; "Evidence of Life."* Enslow.

50. Johnson, Angela. 1998. *The Other Side: Shorter Poems*. New York: Orchard.
51. Johnson, Dave. Ed. 2000. *Movin': Teen Poets Take Voice.* New York: Orchard.
52. Katz, Bobbi. Ed. 2000. *We the People: Poems.* New York: Greenwillow.
53. Koertge, Ron. 2001. *The Brimstone Journals.* Cambridge: Candlewick Press.
54. Lawson, JonArno. 2010. *Think Again*. Kids Can Press.
55. Levithan, David. 2004. *The Realm of Possibility*. New York: Knopf.
56. Lewis, J. Patrick. 2005. *Vherses: A Celebration of Outstanding Women.* Creative.
57. Lewis, J. Patrick. 2007. *The Brothers' War: Civil War Voices in Verse.* National Geographic.
58. Mecum, Ryan. 2008. *Zombie Haiku.* How Books.
59. Marcus, Kimberly. 2011. *exposed.* Random House.
60. Mora, Pat. 2010. *Dizzy in Your Eyes.* Knopf.
61. Mora, Pat. 2000. *My Own True Name: New and Selected Poems for Young Adults.*
62. Myers, Walter Dean. 2004. *Here in Harlem: Poems in Many Voices.* New York: Holiday House.
63. Nelson, Marilyn. 2001. *Carver: A Life in Poems.* Asheville: Front Street.
64. Nelson, Marilyn. 2005. *A Wreath for Emmett Till.* Boston: Houghton Mifflin.
65. Neri, G. and Watson, Jesse Joshua. 2007. *Chess Rumble.* New York: Lee & Low.
66. Nye, Naomi Shihab. Ed. 1995. *The Tree is Older than You Are: A Bilingual Gathering of Poems and Stories from Mexico with Paintings by Mexican Artists.* New York: Simon & Schuster.
67. Nye, Naomi Shihab. Ed. 1998. *The Space Between Our Footsteps: Poems and Paintings From the Middle East.* New York: Simon & Schuster.
68. Nye, Naomi Shihab. Ed. 1999. *What Have You Lost?* New York: Greenwillow.
69. Ochoa, Annette Piña, Betsy Franco, and Traci L. Gourdine, Eds. 2003. *Night is Gone, Day is Still Coming; Stories and Poems by American Indian Teens and Young Adults.* Cambridge, MA: Candlewick.
70. Ostow, Micol. 2011. *family.* New York: Egmont.
71. Panzer, Nora. Ed. 1994. *Celebrate America in Poetry and Art.* New York: Hyperion.
72. Paschen, Elise and Raccah, Dominique. Eds. 2010. *Poetry Speaks; Who I Am.* Naperville, IL: Sourcebooks.
73. Rosenberg, Liz. Ed. 1996. *The Invisible Ladder: An Anthology of Contemporary American Poems for Young Readers.* New York: Henry Holt.
74. Rosenberg, Liz. Ed. 1998. *Earth-shattering Poems.* New York: Henry Holt.

75. Rosenberg, Liz. Ed. 2001. *Light-gathering Poems.* New York: Henry Holt.
76. Sandell, Lisa Ann. 2007. *Song of the Sparrow.* New York: Scholastic.
77. Shakur, Tupac. 1999. *A Rose Grew From Concrete.* New York: Simon & Schuster.
78. Shapiro, Karen Jo. 2007. *I Must Go Down to the Beach Again.* Watertown, MA: Charlesbridge.
79. Sidman, Joyce. 2003. *The World According to Dog: Poems and Teen Voices.* Boston: Houghton Mifflin.
80. Siebert, Diane. 2006. *Tour America: A Journey through Poems and Art.* San Francisco: Chronicle.
81. Smith, Hope Anita. 2003. *The Way a Door Closes.* New York: Henry Holt.
82. Smith, Hope Anita. 2008. *Keeping the Night Watch.* Henry Holt.
83. Sones, Sonya. 1999. *Stop Pretending: What Happened When My Big Sister Went Crazy.* New York: HarperCollins.
84. Sones, Sonya. 2001. *What My Mother Doesn't Know.* New York: Simon & Schuster.
85. Soto, Gary. 1992. *Neighborhood Odes.* San Diego: Harcourt Brace.
86. Soto, Gary. 1995. *Canto Familiar.* San Diego: Harcourt.
87. Soto, Gary. 2009. *Partly Cloudy: Poems of Love and Longing.*
88. Sullivan, Charles, ed. 1994. *Here is My Kingdom: Hispanic-American Literature and Art for Young People.* New York: H.N. Abrams.
89. Tom, Karen, and Kiki. 2001. Eds. *Angst! Teen Verses from the Edge.* New York: Workman Publishing.
90. Vecchione, Patrice. Ed. 2001. *Truth and Lies.* New York: Henry Holt.
91. Vecchione, Patrice. Ed. 2004. *Revenge and Forgiveness.* New York: Henry Holt.
92. Vecchione, Patrice. Ed
93. . 2007. *Faith and Doubt; An Anthology of Poems.* New York: Henry Holt.
94. Wayland, April Halprin. 2002. *Girl Coming in for a Landing.* New York: Knopf.
95. Weatherford, Carole Boston. 2008. *Becoming Billie Holiday.* Honesdale, PA: Wordsong/Boyds Mills Press.
96. Willard, Nancy. 1998. *Step Lightly: Poems for the Journey.* San Diego: Harcourt.
97. Wolff, Virginia Euwer. 1993. *Make Lemonade.* New York: Henry Holt.
98. Wong, Janet. 1999. *Behind the Wheel: Driving Poems.* New York: McElderry.
99. Wong, Joyce Lee. 2006. *Seeing Emily.* New York: Abrams.
100. Worth, Valerie. 1994. *All the Small Poems and Fourteen More.* New York: Farrar, Straus & Giroux.
101. WritersCorps. 2008. *Tell the World.* New York: HarperCollins.

Favorite Poetry for Young People 2011

In examining the nearly one hundred books of poetry published for young people in 2011, I found there was quite a variety in style, tone, content, and format available. In fact, I noticed ten mini-trends (if 2-3 books constitute a trend) that are worth exploring: animals, humor, music, culture, novels in verse, stories in verse, emerging new voices, poetic innovation, ebooks, and book poetry. Some titles feature tried-and-true "formulas" for creating appealing poetry for young people (using the connecting theme of "animals," for example), and others venture into brand new territory (such as creating poems using only the letters from a single word, as in Bob Raczka's Lemonade). Once again, it's heartening to see the field of poetry for young people offer such a bounty of choices and voices. With titles by poetry "fixtures" like Shel Silverstein, as well as National Book Award-winning new writers like Thanhha Lai, we can stock our shelves with gems that will hold up for years and look forward to what's next in poetry for kids and teens.

Engle, Margarita. 2011. *Hurricane Dancers; The First Caribbean Pirate Shipwreck*. Henry Holt.
*A powerful novel in verse set in the early 1500's about a slave named Quebrado, a Spanish pirate named Bernardo de Talavera, and a hostage named Alonso de Ojeda and their intertwining fates when all three are stranded on an island after a hurricane destroys their ship.

Frost, Helen. 2011. *Hidden*. Farrar, Straus & Giroux.
*An inventive verse novel told from two different perspectives—one girl is inadvertently kidnapped during a robbery and get-a-way. The daughter of the kidnapper quietly helps her, but when her father is arrested neither of their lives will ever be the same. Several years later the two girls attend the same summer camp and must confront the past, their feelings, and the repercussions.

George, Kristine O'Connell. 2011. *Emma Dilemma: Big Sister Poems*. Ill. by Nancy Carpenter. Clarion.
*A picture book story-in-poems that introduces the unique relationship between sisters as allies, playmates, and even enemies with a focus on two particular sisters and a crisis of too much togetherness

Henderson, Kathy. 2011. *Hush, Baby, Hush! Lullabies from Around the World*. Ill. by Pam Smy. Seattle: Frances Lincoln.
*A book of traditional lullabies gathered from all over the world with words in the original language plus the English version, together with a melody line and engaging illustrations

Hopkins, Lee Bennett. Ed. 2011. *I am the Book*. Holiday House.
*A collection of thirteen poems written by various top poets all on the subject of books and celebrating the joy of reading

Janeczko, Paul B. 2011. *Requiem; Poems of the Terezín Ghetto*. Candlewick.

*A haunting look into the lives of those imprisoned in the Terezin Concentration Camp during World War II, proudly hailed by Hitler as a sanctuary for artistic Jews

Lai, Thanhha. 2011. *Inside Out and Back Again.* HarperCollins.
*Powerful debut work from a new voice, a loosely autobiographical work about her own experience as a refugee from Vietnam and as a new immigrant to the U.S. in the 1970s

Lewis, J. Patrick and Yolen, Jane. 2011. *Self Portrait with Seven Fingers: A Life of Marc Chagall in Verse.* Creative Editions.
*An art-filled biography in poems that combines glimpses into Chagall's art with factual details and evocative poetry exploring the distinctive life path of an artist

Marcus, Kimberly. 2011. *exposed.* Random House.
*In this debut novel in verse for teens Marcus pens a heartbreaking tale of how one act of violence can tear apart a friendship, a family, and a community.

McCall, Guadalupe Garcia. 2011. *Under the Mesquite.* Lee & Low.
*Another debut novel in verse featuring a young Latina girl with artistic aspirations in a close-knit family coping with the mother's struggle with cancer

Nursery Rhyme Comics; 50 Timeless Rhymes from 50 Celebrated Cartoonists. First Second.
*A clever and comprehensive collection of classic nursery rhymes all freshly interpreted by a variety of top cartoonists

Ostlere, Cathy. 2011. *Karma.* New York: Razorbill.
*Maya and her Sikh father travel from Canada to India with her Hindu mother's ashes on the eve of Prime Minister Indira Gandhi's assassination. In the chaos that ensues, they are separated and this powerful debut verse novel becomes a story of survival, sacrifice, culture clash, and ultimately love.

Raczka, Bob. 2011. *Lemonade and Other Poems Squeezed from a Single Word.* Roaring Brook.
*A clever book filled with puzzle poems built from the letters of a single word; solve the word patterns then enjoy the simple childhood themes

Salas, Laura Purdie. 2011. *BookSpeak!.* Ill. by Josee Bisaillon. Clarion.
*The rhyme, rhythm, and voice of each poem told from the point of view of a book, will not only will this inspire children to read THIS book, but will inspire them to read period.

Thompson, Holly. 2011. *Orchards.* Random House.

*When a young girl takes her life and her circle of peers is complicit, Kana is sent to her mother's childhood home, a small village in Japan, to visit with her family, and reflect on her role and her own identity

Vardell, Sylvia and Wong, Janet. Eds. 2011. *P*TAG*. PoetryTagTime.com.
*In this first ever digital anthology of new poetry for teens, 31 poets speak to the complicated lives of today's teens, with new, quirky, reflective, and soulful poems about love and longing, war and worry, tattoos, piercings, watching people, being watched, broken lives, and more (I know it's a bit self-serving to highlight my own project, but I think these poems are really special and I didn't write ANY of them!)

Wardlaw, Lee. 2011. *Won Ton; A Cat Tale Told in Haiku*. Ill. by Eugene
        Yelchin. Henry Holt.
*The sweet story of a shelter cat as he settles into his new home told in senryu, a form of Japanese poetry, capturing the fickle nature of the feline creature

Wheeler, Lisa. 2011. *Spinster Goose; Twisted Rhymes for Naughty Children*.
        Ill. by Sophie Blackall. Atheneum.
*A clever, satirical twist on classic Mother Goose rhymes in the "Lemony Snicket" tradiition

Wolf, Allan. 2011. *The Watch That Ends the Night; Voices from the Titanic*.
        Cambridge, MA: Candlewick.
*This massive, compelling novel in verse captures this historic and tragic event through multiple perspectives (including the iceberg itself) and varying poetry formats

Zimmer, Tracie Vaughn. 2011. *Cousins of Clouds; Elephant Poems*.
        Houghton Mifflin.
*Through combined poetry, informative paragraphs, and evocative illustrations, the power and myth of the world's largest land animal is revealed in a variety of poetic forms

Favorite Poetry for Young People 2010

Here are my picks for my favorite poetry books of the year. For me, it is all about the poetry "package," if you will. The poems, of course, are number one, and they should be interesting, thoughtful, distinctive, and rhythmic. I also value poetry that reads well out loud since I believe that is so crucial in connecting with children. But I also value the design and illustration of each book, since the presentation of the poems as a set provides an essential context for entering, enjoying, and remembering the poems. So many of today's poetry works do this so well—creating inviting visuals, well-designed layouts, and a distinct combination of art and language. Consider these contributions to the world of poetry for young people this year.

Ada, Alma Flor and Campoy, Isabel. 2010. *Muu, Moo! Rimas de animales/Animal Nursery Rhymes*. New York: Rayo/HarperCollins.
*A blilingual (Spanish/English) collection of 16 playful nursery rhymes taken from Argentina, Puerto Rico, Mexico and Spain together with some original verses, with Zubizarreta (the translator) retaining the musicality of the originals. Simple, rhythmic poems vary in length and featuring not cows, but a conejito (rabbit), a burro (donkey) and una lechuza (an owl), among other appealing animal characters.

Argueta, Jorge. 2010. *Arroz con leche/Rice Pudding: Un poema para cocinar/A Cooking Poem*. Ill. by Fernando Vilela. Toronto: Groundwood.
*Remember Argueta's *Bean Soup (Sopa de frijoles)* last year? Here's a follow up recipe poem picture book for dessert! This time, the lyrical language introduces us to one of the world's staples (rice) and how to prepare this popular and delicious dish. Argueta's fresh phrasing and Vilela's multi-media illustrations are the perfect pairing for this bilingual food-focused poem book in both Spanish and English.

Atkins, Jeannine. 2010. *Borrowed Names; Poems About Laura Ingalls Wilder, Madam C. J. Walker, Marie Curie, and Their Daughters*. New York: Henry Holt.
*Three contemporaneous women from history (Wilder, Walker and Curie) and their relationships with their daughters are showcased in this remarkable collection of poems that weave together like a novel-in-verse. Well researched, lyrical and compelling, these women, their daughters, and their times come to life in unique ways that connect and cross over.

Brown, Calef. 2010. *Hallowilloween; Nefarious Silliness*. Boston: Houghton Mifflin.
*This is classic Calef with his usual interplay of wordplay and artplay in this fun collection of poems perfect for Halloween and beyond. His clever use of point of view and relentless rhyme create irresistible poem portraits about mummies, witches, and "vumpires." Stylized, full-color art creates the perfect stage for his poems, full of details kids will notice and enjoy. Read these aloud together; the humor is completely infectious.

Elliott, David. 2010. *In the Wild.* Ill. by Holly Meade. Cambridge, MA: Candlewick.
In the Wild is a perfect companion to Elliott and Meade's previous work, *On the Farm.* This time the expansive, double-page spreads feature 14 wild cousins such as the lion, elephant, giraffe, zebra, etc. Elliott's short rhymes offer a musical and succinct blend of facts and feelings, with a riddle-like wrinkle spread across Meade's beautiful painted woodblock prints.

Engle, Margarita. 2010. *The Firefly Letters; A Suffragette's Journey to Cuba.* New York: Henry Holt.
*In Engle's fourth historical work in verse, she brings together three memorable female characters from different strata of society as they grapple with issues of freedom and choice. Based on primary sources from Swedish suffragist Fredrika Bremer and set in Cuba in 1851, Engle once again offers multiple overlapping dramatic points of view captured in the most lyrical imagery and language.

Florian, Douglas. 2010. *Poetrees.* New York: Simon & Schuster.
*As a former Girl Scout and leader, I confess I love trees and identifying various species, so I thoroughly enjoyed the art and wordplay in another engaging Florian picture book collection, *Poetrees.* Once again, he is so clever in both his creation and arrangement of art AND words in depicting 18 trees from around the world. And don't forget to check out the "glossatree!"

Hemphill, Stephanie. 2010. *Wicked Girls; A Novel of the Salem Witch Trials.* New York: HarperCollins.
*Hemphill has created a tour de force poetic slice of history with *Wicked Girls*, a totally compelling multi-point of view depiction of the Salem Witch Trials in 1692. Using the varying perspectives of the girls themselves and a formal language that evokes the period, she manages to deftly suggest *The Crucible* meets "Mean Girls," revealing the ageless conflicts and group dynamics that underlie interactions and relationships between girls (and others) across time.

Hopkins, Lee Bennett, comp. 2010. *Amazing Faces.* Ill. by Chris Soentpiet. New York: Lee and Low.
*This appealing new collection of 16 "portrait" poems by an assortment of largely contemporary poets celebrates diversity in our population with details and examples that will resonate with children and readers of all ages and backgrounds. Sumptuously illustrated by Chris Soentpiet, it's the perfect ice-breaker for reading aloud, getting acquainted, and prompting further sharing and writing.

Hopkins, Lee. Bennett, comp. 2010. *Sharing the Seasons.* New York: McElderry.
*Illustrated with David Diaz's vivid color palette, this expansive and generous anthology of 48 poems (12 for each of 4 seasons) gives one time to soak up each poem, a selection and blending of poems and voices. This notion of poems throughout the calendar year has such appeal to adults who want to infuse poetry into daily life, yet the poems rise above the mere curricular

connection (fall = pumpkins, for example) with fresh language and images (e.g., "one brew of wind").

Lawson, JonArno. 2010. *Think Again*. Toronto: Kids Can Press.
*A slim volume of poetry destined for many middle school (and high school) library shelves and surreptitious boy-girl sharing, it's built upon a series of 48 quatrain poems, almost story-like, in revealing the tenderness, angst, confusion, and exhilaration of fledgling first love. Black and white ink drawings by Julie Morstad "people" the book, suggesting the tentative sketching of a young artist doodling and journaling. Lawson's clever wordplay and sometimes syncopated rhythms keep the poems from veering into sentimentality and make them open-ended enough to stand on their own as thoughtful and contemplative.

Levy, Debbie. 2010. *The Year of Goodbyes; A True Story of Friendship, Family and Farewells.* New York: Hyperion.
*Based on her own mother's childhood sharing of 1938 autograph-style/sticker albums in WWII Germany, Levy has created a graphic novel in verse with a childlike look and voice with a strong narrative pull. Be sure to also visit the book's interactive companion web site, The Poesiealbum Project: www.theyearofgoodbyes.com

Mora, Pat. 2010. *Dizzy in Your Eyes; Poems About Love.* New York: Knopf.
*The inter-generational points of view provide a powerful frame for the topic of love for young readers—and readers of all ages. There is clearly a youthful point of view and voice, but the poems reference love of parents, friends, family, pets—acknowledging the depth of feeling in many relationships and at many stages of life. Plus, it's chock full of many poetic forms (and notes about form) which teachers will enjoy.

Paschen, Elise and Raccah, Dominique, comp. 2010. *Poetry Speaks; Who I Am.* Naperville, IL: Sourcebooks.
*The anthology *Poetry Speaks Who I Am* is filled with more than 100 remarkable selections for ages 12–14 from a wide variety of poets. From Dickinson to Collins to Clifton and beyond, this anthology features both classic and contemporary selections and includes an audio CD (be sure to listen to the CD) with poets reading their own work. A journey of discovery through remarkable poets in a graphic teen-friendly format that looks deceptively like a journal of doodlings.

Raczka, Bob. 2010. *Guyku: A Year of Haiku for Boys.* Ill. by Peter Reynolds. Boston: Houghton Mifflin.
*This book really surprised me with its blending of the haiku form (often more formal and prescriptive) and the informal cartoon style of the art and hand-lettered look of the type. That juxtaposition, played out against a clean white background, creates a focused simplicity that is appealing and almost lyrical. The poems themselves are also clever, personal, and loose in feeling, but tightly structured with the clearest of phrasing. In a first person voice, they move us through the year in universal vignettes of boyhood. This book

manages to be boy-friendly poetry, while being an engaging example of contemporary nature haiku, too.

Sidman, Joyce. 2010. *Ubiquitous; Celebrating Nature's Survivors*. Boston: Houghton Mifflin.
*Another powerful blending of poetry (and prose paragraphs) and art with the double-page spreads of Beckie Prange's hand-colored linocut prints and Sidman's distinctive information-rich, yet always evocative poems. You can open to any page and have a poster-like introduction to one of nature's "ubiquitous" phenomenon presented in 3 ways—poem, explanation, and visualization—each complementing the other. "Ubiquitous" is a word that kids will love learning and saying and then the poems (and amazing art and endpapers) will guide them in conceptualizing that construct and give them a window into the natural world that is understandable and uplifting.

Sidman, Joyce. 2010. *Dark Emperor and Other Poems of the Night*. Boston: Houghton Mifflin.
*This collection of poems about the forest at night—owls, moths, porcupines-- is the last in the trio of "ecosystem poetry books" that began with *Song of the Water Boatman* (pond) and continued with *Butterfly Eyes* (meadow). It also offers a parallel layout with beautiful linoleum prints in a double-page spread for each of 12 poems, alongside an accompanying prose paragraph. This marriage of lyrical poetry, science-focused topics, and beautifully executed art has become a Sidman (and collaborating illustrator) trademark!

Singer, Marilyn. 2010. *Mirror, Mirror*. New York: Dutton.
*This picture book collection of clever "reverso" poems reinvents familiar fairy tales in clever, puzzle like fashion. Each tale/poem is two poems, read down the page for one point of view, then up the page for another; such as Red Riding Hood or the Wolf, for example, or Snow White vs. the Wicked Queen, etc. Witty and irreverent, these pithy poems read well out loud and challenge children to imitate the formula, complete with an author's endnote for guidance.

Weinstock, Robert. 2010. *Can You Dig It?* New York: Disney-Hyperion.
*Weinstock is a relative newcomer to creating poetry books for children and has an excellent sensibility for the wild and wacky. Here he once again creates both the dense and cartoon-like art, as well as the clever and quirky poetry, all focused on dinosaurs and paleontology, always a popular topic. He incorporates "big words" and well as sometimes gross humor in strong and rhythmic rhyming poems.

Yolen, Jane and Peters, Andrew Fusek. 2010. *Switching on the Moon; A Very First Book of Bedtime Poems*. Cambridge, MA: Candlewick.
*A companion to *Here's a Little Poem*, Yolen and Peters have created a wonderful early years anthology of poems for bedtime, nap time, and other moments for quiet contemplation. With 60+ poems, the range of voices and styles adds richness and the illustrations by Brian Karas (along with the book's overall design) invite repeated browsing and sharing.

Favorite Poetry for Young People 2009

I think it was a great year for poetry for young people with a tremendous variety of subject matter and format and heaps of quality and innovation. I wrote earlier about trends I observed this year and about the organizing thread of TIME in many poetry books this year, in particular. As a group, all the titles below offer a mini-library of what's new and great about poetry for kids: in form, in format, in look, in impact, in humor, in emotional power, etc. There are so many wonderful works worthy of consideration and sure to hold up in repeated readings over and over again. Just $200 (app.) would buy this entire collection of my recommended list (for example) of some of the best poetry of 2009, a fabulous year's worth of reading for all ages—adults included.

Argueta, Jorge. 2009. *Sopa de frijoles/ Bean Soup.* Ill. by Rafael Yockteng. Toronto, ON: Groundwood.
*It's bilingual (Spanish/English), it's a recipe, it's poetry plus cooking full of metaphors and similes and beans

Burg, Ann. 2009. *All the Broken Pieces.* Scholastic.
*Spare, moving verse novel about a boy wrestling with his identity as a Vietnamese child growing up in the US post war

Florian, Douglas. 2009. *Dinothesaurus.* New York: Simon & Schuster.
*Classic Florian wordplay and information-rich poems about dinosaurs and delectable dinosaur names

Franco, Betsy. 2009. *Curious Collection of Cats.* Ill. by Michael Wertz. San Francisco, CA: Tricycle Press.
*Clever concrete poems about cats and their idiosyncrasies envisioned in popsicle colored art

Frost, Helen. 2009. *Crossing Stones.* New York: Farrar, Straus & Giroux.
*Four teens' lives interweave against a backdrop of WWI, influenza, and women's emerging roles and rights

Hoberman, Mary Ann and Winston, Linda. 2009. *The Tree That Time Built; A Celebration of Nature, Science, and Imagination.* Naperville, IL: Sourcebooks.
*Fascinating exploration of the parallel ways scientists and poets observe and understand the natural world

Hopkins, Lee Bennett. 2009. *City I Love.* Ill. by Marcellus Hall. New York: Abrams.
*Poems can be about cities, too, and here is a playful cityscape of sights, sounds, and smells from cities around the world

Hopkins, Lee Bennett. 2009. *Sky Magic.* Ill. by Mariusz Stawarski. New York: Dutton.

*Color-drenched collection of day-to-night poems perfect for breakfast table or bedtime sharing or in between

Hughes, Langston. 2009. *My People*. Ill. by Charles R Smith Jr. New York: Simon & Schuster.
*A nearly theatrical re-interpretation of the classic Langston Hughes poem through Smith's bold sepia-toned photography

Katz, Bobbi. 2009. *The Monsterologist; A Memoir in Rhyme*. New York: Sterling.
*Ingenious scrapbook design and moveable art showcase clever poems about monsters and the evil genius who knows them best

Lewis, J. Patrick. 2009. *The House*. Illus. by Roberto Innocenti. Minneapolis, MN: Creative Editions.
*Brilliant combination of sensitive, insightful poetry and exquisite fine art tells the story of one house across the centuries

Mordhorst, Heidi. 2009. *Pumpkin Butterfly; Poems from the Other Side of Nature*. Honesdale PA: Wordsong/Boyds Mills Press.
*Subtle, lilting nature poems from Fall to Summer full of metaphor and imagery

Rosen, Michael J. 2009. *The Cuckoo's Haiku and Other Birding Poems*. Ill. by Stan Fellows. Cambridge, MA: Candlewick.
*Who knew haiku could be so gorgeous, informative and inspiring? Birds, seasons, and illustrations all come together beautifully.

Ruddell, Deborah. 2009. *A Whiff of Pine, A Hint of Skunk*. New York: Simon & Schuster.
*Forest life across the seasons in funny-to-contemplative poems

Salas, Laura. 2009. *Stampede! Poems to Celebrate the Wild Side of School!* New York: Clarion.
*Life at school portrayed through children personified as wild animals, a perfect parallel

Schertle, Alice. 2009. *Button Up! Wrinkled Rhymes*. Ill. by Petra Mathers. New York: Harcourt.
*Smart, engaging "mask" poems personify articles of clothing

Sidman, Joyce. 2009. *Red Sings From Treetops; A Year in Colors*. Ill. by Pamela Zagarenski. Boston: Houghton Mifflin.
*Personified colors and color words lead us through the seasons of nature in elegant, evocative poetry

Zimmer, Tracie Vaughn. 2009. *Steady Hands: Poems About Work*. New York: Clarion.
*Thoughtful, descriptive poems about jobs and careers, from the usual to the unique

Favorite Poetry for Young People 2008

The year included an interesting variety, with picture book collections dominating, and new trends in poetry morphed with biography growing strong. There was also more experimentation with poetic form/topic and book layout which is fun for those of us who like to provide diverse models for aspiring writers and artists. This year's list showcases a variety of categories, including poetry written by kids, novels in verse, and even nonfiction works about poets and poetry. I did a bit of research and found that you could purchase hard cover copies of this whole list for only $382-- and have a wonderful mini-library of 2008 poetry for young people that runs the gamut from the hilarious (Frankenstein monster parodies) to the transcendent (Billie Holiday's lyrical life). What a bargain!

Alarcón, Francisco X. 2008. *Animals Poems of the Iguazú / Animalario del Iguazú*. San Francisco: Children's Book Press.
*Animal spirits, Spanish/English, vivid, energetic art

Ashman, Linda. 2008. *Stella, Unleashed*. New York: Sterling.
*Fun and frolicking, frisky rescue dog; dog point of view

Beck, Carolyn. *Buttercup's Lovely Day*. Custer: Orca Books.
*Dawn to dusk day in the life of a contented cow, with lyrical illustrations

Giovanni, Nikki, comp. 2008. *Hip Hop Speaks to Children*. Naperville, IL: Sourcebooks.
*Amazing range, African American voices, fabulous audio CD

Greenberg, Jan, comp. 2008. *Side by Side: New Poems Inspired by Art from Around the World*. New York: Abrams.
*Poetry inspired by art from all around the world, multilingual

Holbrook, Sara and Wolf, Allan. 2008. *More Than Friends: Poems from Him and Her*. Honesdale, PA: Wordsong/ Boyds Mills Press.
*Teen boy and girl perspectives, fun sidebars on poetic form and experimentation

Hopkins, Lee Bennett, comp. 2008. *America at War*. New York: McElderry.
*Poets on war, historical perspective, mural-like art, poignant and powerful

Lawson, Jonarno. 2008. *Black Stars in a White Night Sky*. Honesdale, PA: Boyds Mills/ Wordsong.
*From silly to serious, playful to absurd, poignant to wry

Lewis, J. Patrick. 2008. *The World's Greatest: Poems*. San Francisco: Chronicle.
*Fun facts and factoids become focus of clever poems in varied formats

Nye, Naomi Shihab. 2008. *Honeybee*. New York: Greenwillow.
*Poem gems, vignettes and observations are political, personal, and powerful

Rex, Adam. 2008. *Frankenstein Takes the Cake.* San Diego: Harcourt.
*Hysterically funny riffs on monsters in poems, parodies, and amazing art

Soto, Gary. 2008. *Partly Cloudy; Poems of Love and Longing.* Boston: Houghton Mifflin Harcourt.
*Half and half, he said, she said, young love poems, with crossover character connections

Favorite Poetry for Young People 2007

My favorite children's poetry of 2007 included a great deal of variety: anthologies, biographical poetry, picture book collections, novels in verse, edgy YA work, playful verses for very young children, and more. New voices and new works by old favorites. Great curricular connections in science, social studies, and beyond. Fun experimentation with poetic form and voice. Beautifully written, beautifully illustrated. Serious, humorous, and everything in between. After much deliberation, here's my list of not-to-be-missed poetry for kids in 2007. Be sure your library has multiple copies of each!

Alexander, Elizabeth and Nelson, Marilyn. 2007. *Miss Crandall's School for Young Ladies and Little Misses of Color.* Honesdale, PA: Wordsong/Boyds Mills Press.
*Powerful sonnets tell the story of Prudence Crandall and her school for African American women in the early 1800's

Crisler, Curtis. 2007. *Tough Boy Sonatas.* Honesdale, PA: Wordsong/Boyds Mills Press.
*Gripping, edgy poems about growing up as a young black man in the city

Fisher, Aileen. 2007. *Do Rabbits Have Christmas?* New York: Henry Holt.
*Lovely, fresh gathering of older poems by Fisher about Christmas in nature

Florian, Douglas. 2007. *comets, stars, the moon, and mars.* San Diego: Harcourt.
*Florian's dynamic illustrations and clever, descriptive poetry take us to outer space.

Frank, John. 2007. *How to Catch a Fish.* New York: Roaring Brook.
*Evocative oil paintings and lyrical poetry introduce fishing around the world.

Grandits, John. 2007. *Blue Lipstick: Concrete Poems.* New York: Clarion.
*Musings of a teenage girl in often unorthodox poetic forms

Hemphill, Stephanie. 2007. *Your Own, Sylvia.* New York: Knopf.
*Semi-biographical verse novel written in the style of Sylvia Plath's poetry

Hopkins, Lee Bennett. 2007. *Behind the Museum Door.* New York: Abrams.
*Fun collection of field trip poems that make museum artifacts come alive

Issa, Kobayashi. 2007. *Today and Today.* New York: Scholastic.
*Classic haiku by Issa are arranged to create a lovely chronological story.

Janeczko, Paul, comp. 2007. *Hey, You! Poems to Skyscrapers, Mosquitoes, and Other Fun Things.* New York: HarperCollins.
*These "apostrophe" poems of address give a variety of objects a voice.

Miller, Kate. 2007. *Poems in Black and White.* Asheville: Front Street.

*Striking illustrations and lyrical poems address objects that are black and/or white.

Mora, Pat. 2007. *Yum! Mmmm! Que Rico!: America's Sproutings*. New York: Lee & Low.
*Vibrant illustrations and pungent haiku (along with fun facts) introduce the origins of foods from across the Americas.

Park, Linda Sue. 2007. *Tap Dancing on the Roof; Sijo Poems*. New York: Clarion.
Park brings the Korean form of sijo poetry to the forefront with clever rhymes and helpful background information.

Prelutsky, Jack. 2007. *Good Sports: Rhymes About Running, Jumping, Throwing, and More*. New York: Knopf.
*Participating as well as winning and losing in sports is highlighted in playful rhymes and illustrations.

Sandell, Lisa Ann. 2007. *Song of the Sparrow*. New York: Scholastic.
*Verse novel re-envisions a feminist telling of the "Lady of Shallott" classic.

Schlitz, Laura Amy. 2007. *Good Masters! Sweet Ladies!: Voices from a Medieval Village*. Cambridge: Candlewick.
*Poem portraits of a variety of interconnected characters in a medieval village

Sidman, Joyce. 2007. *This is Just to Say*. Boston: Houghton Mifflin.
*Poems of apology and forgiveness in the voices of a classroom of children

Smith, Charles R., Jr. 2007. *Twelve Rounds to Glory: The Story of Muhammad Ali*. Cambridge: Candlewick.
*A poem biography about boxer Ali told in a shout-out cadence

Spinelli, Eileen. 2007. *Where I Live*. New York: Dial.
*Delicate poems and drawings capture the difficulties of moving and making life transitions.

Vecchione, Patrice. 2007. *Faith and Doubt: An Anthology of Poems*. New York: Henry Holt.
*Powerful poems about belief pack this rich YA anthology

Weatherford, Carole Boston. 2007. *Birmingham, 1963*. Honesdale, PA: Wordsong/Boyds Mills Press.
*Photographs and poems trace the sad events of the church bombing in 1963.

Wong, Janet. 2007. *Twist: Yoga Poems*. New York: McElderry.
*Color-rich illustrations and metaphorical poems make yoga fun.

Worth, Valerie. 2007. *Animal Poems*. Ill. by Steve Jenkins. New York: Farrar, Straus & Giroux.
*Worth's descriptive poems and Steve Jenkins' collage art create vivid animal portraits.

Yolen, Jane and Peters, Andrew Fusek, comp. 2007. *Here's a Little Poem*. Cambridge: Candlewick.
*Fun collection of poems perfectly placed and illustrated for very "little" children

Zimmer, Tracie Vaughn. 2007. *Reaching for Sun*. New York: Bloomsbury.
*Accessible verse novel about a girl growing up with cerebral palsy

PLUS: Hughes, Langston. (75th anniversary edition 2007). *The Dream Keeper* (with seven additional poems). New York: Knopf.

Favorite Poetry for Young People 2006

Once again, 2006 included a variety of works by new and favorite poets-- picture book collections, nature themes, humorous verse, historical poem- stories, a poem biography, poems for the very young, all accompanied by the work of many distinctive illustrators. Stock up with new titles, double up with multiple copies, and speak up sharing poems with kids you care about every day.

Brown, Calef. 2006. *Flamingos on the Roof*. Boston: Houghton Mifflin.
*Zany, syncopated story-poems are accompanied by crazy, cock-eyed story- paintings about all kinds of make-believe creatures.

Bulion, Leslie. 2006. *Hey There, Stink Bug!* Watertown, MA: Charlesbridge.
*The insect world comes to life through poems and facts, with a fun focus on the gross and gruesome.

Engle, Margaret. 2006. *The Poet Slave of Cuba: A Biography of Juan Francisco Manzano*. Ill. by Sean Qualls. New York: Holt.
*The life of nineteenth-century Cuban slave Juan Francisco Manzano is portrayed in vivid free verse from multiple points of view.

Florian, Douglas. 2006. *Handsprings*. New York: Greenwillow.
*Rhyming poems about the colors, sounds, and feelings associated with spring are accompanied by watercolor paintings that energetically capture the mood of the season.

Frost, Helen. 2003. *The Braid*. New York: Farrar, Straus & Giroux.
*The intertwining poem tale of two sisters surviving hardships as Scottish refugees/immigrants in the 1850's

Greenfield, Eloise. 2006. *The Friendly Four*. Ill. by Jan Spivey Gilchrist. New York: HarperCollins.
*Read aloud poems for multiple voices depict four African American neighborhood children (two boys, two girls) who develop a friendship over a summer.

Katz, Bobbi. 2006. *Once Around the Sun*. Ill. by LeUyen Pham. San Diego: Harcourt.
*A-poem-a-month shows city life from the child's point of view combined with lively, energetic scenic illustrations of a diverse community

Larios, Julie. 2006. *Yellow Elephant: A Bright Bestiary*. Ill. by Julie Paschkis. San Diego: Harcourt.
*A kind of BROWN BEAR, BROWN BEAR book of read aloud color-animal poems full of metaphor and description

Lewis, J. Patrick and Rebecca Kai Dotlich. 2006. *Castles: Old Stone Poems*. Honesdale, PA: Wordsong/Boyds Mills.

*A beautiful collection of paintings and poems of historic castles around the world

Lewis, J. Patrick. 2006. *Blackbeard, the Pirate King*. Washington, D.C.: National Geographic.
*With classic pirate illustrations by Pyle and Wyeth, as well as modern incarnations, the fascinating life of Edward Teach is captured in poems, facts, and endnotes.

Myers, Walter Dean. 2006. *Jazz*. Ill. by Christopher Myers. New York: Holiday House.
*A celebration of jazz music and history and a tribute to New Orleans captured with vivid and participatory language

Rex, Adam. 2005. *Frankenstein Makes a Sandwich*. San Diego: Harcourt.
*Rex has written and illustrated an irresistible collection of monster poems told with verve and humor.

Shannon, George. 2006. *Busy in the Garden.* Ill. by Sam Williams. New York: Greenwillow.
*These rollicking rhymes and riddles about garden life will engage even the very youngest children.

Sidman, Joyce. 2006. *Butterfly Eyes and Other Secrets of the Meadow*. Boston: Houghton Mifflin.
*Exquisite riddle rhyme pairs explore the plants and animals of the meadow along with informative prose paragraphs and a glossary.

Siebert, Diane. 2006. *Tour America: A Journey through Poems and Art*. San Francisco: Chronicle Books.
*Tour the U.S. through descriptive, rhyming poems and mixed media art.

Weatherford, Carole Boston. 2006. *Dear Mr. Rosenwald*. Ill. by R. Gregory Christie. New York: Scholastic.
*The true story-in-poems about a small, Southern African American community that builds its own school in the 1920s.

Favorite Poetry for Young People 2005

Nature, history, and the art of poetry itself are some of the dominant themes in this year's poetry. Several of the big names are represented this year (such as Prelutsky, Silverstein) as well as poets of color (such as Alarcón and Soto). The illustrations in many of these collections are also quite striking and add even more interest for young readers. And some collections even invite interaction, including origami and drawing or painting murals. Check 'em all out.

Alarcón, Francisco X. 2005. *Poems to Dream Together/ Poemas para Sonar Juntos.* New York: Lee & Low.
*Alarcón focuses on family and community through bilingual poems about dreams and goals.

George, Kristine O'Connell. 2005. *Fold Me a Poem.* San Diego, CA: Harcourt.
*The poet pairs verses with the art of paper folding, origami.

Hopkins, Lee Bennett. 2005. Days to Celebrate: A Full Year of Poetry, People, Holidays, History, Fascinating Facts, and More. New York: Greenwillow.
*A meaty guide to injecting poetry into daily events based on a variety of connections and happenings

Janeczko, Paul B., comp. 2005. *A Kick in the Head: An Everyday Guide to Poetic Forms.* Cambridge: Candlewick.
*A clear and inviting introduction to a variety of forms of poetry

Kennedy, Caroline, comp. 2005. *A Family of Poems: My Favorite Poetry for Children.* Ill. by Jon J. Muth. New York: Hyperion.
*Kennedy draws together both classic and contemporary poems from around the world—a tribute to her own growing up with poetry.

Lewis, J. Patrick. 2005. *Please Bury Me in the Library.* Ill. by Kyle Stone. San Diego: Harcourt.
*Poems about books, words, libraries, and reading are fun to share

Lewis, J. Patrick. 2005. *Heroes and She-Roes: Poems of Amazing and Everyday Heroes.* Ill. by Jim Cooke. New York: Dial.
*Lewis introduces over 20 famous and not so famous people through rhyming character sketches.

Lewis, J. Patrick. 2005. *Vherses: A Celebration of Outstanding Women.* Ill. by Mark Summer. Mankato: Creative Editions.
*Poem portraits of 14 famous women are compelling and fascinating.

Moore, Lilian. 2004. *Mural on Second Avenue, and Other City Poems.* Ill. by Roma Karas, ill. Cambridge: Candlewick.
*Simple poetic observations of city life

Nelson, Marilyn. 2005. *A Wreath For Emmett Till*. Ill. by Philippe Lardy. Boston: Houghton Mifflin.
*Powerful inter-connected poems tell the true story of the lynching of a teen in Mississippi in the 1960s

Nye, Naomi Shihab. 2005. *A Maze Me: Poems for Girls*. New York: Greenwillow.
*The everyday life and inner world and worries of girls are captured here.

Prelutsky, Jack. 2005. *Read a Rhyme, Write a Rhyme*. Ill. by Meilo So. New York: Random House.
*A direct, practical approach to poetry writing for children including examples, prompts, and tips

Quattlebaum, Marie. 2005. *Winter Friends*. Ill. by Hiroe Nakata. New York: Bantam.
*Energetic poems about a young girl's experiences on a winter's day

Sidman, Joyce. 2005. *Song Of The Water Boatman & Other Pond Poems*. Ill. by Beckie Prange. Boston: Houghton Mifflin.
*A celebration of pond life and the creatures that inhabit the pond

Silverstein, Shel. 2005. *Runny Babbit: A Billy Sook*. New York: HarperCollins.
*Classic Silverstein wordplay and nonsense are sure to appeal.

Soto, Gary. 2005. *Worlds Apart: Fernie and Me*. New York: Putnam.
*Two friends in middle school take imaginary excursions.

Favorite Poetry for Young People 2004

Some of the strongest poetry this year was written for 'tweens and teens, including a memoir by Kathi Appelt, concrete poetry by John Grandits, and gripping verse novels by Paul Janeczko, Walter Dean Myers, and Sonya Sones. There were also lovely picture book poetry collections for young readers, including a very contemporary Mother Goose and haiku by Jack Prelutsky. Look these risky ventures over and enjoy every one.

Appelt, Kathi. 2004. *My Father's Summers: A Daughter's Memoir.* New York: Holt.
This memoir, told in prose poems, offers a movingly descriptive story set in Houston, Texas beginning in 1965. It is a coming of age story as well as a story about family ties that offers one girl's perspective and experience of universal themes.

Crews, Nina. 2004. *Neighborhood Mother Goose.* New York: HarperCollins.
*Familiar Mother Goose rhymes are given a fresh twist with Nina Crew's illustrations, which set them in the cityscape of today. The urban setting and the multi-ethnic characters portrayed in the digitally composed photographs keep time perfectly with the old English verses, making this what *Horn Book* called "a Mother Goose for children growing up in a new century" (2003).

Frost, Helen. 2004. *Spinning Through the Universe.* New York: Farrar, Straus & Giroux.
*Told in alternating voices, this novel in verse explores the lives of Mrs. William's fifth grade class. "It is clear that Frost has been a teacher because her poems truly capture the essence and pathos of a classroom full of unique young people" (*Voice of Youth Advocates*, 2004). An explanation of each poetic form is included at the end of the book.

George, Kristine O'Connell. 2004. *Hummingbird Nest: A Journal of Poems.* Ill. by Barry Moser. New York: Harcourt.
*A hummingbird builds a nest on a family's porch, they get to watch as the bird builds a nest, lays eggs, and the eggs hatch and take their first flight. In journal form, each poem expresses thoughts, observations, and facts about hummingbirds which will move, inform, and spark curiosity in readers.

Grandits, John. 2004. *Technically, It's Not My Fault: Concrete Poems.* Boston: Houghton Mifflin.
*This graphically imaginative book of concrete poems brings humor to the everyday life of sarcastic 11 year-old Robert. *Booklist* calls this a "winning, highly creative collection" that will "convince readers that poetry can be loud, outrageous, gross fun" (2004).

Janeczko, Paul. 2004. *Worlds Afire: The Hartford Circus Fire of 1944.* Cambridge: Candlewick.
*Janeczko presents a novel in verse told from different viewpoints to give readers fictional first hand accounts of an actual circus fire in Hartford, CT which killed 167 people in 1944. "This poetic novel truly captures the terror,

chaos, and horrible aftermath of the tragedy" (*Voice of Youth Advocates*), and its style and drama will appeal to middle school and older readers.

Myers, Walter Dean. 2004. *Here in Harlem: Poems in Many Voices.* New York: Holiday House.
*In a collection of poems inspired by Edgar Lee Master's *Spoon River Anthology*, Myers attempts to capture the essence of Harlem by using the narrative voices of a large cast of characters. These poems can be read aloud, performed, read from cover to cover, or used as writing exercises—as the *Voice of Youth Advocates* state "Possibilities abound for use in the classroom" (2005).

Prelutsky, Jack. 2004. *If Not for the Cat.* Ill. byTed Rand. New York: Harper Collins/Greenwillow.
*In this elegant picture book, seventeen haiku are offered in beautifully illustrated double page spreads. Each haiku describes a different animal and the accompanying illustration shows it in its natural habitat. *Booklist* calls this the "go-to book for haiku to read aloud in classrooms" (2004).

Rosenthal, Betsy R. 2004. *My House is Singing.* Ill. by Margaret Chodos-Irvine. New York: Harcourt.
*Celebrating home and all that it contains is the theme of this colection of poems that are complemented by bright and airy illustrations. The narrator takes us around her home and introduces the reader to her favorite spots as well as unusual items and celebrates the comfort she finds in her home.

Sones, Sonya. 2004. *One of Those Hideous Books Where the Mother Dies.* New York: Simon & Schuster.
*When fifteen-year-old Ruby's mother dies, she is forced to leave her boyfriend, best friend, and home in Boston to go live with her famous movie star father who abandoned her and her mother when she was an infant. This novel in free verse is both a funny Hollywood fairy tale and an insightful look into grief, coping, and family.

SEASONAL AND HOLIDAY POETRY BOOKLISTS

If you're looking for poetry to share that is tied to the calendar and major events and celebrations throughout the year, this is the category for you. Poems are organized by seasons, holidays, and other topics tied to specific occasions and are presented in calendar order from January through December.

Poetry Books about the Seasons
Poetry Books for Valentine's Day
Poetry Books for Presidents Day
Poetry Books about Women's History
Poetry Books about Spring
Poetry Books for Earth Day
Poetry Books about Mothers
Poetry Books about Fathers
Poetry Books for the Fourth of July
Poetry Books about Patriotism
Poetry Books about Summer
Poetry Books about School for Children
Poetry Books about School for Teens
Poetry Books for Halloween
Poetry Books about Monsters
Poetry Books for Thanksgiving
Poetry Books for Hanukkah
Poetry Books for Christmas
Versions and Variants of "The Night Before Christmas"

Poetry Books about the Seasons

The natural world is a natural focus for much poetry written for all ages. Two poets, in fact, Francisco X. Alarcón and Douglas Florian, have created a poetry book for each of the four seasons noted below. Other writers have considered the seasons across the year from a variety of perspective and poetic forms. A selection of those are presented here.

Alarcón's set on the seasons

Alarcón, Francisco X. 1997. *Laughing Tomatoes and Other Spring Poems/Jitomates Risuenos y Otros Poemas de Primavera.* San Francisco, CA: Children's Book Press.

Alarcón, Francisco X. 1998. *From the Bellybutton of the Moon and Other Summer Poems/Del Ombligo de la Luna y Otros Poemas de Verano.* San Francisco: Children's Book Press.

Alarcón, Francisco X. 1999. *Angels Ride Bikes and Other Fall Poems.* San Francisco, CA: Children's Book Press.

Alarcón, Francisco X. 2001. *Iguanas in the Snow and Other Winter Poems/ Iguanas en la Nieve y Otros Poemas de Invierno.* San Francisco, CA: Children's Book Press.

Florian's set on the seasons

Florian, Douglas. 1999. *Winter Eyes.* New York: Greenwillow.

Florian, Douglas. 2002. *Summersaults.* New York: Greenwillow.

Florian, Douglas. 2003. *Autumnblings.* New York: Greenwillow.

Florian, Douglas. 2006. *Handsprings.* New York: Greenwillow.

Other poetry books about all the seasons

Esbensen, Barbara Juster. 1984. *Cold Stars and Fireflies: Poems of the Four Seasons.* New York: Crowell.

Farrar, Sid. 2012. *The Year Comes Round: Haiku Through the Seasons.* Ill. by Ilse Plume. Chicago: Whitman.

Franco, Betsy. 2003. *Mathematickles!* New York: McElderry.

Adoff, Arnold. 1991. *In for Winter, Out for Spring.* San Diego : Harcourt Brace Jovanovich.

Alderson, Sue Ann. 1997. *Pond Seasons.* Toronto: Groundwood.

Booth, David. 1990. *Voices on the Wind: Poems for all Seasons.* New York: Morrow.

Demi. 1992. *In the Eyes of the Cat: Japanese Poetry for all Seasons.* New York: Henry Holt.

Grossnickle, Anna. 2001. *Pieces: A Year in Poems & Quilts.* New York: Greenwillow.

Harrison, David. 2012. *Goose Lake: A Year in the Life of a Lake.* Amazon Digital Services.

Hopkins, Lee Bennett. 1992. *Ring Out, Wild Bells: Poems about Holidays and Seasons.* San Diego : Harcourt Brace Jovanovich.

Hopkins, Lee Bennett. Ed. 1994. *Weather: Poems for All Seasons.* New York: HarperTrophy.

Hopkins, Lee. Bennett Ed. 2010. *Sharing the Seasons.* Margaret McElderry.

Jacobs, Leland B. 1993. *Just Around the Corner: Poems about the Seasons.* New York: Henry Holt.

Katz, Bobbi. 2006. *Once Around the Sun.* Ill. by LeUyen Pham. San Diego, CA: Harcourt.

Livingston, Myra Cohn. 1982. *A Circle of Seasons.* New York: Holiday House.

Manguel, Alberto, Ed. 1990. *Seasons.* New York: Doubleday.

Merriam, Eve. 1992. *The Singing Green: New and Selected Poems for All Seasons.* New York: HarperCollins.

Mordhorst, Heidi. 2009. *Pumpkin Butterfly; Poems from the Other Side of Nature.* Honesdale PA: Wordsong/Boyds Mills Press.

Serio, John N. 2005. *The Seasons.* New York: Sterling.

Thomas, Patricia. 2008. *Nature's Paintbox: A Seasonal Gallery of Art and Verse.* Minneapolis, MN : Millbrook Press.

Whitehead, Jenny. 2007. *Holiday Stew; A Kid's Portion of Holiday and Seasonal Poems.* New York: Henry Holt.

Yolen, Jane. 2002. *Ring of Earth: A Child's Book of Seasons.* San Diego: Harcourt.

Zolotow, Charlotte. 2002. *Seasons; A Book of Poems.* New York: HarperCollins.

Poetry Books for Valentine's Day

Just giving a poem—any poem-- is a lovely Valentine gesture, but if you're looking for poetry for young people specifically ABOUT Valentine's and all kinds of love, you won't have much trouble. Poets have been pouring out their hearts for centuries. Young readers feel this same longing and often gravitate to very emotional "love" poetry—both in their reading and in their writing. You might even be surprised how popular these can be with adolescent readers (both boys and girls). Here's a beginning list.

"Love" poetry for children

Adoff, Arnold. 1997. *Love Letters.* New York: Scholastic.

cummings, e e. 2005. *Love: Selected Poems by e e cummings.* Ill. by Christopher Myers.

Greenfield, Eloise. 2003. *Honey, I Love.* New York: HarperCollins.

Grimes, Nikki. 1999. *Hopscotch Love: A Family Treasury of Love Poems.* New York: Lothrop, Lee & Shepard.

Hopkins, Lee Bennett. 2005. Valentine Hearts: Holiday Poetry. New York: HarperCollins.

Hopkins, Lee Bennett. Ed. 2005. Days to Celebrate: A Full Year of Poetry, People, Holidays, History, Fascinating Facts, and More. New York: Greenwillow.

Katz, Alan. 2010. *Too Much Kissing; And Other Silly Dilly Songs About Parents.* Simon & Schuster.

Lear, Edward. 2007. *The Owl and the Pussycat.* Toronto: Kids Can Press.

Levine, Gail Carson. 2012. *Forgive Me, I Meant to Do It: False Apology Poems.* Ill. by Matthew Cordell. HarperCollins.

Livingston, Myra Cohn. 1985. *Celebrations.* New York: Holiday House.

Livingston, Myra Cohn. Ed. 1987. *Valentine Poems.* Holiday House.

Marzollo, Jean. 2000. *I Love You: A Rebus Poem.* New York: Scholastic.

Mora, Pat. 2001. Ed. *Love to Mamá: A Tribute to Mothers.* New York: Lee & Low.

Pearson, Susan. 2006. *Slugs in Love.* New York: Marshall Cavendish.

Prelutsky, Jack. 1996. *It's Valentine's Day.* New York: HarperTrophy.

Sidman, Joyce. 2007. *This is Just to Say: Poems of Apology and Forgiveness.* Ill. by Pamela Zagarenski. Boston: Houghton Mifflin.

Singer, Marilyn. 2011. *Twosomes: Love Poems from the Animal Kingdom.* New York: Knopf.

Steptoe, Javaka. Ed. 1997. *In Daddy's Arms I Am Tall: African Americans Celebrating Fathers.* New York: Lee & Low.

Strachan, Linda. 2003. *What Colour is Love?* London: Bloomsbury.

Thomas, Joyce Carol. 2001. *A Mother's Heart, A Daughter's Love: Poems for Us to Share.* New York: HarperCollins.

Walker, Rob D. 2009. *Mama Says: A Book of Love For Mothers and Sons.* Ill. by Leo and Diane Dillon. New York: Scholastic.

Wilson, Karma. 2003. *Bear Hugs: Romantically Ridiculous Animal Rhymes.* New York: McElderry Books.

Yolen, Jane. 2009. *How Do Dinosaurs Say I Love You?* New York: Scholastic.

Young, Ed. 1997. *Voices of the Heart.* New York: Scholastic.

"Love" poetry or young adults

Block, Francesca Lia. 2008. *How to (Un)Cage a Girl.* New York: Joanna Cotler.

Fletcher, Ralph J. 1998. *Room Enough for Love: the Complete Poems of I Am Wings* and *Buried Alive: Poems.* New York: Aladdin.

Franco, Betsy. 2008. *Falling Hard: Teenagers on Love.* Somerville, MA: Candlewick Press.

Hemphill, Stephanie. 2012. *Sisters of Glass.* New York: Knopf.

Herrera, Juan Felipe. 1999. *Crashboomlove.* Albuquerque: University of New Mexico Press.

Herrick, Steven. 2004. *A Place Like This.* New York: Simon Pulse.

Herrick, Steven. 2004. *Love, Ghosts, & Facial Hair.* New York: Simon Pulse.

Holbrook, Sara and Wolf, Allan. 2008. *More Than Friends; Poems from Him and Her.* Honesdale, PA: Wordsong/Boyds Mills Press.

Janeczko, Paul B. Ed. 2004. *Blushing: Expressions of Love in Poems and Letters.* New York: Scholastic.

Merriam, Eve. 1983. *If Only I Could Tell You: Poetry for Young Lovers and Dreamers.* New York: Knopf.

Mora, Pat. 2010. *Dizzy in Your Eyes.* New York: Knopf.

Myers, Walter Dean. 2009. *Amiri and Odette: A Dance for Two.* New York: Scholastic.

Pockell, Leslie. Ed. 2003. *The 100 Best Love Poems of All Time.* New York: Warner.

Sayer, Viv. Ed. 2008. *Poems of Love and Longing.* London: Pont Books.

Soto, Gary. 1990. *A Fire in My Hands.* New York: Scholastic.

Soto, Gary. 2009. *Partly Cloudy: Poems of Love and Longing.* Orlando: Harcourt.

Tregay, Sarah. 2012. *Love & Leftovers.* New York: Katherine Tegen.

Vecchione, Patrice. Ed. 2004. *Revenge and Forgiveness.* New York: Henry Holt.

Poetry Books for Presidents Day

When it's time to remember our government's leaders, reading a poem aloud is a time-honored tradition. Below, is a selection of appropriate and relevant books for young people from which to choose.

Bates, Katharine Lee. 1994. *O Beautiful for Spacious Skies*. New York: Chronicle.

Chandra, Deborah and Madeleine Comora. 2003. *George Washington's Teeth*. New York: Farrar, Straus & Giroux.

Cohn, Amy L. Ed. 1993. *From Sea to Shining Sea: A Treasury of American Folklore and Folk Songs*. New York: Scholastic.

Corcoran, Jill. Ed. 2012. *Dare to Dream… Change the World*. San Diego, CA: Kane Miller.

Gunning, Monica. 2004. *America, My New Home*. San Francisco, CA: Children's Book Press.

Hopkins, Lee Bennett. Ed. 1993. *Beat the Drum, Independence Day has Come: Poems for the Fourth of July*. Honesdale, PA: Wordsong/Boyds Mills.

Hopkins, Lee Bennett. Ed. 1999. *Lives: Poems about Famous Americans*. New York: HarperCollins.

Hopkins, Lee Bennett. Ed. 1994. *Hand in Hand: An American History through Poetry*. New York: Simon & Schuster.

Hopkins, Lee Bennett. 2005. *Days to Celebrate: A Full Year of Poetry, People, Holidays, History, Fascinating Facts, and More*. New York: Greenwillow.

Hughes, Langston. 2012. *I, Too, Am America*. Ill. by Bryan Collier. New York: Simon & Schuster.

Katz, Bobbi. 2000. *We the People: Poems*. New York: Greenwillow.

Katz, Susan. 2012. *The President's Stuck in the Bathtub: Poems About U.S. Presidents*. Clarion.

Lewis, J. Patrick. 2005. *Monumental Verses*. Washington, D.C.: National Geographic.

Livingston, Myra Cohn. 1993. *Abraham Lincoln: A Man for All the People: A Ballad*. New York: Holiday House.

Myers, Walter Dean. 2011. *We are America; A Tribute from the Heart*. Ill. by Christopher Myers. New York: HarperCollins.

Philip, Neil. Ed. 1995. *Singing America*. New York: Viking.

Rappaport, Doreen. 2008. *Lady Liberty*. Somerville, MA: Candlewick.

Shields, Carol Diggory. 2002. *American History, Fresh Squeezed*. Brooklyn, NY: Handprint Books.

Siebert, Diane. 2006. *Tour America: A Journey through Poems and Art*. San Francisco: Chronicle.

Smith, Charles R. Jr. 2003. *I am America*. New York: Scholastic.

Swamp, Chief Jake. 1995. *Giving Thanks: A Native American Good Morning Message*. New York: Lee & Low.

Whipple, Laura. Ed. 1994. *Celebrating America: A Collection of Poems and Images of the American Spirit*. New York: Philomel Books.

Wong, Janet. 2012. *Declaration of Interdependence: Poems for an Election Year*. PoetrySuitcase.

Poetry Books about Women's History

Here is a select list of poetry books that celebrate the unique qualities of girls and women. Some take an historical approach, others consider the roles of girls and women and their place in the world. They offer food for thought for girl readers—and boys—who are growing in their sense of identity and voice.

Adoff, Arnold. 1979. *I Am the Running Girl.* New York: Harper & Row.

Alexander, Elizabeth and Nelson, Marilyn. 2007. *Miss Crandall's School for Young Ladies and Little Misses of Color.* Honesdale, PA: Wordsong.

Atkins, Jeannine. 2010. *Borrowed Names; Poems About Laura Ingalls Wilder, Madam C. J. Walker, Marie Curie, and Their Daughters.* Henry Holt.

Bernier-Grand, Carmen T. 2007. *Frida: ¡Viva la vida! Long Live Life!* New York: Marshall Cavendish.

Bush, Timothy. 2000. *Ferocious Girls, Steamroller Boys, and Other Poems in Between.* New York: Orchard Books.

Clinton, Catherine. Ed. 2003. *A Poem of Her Own; Voices of American Women Yesterday and Today.* New York: Henry N. Abrams.

Engle, Margarita. 2010. *The Firefly Letters; A Suffragette's Journey to Cuba.* Henry Holt.

Engle, Margarita. 2008. *The Surrender Tree.* New York: Holt.

Franco, Betsy. Ed. 2001. *Things I Have to Tell You: Poems And Writing by Teenage Girls.* Cambridge: Candlewick Press.

Frost, Helen. 2009. *Crossing Stones.* New York: Farrar, Straus & Giroux.

George, Kristine O'Connell. 2011. *Emma Dilemma: Big Sister Poems.* Ill. by Nancy Carpenter. Clarion.

Glaser, Isabel Joshlin. Ed. 1995. *Dreams of Glory: Poems Starring Girls.* New York: Atheneum Books For Young Readers.

Grimes, Nikki. 1994. *Meet Danitra Brown.* New York: Lothrop, Lee & Shepard.

Hemphill, Stephanie. 2010. *Wicked Girls; A Novel of the Salem Witch Trials.* HarperCollins.

Hemphill, Stephanie. 2012. *Sisters of Glass.* New York: Knopf.

Hollyer, Belinda. 2006. Ed. *She's All That! Poems About Girls.* Boston: Kingfisher.

Hopkins, Lee Bennett. Ed. 1973. *Girls Can, Too! A Book of Poems.* New York: Franklin Watts.

Lewis, J. Patrick. 2005. *Heroes and She-roes: Poems of Amazing and Everyday Heroes.* New York: Dial Books For Young Readers.

Lewis, J. Patrick. 2005. *Vherses: A Celebration of Outstanding Women.* Mankato: Creative Editions.

Little, Jean. 1990. *Hey, World, Here I Am!* New York: Harper & Row.

McCall, Guadalupe Garcia. 2011. *Under the Mesquite.* Lee & Low.

Mora, Pat. 2001. Ed. *Love to Mama: A Tribute to Mothers.* New York: Lee & Low Books.

Morrison, Lillian. 2001. *More Spice Than Sugar.* Boston: Houghton Mifflin.

Nelson, Marilyn. 2009. *Sweethearts of Rhythm; The Story of the Greatest All-Girl Swing Band in the World.* New York: Dial.

Nye, Naomi Shihab. 2005. *A Maze Me; Poems for Girls*. New York: Greenwillow Books.

Paul, Ann Whitford. 1999. *All by Herself: 14 Girls Who Made a Difference: Poems*. San Diego: Harcourt Brace.

Philip, Neil. Ed. 2000. *It's a Woman's World: A Century of Women's Voices in Poetry*. New York: Dutton Children's Books.

Singer, Marilyn. 1996. *All We Needed to Say: Poems About School from Tanya and Sophie*. New york: Atheneum Books for Young Readers.

Smith, Charles R., Jr. 2003. *Hoop Queens*. Boston: Candlewick Press.

Thomas, Joyce Carol. 2002. *Crowning Glory*. New York: HarperCollins.

Wayland, April Halprin. 2002. *Girl Coming in for a Landing: A Novel in Poems*. New York: Knopf.

Weatherford, Carole Boston. 2007. *Birmingham, 1963*. Honesdale, PA: Wordsong/Boyds Mills Press.

Weatherford, Carole Boston. 2008. *Becoming Billie Holiday*. Honesdale, PA: Wordsong/Boyds Mills Press.

Williams, Vera B. 2001. *Amber Was Brave, Essie Was Smart*. New York: Greenwillow Books.

Wong, Janet S. 1999. *The Rainbow Hand: Poems about Mothers and Children*. New York: McElderry.

Poetry Books about Spring

People often think poetry is all about springtime and daffodils and tulips—and not in a good way—but poetry can be about so many different topics. Of course poetry can also be about springtime and related topics, as the following book titles demonstrate.

Adoff, Arnold. 1991. *In for Winter, Out for Spring*. San Diego, CA: Harcourt Brace.

Alarcón, Francisco X. 1997. *Laughing Tomatoes and Other Spring Poems/Jitomates Risuenos y Otros Poemas de Primavera*. San Francisco, CA: Children's Book Press.

Blackaby, Susan. 2010. *Nest, Nook & Cranny*. Watertown, MA: Charlesbridge.

Booth, David. 1990. *Voices on the Wind: Poems for All Seasons*. New York: Morrow.

Brenner, Barbara. Ed. 1994. *The Earth is Painted Green: A Garden of Poems about Our Planet*. New York: Scholastic.

Bruchac, Joseph. 1992. *Thirteen Moons on Turtle's Back: A Native American Year of Moons*. New York: Philomel Books.

Bruchac, Joseph. 1995. *The Earth under Sky Bear's Feet: Native American Poems of the Land*. New York: Philomel Books.

Esbensen, Barbara Juster. 1984. *Cold Stars and Fireflies: Poems of the Four Seasons*. New York: Crowell.

Fletcher, Ralph J. 1997. *Ordinary Things: Poems from a Walk in Early Spring*. New York: Atheneum.

Florian, Douglas. 2006. *Handsprings*. New York: Greenwillow.

George, Kristine O'Connell. 2004. *Hummingbird Nest: A Journal of Poems*. New York: Harcourt.

Harley, Avis. 2008. *The Monarch's Progress: Poems with Wings*. Honesdale, PA: Boyds Mills/Wordsong.

Havill, Juanita. 2006. *I Heard It from Alice Zucchini: Poems About the Garden*. San Francisco: Chronicle Books.

Hopkins, Lee. Bennett. Ed. 2010. *Sharing the Seasons*. New York: Margaret McElderry.

Katz, Bobbi. Ed. 1992. *Puddle-wonderful: Poems to Welcome Spring*. New York: Random House.

Merriam, Eve. 1992. *The Singing Green: New and Selected Poems for All Seasons*. New York: HarperCollins.

Nicholls, Judith. 2003. *The Sun in Me: Poems about the Planet*. Somerville, MA: Barefoot Books.

Oelschlager, Vanita. 2009. *Ivy in Bloom: The Poetry of Spring from Great Poets and Writers of the Past*. Ill. by Kristin Blackwood. Akron, OH: Vanitabooks.

Roemer, Heidi. 2009. *Whose Nest is This?* NorthWord.

Rosen, Michael J. 2009. *The Cuckoo's Haiku and Other Birding Poems*. Ill. by Stan Fellows. Somerville, MA: Candlewick.

Schnur, Steven. 1999. *Spring: An Alphabet Acrostic*. New York: Clarion.

Shannon, George. Ed. 1996. *Spring: A Haiku Story*. New York: Greenwillow.

Sidman, Joyce. 2006. *Butterfly Eyes and Other Secrets of the Meadow*. Ill. by

Beth Krommes. Boston: Houghton Mifflin.

Thomas, Patricia. 2008. *Nature's Paintbox: A Seasonal Gallery of Art and Verse.* Minneapolis, MN: Millbrook Press.

Wolf, Sallie. 2010. *The Robin Makes a Laughing Sound.* Charlesbridge.

Yolen, Jane. 2002. *Ring of Earth: A Child's Book of Seasons.* San Diego: Harcourt.

Yolen, Jane. 2009. *A Mirror to Nature.* Ill. by Jason Stemple. Honesdale, PA: Wordsong/Boyds Mills Press.

Zolotow, Charlotte. 2002. *Seasons; A Book of Poems.* New York: HarperCollins.

Poetry Books for Earth Day

Poets have written about nature and the natural world for centuries. It's a favorite topic of writers of poetry for children, too. The following poetry books for young people focus even further on the earth and Earth Day themes such as respect for the land, extinction of species, conservation of resources—all with beautiful imagery and lyrical language.

Ada, Alma Flor. 1997. *Gathering the Sun*. New York: Lothrop, Lee, & Shepard.

Argueta, Jorge. 2006. *Talking with Mother Earth; Poems; Hablando con Madre Tierra*. Toronto: Groundwood.

Asch, Frank. 1996. *Sawgrass Poems: A View of the Everglades*. San Diego, CA: Harcourt Brace.

Asch, Frank. 1998. *Cactus Poems*. San Diego, CA: Harcourt Brace.

Begay, Shonto. 1995. *Navajo: Visions and Voices Across the Mesa*. New York: Scholastic.

Brenner, Barbara. Ed.1994. *The Earth is Painted Green: A Garden of Poems about Our Planet*. New York: Scholastic.

Bruchac, Joseph. 1995. *The Earth under Sky Bear's Feet: Native American Poems of the Land*. New York: Philomel Books.

Bruchac, Joseph. 1996. *Between Earth and Sky: Legends of Native American Sacred Places*. San Diego, CA: Harcourt Brace.

Cooling, Wendy. Ed. 2010. *All the Wild Wonders: Poems of Our Earth*. Ill. by Piet Grobler. London: Frances Lincoln Children's Books.

Coombs, Kate. 2012. *Water Sings Blue: Ocean Poems*. Ill. by Meilo So. Chronicle.

Davies, Nicola. 2012. *Outside Your Window: A First Book of Nature*. Ill. by Mark Hearld. Somerville, MA: Candlewick.

Farrar, Sid. 2012. *The Year Comes Round: Haiku Through the Seasons*. Ill. by Ilse Plume. Chicago, IL: Whitman.

Fisher, Aileen. 1997. *Sing of the Earth and Sky: Poems about Our Planet and the Wonders Beyond*. Honesdale, PA: Boyds Mills Press.

Fletcher, Ralph J. 1991. *Water Planet: Poems about Water*. Paramus, N.J.: Arrowhead Books.

Florian, Douglas. 2012. *Unbeelievables: Honeybee Poems and Paintings*. Beach Lane.

George, Kristine O'Connell. 1998. *Old Elm Speaks: Tree Poems*. New York: Clarion.

Harley, Avis. 2006. *Sea Stars: Saltwater Poems*. Honesdale, PA: Wordsong/Boyds Mills Press.

Harley, Avis. 2008. *The Monarch's Progress: Poems with Wings*. Honesdale, PA: Boyds Mills/Wordsong.

Havill, Juanita. 2006. *I Heard It from Alice Zucchini: Poems About the Garden*. San Francisco: Chronicle Books.

Havill, Juanita. 2008. *Grow*. Atlanta, GA: Peachtree.

Hopkins, Lee. Bennett. Ed. 2010. *Sharing the Seasons*. New York: Margaret McElderry.

Hopkins, Lee Bennett. Ed.1999. *Spectacular Science: A Book of Poems*. New York: Simon & Schuster.

Hopkins, Lee Bennett. Ed. 2012. *Nasty Bugs*. Ill. by Will Terry. New York: Dial.

Johnston, Tony. 1999. *An Old Shell: Poems of the Galapagos*. New York: Farrar, Straus & Giroux.

Kurtz, Jane. 2000. *River Friendly, River Wild*. New York: Simon & Schuster.

Levy, Constance. 1994. *A Tree Place and Other Poems*. New York: McElderry.

Levy, Constance. 1998. *A Crack in the Clouds*. New York: Margaret K. McElderry.

Levy, Constance. 2002. *Splash! Poems of Our Watery World*. New York: Orchard.

Lewis, J. Patrick. 1991. *Earth Verses and Water Rhymes*. New York; Simon & Schuster.

Lewis, J. Patrick. 2003. *Swan Song: Poems of Extinction*. Creative Editions.

Lewis, J. Patrick. 2009. *The House*. Illus. by Roberto Innocenti. Minneapolis, MN: Creative Editions.

Lewis, J. Patrick. Ed. 2012. *Book of Animal Poetry*. Washington DC: National Geographic.

Lindbergh, Reeve. 1990. *Johnny Appleseed*. Boston: Joy Street Books.

Littlechild, George. 1993. *This Land Is My Land*. San Francisco, CA: Children's Book Press.

Livingston, Myra Cohn. 1986. *Earth Songs*. New York: Holiday House.

Michael, Pamela, Ed. 2008. *River of Words*. Minneapolis, MN: Milkweed.

Mora, Pat. 1994. *The Desert is My Mother/El Desierto es Mi Madre*. Houston, TX: Pinata Books.

Mora, Pat. 1998. *This Big Sky*. New York: Scholastic.

Nicholls, Judith. Ed.1993. *Earthways, Earthwise: Poems on Conservation*. Oxford, NY: Oxford University Press.

Nicholls, Judith. 2003. *The Sun in Me: Poems about the Planet*. Cambridge, MA: Barefoot Books.

Nye, Naomi Shihab. 2008. *Honeybee*. New York: Greenwillow.

Peck, Jan and Davis, David. Eds. 2011. *The Green Mother Goose; Saving the World One Rhyme at a Time*. Ill. by Carin Berger. Sterling.

Peters, Lisa Westberg. 2003. *Earthshake: Poems from the Ground Up*. Ill. by Cathie Felstead. New York: HarperCollins.

Philip, Neil. Ed.1996. *Earth Always Endures: Native American Poems*. New York: Viking.

Roberts, Elizabeth, and Elias Amidon. 1991. *Earth Prayers: 365 Prayers, Poems and Invocations for Honoring the Earth*. San Francisco, CA: HarperCollins.

Rogasky, Barbara. Ed.2001. *Leaf by Leaf*. New York: Scholastic.

Rosenberg, Liz, ed. 1998. *Earth-shattering Poems*. New York: Henry Holt.

Shannon, George. 2006. *Busy in the Garden*. Ill. by Sam Williams. New York: Greenwillow.

Singer, Marilyn. 2002. *Footprints on the Roof: Poems about the Earth*. New York: Knopf.

Singer, Marilyn. 2003. *How to Cross a Pond: Poems about Water*. New York: Knopf.

Singer, Marilyn. 2005. *Central Heating: Poems about Fire and Warmth*. New York: Knopf.

Singer, Marilyn. 2012. *A Strange Place to Call Home: The World's Most Dangerous Habitats and the Animals That Call Them Home*. Ill. by Ed Young. Chronicle.

Wassenhove, Sue Van. 2008. *The Seldom-Ever-Shady Glades*. Honesdale, PA: Boyds Mills/Wordsong.

Wong, Janet. 2011. *Once Upon A Tiger; New Beginnings for Endangered Animals*. OnceUponaTiger.com.

Yolen, Jane. Ed.1996. *Mother Earth, Father Sky: Poems of Our Planet*. Honesdale, PA: Wordsong/Boyds Mills Press.

Yolen, Jane. 1998. *The Originals*. New York: Philomel.

Poetry Books about Mothers

What better tribute for a mother, aunt or grandmother than a well-chosen poem? Poets have given us words with which to honor the women in our lives with the following selected books for young readers.

Atkins, Jeannine. 2010. *Borrowed Names; Poems About Laura Ingalls Wilder, Madam C. J. Walker, Marie Curie, and Their Daughters.* Henry Holt.

Castillo, Ana. 2000. *My Daughter, My Son, the Eagle, the Dove: An Aztec Chant.* New York: Dutton.

Clinton, Catherine. Ed. 2003. *A Poem of Her Own; Voices of American Women Yesterday and Today.* New York: Abrams.

Coyne, Rachel. 1998. *Daughter Have I Told You?* New York: Henry Holt.

Dotlich, Rebecca Kai. 2004. *Mama Loves.* New York: HarperCollins.

Fletcher, Ralph. 1999. *Relatively Speaking: Poems about Family.* New York: Orchard.

Grimes, Nikki. 1999. *Hopscotch Love: A Family Treasury of Love Poems.* New York: Lothrop, Lee & Shepard.

Grimes, Nikki. 2000. *Stepping out with Grandma Mac.* New York: Simon & Schuster.

Hoberman, Mary Ann. 1993. *Fathers, Mothers, Sisters, Brothers: A Collection of Family Poems.* New York: Puffin Books.

Hoberman, Mary Ann. 2009. *All Kinds of Families.* New York: Little, Brown.

Hopkins, Lee Bennett. Ed. 2005. *Days to Celebrate: A Full Year of Poetry, People, Holidays, History, Fascinating Facts, and More.* New York: Greenwillow.

Hopkins, Lee Bennett. 1995. *Been to Yesterdays: Poems of a Life.* Honesdale, PA: Wordsong/Boyds Mills.

Hollyer, Belinda. 2003. Ed. *The Kingfisher Book of Family Poems.* New York: Kingfisher.

Lewis, J. Patrick. 2005. *Vherses: A Celebration of Outstanding Women.* Mankato, MN: Creative Editions.

Livingston, Myra Cohn. Ed. 1988. *Poems for Mothers.* New York: Holiday House.

McCall, Guadalupe Garcia. 2011. *Under the Mesquite.* New York: Lee & Low.

Micklos, John Jr. 2001. *Mommy Poems.* Honesdale, PA : Wordsong/Boyds Mills.

Mora, Pat. 1994. *The Desert is My Mother/El Desierto es Mi Madre.* Houston, TX: Pinata Books.

Mora, Pat. 2001. Ed. *Love to Mamá: a Tribute to Mothers.* New York: Lee & Low Books.

Myers, Walter Dean. 1998. *Angel to Angel: a Mother's Gift of Love.* New York: HarperCollins.

Nye, Naomi Shihab. Ed. 1992. *This Same Sky: A Collection of Poems from Around the World.* New York: Four Winds Press.

Rosenberg, Liz. 2001. Ed. *Roots & Flowers: Poets and Poems on Family.* New York: Henry Holt.

Smith, Hope Anita. 2009. *Mother; Poems.* New York: Henry Holt.

Strickland, Dorothy S. and Michael R. Strickland. Ed. 1994. *Families: Poems Celebrating the African-American Experience.* Honesdale, PA: Wordsong/Boyds Mills.

Thomas, Joyce Carol. 2001. *A Mother's Love: Poems for us to Share.* New York: Joanna Cotler.

Walker, Rob D. 2009. *Mama Says: A Book of Love For Mothers and Sons.* Ill. by Leo and Diane Dillon. New York: Scholastic.

Wong. Janet S. 1999. *The Rainbow Hand: Poems about Mothers and Children.* New York: McElderry.

Yolen, Jane and Heidi E.Y. Stemple. 2001. *Dear Mother, Dear Daughter: Poems for Young People.* Honesdale, PA: Wordsong/Boyds.

Poetry Books about Fathers

Although mothers get many poetic tributes, fathers deserve their chance, too. Whether it's for Father's Day, dad's birthday, or other occasions, sharing a poem with a focus on fathers can make for a memorable moment. Here is a selection of books with poems about fathers.

Appelt, Kathi. 2004. *My Father's Summers: A Daughter's Memoirs*. New York: Henry Holt.

Clifton, Lucille. 1983. *Everett Anderson's Goodbye*. New York: Holt, Rinehart, and Winston.

Fletcher, Ralph J. 1999. *Relatively Speaking: Poems about Family*. New York: Orchard.

Grimes, Nikki. 1999. *Hopscotch Love: A Family Treasury of Love Poems*. New York: Lothrop, Lee & Shepard.

Grimes, Nikki. 1999. *My Man Blue: Poems*. New York: Dial Books.

Grimes, Nikki. 2002. *When Daddy Prays*. Grand Rapids: Eerdmans.

Hoberman, Mary Ann. 1991. *Fathers, Mothers, Sisters, Brothers: A Collection of Family Poems*. Boston: Joy Street.

Hoberman, Mary Ann. 2009. *All Kinds of Families*. New York: Little, Brown.

Hollyer, Belinda. 2003. Ed. *The Kingfisher Book of Family Poems*. New York: Kingfisher.

Hopkins, Lee Bennett. 2005. Ed. *Days to Celebrate: A Full Year of Poetry, People, Holidays, History, Fascinating Facts, and More*. New York: Greenwillow.

Livingston, Myra Cohn. Ed. 1989. *Poems for Fathers*. New York: Holiday House.

Micklos, John Jr. 2000. *Daddy Poems*. Honesdale, PA: Wordsong/Boyds Mills.

Moss, Jeff. 1997. *The Dad of the Dad of the Dad of Your Dad*. New York: Ballantine.

Rosenberg, Liz. 2001. *Roots & Flowers: Poets and Poems on Family*. New York: Henry Holt.

Sidman, Joyce. 2000. *Just Us Two: Poems about Animal Dads*. Brookfield: Millbrook.

Smith, Hope Anita. 2003. *The Way a Door Closes*. New York: Henry Holt.

Smith, Hope Anita. 2008. *Keeping the Night Watch*. New York: Henry Holt.

Steptoe, Javaka. Ed. 1997. In *Daddy's Arms I Am Tall: African Americans Celebrating Fathers*. New York: Lee & Low Books.

Strickland, Dorothy S. and Michael R. Strickland. Eds. 1994. *Families: Poems Celebrating the African-American Experience*. Honesdale, PA: Wordsong/Boyds Mills.

Poetry Books for the Fourth of July

Celebrating the 4th of July evokes thoughts of summer vacation, family time, fireflies and fireworks, etc. Here is a sampling of poetry books on these topics and more. Check the special list of "patriotic poetry" for additional poetry book possibilities.

Ada, Alma Flor. 1997. *Gathering the Sun*. New York: Lothrop, Lee, & Shepard.
Alarcón, Francisco X. 1998. *From the Bellybutton of the Moon and Other Summer Poems/Del Ombligo de la Luna y Otros Poemas de Verano*. San Francisco: Children's Book Press.
Appelt, Kathi. 2004. *My Father's Summers: A Daughter's Memoirs*. New York: Henry Holt.
Argueta, Jorge. 2012. *Guacamole; Un poema para cocinar/ A Cooking Poem*. Ill. by Margarita Sada. Toronto: Groundwood.
Bates, Katharine Lee. 2003. *America the Beautiful*. Ill. by Wendell Minor. New York: Putnam.
Borden, Louise. 2002. *America Is*—New York: Margaret K. McElderry Books.
Bryan, Ashley. 1992. *Sing to the Sun*. New York: HarperCollins.
Bulion, Leslie. 2006. *Hey There, Stink Bug!* Watertown, MA: Charlesbridge.
Carlson, Lori M. Ed. 1998. *Sol a Sol: Bilingual Poems*. New York: Henry Holt.
Coombs, Kate. 2012. *Water Sings Blue: Ocean Poems*. Ill. by Meilo So. San Francisco: Chronicle.
Dotlich, Rebecca Kai. 1998. *Lemonade Sun and Other Summer Poems*. Honesdale, PA: Wordsong/Boyds Mills Press.
Esbensen, Barbara Juster. 1984. *Cold Stars and Fireflies: Poems of the Four Seasons*. New York: Crowell.
Florian, Douglas. 2002. *Summersaults: Poems and Paintings*. New York: Greenwillow.
Frank, John. 2007. *How to Catch a Fish*. New Milford, CT: Roaring Brook.
George, Kristine O'Connell. 2001. *Toasting Marshmallows: Camping Poems*. New York: Clarion.
Giovanni, Nikki. 1981. *Vacation Time: Poems for Children*. New York: Morrow.
Graham, Joan Bransfield. 1994. *Splish Splash*. Boston: Houghton Mifflin.
Graham, Joan Bransfield. 1999. *Flicker Flash*. Boston: Houghton Mifflin.
Greenfield, Eloise. 1988. *Under the Sunday Tree*. New York: Harper & Row.
Harrison, David. 2009. *Vacation, We're Going to the Ocean!* Ill. by Rob Shepperson. Honesdale, PA: Wordsong/Boyds Mills Press.
Hopkins, Lee Bennett. Ed. 1993. *Beat the Drum, Independence Day has Come: Poems for the Fourth of July*. Honesdale, PA: Wordsong/Boyds Mills Press.
Hopkins, Lee Bennett. Ed. 2012. *Nasty Bugs*. Ill. by Will Terry. New York: Dial.
Holub, Joan. 2003. *Fourth of July Sparkly Sky*. New York: Little Simon.
Katz, Alan. 2011. *Mosquitoes Are Ruining My Summer! And Other Silly Dilly Camp Songs*. New York: McElderry.
Knowlton, Laurie Lazzaro. 2002. *Red, White, and Blue*. Grenta, LA: Pelican Publishing.

Lessac, Frane. Ed. 2003. *Camp Granada: Sing-Along Camp Songs*. New York: Henry Holt.

Lewis, J. Patrick. 1994. *July is a Mad Mosquito*. New York: Atheneum.

Moore, Lilian. Ed. 1992. *Sunflakes: Poems for Children*. New York: Clarion.

Mora, Pat. 1998. *This Big Sky*. New York: Scholastic.

Nicholls, Judith. 2003. *The Sun in Me: Poems about the Planet*. Somerville, MA: Barefoot Books.

Schnur, Steven. 2001. *Summer: An Alphabet Acrostic*. New York: Clarion.

Siebert, Diane. 2006. *Tour America: A Journey through Poems and Art*. San Francisco: Chronicle.

Singer, Marilyn. 1989. *Turtle in July*. New York: Macmillan.

Singer, Marilyn. 1994. *Family Reunion*. New York: Atheneum.

Singer, Marilyn. 2003. *Fireflies at Midnight*. New York: Atheneum.

Spinelli, Eileen. 2007. *Summerhouse Time*. New York: Knopf.

Weatherford, Carole Boston. 2001. *Sidewalk Chalk; Poems of the City*. Honesdale, PA: Wordsong/Boyds Mills Press.

Wong, Janet. 2008. *Minn and Jake's Almost Terrible Summer*. New York: Farrar, Straus & Giroux.

Zimmer, Tracie Vaughn. 2005. *Sketches from a Spy Tree*. New York: Clarion.

Poetry Books about Patriotism

Poets have written about pride in homeland, about the search for a national identity, the value of one's cultural heritage, and finding a place in an adopted country, among other patriotic topics, for many generations. How has this been expressed in poetry for young people? Here are a few outstanding examples.

Burg, Ann. 2009. *All the Broken Pieces*. New York: Scholastic.

Clinton, Catherine. 1998. *I, Too, Sing America: Three Centuries of African American Poetry*. Boston: Houghton Mifflin.

Cohn, Amy L. Ed. 1993. *From Sea to Shining Sea: A Treasury of American Folklore and Folk Songs*. New York: Scholastic.

Greenberg, Jan. 2001. Ed. *Heart to Heart: New Poems Inspired by Twentieth-Century American Art*. New York: Abrams.

Gunning, Monica. 2004. *America, My New Home*. San Francisco, CA: Children's Book Press.

Hopkins, Lee Bennett, Ed. 1993. *Beat the Drum, Independence Day has Come: Poems for the Fourth of July*. Honesdale, PA: Wordsong/Boyds Mills Press.

Hopkins, Lee Bennett, Ed. 1994. *Hand in Hand: An American History through Poetry*. New York: Simon & Schuster.

Hopkins, Lee Bennett, Ed. 1999. *Lives: Poems about Famous Americans*. New York: HarperCollins.

Hopkins, Lee Bennett. Ed. 2000. *My America: A Poetry Atlas of the U.S*. New York: Simon & Schuster.

Hopkins, Lee Bennett, Ed. 2002. *Home to Me: Poems Across America*. New York: Orchard.

Hopkins, Lee Bennett. Ed. 2008. *America at War*. New York: McElderry.

Hughes, Langston. 2012. *I, Too, Am America*. Ill. by Bryan Collier. Simon & Schuster.

Izuki, Steven. 1994. *Believers in America: Poems about Americans of Asian and Pacific Islander Descent*. Chicago, IL: Children's Press.

Katz, Bobbi. 2000. *We the People: Poems*. New York: Greenwillow.

Lai, Thanhha. 2011. *Inside Out and Back Again*. New York: HarperCollins.

Lewis, J. Patrick. 2005. *Good Mornin', Miss America: The U.S.A. in Verse*. School Specialty Publishing.

Lewis, J. Patrick. 2007. *The Brothers' War: Civil War Voices in Verse*. Washington, DC: National Geographic.

Littlechild, George. 1993. *This Land Is My Land*. San Francisco, CA: Children's Book Press.

Longfellow, Henry Wadsworth. 2001. *The Midnight Ride of Paul Revere*. Ill. by Christopher Bing. New York: Handprint Books.

Mak, Kam. 2001. *My Chinatown: One Year in Poems*. New York: HarperCollins.

Meltzer, Milton. Ed. 2003. *Hour of Freedom: American History in Poetry*. Honesdale, PA: Wordsong/Boyds Mills Press.

Myers, Walter Dean. 2011. *We are America; A Tribute from the Heart*. Ill. by Christopher Myers. New York: HarperCollins.

Panzer, Nora, Ed. 1994. *Celebrate America in Poetry and Art*. New York: Hyperion.

Philip, Neil. Ed. 1995. *Singing America*. New York: Viking.

Philip, Neil. Ed. 1998. *War and the Pity of War*. New York: Clarion.

Robb, Laura. Ed. 1997. *Music and Drum: Voices of War and Peace, Hope and Dreams*. New York: Philomel.

Salas, Laura Purdie. 2008. *Tiny Creams, Sprouting Tall: Poems About the United States*. Minneapolis, MN: Capstone.

Shange, Ntozake. 2012. *Freedom's a-Callin Me*. Ill. by Rod Brown. Amistad/Collins.

Siebert, Diane. 2006. *Tour America: A Journey through Poems and Art*. San Francisco: Chronicle.

Smith, Charles R. Jr. 2003. *I am America*. New York: Scholastic.

Swamp, Chief Jake. 1995. *Giving Thanks: A Native American Good Morning Message*. New York: Lee & Low.

Testa, Maria. 2005. *Something about America*. Cambridge, MA: Candlewick.

Whipple, Laura. Ed. 1994. *Celebrating America: A Collection of Poems and Images of the American Spirit*. New York: Philomel Books.

Wong, Janet. 2012. *Declaration of Interdependence. Poems for an Election Year*. PoetrySuitcase.

Poetry Books about Summer

Summer time is the perfect time to catch up on all kinds of poetry reading of course, but we can kick off our summertime events and gatherings with poems written specifically about summer and typical summer activities. Here are a few examples to get us started.

Alarcón, Francisco X. 1998. *From the Bellybutton of the Moon and Other Summer Poems/Del Ombligo de la Luna y Otros Poemas de Verano.* San Francisco: Children's Book Press.

Appelt, Kathi. 2004. *My Father's Summers: A Daughter's Memoirs.* New York: Henry Holt.

Bruchac, Joseph. 1995. *The Earth under Sky Bear's Feet: Native American Poems of the Land.* New York: Philomel Books.

Carlson, Lori M. Ed. 1998. *Sol a Sol: Bilingual Poems.* New York: Henry Holt.

Cohn, Amy L., comp. 1993. *From Sea to Shining Sea: A Treasury of American Folklore and Folk Songs.* New York: Scholastic.

Dotlich: Rebecca Kai 1998. *Lemonade Sun and Other Summer Poems* Honesdale: Wordsong/Boyds Mills Press.

Dotlich, Rebecca Kai. 2004. *Over in the Pink House: New Jump Rope Rhymes.* Honesdale, PA: Wordsong/Boyds Mills Press.

Esbensen, Barbara Juster. 1984. *Cold Stars and Fireflies: Poems of the Four Seasons.* New York: Crowell.

Fletcher, Ralph. 2001. *Have You Been to the Beach Lately?* New York: Orchard Books.

Florian, Douglas. 2002. *Summersaults: Poems and Paintings* New York: Greenwillow Books.

Frank, John. 2007. *How to Catch a Fish.* New Milford: Roaring Brook Press.

George, Kristine O'Connell. 2001. *Toasting Marshmallows: Camping Poems* New York: Clarion Books.

Giovanni, Nikki. 1981. *Vacation Time: Poems for Children.* New York: Morrow.

Graham, Joan Bransfield. 1994. *Splish Splash.* New York: Houghton Mifflin.

Grimes, Nikki. 2004. *Tai Chi morning: Snapshots of China.* Chicago: Cricket Books.

Hopkins, Lee Bennett. Ed. 1993. *Beat the Drum, Independence Day has Come: Poems for the Fourth of July.* Honesdale, PA: Wordsong/Boyds Mills Press.

Hopkins, Lee Bennett. Ed. 2005. *Days to Celebrate: A Full Year of Poetry, People, Holidays, History, Fascinating Facts, and More.* New York: Greenwillow.

Hopkins, Lee Bennett. Ed. 2006 *Got Geography!* New York: Greenwillow.

Hopkins, Lee Bennett. 2007. *Behind the Museum Door.* New York: Abrams.

Hopkins, Lee. Bennett Ed. 2010. *Sharing the Seasons.* Margaret McElderry.

Katz, Alan. 2011. *Mosquitoes Are Ruining My Summer! And Other Silly Dilly Camp Songs.* New York: McElderry.

Lansky, Bruce. Ed. 2009. *What I Did on My Summer Vacation: Kids' Favorite Funny Summer Vacation Poems.* Minnetonka, MN: Meadowbrook Press.

Lessac, Frane. 2003. *Camp Granada: Sing-Along Camp Songs* New York: Holt.

Levy, Constance. 2002. *Splash! Poems of Our Watery World.* New York: Orchard.

Lewis, J. Patrick. 2002. *A World of Wonders: Geographic Travels in Verse and Rhyme.* New York: Dial.

Lewis, J. Patrick. 1994. *July is a Mad Mosquito.* New York: Atheneum.

Lewis, J. Patrick. 2005. *Monumental Verses.* Washington, D.C.: National Geographic.

McCord, David. 1999. *Every Time I Climb a Tree.* New York: Little Brown.

Moore, Lilian. comp. 1992. *Sunflakes: Poems for Children.* New York: Clarion.

Mora, Pat. 1998. *This Big Sky.* New York: Scholastic.

Schnur, Steven. 2001. *Summer: An Alphabet Acrostic.* New York: Clarion.

Shaw, Alison, comp. 1995. *Until I Saw the Sea: A Collection of Seashore Poems.* New York: Henry Holt.

Siebert, Diane. 2006. *Tour America: A Journey through Poems and Art.* San Francisco: Chronicle.

Singer, Marilyn. 2000. *Fireflies at Midnight.* New York: Atheneum.

Singer, Marilyn. 1992. *In My Tent.* New York: Macmillan.

Singer, Marilyn. 1989. *Turtle in July.* New York: Macmillan.

Spinelli, Eileen. 2007. *Summerhouse Time.* New York: Alfred A. Knopf.

Weatherford, Carole Boston. 2001. *Sidewalk Chalk; Poems of the City.* Honesdale, PA: Wordsong/Boyds Mills Press.

Wong, Janet. 2008. *Minn and Jake's Almost Terrible Summer.* New York: Farrar, Straus & Giroux.

Zimmer, Tracie Vaughn. 2005. *Sketches from a Spy Tree.* New York: Clarion.

Wong, Janet S. 1999. *Behind the Wheel: Poems about Driving.* New York: Margaret K. McElderry Books.

Yolen, Jane. 2000. *Color Me a Rhyme: Nature Poems for Young People.* Honesdale, PA: Wordsong/Boyds Mills Press.

Poetry Books about School for Children

Children often particularly enjoy poetry about school since most of their daily lives are spent there. The ups and downs of classroom life make fine grist for both humorous and serious poetry. Look for these books of poems about school and share them throughout the school year.

Abeel, Samantha.1993. *Reach for the Moon*. Duluth, MN: Pfeifer-Hamilton.

Bagert, Brod. 1999. *Rainbows, Head Lice, and Pea-Green Tile: Poems in the Voice of the Classroom Teacher*. Gainesville, FL: Maupin House.

Bagert, Brod. 2008. *School Fever*. New York: Dial Books for Young Readers.

Dakos, Kalli. 1990. *If You're Not Here, Please Raise Your Hand: Poems about School.* New York: Four Winds Press.

Dakos, Kalli. 1993. *Don't Read This Book Whatever You Do!: More Poems about School*. New York: Trumpet Club.

Dakos, Kalli. 1995. *Mrs. Cole on an Onion Roll and Other School Poems.* New York: Simon & Schuster.

Dakos, Kalli. 1996. *The Goof Who Invented Homework and Other School Poems*. New York: Dial.

Dakos, Kalli. 1999. *The Bug in Teacher's Coffee*. New York: HarperCollins.

Dakos, Kalli. 2003. *Put Your Eyes Up Here: And Other School Poems*. New York: Simon & Schuster.

Dakos, Kalli. 2011. *A Funeral in the Bathroom and Other School Bathroom Poems*. Albert Whitman.

Franco, Betsy. 2009. *Messing Around the Monkey Bars and Other School Poems for Two Voices*. Ill. by Jessie Hartland. Somerville, MA: Candlewick.

Frost, Helen. 2004. *Spinning Through the Universe*. New York: Farrar, Straus & Giroux.

Harrison, David L. 1993. *Somebody Catch My Homework*. Honesdale, PA: Wordsong/Boyds Mills Press.

Harrison, David L. 2003. *The Mouse was out at Recess*. Honesdale, PA: Wordsong/Boyds Mills Press.

Heide, Florence Parry and Pierce, Roxanne Heide. 1996. *Oh, Grow Up! Poems To Help You Survive Parents, Chores, School, And Other Afflictions*. New York: Orchard.

Holbrook, Sara. 1996. *The Dog Ate My Homework*. Honesdale, PA: Boyds Mills Press.

Hopkins, Lee Bennett. Ed. 1996. *School Supplies: A Book of Poems*. New York: Simon & Schuster.

Horton, Joan. 2004. *I Brought my Rat for Show-and-Tell and Other Funny School Poems*. New York: Grosset & Dunlap.

Katz, Alan. 2008. *Smelly Locker; Silly Dilly School Songs*. New York: Simon & Schuster.

Kennedy, Dorothy M. Ed. 1993. *I Thought I'd Take My Rat To School: Poems for September to June*. New York: Little, Brown.

Krensky, Stephen. 2004. *There Once was a Very Odd School and Other Lunch-Box Limericks*. New York: Dutton.

Lansky, Bruce. Ed. 1997. *No More Homework! No More Tests! Kids Favorite Funny School Poems.* Minnetonka, MN: Meadowbrook Press.

Lewis, J. Patrick. 2009. *Countdown to Summer: A Poem for Every Day of the School Year.* Ill. by Ethan Long. New York: Little, Brown.

Opie, Iona and Peter Opie. Eds. 1992. *I Saw Esau: The Schoolchild's Pocket Book.* Cambridge, MA: Candlewick.

Paraskevas, Betty. 1995. *Gracie Graves and the Kids from Room 402.* San Diego, CA: Harcourt.

Prelutsky, Jack. Ed. 2003. *I Like It Here at School.* New York: Scholastic.

Prelutsky, Jack. 2006. *What a Day it was at School!: Poems.* New York: Greenwillow.

Prelutsky, Jack. Ed. 2010. *There's No Place Like School.* New York: HarperCollins.

Salas, Laura Purdie. 2008. *Do Buses Eat Kids? Poems About School.* Minneapolis, MN: Capstone.

Salas, Laura. 2009. *Stampede! Poems to Celebrate the Wild Side of School!* New York: Clarion.

Shields, Carol Diggory. 1995. *Lunch Money and Other Poems About School.* New York: Dutton.

Shields, Carol Diggory. 2003. *Almost Late to School: And More School Poems.* New York: Dutton.

Sierra, Judy. 2000. *There's a Zoo in Room 22.* San Diego: Harcourt.

Sierra, Judy. 2005. *Schoolyard Rhymes: Kids' Own Rhymes for Rope Skipping, Hand Clapping, Ball Bouncing, and Just Plain Fun.* New York: Knopf.

Singer, Marilyn. 1996. *All We Needed to Say: Poems about School from Tanya and Sophie.* New York: Atheneum.

Stockland, Patricia M. 2004. *Recess, Rhyme, and Reason: A Collection of Poems about School.* Minneapolis: Compass Point Books.

Thurston, Cheryl Miller. 1987. *Hide Your Ex-lax under the Wheaties: Poems about Schools, Teachers, Kids, and Education.* Fort Collins, CO: Cottonwood Press.

Weatherford, Carole Boston. 2006. *Dear Mr. Rosenwald.* New York: Scholastic.

Winters, Kay. 1996. *Did You See What I Saw? Poems About School.* New York: Viking.

Poetry Books about School for Teens

School is a big part of the lives of teenagers, too. Here is a selection of poetry books for tweens and teens that are set in the daily life of school, past and present.

Alexander, Elizabeth and Nelson, Marilyn. 2007. *Miss Crandall's School for Young Ladies and Little Misses of Color.* Honesdale, PA: Wordsong/Boyds Mills Press.

Bagert, Brod. 2006. *Hormone Jungle; Coming of Age in Middle School.* Gainesville, FL: Maupin House.

George, Kristine O'Connell. 2002. *Swimming Upstream: Middle School Poems.* New York: Clarion.

Glenn, Mel. 1982. *Class Dismissed! High School Poems.* New York: Clarion.

Glenn, Mel. 1986. *Class Dismissed II.* New York: Clarion.

Glenn, Mel. 1988. *Back to Class.* New York: Clarion.

Glenn, Mel. 1991. *My Friend's Got This Problem, Mr. Candler: High School Poems.* New York: Clarion.

Glenn, Mel. 1996. *Who Killed Mr. Chippendale?* New York: Lodestar Books/Dutton.

Glenn, Mel. 1997. *Jump Ball: A Basketball Season in Poems.* New York: Lodestar Books/Dutton.

Glenn, Mel. 1997. *The Taking of Room 114: A Hostage Drama in Poems.* New York: Lodestar Books/Dutton.

Glenn, Mel. 1999. *Foreign Exchange: A Mystery in Poems.* New York: Morrow.

Glenn, Mel. 2000. *Split Image.* New York: HarperCollins.

Grimes, Nikki. 2002. *Bronx Masquerade.* New York: Dial.

Grimes, Nikki. 2011. *Planet Middle School.* New York: Bloomsbury.

Koertge, Ron. 2001. *The Brimstone Journals.* Somerville, MA: Candlewick.

Korman, Gordon and Bernice Korman. 1992. *The D- Poems of Jeremy Bloom: A Collection of Poems about School, Homework, and Life (Sort of).* New York: Scholastic.

Poetry Books for Halloween

Halloween is a popular topic for poetry books for young people, along with a look at fall and autumn seasonal changes. Here is just a sampling.

Alarcón, Francisco X. 1999. *Angels Ride Bikes and Other Fall Poems.* San Francisco, CA: Children's Book Press.

Brown, Calef. 2010. *Hallowilloween: Nefarious Silliness.* Boston: Houghton Mifflin.

Dahl, Roald. 2005. *Vile Verses.* New York: Viking.

Farrar, Sid. 2012. *The Year Comes Round: Haiku Through the Seasons.* Ill. by Ilse Plume. Chicago: Whitman.

Florian, Douglas. 1993. *Monster Motel: Poems and Paintings.* San Diego, CA: Harcourt Brace.

Florian, Douglas. 2003. *Autumnblings: Poems & Paintings.* New York: Greenwillow.

Frank, John. 2003. *A Chill in the Air: Nature Poems for Fall and Winter.* New York: Simon & Schuster.

Ghigna, Charles. 2003. *Halloween Night: Twenty-One Spooktacular Poems.* Philadelphia: Running Kids Press.

Gibbs, Susie. Ed. 2003. *Poems to Make Your Friends Scream!.* Oxford: Oxford University Press.

Gibbs, Susie. Ed. 2007. *Scary Poems to Make You Shiver.* Oxford: Oxford University Press.

Gibbs, Susie. Ed. 2006. *Revolting Poems to Make you Squirm.* Oxford: Oxford University Press.

Hopkins, Lee Bennett. Ed. 2005. *Days to Celebrate: A Full Year of Poetry, People, Holidays, History, Fascinating Facts, and More.* New York: Greenwillow.

Hopkins, Lee Bennett. 2006. *Halloween Howls; An I Can Read Book.* New York: HarperCollins.

Hopkins, Lee. Bennett Ed. 2010. *Sharing the Seasons.* Margaret McElderry.

Katz, Bobbi. 2009. *The Monsterologist; A Memoir in Rhyme.* Ill. by Adam McCauley. New York: Sterling.

Kutner, Merrily. 2007. *The Zombie Nite Café.* Ill. by Ethan Long. Holiday House.

Lewis, J. Patrick. 2009. *Countdown to Summer: 180 Poems for Every Day of the School Year.* New York: Little, Brown.

Livingston, Myra Cohn. Ed. 1989. *Halloween Poems.* New York: Holiday House.

McNaughton, Colin. 2002. *Making Friends with Frankenstein.* Somerville, MA: Candlewick.

Mecum, Ryan. 2008. *Zombie Haiku.* Cincinnati, OH: How Books.

Mecum, Ryan. 2009. *Vampire Haiku.* Cincinnati, OH: How Books.

Merriam, Eve. 2002. *Spooky A B C.* New York: Simon & Schuster.

Moore, Lilian. 1973. *Spooky Rhymes and Riddles.* New York: Scholastic.

Mordhorst, Heidi. 2009. *Pumpkin Butterfly; Poems from the Other Side of Nature.* Honesdale PA: Wordsong/Boyds Mills Press.

Neugebauer, Charise. 2002. *Halloween Circus.* New York: NorthSouth Books.

Prelutsky, Jack. 1976. *Nightmares: Poems to Trouble Your Sleep*. New York: Greenwillow. Reprinted, New York: Mulberry Books, 1993.

Prelutsky, Jack. 1977. *It's Halloween*. New York: Greenwillow.

Rex, Adam. 2006. *Frankenstein Makes a Sandwich*. San Diego, CA: Harcourt.

Rex, Adam. 2008. *Frankenstein Takes the Cake*. New York: Harcourt Houghton Mifflin.

Rogasky, Barbara. Ed. 2001. *Leaf by Leaf*. New York: Scholastic.

Salas, Laura Purdie. 2008. *Shrinking Days, Frosty Nights: Poems About Fall*. Minneapolis, MN: Capstone.

Sierra, Judy. 2005. *Gruesome Guide to World Monsters*. Somerville, MA: Candlewick.

Rogasky, Barbara. Ed. 2001. *Leaf by Leaf*. New York: Scholastic.

Schnur, Steven. 1997. *Autumn: An Alphabet Acrostic*. New York: Clarion.

Sierra, Judy. 2008. *Beastly Rhymes to Read After Dark*. Ill. by Brian Biggs. New York: Knopf.

Singer, Marilyn. 2001. *Monster Museum*. New York: Hyperion.

Singer, Marilyn. 2004. *Creature Carnival*. New York: Hyperion.

Sklanksy, Amy E. 2004. *Skeleton Bones & Goblin Groans: Poems for Halloween*. New York: Henry Holt .

Swaim, Jessica. 2010. *Scarum Fair*. Ill. by Carol Ashley. Honesdale, PA: Wordsong/Boyds Mills Press.

Whitehead, Jenny. 2007. *Holiday Stew; A Kid's Portion of Holiday and Seasonal Poems*. New York: Henry Holt.

Poetry Books about Monsters

Young readers and listeners may be surprised that poetry can be about monsters ogres, and other scary creatures. Here are a few of the most popular books of "monster" poetry, some hilarious and some scary—so beware.

Ashman, Linda. 2003. *The Essential Worldwide Monster Guide.* New York: Simon & Schuster.

Ciardi, John. 1966. *The Monster Den; or, Look What Happened at My House --and to It.* Philadelphia: Lippincott. 1991. Reprinted: Honesdale, PA: Wordsong.

Dahl, Roald. 2002. *Roald Dahl's Revolting Rhymes.* New York: Knopf.

Dahl, Roald. 2005. *Vile Verses.* New York: Viking.

Florian, Douglas. 1993. *Monster Motel: Poems and Paintings.* San Diego, CA: Harcourt Brace.

Foster, John. Ed. 2002. *Monster Poems.* Oxford, UK: Oxford University Press.

Gibbs, Susie. Ed. 2006. *Revolting Poems to Make you Squirm.* Oxford: Oxford University Press.

Hoberman, Mary Ann. 2007. *You Read to Me, I'll Read to You: Very Scary Stories to Read Together.* New York: Little, Brown.

Hopkins, Lee Bennett. 1977. *Monsters, Ghoulies, and Creepy Creatures: Fantastic Stories and Poems.* New York: Albert Whitman.

Katz, Bobbi. 2009. *The Monsterologist; A Memoir in Rhyme.* Ill. by Adam McCauley. New York: Sterling.

Kutner, Merrily. 2007. *The Zombie Nite Café.* Ill. by Ethan Long. Holiday House.

Lansky, Bruce. 2006. *Dinner with Dracula: A Spine-Tingling Collection of Frighteningly Funny Poems.* New York: Meadowbrook Press.

Larios, Julie. 2008. *Imaginary Menagerie: A Book of Curious Creatures.* New York: Houghton Mifflin Harcourt.

Lewis, J. Patrick. 2006. *Blackbeard, the Pirate King.* Washington, D.C.: National Geographic.

McNaughton, Colin. 2002. *Making Friends with Frankenstein.* Somerville, MA: Candlewick.

Mecum, Ryan. 2008. *Zombie Haiku.* Cincinnati, OH: How Books.

Mecum, Ryan. 2009. *Vampire Haiku.* Cincinnati, OH: How Books.

Moore, Lilian. 2006. *Beware, Take Care: Fun and Spooky Poems.* New York: Henry Holt.

Prelutsky, Jack. 2001. *Awful Ogre's Awful Day.* New York: Greenwillow.

Prelutsky, Jack. 1999. *The Gargoyle on the Roof.* New York: Greenwillow.

Prelutsky, Jack. 2000. *Monday's Troll.* New York: HarperTrophy.

Prelutsky, Jack. 1976. *Nightmares: Poems to Trouble Your Sleep.* New York: Greenwillow. Reprinted, New York: Mulberry Books, 1993.

Rex, Adam. 2006. *Frankenstein Makes a Sandwich.* San Diego, CA: Harcourt.

Rex, Adam. 2008. *Frankenstein Takes the Cake.* New York: Harcourt Houghton Mifflin.

Sierra, Judy. 2001. *Monster Goose.* San Diego: Gulliver Books.

Sierra, Judy. 2005. *Gruesome Guide to World Monsters*. Somerville, MA: Candlewick.

Sierra, Judy. 2006. *Thelonius Monster's Sky-High Fly-Pie*. New York: Knopf.

Sierra, Judy. 2008. *Beastly Rhymes to Read After Dark*. Ill. by Brian Biggs. New York: Knopf.

Singer, Marilyn. 2004. *Creature Carnival*. New York: Hyperion.

Singer, Marilyn. 2001. *Monster Museum*. New York: Hyperion.

Sklansky, Amy E. 2004. *Skeleton Bones & Goblin Groans; Poems for Halloween*. New York: Henry Holt.

Swaim, Jessica. 2010. *Scarum Fair*. Ill. by Carol Ashley. Honesdale, PA: Wordsong/Boyds Mills Press.

Wheeler, Lisa. 2011. *Spinster Goose; Twisted Rhymes for Naughty Children*. Ill. by Sophie Blackall. New York: Atheneum.

Whipple, Laura. Ed. 1996. *Eric Carle's Dragons, Dragons*. New York: Philomel.

Poetry Books for Thanksgiving

Here is a sampling of poetry books about giving thanks, celebrating Thanksgiving, and enjoying food, friends, and family times.

Alarcón, Francisco X. 1999. *Angels Ride Bikes and Other Fall Poems.* San Francisco, CA: Children's Book Press.

Bruchac, Joseph. 1996. *The Circle of Thanks.* Mahwah, NJ: BridgeWater Books

Carlstrom, Nancy White. 2002. *Thanksgiving Day at Our House: Thanksgiving Poems for the Very Young.* New York: Aladdin.

Child, Lydia Maria. 2004. *Over the River & Through the Woods.* New York: Hyperion.

Florian, Douglas. 2003. *Autumnblings: Poems & Paintings.* New York: Greenwillow.

Grimes, Nikki. 2006. *Thanks a Million: Poems.* New York: Amistad.

Hopkins, Lee Bennett. Ed. 1992. *Ring Out, Wild Bells: Poems about Holidays and Seasons.* New York: Harcourt Brace.

Hopkins, Lee Bennett. 2000. *Yummy! Eating Through a Day: Poems.* New York: Simon & Schuster.

Hopkins, Lee Bennett. Ed. 2005. *Days to Celebrate: A Full Year of Poetry, People, Holidays, History, Fascinating Facts, and More.* New York: Greenwillow.

Lewis, J. Patrick. 2009. *Countdown to Summer: 180 Poems for every day of the School Year.* New York: Little, Brown.

Livingston, Myra Cohn. Ed. 1985. *Thanksgiving Poems.* New York: Holiday House.

Melmed, Laura Krauss. 2001. *This First Thanksgiving Day: A Counting Story.* New York: HarperCollins.

Mora, Pat. 2007. *Yum! Mmmm! Que Rico!: America's Sproutings.* New York: Lee & Low.

Mordhorst, Heidi. 2009. *Pumpkin Butterfly; Poems from the Other Side of Nature.* Honesdale PA: Wordsong/Boyds Mills Press.

Philip, Neil. 2004. *Hot Potato: Mealtime Rhymes.* New York: Clarion.

Prelutsky, Jack. 2007. *It's Thanksgiving!* New York: HarperCollins.

Rogasky, Barbara. Ed. 2001. *Leaf by Leaf.* New York: Scholastic.

Rosen, Michael, J., Ed. 1996. Food Fight: Poets Join the Fight Against Hunger with Poems about Their Favorite Foods. San Diego, CA: Harcourt Brace.

Salas, Laura Purdie. 2008. *Shrinking Days, Frosty Nights: Poems About Fall.* Minneapolis, MN: Capstone.

Schnur, Steven. 1997. Autumn: An Alphabet Acrostic. New York: Clarion.

Shore, Diane. 2008. *This is the Feast.* New York: HarperCollins Publishers.

Swamp, Chief Jake. 1995. *Giving Thanks: A Native American Good Morning Message.* New York: Lee & Low.

Thomas, Joyce Carol. 1995 *Gingerbread Days.* New York: HarperCollins.

Vardell, Sylvia and Wong, Janet. Eds. 2011. *Gift Tag.* PoetryTagTime.com.

Weinstock, Robert. 2009. *Food Hates You, Too.* New York: Disney-Hyperion.

Whitehead, Jenny. 2007. *Holiday Stew; A Kid's Portion of Holiday and Seasonal Poems.* New York: Henry Holt.

Wilson, Karma. 2007. *Give Thanks to the Lord*. Grand Rapids, MI: Zonderkids.

Wing, Natasha. 2001. *The Night Before Thanksgiving*. New York: Grosset and Dunlap.

Wong, Janet. 1996. *A Suitcase of Seaweed, and Other Poems*. New York: McElderry.

Young, Ed. 1997. *Voices of the Heart*. New York: Scholastic.

Poetry Books for Hanukkah

Gathering with family and friends to celebrate Hanukkah is the focus of several collections of poetry including these.

Chorao, Kay. 2009. *Rhymes Round the World.* New York: Dutton Children's Books.

Florian, Douglas. 1999. *Winter Eyes: Poems and Paintings.* New York: Greenwillow.

Jules, Jacqueline. 2001. *Clap and Count! Action Rhymes for the Jewish Year.* Rockville, MD: Kar-Ben.

Hines, Anna Grossnickle. 2005. *Winter Lights: A Season in Poems & Quilts.* New York: Greenwillow.

Hopkins, Lee Bennett. 2004. *Hanukkah Lights: Holiday Poetry.* New York: HarperCollins.

Hopkins, Lee Bennett. Ed. 2005. *Days to Celebrate: A Full Year of Poetry, People, Holidays, History, Fascinating Facts, and More.* New York: Greenwillow.

Hopkins, Lee Bennett. Ed. 1992. *Ring Out, Wild Bells: Poems about Holidays and Seasons.* New York: Harcourt Brace.

Jules, Jacqueline. 2001. *Clap and Count! Action Rhymes for the Jewish Year.* Rockville, MD: Kar-Ben.

Livingston, Myra Cohn. Ed. 1986. *Poems for the Jewish Holidays.* New York: Holiday House.

Peters, Andrew Fusek. 2000. *Poems about Festivals.* London, UK: Hodder Wayland.

Roemer, Heidi. 2004. Come to my Party and other Shape Poems. New York: Henry Holt.

Whitehead, Jenny. 2007. Holiday Stew; A Kid's Portion of Holiday and Seasonal Poems. New York: Henry Holt.

Vardell, Sylvia and Wong, Janet. Eds. 2011. *Gift Tag.* PoetryTagTime.com.

Yolen, Jane. 1998. *Snow, Snow: Winter Poems for Children.* Honesdale, PA: Wordsong/Boyds Mills.

Ziefert, Harriet. 2008. *Hanukkah Haiku.* Maplewood, NJ: Blue Apple Books.

Poetry Books for Christmas

The Christmas holiday is often a time to pause, reflect, and ponder a poem. Here is a list of poetry books that focus on Christmas, with a separate list for versions and variants of the classic Christmas poem, "The Night Before Christmas."

Aigner-Clark, Julie. 2001. *Baby Santa's Christmas Joy! A Celebration of the Holiday Spirit in Poetry, Photography, and Music.* New York: Hyperion.

Alarcón, Francisco X. 2001. *Iguanas in the Snow and Other Winter Poems/ Iguanas en la Nieve y Otros Poemas de Invierno.* San Francisco, CA: Children's Book Press.

Angelou, Maya. 2008. *Amazing Peace: A Christmas Poem.* New York: Schwartz & Wade.

Bennett, Jill. 2003. *Poems for Christmas.* New York: Scholastic.

Bronson, Linda. 2002. *Sleigh Bells and Snowflakes: A Celebration of Christmas.* New York: Henry Holt.

Bunting, Eve and Leonid Gore. 2000. *Who was Born this Special Day?* New York: Atheneum.

Causley, Charles. 2000. *Bring in the Holly.* London: Frances Lincoln.

Cookson, Paul. 2000. *Christmas Poems.* London: Macmillan.

Cummings, E.E. 2001. *Little Tree.* New York: Hyperion.

Cunningham, Julia. 2001. *The Stable Rat, and Other Christmas Poems.* New York: Greenwillow.

Delacre, Lulu. Ed. 1992. *Las Navidades: Popular Christmas Songs from Latin America.* New York: Scholastic.

Fisher, Aileen. 2007. *Do Rabbits Have Christmas?* New York: Henry Holt.

Florian, Douglas. 1999. *Winter Eyes: Poems and Paintings.* New York: Greenwillow.

Frank, John. 2003. *A Chill in the Air: Nature Poems for Fall and Winter.* New York: Simon & Schuster.

Ghigna, Charles and Ghigna, Debra. 2000. *Christmas is Coming!* Watertown, MA: Charlesbridge.

Grimes, Nikki. 2002. *Under the Christmas Tree.* New York: HarperCollins.

Harrison, Michael and Christopher Stuart-Clark. Eds. 2000. *The Young Oxford Book of Christmas Poems.* Oxford: Oxford University Press.

Hines, Anna Grossnickle. 2005. *Winter Lights: A Season in Poems & Quilts.* New York: Greenwillow.

Hopkins, Lee Bennett. Ed. 1992. *Ring Out, Wild Bells: Poems about Holidays and Seasons.* New York: Harcourt Brace.

Hopkins, Lee Bennett. Ed. 2004. *Christmas Presents: Holiday Poetry.* New York: HarperCollins.

Hopkins, Lee Bennett. Ed. 2005. Days to Celebrate: A Full Year of Poetry, People, Holidays, History, Fascinating Facts, and More. New York: Greenwillow.

Hudson, Cheryl Willis. Ed. 2002. *Hold Christmas In Your Heart: African American Songs, Poems, and Stories for the Holidays.* New York: Scholastic.

Hughes, Langston. 1998. *Carol of the Brown King: Nativity Poems.* Ill. by Ashley Bryan. New York: Atheneum.

Johnston, Tony. 2005. *Noel.* Minneapolis, MN: Carolrhoda Books.

Katz, Alan. 2005. *Where Did They Hide My Presents? Silly Dilly Christmas Songs.* New York: McElderry.

Kortepeter, Paul. 2002. *A Child's Book of Christmas.* New York: Dutton.

Lewis, J. Patrick. 2007. *Under the Kissletoe: Christmastime Poems.* Honesdale, PA: Wordsong.

Nesbitt, Kenn and Linda Knaus. 2006. *Santa Got Stuck in the Chimney: 20 Funny Poems Full of Christmas Cheer.* Minnetonka, MN: Meadowbrook Press.

Prelutsky, Jack. 2008. *It's Christmas!* New York: HarperCollins.

Vardell, Sylvia and Wong, Janet. Eds. 2011. *Gift Tag.* PoetryTagTime.com.

Watson, Clyde. 2003. *Father Fox's Christmas Rhymes.* New York: Farrar Straus & Giroux.

Wells, Carolyn. 2002. *Christmas ABC.* New York: Abrams.

Whitehead, Jenny. 2007. *Holiday Stew; A Kid's Portion of Holiday and Seasonal Poems.* New York: Henry Holt.

Worth, Valerie. 1992. *At Christmastime.* New York: HarperCollins.

Versions and Variants of "The Night Before Christmas"

Clement Clarke Moore is said to have written the poem, "A Visit from St. Nicholas," for his own children and recited it to them on Christmas Eve in 1822. It was then published anonymously, became increasingly popular and is still shared today as a Christmas tradition. It has also been interpreted, re-cast, and even parodied by many others as shown in the books listed here.

Adams, Jennifer. 2004. *The Night Before Christmas in Idaho.* Salt Lake City, UT: Gibbs Smith.

Beard, Henry. 2005. *A Cat's Night Before Christmas.* New York: Broadway Books.

Beard, Henry. 2005. *A Dog's Night Before Christmas.* New York: Broadway Books.

Cutlip, Kimbra. 2002. *Firefighter's Night Before Christmas.* Gretna, LA: Pelican.

Davis, David. 2003. *Nurse's Night Before Christmas.* Gretna, LA: Pelican.

Davis, David. 2003. *Librarian's Night Before Christmas.* Gretna, LA: Pelican.

Gribnau, Joe. 2007. *Rocky Mountain Night Before Christmas.* Gretna, LA: Pelican.

Holland, Trish and Christine Ford. 2006. *The Soldiers' Night Before Christmas.* New York: Random House.

Layne, Steven L. 2001. *The Teacher's Night Before Christmas.* Gretna, LA: Pelican.

Layne, Steven L. 2006. *Preacher's Night Before Christmas.* Gretna, LA: Pelican.

Layne, Steven L. 2004. *The Principal's Night Before Christmas.* Gretna, LA: Pelican.

Macy, Carolyn. 2008. *Hawaiian Night Before Christmas.* Gretna, LA: Pelican.

McWilliams, Amanda. 2004. *Ozark Night Before Christmas.* Gretna, LA: Pelican.

Metropolitan Museum of Art. 2003. *'Twas the Night Before Christmas, and other Seasonal Favorites.* New York: Abrams.

Moore, Clement C. 2002. *The Night Before Christmas.* New York: HarperCollins.

Moore, Clement C. 2003. *The Night Before Christmas: A Goblin Tale.* New York: Dial.

Moore, Clement Clark. 2002. *'Twas the Night Before Christmas; or, Account of A Visit from St. Nicholas.* Ill. by Matt Tavares. Somerville, MA: Candlewick Press.

Moore, Clement Clarke. 2000. *The Teddy Bear's Night Before Christmas.* London: Scholastic.

Moss, Jenny Jackson. 2000. *Cajun Night after Christmas.* Gretna, LA: Pelican.

Robinson, Gary. 2007. *Native American Night Before Christmas.* Santa Fe, NM: Clear Light Publishing.

Simmons, Lynn Sheffield. 2007. *Sugar Lump, the Orphan Calf's Night Before Christmas.* Gretna, LA: Pelican.

Smith, Johanna. 2004. *The Night Before Christmas in Michigan.* Salt Lake City, UT: Gibbs Smith.

Sullivan, E.J. 2003. *The Redneck Night Before Christmas.* Canada: Crane Hill Publishers.

Terrill, Beth. 2007. *The Barnyard Night Before Christmas.* New York: Random House.

Townsend, Una Belle. 2008. *Racecar Driver's Night Before Christmas.* Gretna, LA: Pelican.

Turner, Thomas N. 2003. *Country Music Night Before Christmas.* Gretna, LA: Pelican.

Williamson, Chet. 2002. *Pennsylvania Dutch Night Before Christmas.* Gretna, LA: Pelican.

Yates, Phillip. 2008. *A Pirate's Night Before Christmas.* New York: Sterling.

MULTICULTURAL AND INTERNATIONAL POETRY BOOKLISTS

Poetry by poets of color and about multiple cultures appears on all the lists throughout this book, but it can also be valuable to showcase multicultural and international poetry specifically, so that's how the poetry lists are organized in this category. In addition, lists of bilingual poetry as well as poetry that targets the needs of students acquiring English as a new language are also provided here.

African American Poetry for Young People
Asian American Poetry for Young People
Hispanic/Latino/Latina Poetry for Young People
Native American Poetry For Young People
International Poetry for Young People
Bilingual Poetry for Young People
Poetry Books for (ESL/ELL) English Language Learners

African American Poetry for Young People

African American writers have been creating poetry for many generations. Poetry for young readers, in particular, is a more recent development with many wonderful gems now available to share with children and teens. Consider some of these outstanding examples of African American poetry collections.

Adedjouma, D. Ed.. 1996. *The Palm of My Heart: Poetry by African American Children.* New York: Lee & Low.

Adoff, Arnold, comp. 1974. *My Black Me: A Beginning Book of Black Poetry.* New York: Dutton. Reprinted, 1994.

Adoff, Arnold. 2010. *Roots and Blues, A Celebration.* Houghton Mifflin Harcourt.

Adoff, Jaime. 2005. *Jimi & Me.* New York: Hyperion.

Adoff, Jaime. 2008. *The Death of Jayson Porter.* New York: Jump at the Sun/Hyperion.

Alexander, Elizabeth and Nelson, Marilyn. 2007. *Miss Crandall's School for Young Ladies and Little Misses of Color.* Honesdale, PA: Wordsong.

Angelou, Maya. 1993. *Life Doesn't Frighten Me.* New York: Steward, Tabori, & Chang.

Brooks, Gwendolyn. 1956/1984. *Bronzeville Boys and Girls.* New York: HarperCollins.

Bryan, Ashley. 1997. *Ashley Bryan's ABC of African American Poetry.* New York: Atheneum.

Clinton, Catherine. Ed. 1998. *I, Too, Sing America: Three Centuries of African American Poetry.* Boston: Houghton Mifflin.

Crisler, Curtis. 2007. *Tough Boy Sonatas.* Honesdale, PA: Wordsong/Boyds Mills.

Dunbar, Paul Laurence. Reissued, 1999. *Jump Back Honey.* New York: Hyperion.

Feelings. Tom. 1993. *Soul Looks Back in Wonder.* New York: Dial.

Giovanni, Nikki. 1994. *Knoxville, Tennessee.* New York: Scholastic.

Giovanni, Nikki. 1996. *The Sun Is So Quiet.* New York: Henry Holt.

Giovanni, Nikki. 1997. *It's Raining Laughter.* New York: Dial.

Giovanni, Nikki. Coll. 2008. *Hip Hop Speaks to Children.* Naperville, IL: Sourcebooks.

Greenfield, Eloise. 2004. *In the Land of Words.* New York: HarperCollins.

Greenfield, Eloise. 2006. *The Friendly Four.* Ill. by Jan Spivey Gilchrist. New York: HarperCollins.

Greenfield, Eloise. 2008. *Brothers and Sisters: Family Poems.* New York: Amistad/HarperCollins.

Greenfield, Eloise. 2011. *The Great Migration: Journey to the North.* Ill. by Jan Spivey Gilchrist. Amistad/HarperCollins.

Grimes, Nikki. 1994. *Meet Danitra Brown.* New York: Lothrop, Lee & Shepard.

Grimes, Nikki. 1997. *It's Raining Laughter: Poems.* New York: Dial.

Grimes, Nikki. 1998. *A Dime a Dozen.* New York: Dial.

Grimes, Nikki. 1998. *Jazmin's Notebook.* New York: Dial.

Grimes, Nikki. 1999. *Hopscotch Love: A Family Treasury of Love Poems*. New York: Lothrop, Lee & Shepard.

Grimes, Nikki. 1999. *My Man Blue: Poems*. New York: Dial.

Grimes, Nikki. 2000. *Is It Far to Zanzibar: Poems about Tanzania*. New York: Lothrop, Lee & Shepard.

Grimes, Nikki. 2000. *Stepping out with Grandma Mac*. New York: Simon & Schuster.

Grimes, Nikki. 2002. *Bronx Masquerade.* New York: Dial.

Grimes, Nikki. 2004. *What is Goodbye?* New York: Jump at the Sun/Hyperion.

Grimes, Nikki. 2005. *Dark Sons*. New York: Hyperion. NOVEL IN VERSE

Gunning, Monica. 2004. *A Shelter In Our Car*. San Francisco, CA: Children's Book Press.

Gunning, Monica. 2004. *America, My New Home*. San Francisco, CA: Children's Book Press.

Hudson, Wade. Ed. 1993. *Pass It On: African American Poetry for Children*. New York: Scholastic.

Hughes, Langston. (75th anniversary edition) 2007. *The Dream Keeper* (and seven additional poems). New York: Knopf.

Hughes, Langston. 2012. *I, Too, Am America*. Ill. by Bryan Collier. Simon & Schuster.

Hughes, Langston. 2009. *My People*. Ill. by Charles R Smith Jr. New York: Simon & Schuster.

Hughes, Langston. 2009. *The Negro Speaks of Rivers*. Ill. by E. B. Lewis. New York: Disney-Hyperion.

Iyengar, Malathi Michelle. 2009. *Tan to Tamarind: Poems About the Color Brown*. Ill. by Jamel Akib. San Francisco, CA: Children's Book Press.

Johnson, Angela. 1998. *The Other Side: Shorter Poems*. New York: Orchard.

Johnson, James Weldon. 1995. *Lift Ev'ry Voice and Sing*. New York: Scholastic.

McKissack, Patricia. 2011. *Never Forgotten*. Ill. by Leo and Diane Dillon. New York: Schwartz & Wade.

McKissack, Patricia. 2008. *Stitchin' and Pullin'; A Gee's Bend Quilt*. Illus. by Cozbi A. Cabrera. New York: Random House.

Medearis, Angela Shelf. 1995. *Skin Deep and Other Teenage Reflections: Poems*. New York: Macmillan.

Myers, Walter Dean. 1993. *Brown Angels: An Album of Pictures and Verse*. New York: HarperCollins.

Myers, Walter Dean. 1995. *Glorious Angels: A Celebration of Children*. New York: HarperCollins.

Myers, Walter Dean. 1997. *Harlem: A Poem*. New York: Scholastic.

Myers, Walter Dean. 1998. *Angel to Angel*. New York: HarperCollins.

Myers, Walter Dean. 2003. *Blues Journey*. New York: Holiday House.

Myers, Walter Dean. 2004. *Here in Harlem: Poems in Many Voices*. New York: Holiday House.

Myers, Walter Dean. 2006. *Jazz*. Ill. by Christopher Myers. New York: Holiday House.

Myers, Walter Dean. 2009. *Amiri and Odette: A Love Story*. Ill. by Javaka Steptoe. New York: Scholastic.

Myers, Walter Dean. 2011. *We are America; A Tribute from the Heart*. Ill. by Christopher Myers. HarperCollins.

Nelson, Marilyn. 1997. *The Fields Of Praise: New and Selected Poems*. Baton Rouge: Louisiana State University Press.

Neri, G. and Watson, Jesse Joshua. 2007. *Chess Rumble*. New York, NY: Lee & Low.

Newsome, Effie Lee. 1999. *Wonders: The Best Children's Poems by Effie Lee Newsome*. Honesdale, PA: Boyds Mills.

Okutoro, L. O. 1999. *Quiet Storm: Voices from Young Black Poets*. New York: Hyperion.

Shakur, Tupac. 1999. *A Rose That Grew from Concrete*. New York: Pocket Books.

Smith, Charles R. Jr. 2002. *Perfect Harmony: A Musical Journey with the Boys Choir of Harlem*. New York: Hyperion/Jump at the Sun.

Smith, Charles R. Jr. 2003. *Hoop Queens*. Somerville, MA: Candlewick.

Smith, Charles R. Jr. 2003. *I am America*. New York: Scholastic.

Smith, Charles R. Jr. 2004. *Hoop Kings*. Somerville, MA: Candlewick.

Smith, Charles R. Jr. 2007. *Twelve Rounds to Glory: The Story of Muhammad Ali*. Somerville, MA: Candlewick.

Smith, Charles R., Jr. 2010. *Black Jack; The Ballad of Jack Johnson*. Roaring Brook.

Smith, Charles R., Jr. 2012. *Stars in the Shadows: The Negro League All-Star Game of 1934*. Ill. by Frank Morrison. Atheneum.

Smith, Hope Anita. 2003. *The Way a Door Closes*. New York: Henry Holt.

Smith, Hope Anita. 2008. *Keeping the Night Watch*. New York: Henry Holt.

Smith, Hope Anita. 2009. *Mother; Poems*. New York: Henry Holt.

Smith, Jr., Charles R. 2004. *Diamond Life: Baseball Sights, Sounds, and Swings*. New York: Orchard.

Steptoe, Javaka. Ed. 1997. *In Daddy's Arms I Am Tall: African Americans Celebrating Fathers*. New York: Lee & Low.

Strickland, Dorothy S. and Michael R. Strickland. Eds. 1994. *Families: Poems Celebrating the African-American Experience*. Honesdale, PA: Wordsong/Boyds Mills.

Thomas, Joyce Carol. 1993. *Brown Honey in Broomwheat Tea: Poems*. New York: HarperCollins.

Thomas, Joyce Carol. 1995. *Gingerbread Days*. New York: HarperCollins.

Thomas, Joyce Carol. 2000. *Hush Songs: African American Lullabies*. New York: Hyperion.

Thomas, Joyce Carol. 2001. *A Mother's Heart, A Daughter's Love: Poems for Us to Share*. New York: HarperCollins.

Thomas, Joyce Carol. 2002. *Crowning Glory*. New York: HarperCollins.

Thomas, Joyce Carol. 2007. *Shouting!* New York: Hyperion.

Thomas, Joyce Carol. 2008. *The Blacker the Berry*. Illus. by Floyd Cooper. New York: Amistad.

Weatherford, Carole Boston. 2001. *Sidewalk Chalk; Poems of the City*. Honesdale, PA: Wordsong/Boyds Mills Press.

Weatherford, Carole Boston. 2002. *Remember the Bridge: Poems of a People*. New York: Philomel.

Weatherford, Carole Boston. 2006. *Dear Mr. Rosenwald*. Ill. by R. Gregory Christie. New York: Scholastic.

Weatherford, Carole Boston. 2007. *Birmingham, 1963*. Honesdale, PA: Wordsong/Boyds Mills Press.

Weatherford, Carole Boston. 2008. *Becoming Billie Holiday*. Honesdale, PA: Wordsong/Boyds Mills Press.

Woodson, Jacqueline. 2003. *Locomotion*. New York: Putnam.

Asian American Poetry for Young People

Asian and Asian American poetry for young people is not just haiku; there are many lovely, ancient and contemporary works to share with children. Here is a sampling of poetry for young people by Asian and Asian American poets.

Cheng, Andrea. 2005. *Shanghai Messenger*. New York: Lee & Low.

Demi, comp. 1994. *In the Eyes of the Cat: Japanese Poetry for All Seasons*. Translated by Tze-Si Huang. New York: Henry Holt.

Gollub, Matthew. 1998. *Cool Melons Turn to Frogs: The Life and Poems of Issa*. New York: Lee & Low Books.

Ho, Minfong. 1996. *Maples in the Mist: Poems for Children from the Tang Dynasty*. New York: Lothrop, Lee, & Shepard.

Issa, Kobayashi. 2007. *Today and Today*. New York: Scholastic.

Izuki, Steven. 1994. *Believers in America: Poems about Americans of Asian and Pacific Islander Descent*. Chicago, IL: Children's Press.

Lai, Thanhha. 2011. *Inside Out and Back Again*. New York: HarperCollins.

Mak, Kam. 2001. *My Chinatown: One Year in Poems*. New York: HarperCollins.

Park, Linda Sue. 2007. *Tap Dancing on the Roof; Sijo Poems*. New York : Clarion.

Thompson, Holly. 2011. *Orchards*. New York: Random House.

Wong, Janet S. 1994. *Good Luck Gold and Other Poems*. New York: McElderry.

Wong, Janet S. 1996/2008. *A Suitcase of Seaweed, and Other Poems*. New York: Booksurge.

Wong, Janet S. 1999. *Behind the Wheel: Poems about Driving*. New York: McElderry.

Wong, Janet S. 1999. *The Rainbow Hand: Poems about Mothers and Children*. New York: McElderry.

Wong, Janet S. 2000. *Night Garden: Poems from the World of Dreams*. New York: McElderry.

Wong, Janet S. 2003. *Knock on Wood: Poems about Superstitions*. New York: McElderry.

Wong, Janet S. 2003. *Minn and Jake*. New York: Farrar, Straus & Giroux.

Wong, Janet S. 2007. *Twist: Yoga Poems*. New York: McElderry.

Wong, Janet. 2008. *Minn and Jake's Almost Terrible Summer*. New York: Farrar, Straus & Giroux.

Wong, Janet. 2011. *Once Upon A Tiger; New Beginnings for Endangered Animals*. OnceUponaTiger.com.

Wong, Janet. 2012. *Declaration of Interdependence: Poems for an Election Year*. PoetrySuitcase.

Wong, Joyce Lee. 2006. *Seeing Emily*. New York: Abrams.

Yep, Laurence, ed. 1993. American Dragons: Twenty-five Asian American Voices. *New York: HarperCollins.*

Yu, Chin. 2005. Little Green; Growing Up During the Chinese Cultural Revolution. New York: Simon & Schuster.

Hispanic/Latino/Latina Poetry for Young People

There are more and more poets of Hispanic/Latino background writing poetry for children. Some are of Hispanic heritage and others collect poetry from Latin American countries. Here's a list of some of my favorites for sharing with young people.

Ada, Alma Flor and Campoy, Isabel. 2010. *Muu, Moo! Rimas de animales/Animal Nursery Rhymes.* New York: Rayo/HarperCollins.

Ada, Alma Flor and Campoy, F. Isabel. 2011. *Ten Little Puppies; Diez perritos.* New York: Rayo/HarperCollins.

Ada, Alma Flor, and Isabel Campoy, comp. 2003. *Pio Peep! Traditional Spanish Nursery Rhymes.* New York: HarperCollins.

Ada, Alma Flor. 1997. *Gathering the Sun.* New York: Lothrop, Lee, & Shepard.

Alarcón, Francisco X. 1997. *Laughing Tomatoes and Other Spring Poems/Jitomates Risuenos y Otros Poemas de Primavera.* San Francisco, CA: Children's Book Press.

Alarcón, Francisco X. 1998. *From the Bellybutton of the Moon and Other Summer Poems/Del Ombligo de la Luna y Otros Poemas de Verano.* San Francisco: Children's Book Press.

Alarcón, Francisco X. 1999. *Angels Ride Bikes and Other Fall Poems.* San Francisco, CA: Children's Book Press.

Alarcón, Francisco X. 2001. *Iguanas in the Snow and Other Winter Poems/ Iguanas en la Nieve y Otros Poemas de Invierno.* San Francisco, CA: Children's Book Press.

Alarcón, Francisco X. 2005. *Poems to Dream Together/ Poemas para Sonar Juntos.* New York: Lee & Low.

Alarcón, Francisco X. 2008. *Animals Poems of the Iguazú / Animalario del Iguazú.* San Francisco, CA: Children's Book Press.

Argueta, Jorge. 2001. *A Movie in My Pillow/Una película en mi almohada.* San Francisco, CA: Children's Book Press.

Argueta, Jorge. 2009. *Sopa de frijoles/ Bean Soup.* Ill. by Rafael Yockteng. Toronto, ON: Groundwood.

Argueta, Jorge. 2010. *Arroz con leche; Rice Pudding.* Ill. by Fernando Vilela. Toronto, ON: Groundwood.

Argueta, Jorge. 2012. *Guacamole; Un poema para cocinar/ A Cooking Poem.* Ill. by Margarita Sada. Toronto: Groundwood.

Bernier-Grand, Carmen T. 2006. *César; ¡Sí, Se Puede! Yes, We can!* New York: Marshall Cavendish.

Bernier-Grand, Carmen T. 2007. *Frida: ¡Viva la vida! Long Live Life!* New York: Marshall Cavendish.

Bernier-Grand, Carmen T. 2009. *Diego; Bigger Than Life.* Ill. by David Diaz. New York: Marshall Cavendish.

Carlson, Lori M, comp. 1998. *Sol a Sol: Bilingual Poems.* New York: Henry Holt.

Carlson, Lori M, comp. 2005. *Red Hot Salsa; Bilingual Poems on Being Young and Latino in the United States.* New York: Henry Holt.

Carlson, Lori M., comp. 1994. *Cool Salsa: Bilingual Poems on Growing Up Latino in the United States.* New York: Henry Holt.

Cofer, Judith Ortiz. 2004. *Call Me Maria; A Novel in Letters, Poems, and Prose*. New York: Orchard.

Cumpian, Carlos. 1994. *Latino Rainbow: Poems about Latino Americans*. Chicago: Children's Press.

De Gerez, Toni, comp. 1984. *My Song is a Piece of Jade: Poems of Ancient Mexico in English and Spanish/ Mi Canción es un Pedazo de Jade: Poemas del México Antiguo en Inglés y Español*. New York: Little Brown.

Delacre, Lulu, comp. 1992. *Arroz con Leche: Popular Songs and Rhymes from Latin America*. New York: Scholastic.

Delacre, Lulu, comp. 1992. *Las Navidades: Popular Christmas Songs from Latin America*. New York: Scholastic.

Delacre, Lulu. 2004. *Arrorró Mi Niño: Latino Lullabies and Gentle Games*. New York: Scholastic.

Durango, Julia. 2011. *Under the Mambo Moon*. Watertown, MA: Charlesbridge.

Engle, Margaret. 2006. *The Poet Slave of Cuba: A Biography of Juan Francisco Manzano*. New York: Holt.

Engle, Margarita. 2008. *The Surrender Tree*. New York: Holt.

Engle, Margarita. 2009. *Tropical Secrets: Holocaust Refugees in Cuba*. New York: Holt.

Engle, Margarita. 2010. *The Firefly Letters; A Suffragette's Journey to Cuba*. New York: Holt.

Engle, Margarita. 2011. *Hurricane Dancers; The First Caribbean Pirate Shipwreck*. New York: Holt.

Engle, Margarita. 2012. *The Wild Book*. Boston: Houghton Mifflin.

Gonzalez, Ray, ed. 1999. *Touching the Fire: Fifteen Poets of Today's Latino Renaissance*. New York: Anchor Books/Doubleday.

Herrera, Juan Felipe. 1998. *Laughing Out Loud, I Fly: Poems in English and Spanish*. New York: HarperCollins.

Herrera, Juan Felipe. 1999. *Crashboomlove*. Albuquerque: University of New Mexico Press.

Herrera, Juan Felipe. 2000. *The Upside Down Boy/El niño de cabeza*. San Francisco, CA: Children's Book Press.

Herrera, Juan Felipe. 2001. *Calling The Doves/El Canto De Las Palomas*. San Francisco, CA: Children's Book Press.

Herrera, Juan Felipe. 2003. *Super Cilantro Girl*. San Francisco, CA: Children's Book Press.

Herrera, Juan Felipe. 2004. *Featherless/Desplumado*. San Francisco, CA: Children's Book Press.

Herrera, Juan Felipe. 2005. *Cinnamon Girl: Letters Found Inside A Cereal Box*. New York: Rayo/HarperCollins.

Herrera, Juan Felipe. 2005. *Downtown Boy*. New York: Scholastic.

Herrera, Juan Felipe. 2011. *Skate Fate*. New York: HarperCollins.

Johnston, Tony. 1996. *My Mexico-Mexico Mio*. New York: Putnam's Sons.

Lee, Claudia M. Ed. 2011. *Mandaderos de la lluvia/Messengers of Rain*. Ill. by Rafael Yockteng. Toronto: Groundwood. (new bilingual edition).

Luján, Jorge. 2008. *Colors! Colores!* Ill. by Piet Grobler. Toronto: Groundwood.

Luján, Jorge. 2010. *Brunhilda and the Ring*. Translated by Hugh Hazelton. Toronto: Groundwood.

Luján, Jorge. 2012. *Con el sol en los ojos/ With the Sun in My Eyes*. Ill. by Morteza Zahedi. Toronto: Groundwood.

McCall, Guadalupe Garcia. 2011. *Under the Mesquite*. New York: Lee & Low.

Medina, Jane. 2004. *The Dream on Blanca's Wall*. Honesdale, PA: Boyd's Mill Press.

Medina, Jane. 1999. *My Name is Jorge on Both Sides of the River: Poems*. Honesdale, PA: Boyds Mills Press.

Mora, Pat. 1996. *Confetti: Poems for Children*. New York: Lee & Low Books.

Mora, Pat. 1998. *Delicious Hullabaloo/Pachanga Deliciosa*. Houston, TX: Pinata Books.

Mora, Pat. 1994. *The Desert is My Mother/El Desierto es Mi Madre*. Houston, TX: Pinata Books.

Mora, Pat. 2001. *Love to Mama: A Tribute to Mothers*. New York: Lee & Low Books.

Mora, Pat. 2000. *My Own True Name: New and Selected Poems for Young Adults, 1984-1999*. Houston, TX: Pinata Books.

Mora, Pat. 1998. *This Big Sky*. New York: Scholastic.

Mora, Pat. 1996. *Uno Dos Tres, One, Two, Three*. New York: Clarion Books.

Mora, Pat. 2007. *Yum! Mmmm! Que Rico!: America's Sproutings*. New York: Lee & Low.

Mora, Pat. 2010. *Dizzy in My Eyes*. New York: Knopf.

Nye, Naomi Shihab, comp. 1995. *The Tree is Older than You Are: A Bilingual Gathering of Poems and Stories from Mexico with Paintings by Mexican Artists*. New York: Simon & Schuster.

Orozco, José Luis. 2002. *Diez Deditos: Ten Little Fingers and Other Play Rhymes and Action Songs from Latin America*. New York: Dutton.

Orozco, José Luis.1994. Fiestas: A Year of Latin American Songs of Celebration. New York: Dutton.

Orozco, Jose-Luis. 1994. De Colores and Other Latin-American Folk Songs for Children. New York: Dutton.

Ruesga, Rita Rosa. 2011. *Cantaba la rana/The Frog Was Singing*. Ill. by Soledad Sebastián. New York: Scholastic.

Shahan, Sherry. 2009. *Fiesta!; A Celebration of Latino Festivals*. Ill. by Paula Barragan. Atlanta, GA: August House.

Soto, Gary. 1990. *A Fire in My Hands*. New York: Scholastic.

Soto, Gary. 1992. *Neighborhood Odes*. San Diego, CA: Harcourt Brace Jovanovich.

Soto, Gary. 1995. *Canto Familiar*. San Diego, CA: Harcourt Brace.

Soto, Gary. 2002. *Fearless Fernie: Hanging Out with Fernie & Me*. New York: Putnam.

Soto, Gary. 2005. *Worlds Apart: Fernie and Me*. New York: Putnam.

Soto, Gary. 2008. *Partly Cloudy; Poems of Love and Longing*. Boston: Houghton Mifflin Harcourt.

Sullivan, Charles. Ed. 1994. *Here is My Kingdom: Hispanic-American Literature and Art for Young People*. New York: Abrams.

Native American Poetry For Young People

Voices from Native American or Indian tribes and traditions offer poetry in many forms. Here is a selection of these poetry books for young people.

Begay, Shonto. 1995. *Navajo; Visions and Voices Across the Mesa*. New York: Scholastic.

Bierhorst, John. Ed. 1994. *On the Road of Stars; Native American Night Poems and Sleep Charms*. New York: Macmillan.

Bierhorst, John. Ed. 1998. *In the Trail of The Wind*. New York: Farrar, Straus, & Giroux.

Bruchac, Joseph. 1996. *Between Earth and Sky*. San Diego: Harcourt Brace.

Bruchac, Joseph. 1996. *The Circle of Thanks*. Mahwah, NJ: Bridgewater Books.

Bruchac, Joseph. 1995. *The Earth Under Sky Bear's Feet: Native American Poems of the Land*. New York: Philomel.

Bruchac, Joseph. 1996. *Four Ancestors: Stories, Songs, and Poems from Native North America*. Mahwah, NJ: Bridgewater Books.

Bruchac, Joseph. 1992. *Thirteen Moons on Turtle's Back: A Native American Year of Moons*. New York: Philomel.

Carvell, Marlene. 2005. *Sweetgrass Basket*. New York: Dutton.

Castillo, Ana. 2000. *My Daughter, My Son, the Eagle, the Dove: An Aztec Chant*. New York: Dutton.

Francis, Lee. 1999. *When The Rain Sings: Poems by Young Native Americans*. New York: Simon & Schuster.

Geis, Jacqueline. 1992. *Where the Buffalo Roam*. Nashville, TN: Ideals Children's Books.

Hirschfelder, A. and Singer, B. Eds. 1992. *Rising Voices: Writings of Young Native Americans*. New York: Scribner's.

Jones, Hettie. Ed. 1971. *The Tree Stands Shining: Poetry of the North American Indian*. New York: Dial.

Littlechild, George. 1993. *This Land Is My Land*. San Francisco, CA: Children's Book Press.

McLaughlin, Timothy. Ed. 2012. *Walking on Earth and Touching the Sky; Poetry and Prose by Lakota Youth at Red Cloud Indian School*. New York: Abrams.

Ochoa, Annette Piña, Betsy Franco, And Traci L. Gourdine. Ed. 2003. *Night Is Gone, Day Is Still Coming; Stories and Poems by American Indian Teens and Young Adults*. Somerville, MA: Candlewick.

Philip, Neil. Ed. 1996. *Earth Always Endures: Native American Poems*. New York: Viking.

Philip, Neil. Ed. 1997. *In a Sacred Manner I Live: Native American Wisdom*. New York: Clarion.

Slapin, Beverly, And Doris Seale. Eds. 1998. *Through Indian Eyes: The Native American Experience in Books for Children*. Berkeley, CA: Oyate.

Sneve, Virginia. D. H. Ed. 1989. *Dancing Teepees: Poems of American Indian Youth*. New York: Holiday House.

Swamp, C. J. 1995. *Giving Thanks; A Native American Good Morning Message*. New York: Lee & Low.

Swann, B. 1998. *Touching the Distance: Native American Riddle-Poems.* San Diego, CA: Browndeer Press/Harcourt Brace.

Wood, Nancy. 1995. *Dancing Moons.* New York: Doubleday.

Wood, Nancy. 1998. *Sacred Fire.* New York: Doubleday.

Wood, Nancy. 1993. *Spirit Walker.* New York: Doubleday.

International Poetry for Young People

As we seek poetry for children from many cultural perspectives, we can expand beyond the cultures in the U.S. and include poetry from other countries. Some of the following works are imported from across the oceans and others are anthologies of global poems collected by poets within the U.S. Sharing poems from these collections can put a face on a news story from far away lands.

Agard, John and Grace Nichols, Eds. 1994. *A Caribbean Dozen: Poems from Caribbean Poets.* Somerville, MA: Candlewick.

Agard, John, and Nichols, Grace. Eds. 1995. *No Hickory, No Dickory, No Dock: Caribbean Nursery Rhymes.* Somerville, MA: Candlewick.

Aldana, Patricia. Ed. 2004. *Under the Spell of the Moon.* Toronto, Canada: Groundwood.

Argante, Jenny. Ed. 2007. *Poetry Pudding; A Delicious Collection of Rhyme and Wit.* Ill. by Debbie Tipuna. Auckland, NZ: Reed Publishing, p. 168.

Beck, Carolyn. *Buttercup's Lovely Day.* Custer, WA: Orca Books.

Benjamin, Floella. Ed. 1995. *Skip Across the Ocean: Nursery Rhymes from Around the World.* New York: Orchard.

Brenner, Barbara. Ed. 2000. *Voices Poetry and Art from Around the World.* Washington, DC: National Geographic Society.

Brownlee, Liz. 2012. *Animal Magic.* Ill. by Rose Sanderson. London: Iron Press.

Cashman, Seamus. Ed. 2004. *Something Beginning with P: New Poems from Irish Poets.* Dublin: O'Brien Press.

Chorao, Kay. 2009. *Rhymes Round the World.* New York: Dutton.

Cooling, Wendy. Ed. 2004. *Come to the Great World; Poems from Around the Globe.* New York: Holiday House.

Cooling, Wendy. Ed. 2010. *All the Wild Wonders: Poems of Our Earth.* Ill. by Piet Grobler. London: Frances Lincoln Children's Books.

Denton, Graham. 2006. *Silly Superstitions.* London: Macmillan Children's Books.

Denton, Graham. 2009. *Orange Silver Sausage.* London: Walker Books.

Denton, Graham. 2010. *My Cat is in Love with the Goldfish.* London: A&C Black.

Denton, Graham. 2009. *Wild! Rhymes that Roar.* London: Macmillan.

Foster, John. Ed. 1997. *Let's Celebrate: Festival Poems.* New York: Oxford University Press.

Greenberg, Jan. Ed. 2008. *Side by Side: New Poems Inspired by Art from Around the World.* New York: Abrams.

Gunning, Monica. 1993. *Not a Copper Penny in Me House.* Honesdale, PA: Wordsong/Boyds Mills Press.

Gunning, Monica. 1998. *Under The Breadfruit Tree: Island Poems.* Honesdale, PA: Boyds Mills Press.

Hallworth, Grace. Ed. 1996. *Down by the River: Afro-Caribbean Rhymes, Games, and Songs for Children.* New York: Scholastic.

Henderson, Kathy. 2011. *Hush, Baby, Hush! Lullabies from Around the World.* Ill. by Pam Smy. Seattle: Frances Lincoln.

Herrick, Steven. 2004. *By the River*. Asheville, NC: Front Street.

Herrick, Steven. 2004. *The Simple Gift*. New York: Simon & Schuster.

Herrick, Steven. 2006. *The Wolf*. Asheville, NC: Front Street.

Herrick, Steven. 2008. *Naked Bunyip Dancing*. Honesdale, PA: Boyds Mills/Wordsong.

Herrick, Steven. 2009. *Cold Skin*. Asheville, NC: Front Street.

Houle, Michelle M. Ed. 2010. *Poetry Rocks: Modern British Poetry; "The World is Never the Same."* Enslow.

Lawson, JonArno. 2008. *Black Stars in a White Night Sky*. Honesdale, PA: Boyds Mills/Wordsong.

Lawson, JonArno. 2010. *Think Again*. Kids Can Press.

Lee, Dennis. 1997. *Dinosaur Dinner with a Slice of Alligator Pie*. New York: Random House.

Lee, Dennis. 1991. *The Ice Cream Store*. New York: Scholastic. Reprint, New York: HarperCollins, 1999.

Lee, Dennis. 2001. *Alligator Pie*. Toronto: Key Porter Books.

Lee, Dennis. 2001. *Bubblegum Delicious*. New York: HarperCollins.

Lee, Dennis. 2002. *Garbage Delight: Another Helping*. Toronto: Key Porter Books.

Luján, Jorge. 2008. *Colors! Colores!* Ill. by Piet Grobler. Toronto: Groundwood.

Luján, Jorge. 2012. *Con el sol en los ojos/ With the Sun in My Eyes*. Ill. by Morteza Zahedi. Toronto: Groundwood.

Mado, Michio. 1992. *The Animals: Selected Poems*. New York: McElderry.

Mado, Michio. 1998. The Magic Pocket. *New York: McElderry.*

Nye, Naomi Shihab. Ed. 1992. *This Same Sky: A Collection of Poems from Around the World*. New York: Four Winds Press.

Nye, Naomi Shihab. Ed. 1995. *The Tree is Older than You Are: A Bilingual Gathering of Poems and Stories from Mexico with Paintings by Mexican Artists*. New York: Simon & Schuster.

Nye, Naomi Shihab. Ed. 1998. *The Space Between Our Footsteps: Poems and Paintings From the Middle East*. New York: Simon & Schuster.

Nye, Naomi Shihab. 1998. *The Flag of Childhood: Poems from the Middle East*. New York: Simon & Schuster.

Nye, Naomi Shihab. 2002. *Nineteen Varieties of the Gazelle*. New York: Greenwillow.

Olaleye, I. 1995. *The Distant Talking Drum: Poems from Nigeria*. Honesdale, PA: Wordsong.

Pomerantz, Charlotte. 1982. *If I Had a Paka: Poems in Eleven Languages*. New York: Greenwillow.

Rasmussen, Halfdan. 2011. *A Little Bitty Man and Other Poems for the Very Young*. Translated by Marilyn Nelson and Pamela Espeland. Somerville, MA: Candlewick.

Rosen, Michael. Ed.1991. *A World of Poetry*. London: Kingfisher Books.

Rosen, Michael. Ed. 1992. *Itsy-bitsy Beasties: Poems from Around the World*. Minneapolis, MN: Carolrhoda Books.

Sayer, Viv. Ed. 2008. *Poems of Love and Longing*. Pont Books.

Schmidt, Annie M. G. 2011. *A Pond Full of Ink*, translated by David Colmer. Amsterdam: Querido Children's Books.

Swann, Brian. 1998. *The House with No Door: African Riddle-poems.* San Diego, CA: Browndeer Press.

Warren, Celia. Ed. 2011. *RSPB Anthology of Wildlife Poetry.* London: A&C Black.

Wright, Danielle. Ed. 2008. *My Village; Rhymes from Around the World.* Wellington, NZ: Gecko Press.

Yolen, Jane. Ed. 1992. *Street Rhymes from Around the World.* Honesdale, PA: Wordsong/Boyds Mills Press.

Yolen, Jane. Ed. 1994. *Sleep Rhymes around the World.* Honesdale, PA: Wordsong/Boyds Mills Press.

Bilingual Poetry for Young People

Young people who read or speak a language in addition to English will enjoy seeing poetry in their native (or adopted) language. There are many collections of poetry in Spanish and English available, as well as in other languages, as evidenced by this sample listing below. Try reading them aloud with two readers, one reading each language simultaneously (e.g., Spanish; English), as if written for two voices.

Ada, Alma Flor and Campoy, Isabel. 2010. *Muu, Moo! Rimas de animales/Animal Nursery Rhymes*. Rayo/HarperCollins.

Ada, Alma Flor, and Isabel Campoy. Ed. 2003. *Pio Peep! Traditional Spanish Nursery Rhymes*. New York: HarperCollins.

Ada, Alma Flor and Campoy, F. Isabel. 2011. *Ten Little Puppies; Diez perritos*. Rayo/HarperCollins.

Ada, Alma Flor. 1997. *Gathering the Sun*. New York: Lothrop, Lee, & Shepard.

Alarcón, Francisco X. 1997. *Laughing Tomatoes and Other Spring Poems/Jitomates Risuenos y Otros Poemas de Primavera*. San Francisco, CA: Children's Book Press.

Alarcón, Francisco X. 1998. *From the Bellybutton of the Moon and Other Summer Poems/Del Ombligo de la Luna y Otros Poemas de Verano*. San Francisco: Children's Book Press.

Alarcón, Francisco X. 1999. *Angels Ride Bikes and Other Fall Poems*. San Francisco, CA: Children's Book Press.

Alarcón, Francisco X. 2001. *Iguanas in the Snow and Other Winter Poems/ Iguanas en la Nieve y Otros Poemas de Invierno*. San Francisco, CA: Children's Book Press.

Alarcón, Francisco X. 2005. *Poems to Dream Together/ Poemas para Sonar Juntos*. New York: Lee & Low.

Alarcón, Francisco X. 2008. *Animals Poems of the Iguazú / Animalario del Iguazú*. San Francisco, CA: Children's Book Press.

Argueta, Jorge. 2001. *A Movie in My Pillow/Una película en mi almohada*. San Francisco, CA: Children's Book Press.

Argueta, Jorge. 2006. *Talking with Mother Earth; Poems; Hablando con Madre Tierra*. Toronto: Groundwood.

Argueta, Jorge. 2009. *Sopa de frijoles/ Bean Soup*. Ill. by Rafael Yockteng. Toronto, ON: Groundwood.

Argueta, Jorge. 2010. *Arroz con leche; Rice Pudding*. Ill. by Fernando Vilela. Toronto, ON: Groundwood.

Argueta, Jorge. 2012. *Guacamole; Un poema para cocinar/ A Cooking Poem*. Ill. by Margarita Sada. Groundwood.

Bernier-Grand, Carmen T. 2006. *César; ¡Sí, Se Puede! Yes, We can!* New York: Marshall Cavendish.

Bernier-Grand, Carmen T. 2007. *Frida: ¡Viva la vida! Long Live Life!* New York: Marshall Cavendish.

Bernier-Grand, Carmen T. 2009. *Diego; Bigger Than Life*. Ill. by David Diaz. New York: Marshall Cavendish.

Carlson, Lori M. Ed. 1998. *Sol a Sol: Bilingual Poems*. New York: Henry Holt.

Carlson, Lori M. Ed. 2005. *Red Hot Salsa; Bilingual Poems on Being Young and Latino in the United States.* New York: Henry Holt.

Carlson, Lori M.. Ed. 1994. *Cool Salsa: Bilingual Poems on Growing Up Latino in the United States.* New York: Henry Holt.

Cashman, Seamus. 2004. *Something Beginning with P: New Poems from Irish Poets.* Dublin: O'Brien Press.

De Gerez, Toni. Ed. 1984. *My Song is a Piece of Jade: Poems of Ancient Mexico in English and Spanish/ Mi Canción es un Pedazo de Jade: Poemas del México Antiguo en Inglés y Español.* Boston: Little, Brown.

Delacre, Lulu. Ed. 1992. *Arroz con Leche: Popular Songs and Rhymes from Latin America.* New York: Scholastic.

Delacre, Lulu. Ed. 1992. *Las Navidades: Popular Christmas Songs from Latin America.* New York: Scholastic.

Delacre, Lulu. 2004. *Arrorró Mi Niño: Latino Lullabies and Gentle Games.* New York: Scholastic.

Henderson, Kathy. 2011. *Hush, Baby, Hush! Lullabies from Around the World.* Ill. by Pam Smy. Seattle: Frances Lincoln.

Herrera, Juan Felipe. 2000. *The Upside Down Boy/El niño de cabeza.* San Francisco, CA: Children's Book Press.

Herrera, Juan Felipe. 2001. *Calling The Doves/El Canto De Las Palomas.* San Francisco, CA: Children's Book Press.

Herrera, Juan Felipe. 2004. *Featherless/Desplumado.* San Francisco, CA: Children's Book Press.

Lee, Claudia M. Ed. 2011. *Mandaderos de la lluvia/Messengers of Rain.* Ill. by Rafael Yockteng. Toronto: Groundwood.

Luján, Jorge. 2008. *Colors! Colores!* Ill. by Piet Grobler. Toronto: Groundwood.

Luján, Jorge. 2012. *Con el sol en los ojos/ With the Sun in My Eyes.* Ill. by Morteza Zahedi. Toronto: Groundwood.

Mado, Michio. 1992. *The Animals: Selected Poems.* New York: McElderry.

Mado, Michio. 1998. The Magic Pocket. *New York: McElderry.*

Medina, Jane. 1999. *My Name is Jorge on Both Sides of the River: Poems.* Honesdale, PA: Boyds Mills Press.

Medina, Jane. 2004. *The Dream on Blanca's Wall.* Honesdale, PA: Boyd's Mill Press.

Mora, Pat. 1994. *The Desert is My Mother/El Desierto es Mi Madre.* Houston, TX: Pinata Books.

Mora, Pat. 1996. *Uno Dos Tres/One, Two, Three.* New York: Clarion.

Mora, Pat. 1998. *Delicious Hullabaloo/Pachanga Deliciosa.* Houston, TX: Pinata Books.

Nye, Naomi Shihab. Ed. 1995. *The Tree is Older than You Are: A Bilingual Gathering of Poems and Stories from Mexico with Paintings by Mexican Artists.* New York: Simon & Schuster.

Orozco, José Luis. 2002. *Diez Deditos: Ten Little Fingers and Other Play Rhymes and Action Songs from Latin America.* New York: Dutton.

Orozco, José Luis.1994. *Fiestas: A Year of Latin American Songs of Celebration.* New York: Dutton.

Orozco, Jose-Luis. 1994. *De Colores and Other Latin-American Folk Songs for Children*. New York: Dutton.

Pomerantz, Charlotte. 1982. *If I Had a Paka: Poems in Eleven Languages*. New York: Greenwillow.

Yolen, Jane. Ed. 1992. *Street Rhymes from Around the World*. Honesdale, PA: Wordsong/Boyds Mills Press.

Yolen, Jane. Ed. 1994. *Sleep Rhymes around the World*. Honesdale, PA: Wordsong/Boyds Mills Press.

Poetry Books for (ESL/ELL) English Language Learners

Children who are learning English as a second, third, or additional language enjoy the simplicity and clarity of poetry when examples are chosen with them in mind. Ideally, poems should have a clear focus and accessible vocabulary. If you can also find poetry that represents the cultures of the children, that adds a connection of relevancy, too. Humorous poetry, on the other hand, is not necessarily the best choice as it requires culturally specific knowledge that may not yet be familiar. Here are selected books based on "Matching Books and Readers: Selecting Literature for English Learners" by Nancy Hadaway, Terrell Young and me.

Alarcón, Francisco X. 1997. *Laughing Tomatoes and Other Spring Poems/Jitomates Risuenos y Otros Poemas de Primavera.* San Francisco, CA: Children's Book Press.

Alarcón, Francisco X. 1998. *From the Bellybutton of the Moon and Other Summer Poems/Del Ombligo de la Luna y Otros Poemas de Verano.* San Francisco: Children's Book Press.

Alarcón, Francisco X. 1999. *Angels Ride Bikes and Other Fall Poems.* San Francisco, CA: Children's Book Press.

Alarcón, Francisco X. 2001. *Iguanas in the Snow and Other Winter Poems/ Iguanas en la Nieve y Otros Poemas de Invierno.* San Francisco, CA: Children's Book Press.

Alarcón, Francisco X. 2005. *Poems to Dream Together/ Poemas para Sonar Juntos.* New York: Lee & Low.

Alarcón, Francisco X. 2008. *Animals Poems of the Iguazú / Animalario del Iguazú.* San Francisco, CA: Children's Book Press.

Anholt, Catherine, and Laurence Anholt. 1998. *Big Book of Families.* Cambridge, MA: Candlewick.

Argueta, Jorge. 2009. *Sopa de frijoles/ Bean Soup.* Ill. by Rafael Yockteng. Toronto, ON: Groundwood.

Argueta, Jorge. *Arroz con leche; Rice Pudding.* Ill. by Fernando Vilela. Toronto, ON: Groundwood.

Bruchac, Joseph. 1992. *Thirteen Moons on Turtle's Back: A Native American Year of Moons.* New York: Philomel Books.

Bruchac, Joseph. 1995. *The Earth under Sky Bear's Feet: Native American Poems of the Land.* New York: Philomel Books.

Bruchac, Joseph. 1996. *Between Earth and Sky: Legends of Native American Sacred Places.* San Diego, CA: Harcourt Brace.

Bryan, Ashley. 1997. *Ashley Bryan's ABC of African American Poetry.* New York: Atheneum.

Calmenson, Stephanie. 2002. *Welcome, Baby! Baby Rhymes for Baby Times.* New York: HarperCollins.

Cheng, Andrea. 2008. *Where the Steps Were.* Honesdale, PA: Boyds Mills/Wordsong.

Cooling, Wendy. 2004. *Come to the Great World; Poems from Around the Globe.* New York: Holiday House.

Crews, Nina. 2004. *The Neighborhood Mother Goose.* New York: Greenwillow.

Crews, Nina. 2011. *Neighborhood Sing Along.* HarperCollins.

Delacre, L. 1989. Arroz con leche: *Popular Songs and Rhymes from Latin America*. New York: Scholastic.

Ehlert, Lois. 2008. *Oodles Of Animals*. Harcourt.

Ehlert, Lois. 2010. *Lots of Spots*. Beach Lane Books.

Elliott, David. 2008. *On the Farm*. Cambridge, MA: Candlewick.

Elliott, David. 2010. *In the Wild*. Cambridge, MA: Candlewick.

Engle, Margarita. 2008. *The Surrender Tree*. New York: Holt.

Engle, Margarita. 2011. *Hurricane Dancers; The First Caribbean Pirate Shipwreck*. Henry Holt.

Florian, D. 1994. *Bing Bang Boing*. San Diego: Harcourt.

Florian, D. 1998. *Insectlopedia*. San Diego: Harcourt.

Florian, Douglas. 1999. *Laugh-eteria: Poems and Drawings*. San Diego: Harcourt.

Florian, Douglas. 2005. *Zoo's Who*. San Diego, CA: Harcourt.

George, Kristine O'Connell. 2005. *Fold Me a Poem*. San Diego, CA: Harcourt Brace.

Gibson, Amy. 2011. *Around the World on Eighty Legs: Animals Poems*. Ill. by Daniel Salmieri. New York: Scholastic.

Giovanni, Nikki. Coll. 2008. *Hip Hop Speaks to Children*. Naperville, IL: Sourcebooks.

Graham, J.B. 1994. *Splish Splash*. Boston: Houghton Mifflin.

Greenfield, E. 1978. *Honey, I Love*. New York: HarperCollins.

Greenfield, E. 1991. *Night on Neighborhood Street*. New York: Dial.

Greenfield, Eloise. 2008. *Brothers and Sisters: Family Poems*. New York: Amistad/HarperCollins.

Grimes, Nikki. 1999. *Hopscotch Love: A Family Treasury of Love Poems*. New York: Lothrop, Lee & Shepard.

Grimes, N. 2000. *Shoe Magic*. New York: Orchard Books.

Gunning, Monica. 2004. *A Shelter In Our Car*. San Francisco, CA: Children's Book Press.

Gunning, Monica. 2004. *America, My New Home*. San Francisco, CA: Children's Book Press.

Harley, Avis. 2000. *Fly with Poetry; An ABC of Poetry*. Honesdale, PA: Wordsong/Boyds Mills.

Harley, Avis. 2001. *Leap into Poetry: More ABCs of Poetry*. Honesdale, PA: Wordsong/Boyds Mills.

Heard, Georgia. 2009. *Falling Down the Page; A Book of List Poems*. New York: Roaring Brook.

Heide, Florence Parry, comp. 1999. *It's About Time!* New York: Clarion.

Henderson, Kathy. 2011. *Hush, Baby, Hush! Lullabies from Around the World*. Ill. by Pam Smy. Seattle: Frances Lincoln.

Herrera, J.F. 1998. *Laughing Out Loud, I Fly: Poems in English in Spanish*. New York: HarperCollins.

Hines, Anna Grossnickle. 2011. *Peaceful Pieces: A Year in Poems and Quilts*. New York: Greenwillow.

Ho, Minfong. 1996. *Maples in the Mist: Poems for Children from the Tang Dynasty*. New York: Lothrop, Lee, & Shepard.

Hoberman, Mary Ann. 1998. *The Llama Who Had No Pajama: 100 Favorite Poems*. San Diego: Harcourt.

Hoberman, Mary Ann. 2009. *All Kinds of Families*. New York: Little, Brown.

Hopkins, Lee Bennett, comp. 1996. *School Supplies: A Book of Poems.* New York: Simon & Schuster.

Hopkins, Lee Bennett, comp. 1997. *Marvelous Math: A Book of Poems*. New York: Simon & Schuster.

Hopkins, Lee Bennett, comp. 1999. *Spectacular Science: A Book of Poems.* New York: Simon & Schuster.

Hopkins, Lee Bennett, comp. 2010. *Amazing Faces.* Ill. By Chris Soentpiet. Lee and Low.

Hudson, Wade, comp. 1993. *Pass It On: African-American Poetry for Children*. New York: Scholastic.

Janeczko, Paul B., ed. 2005. *A Kick in the Head: An Everyday Guide to Poetic Forms.* Cambridge, MA: Candlewick.

Johnston, T. 1996. *My Mexico~Mexico Mio*. New York: Penguin Putnam.

Lai, Thanhha. 2011. *Inside Out and Back Again.* HarperCollins.

Lewis, J. Patrick. 2002. *A World of Wonders: Geographic Travels in Verse and Rhyme.* New York: Dial.

Lewis, J. Patrick. 2005. *Monumental Verses.* Washington, D.C.: National Geographic.

Luján, Jorge. 2008. *Colors! Colores!* Ill. by Piet Grobler. Toronto: Groundwood.

Martin, Bill, Jr. and Sampson, Michael. Comp. 2008. *The Bill Martin Jr. Big Book of Poetry*. New York: Simon & Schuster.

Moore, Lilian. 2004. *Mural on Second Avenue, and Other City Poems.* Cambridge, MA: Candlewick.

Mora, Pat. 1996. *Confetti: Poems for Children. New York: Lee & Low.*

Mora, Pat. 2001. *Love to Mama: A Tribute to Mothers.* New York: Lee & Low.

Mora, Pat. 2007. *Yum! Mmmm! Que Rico!: America's Sproutings*. New York: Lee & Low.

Myers, Walter Dean. 2011. *We are America; A Tribute from the Heart*. Ill. by Christopher Myers. HarperCollins.

Orozco, José Luis.1994. *Fiestas: A Year of Latin American Songs of Celebration.* New York: Dutton.

Paschen, Elise and Raccah, Dominique, comp. 2005. *Poetry Speaks to Children.* Naperville, IL: Sourcebooks.

Prelutsky, Jack. 1995. *It's Christmas.* New York: HarperTrophy.

Prelutsky, Jack, comp. 1997. *The Beauty of the Beast: Poems from the Animal Kingdom.* New York: Knopf.

Prelutsky, Jack. 2007. *Good Sports; Rhymes About Running, Jumping, Throwing, and More.* New York: Knopf.

Roemer, Heidi. 2004. *Come to My Party and Other Shape Poems.* New York: Henry Holt.

Salas, Laura Purdie. 2008. *Lettuce Introduce You: Poems About Food (A+ Books).* Minneapolis, MN: Capstone.

Salas, Laura Purdie. 2011. *BookSpeak!*. Ill. by Josee Bisaillon. Clarion.

Schertle, Alice. 2009. *Button Up! Wrinkled Rhymes.* Ill. by Petra Mathers. New York: Harcourt.

Schnur, Steven. 1997. *Autumn: An Alphabet Acrostic.* New York: Clarion.

Schnur, Steven. 1999. *Spring: An Alphabet Acrostic.* New York: Clarion.

Schnur, Steven. 2001. *Summer: An Alphabet Acrostic.* New York: Clarion.

Schnur, Steven. 2002. *Winter: An Alphabet Acrostic.* New York: Clarion.

Shahan, Sherry. 2009. *Fiesta!; A Celebration of Latino Festivals*. Ill. by Paula Barragan. Atlanta, GA: August House.

Shannon, George. 2006. *Busy in the Garden*. Ill. by Sam Williams. New York: Greenwillow.

Sidman, Joyce. 2007. *This is Just to Say: Poems of Apology and Forgiveness*. Ill. by Pamela Zagarenski. Boston: Houghton Mifflin.

Siebert, Diane. 2006. *Tour America: A Journey through Poems and Art*. San Francisco: Chronicle.

Singer, Marilyn. 2003. *How to Cross a Pond: Poems about Water*. New York: Knopf.

Singer, Marilyn. 2005. *Central Heating: Poems about Fire and Warmth*. New York: Knopf.

Smith, Charles R. Jr. 2003. *I am America*. New York: Scholastic.

Smith, Hope Anita. 2009. *Mother; Poems*. New York: Henry Holt.

Soto, Gary. 1992. *Neighborhood Odes*. San Diego, CA: Harcourt Brace Jovanovich.

Soto, Gary. 1995. *Canto Familiar*. San Diego, CA: Harcourt Brace.

Thomas, Joyce Carol. 2008. *The Blacker the Berry*. Illus. by Floyd Cooper. New York: Amistad.

Weatherford, Carole Boston. 2002. *Remember the Bridge: Poems of a People*. New York: Philomel.

Wong, Janet S. 1994. *Good Luck Gold and Other Poems*. New York: Margaret K. McElderry Books.

Wong, Janet S. 1996/2008. *A Suitcase of Seaweed, and Other Poems*. New York: Booksurge.

Wong, Janet S. 2003. *Knock on Wood: Poems about Superstitions*. New York: McElderry.

Wong, Janet S. 2007. *Twist: Yoga Poems*. New York: McElderry.

Wong, Joyce Lee. 2006. *Seeing Emily*. New York: Abrams.

Worth, Valerie. 2007. *Animal Poems*. Ill. by Steve Jenkins. New York: Farrar, Straus & Giroux.

Yolen, Jane, comp. 1996. *Mother Earth, Father Sky: Poems of Our Planet*. Honesdale, PA: Wordsong/Boyds Mills Press.

THEMATIC OR TOPICAL POETRY BOOKLISTS

Sometimes we need to find poems for a particular purpose such as helping children through worries, adjustments or difficult times. Sometimes poetry can introduce reassuring topics such as the importance of family and friends. And sometimes we simply want to laugh and share funny poetry. Indeed, studies show that children often rate humorous poems as their favorites. Here are lists of poetry books for each of these purposes.

Humorous Poetry Books for Young People
Poetry Books about Family
Poetry Books about Friendship
Poetry Books about Superstitions, Beliefs, Luck, Magic, Dreams, and Nightmares
Poetry Books about Coping with Disability, Illness, Homelessness, and Death
Comforting Poetry Books for Difficult Times

Humorous Poetry Books for Young People

According to studies of children's poetry preferences, humorous poetry consistently ranks as one of their favorites. Here are examples of many popular collections of funny poems, keeping in mind that some things that are funny to one audience (wordplay, puns, zombies), may not be to another.

Bagert, Brod. 1993. *Chicken Socks and Other Contagious Poems.* Honesdale, PA: Wordsong/Boyds Mills.

Bagert, Brod. 2000. *Giant Children.* Honesdale, PA: Wordsong/Boyds Mills.

Bagert, Brod. 2008. *School Fever.* Ill. by Robert Neubecker. New York: Dial.

Brown, Calef. 2006. *Flamingos on the Roof.* Boston: Houghton Mifflin.

Brown, Calef. 2008. *Soup For Breakfast.* Boston: Houghton Mifflin.

Brown, Calef. 2010. *Hallowilloween: Nefarious Silliness.* Boston: Houghton Mifflin.

Ciardi, John. 1962/1987. *You Read to Me, I'll Read to You.* Reprinted. New York: HarperTrophy, 1987.

Ciardi, John. 1966/1991. *The Monster Den.* Reprinted: Honesdale, PA: Wordsong.

Dahl, Roald. 2002. *Roald Dahl's Revolting Rhymes.* New York: Knopf.

Dahl, Roald. 2005. *Vile Verses.* New York: Viking.

Dakos, Kalli. 1996. *The Goof Who Invented Homework and Other School Poems.* New York: Dial.

Dakos, Kalli. 2003. *Put Your Eyes Up Here: And Other School Poems.* New York: Simon & Schuster.

Dakos, Kalli. 2011. *A Funeral in the Bathroom and Other School Bathroom Poems.* Albert Whitman.

Florian, Douglas. 1999. *Laugh-eteria: Poems and Drawings.* San Diego, CA: Harcourt Brace.

Florian, Douglas. 2001. *Bow Wow Meow Meow.* San Diego: Harcourt.

Florian, Douglas. 2002. *Summersaults: Poems and Paintings.* New York: Greenwillow.

Florian, Douglas. 2009. *Dinothesaurus.* New York: Simon & Schuster.

Franco, Betsy. 2003. *Mathematickles!* New York: Margaret K. McElderry Books.

Franco, Betsy. 2009. *A Curious Collection of Cats.* Ill. by Michael Wertz. San Francisco, CA: Tricycle Press.

Franco, Betsy. 2011. A *Dazzling Display of Dogs.* Ill. by Michael Wertz. Berkeley, CA: Tricycle.

Hauth, Katherine. 2011. *What's for Dinner? Quirky, Squirmy Poems from the Animal World.* Charlesbridge.

Hoberman, Mary Ann. 1998. *The Llama Who Had No Pajama: 100 Favorite Poems.* San Diego: Harcourt.

Hoberman, Mary Ann. 2001. *You Read to Me, I'll Read to You; Very Short Stories to Read Together.* Ill. by Michael Emberley. Boston: Little, Brown.

Hopkins, Lee Bennett. Ed. 1984. *Surprises.* New York: HarperTrophy.

Hopkins, Lee Bennett. Ed. 2011. *Dizzy Dinosaurs; An I Can Read Book.* New York: HarperCollins.

Katz, Alan. 2008. *Oops.* New York: McElderry.

Katz, Alan. 2011. *Poems I Wrote When No One Was Looking*. New York: Simon & Schuster.

Katz, Bobbi. 2001. *A Rumpus of Rhymes: A Book of Noisy Poems*. New York: Dutton.

Katz, Bobbi. 2009. *The Monsterologist; A Memoir in Rhyme*. Ill. by Adam McCauley. New York: Sterling.

Katz, Susan. 2012. *The President's Stuck in the Bathtub: Poems About U.S. Presidents*. New York: Clarion.

Kennedy, Dorothy M.. Ed. 1993. *I Thought I'd Take My Rat to School: Poems for September to June*. New York: Little, Brown.

Kennedy, X.J. 1989. *Ghastlies, Goops, & Pincushions: Nonsense Verse*. New York: McElderry.

Kennedy, X.J. 1997. *Uncle Switch: Loony Limericks*. New York: McElderry.

Kennedy, X.J. 2002. *Exploding Gravy, Poems to Make You Laugh*. Boston: Little, Brown.

Lansky, Bruce. Ed. 1994. *A Bad Case of the Giggles: Kid's Favorite Funny Poems*. Deephaven, MN: Meadowbrook Press.

Lansky, Bruce. Ed. 1997. *No More Homework! No More Tests! Kids Favorite Funny School Poems*. Minnetonka, MN: Meadowbrook Press.

Lansky, Bruce. Ed. 1998. *Miles of Smiles: Kids Pick the Funniest Poems, Book #3*. New York: Scholastic.

Lee, Dennis. 2001. *Alligator Pie*. Toronto: Key Porter Books.

Lee, Dennis. 2001. *Bubblegum Delicious*. New York: HarperCollins.

Lee, Dennis. 2002. *Garbage Delight: Another Helping*. Toronto: Key Porter Books.

Levy, Debbie. 2010. *Maybe I'll Sleep in the Bathtub Tonigh*t. Sterling.

Lewis, J. Patrick and Janeczko, Paul B. 2006. *Wing Nuts: Screwy Haiku*. New York: Little, Brown.

Lewis, J. Patrick. 2006. *Once Upon a Tomb: Gravely Humorous Verses*. Candlewick.

Lewis, J. Patrick. 2009. *The Underwear Salesman: And Other Jobs for Better or Verse*. Ill. by Serge Bloch. New York: Simon & Schuster/Atheneum.

Lewis, J. Patrick and Yolen, Jane. 2012. *Last Laughs: Animal Epitaphs*. Ill. by Jeffrey Timmins. Watertown, MA: Charlesbridge.

McNaughton, Colin. 2002. *Making Friends with Frankenstein*. Somerville, MA: Candlewick.

Mecum, Ryan. 2008. *Zombie Haiku*. Cincinnati, OH: How Books.

Mecum, Ryan. 2009. *Vampire Haiku*. Cincinnati, OH: How Books.

Merriam, Eve. 1989. *A Poem for a Pickle: Funnybone Verses*. New York: Morrow.

Merriam, Eve. 1989. *Chortles: New and Selected Wordplay Poems*. New York: Morrow.

Prelutsky, Jack. 1984. *The New Kid on the Block*. New York: Greenwillow.

Prelutsky, Jack. 1990. *Something Big Has Been Here*. New York: Scholastic.

Prelutsky, Jack. 1996. *A Pizza the Size of the Sun*. New York: Greenwillow.

Prelutsky, Jack. 2000. *It's Raining Pigs & Noodles*. New York: Greenwillow.

Prelutsky, Jack. 2008. *My Dog May Be a Genius*. New York: Greenwillow.

Rex, Adam. 2005. *Frankenstein Makes a Sandwich*. San Diego, CA: Harcourt.

Rex, Adam. 2006. *Frankenstein Makes a Sandwich.* San Diego, CA: Harcourt.

Rex, Adam. 2008. *Frankenstein Takes the Cake.* New York: Harcourt Houghton Mifflin.

Shields, Carol Diggory. 1995. *Lunch Money and Other Poems about School.* New York: Dutton.

Shields, Carol Diggory. 2003. *Almost Late To School: And More School Poems.* New York: Dutton.

Silverstein, Shel. 1974. *Where the Sidewalk Ends.* New York: HarperCollins.

Silverstein, Shel. 1981. *A Light in the Attic.* New York: HarperCollins.

Silverstein, Shel. 1996. *Falling Up.* New York: HarperCollins.

Silverstein, Shel. 2005. *Runny Babbit: A Billy Sook.* New York: HarperCollins.

Silverstein, Shel. 2008. *Don't Bump the Glump!* New York: HarperCollins.

Silverstein, Shel. 2011. *Every Thing On It.* New York: HarperCollins.

Singer, Marilyn. 2001. *Monster Museum.* New York: Hyperion.

Singer, Marilyn. 2004. *Creature Carnival.* New York: Hyperion.

Singer, Marilyn. 2012. *The Boy Who Cried Alien.* Ill. by Brian Biggs. New York: Hyperion.

Singer, Marilyn. 2012. *The Superheroes Employment Agency.* Ill. by Noah Z. Jones. New York: Clarion.

Viorst, Judith. 1981. *If I Were in Charge of the World and Other Worries: Poems for Children and Their Parents.* New York: Atheneum.

Viorst, Judith. 1995. *Sad Underwear: And Other Complications More Poems for Children and Their Parents.* New York: Atheneum.

Weinstock, Robert. 2009. *Food Hates You, Too.* New York: Disney-Hyperion.

Weinstock, Robert. 2010. *Can You Dig It?* New York: Disney-Hyperion.

Westcott, Nadine Bernard. Ed. 1994. *Never Take a Pig to Lunch and Other Poems about the Fun of Eating.* New York: Orchard.

Weston, Robert Paul. 2008. *Zorgamazoo.* New York: Razorbill/Penguin.

Wheeler, Lisa. 2011. *Spinster Goose; Twisted Rhymes for Naughty Children.* Ill. by Sophie Blackall. New York: Atheneum.

Wilbur, Richard. 2000. Opposites, More Opposites, and a Few Differences. Orlando: Harcourt.

Wolf, Allan. 2003. *The Blood-Hungry Spleen and Other Poems about Our Parts.* Somerville, MA: Candlewick.

Yolen, Jane. 2000. *How Do Dinosaurs Say Good Night?* New York: Scholastic.

Yolen, Jane. 2009. *How Do Dinosaurs Say I Love You?* New York: Scholastic.

Poetry Books about Family

The family unit is such an important part of the lives of children as they're developing as well as for teens trying to establish their own independent identity. Poetry can capture familiar experiences and emotions and celebrate the good times as well as reflect the special challenges of these relationships and comfort us through the bad times. Here is a selection of poetry books about family, families, and sibling relationships.

Adoff, Arnold. 1973. *Black is Brown is Tan.* New York: Harper & Row.

Ahlberg, Allan and Ingram, Bruce. 2010. *Everybody Was a Baby Once.* Candlewick.

Anholt, Catherine, and Laurence Anholt. 1998. *Big Book of Families.* Somerville, MA: Candlewick.

Calmenson, Stephanie. 2002. *Welcome, Baby! Baby Rhymes for Baby Times.* New York: HarperCollins.

Dotlich, Rebecca Kai. 2002. *A Family like Yours.* Honesdale, PA: Wordsong/Boyds Mills.

Dotlich, Rebecca Kai. 2004. *Mama Loves.* New York: HarperCollins.

Dotlich, Rebecca Kai. 2005. *Grandpa Loves.* New York: HarperCollins.

Fletcher, Ralph J. 1999. *Relatively Speaking: Poems about Family.* New York: Orchard. Grimes, Nikki. 2002. *When Daddy Prays.* Grand Rapids, MI: Eerdmans.

Grimes, Nikki. 1999. *Hopscotch Love: A Family Treasury of Love Poems.* New York: Lothrop, Lee & Shepard.

Grimes, Nikki. 1999. *My Man Blue: Poems.* New York: Dial.

Grimes, Nikki. 2000. *Stepping out with Grandma Mac.* New York: Simon & Schuster.

Gunning, Monica. 2004. *A Shelter In Our Car.* San Francisco, CA: Children's Book Press.

Harrison, David L. 1996. *A Thousand Cousins: Poems of Family Life.* Honesdale, PA: Wordsong/Boyds Mills Press.

Harrison, David. 2009. *Vacation, We're Going to the Ocean!* Ill. by Rob Shepperson. Honesdale, PA: Wordsong/Boyds Mills Press.

Heide, Florence Parry, and Roxanne Heide Pierce. 1996. *Oh, Grow Up!: Poems to Help You Survive Parents, Chores, School, and Other Afflictions.* New York: Orchard.

Hittleman, Carol G. and Daniel R. Hittleman. *A Grand Celebration: Grandparents in Poetry.* Honesdale, PA: Wordsong/Boyds Mills.

Hoberman, Mary Ann. 1991. *Fathers, Mothers, Sisters, Brothers: A Collection of Family Poems.* Boston: Joy Street Books.

Hoberman, Mary Ann. 2009. *All Kinds of Families.* New York: Little, Brown.

Hollyer, Belinda. Ed. 2003. *The Kingfisher Book of Family Poems.* New York: Kingfisher.

Hopkins, Lee Bennett. Ed. 1998. *Climb Into My Lap: First Poems To Read Together.* New York: Simon & Schuster.

Hopkins, Lee Bennett. Ed. 1998. *Families, Families.* New York: Sadlier-Oxford.

Hopkins, Lee Bennett. Ed. 2010. *Amazing Faces.* Ill. By Chris Soentpiet. Lee and Low.

Kipling, Rudyard. 2007. *If: A Father's Advice to his Son.* Ill. by Charles R. Smith, Jr. New York: Atheneum.

Livingston, Myra Cohn. Ed. 1988. *Poems for Mothers.* New York: Holiday House.

Livingston, Myra Cohn. Ed. 1989. *Poems for Fathers.* New York: Holiday House.

Micklos, Jr, John. 2001. *Mommy Poems.* Honesdale, PA: Wordsong/Boyds Mills Press.

Mora, Pat. 1994. *The Desert is My Mother/El Desierto es Mi Madre.* Houston, TX: Pinata Books.

Mora, Pat. Ed. 2001. *Love to Mamá.* New York: Lee & Low.

Myers, Walter Dean. 1998. *Angel to Angel.* New York: HarperCollins.

Rosenberg, Liz. 2001. *Roots & Flowers: Poets and Poems on Family.* New York: Henry Holt.

Singer, Marilyn. 1994. *Family Reunion.* New York: Atheneum.

Smith, Hope Anita. 2003. *The Way a Door Closes.* New York: Henry Holt.

Smith, Hope Anita. 2009. *Mother: Poems.* New York: Henry Holt.

Steptoe, Javaka. Ed. 1997. *In Daddy's Arms I Am Tall: African Americans Celebrating Fathers.* New York: Lee & Low.

Sweeny, Jacqueline. Ed. 2003. *Poems about Family.* New York: Benchmark Books.

Thomas, Joyce Carol. 2001. *A Mother's Heart, A Daughter's Love: Poems for Us to Share.* New York: HarperCollins.

Thomas, Joyce Carol. 2008. *The Blacker the Berry.* Illus. by Floyd Cooper. New York: Amistad.

Thompson, Holly. 2011. *Orchards.* New York: Random House.

Walker, Rob D. 2009. *Mama Says: A Book of Love For Mothers and Sons.* Ill. by Leo and Diane Dillon. New York: Scholastic.

Wong, Janet S. 1999. *The Rainbow Hand: Poems about Mothers and Children.* New York: McElderry.

Zimmer, Tracie Vaughn. 2008. *42 Miles.* New York: Clarion.

Poetry about Siblings

George, Kristine O'Connell. 2011. *Emma Dilemma: Big Sister Poems.* New York: Clarion.

Grandits, John. 2004. *Technically, It's Not My Fault: Concrete Poems.* New York: Clarion.

Grandits, John. 2007. *Blue Lipstick: Concrete Poems.* New York: Clarion.

Greenfield, Eloise. 2009. *Brother & Sisters: Family Poems.* New York: HarperCollins.

Grimes, Nikki. 2004. *What is Goodbye?* New York: Jump at the Sun/Hyperion.

Hoberman, Mary Ann. 2000. *And to Think We Thought that We'd Never Be Friends.* New York: Random House.

Lewis, J. Patrick and Yolen, Jane. 2012. *Take Two! A Celebration of Twins.* Somerville, MA: Candlewick.

Micklos, John, Jr. 2006. *No Boys Allowed: Poems about Brothers and Sisters.* Honesdale, PA: Wordsong/Boyds Mills.

Sones, Sonya. 2000. *Stop Pretending.* New York: HarperCollins.

Williams, Vera B. 2001. *Amber was Brave, Essie was Smart*. New York: Greenwillow.

Woodson, Jacqueline. 2003. *Locomotion*. New York: Putnam.

Poetry Books about Friendship

Friends and friendship are such an important part of childhood and growing up. Many poetry books focus on this topic, including the following.

Cheng, Andrea. 2008. *Where the Steps Were.* Honesdale, PA: Boyds Mills/Wordsong.

Glenn, Mel. 1991. My Friend's Got This Problem, Mr. Candler: High School Poems. New York: Clarion.

Greenfield, Eloise. 2006. *The Friendly Four.* Ill. by Jan Spivey Gilchrist. New York: HarperCollins.

Grimes, Nikki. 1994. *Meet Danitra Brown.* New York: Lothrop, Lee & Shepard.

Grimes, Nikki. 2002. *Danitra Brown Leaves Town.* New York: HarperCollins.

Grimes, Nikki. 2005. *Danitra Brown, Class Clown.* New York: Lothrop, Lee & Shepard.

Herrick, Steven. 2008. *Naked Bunyip Dancing.* Honesdale, PA: Boyds Mills/Wordsong.

Hoberman, Mary Ann. 2000. *And to Think We Thought that We'd Never be Friends.* New York: Random House.

Holbrook, Sara. 2011. *Weird? (Me, Too!) Let's Be Friends.* Ill. by Karen Sandstrom. Wordsong/Boyds Mills Press.

Janeczko, Paul B. 1999. *Very Best (Almost Friends): Poems of Friendship.* Somerville, MA: Candlewick.

Levy, Debbie. 2010. *The Year of Goodbyes; A True Story of Friendship, Family and Farewells.* New York: Hyperion.

Livingston, Myra Cohn. Ed. 1992. *A Time to Talk: Poems about Friendship.* New York: Margaret K. McElderry.

Mavor, Salley. 1997. *You and Me: Poems of Friendship.* New York: Orchard Books.

Myers, Walter Dean. 2004. *Here in Harlem: Poems in Many Voices.* New York: Holiday House.

Nicholls, Judith. 2006. *Someone I Like: Poems about People.* Somerville, MA: Barefoot Books.

Quattlebaum, Mary. 2005. *Winter Friends.* New York: Doubleday Books for Young Readers.

Singer, Marilyn. 1996. *All We Needed to Say: Poems about School from Tanya and Sophie.* New York: Atheneum.

Singer, Marilyn. 2011. *Twosomes: Love Poems from the Animal Kingdom.* New York: Knopf.

Soto, Gary. 2002. *Fearless Fernie: Hanging out with Fernie and Me.* New York: Putnam.

Soto, Gary. 2005. *Worlds Apart: Fernie and Me.* New York: Putnam.

Sweeney, Jacqueline. Ed. 2002. *Poems about Friends.* New York: Marshall Cavendish.

Walsh, Caroline. 1995. *The Little Book of Friendship.* New York: Kingfisher.

Wong, Janet S. 2003. *Minn and Jake.* New York: Farrar, Straus & Giroux.

Wong, Janet. 2008. *Minn and Jake's Almost Terrible Summer.* New York: Farrar, Straus & Giroux.

Poetry Books about Superstitions, Beliefs, Luck, Magic, Dreams, and Nightmares

Many works of poetry promote a sense of wonder. These titles focus especially on the world of superstitions, beliefs, luck, magic, dreams and nightmares.

Alarcón, Francisco X. 2005. *Poems to Dream Together/ Poemas para Sonar Juntos*. New York: Lee & Low.

Berry, James. 1991. *Isn't My Name Magical?: Sister and Brother Poems*. New York: Simon & Schuster.

Brownlee, Liz. 2012. *Animal Magic*. Ill. by Rose Sanderson. London: Iron Press.

Corcoran, Jill. Ed. 2012. *Dare to Dream… Change the World*. San Diego, CA: Kane Miller.

Denton, Graham. 2006. *Silly Superstitions*. London: Macmillan Children's Books.

Field, Edward. 1998. *Magic Words: Poems*. San Diego, CA: Gulliver Books/Harcourt Brace.

Grimes, Nikki. 2000. *Shoe Magic*. New York: Orchard.

Hopkins, Lee Bennett. Ed. 2009. *Sky Magic*. Ill. by Mariusz Stawarski. New York: Dutton.

Hughes, Langston. (75th anniversary edition) 2007. *The Dream Keeper* (and seven additional poems). New York: Knopf.

Kennedy, X.J. 1989. *Ghastlies, Goops, & Pincushions: Nonsense Verse*. New York: McElderry.

Larios, Julie. 2008. *Imaginary Menagerie: A Book of Curious Creatures*. New York: Houghton Mifflin Harcourt.

Mado, Michio. 1998. The Magic Pocket. *New York: McElderry.*

Medina, Jane. 2004. *The Dream on Blanca's Wall*. Honesdale, PA: Boyd's Mill Press.

Prelutsky, Jack. 1976/1993. *Nightmares: Poems to Trouble Your Sleep*. New York: Greenwillow. Reprinted, New York: Mulberry Books.

Schertle, Alice. 1999. *A Lucky Thing*. San Diego, CA: Harcourt Brace.

Schwartz, Alvin. 1992. *And the Green Grass Grew All Around: Folk Poetry from Everyone*. New York: HarperCollins.

Whipple, Laura. Ed. 1996. *Eric Carle's Dragons, Dragons*. New York: Philomel.

Wong, Janet S. 1994. *Good Luck Gold and Other Poems*. New York: Margaret K. McElderry Books.

Wong, Janet S. 2003. *Knock on Wood: Poems about Superstitions*. New York: Margaret K. McElderry Books.

Wong, Janet S. 2000. *Night Garden: Poems from the World of Dreams*. New York: Margaret K. McElderry

Yolen, Jane. 1996. *Sacred Places*. San Diego, CA: Harcourt Brace.

Poetry Books about Coping with Disability, Illness, Homelessness, and Death

All kinds of poetry can be therapeutic during difficult times, but the following poetry books for young people particularly focus on coping with disability, illness, homelessness, and death.

Adoff, Arnold. 2000. *Touch the Poem.* New York: Blue Sky Press.

Akaza, Norihisa. 1994. *Smell of the Rain, Voices of the Stars.* Orlando: Harcourt Brace.

Abeel, Samantha. 2001. *Reach for the Moon.* New York: Orchard Books.

Bartlett, Jennifer; Black, Sheila and Northen, Michael. Eds. 2011. *Beauty is a Verb; The New Poetry of Disability.* El Paso, TX: Cinco Puntos Press.

Bernier-Grand, Carmen T. 2007. *Frida: Viva la Frida = Long Live Life.* New York: Marshall Cavendish.

Bouchard, Dave. 1997. *If Sarah will take me.* Victoria: Orca Book Publishers.

Brown, Dale S. 1995. *I Know I Can Climb the Mountain.* Columbus: Mountain Books & Music.

Corcoran, Jill. Ed. 2012. *Dare to Dream… Change the World.* San Diego, CA: Kane Miller.

Crist-Evans, Craig. 2004. *North of Everything.* Somerville, MA: Candlewick.

Elliott, Zetta. 2008. *Bird.* Ill. by Shadra Strickland. New York: Lee & Low.

Engle, Margarita. 2012. *The Wild Book.* Boston: Houghton Mifflin.

Fields, Terri. 2002. *After the Death of Anna Gonzales.* New York: Holt.

Frost, Helen. 2003. *Keesha's House.* New York: Farrar, Straus & Giroux.

Frost, Helen. 2008. *Diamond Willow.* New York: Farrar, Straus & Giroux.

Frost, Helen. 2011. *Hidden.* New York: Farrar, Straus & Giroux.

Grandits, John. 2004. *Technically, It's Not My Fault: Concrete Poems.* New York: Clarion.

Grimes, Nikki. 2004. *What is Goodbye?* New York: Jump at the Sun/Hyperion.

Gunning, Monica. 2004. *A Shelter In Our Car.* San Francisco, CA: Children's Book Press.

Heard, Georgia. 2002. *This Place I Know: Poems of Comfort.* Somerville, MA: Candlewick.

Herrick, Steven. 2004. *The Simple Gift.* New York: Simon & Schuster.

Hesse, Karen. 1997. *Out of the Dust.* New York: Scholastic.

Hopkins, Lee Bennett. Ed. 1992. *Through Our Eyes: Poems and Pictures about Growing Up.* New York: Trumpet.

Johnson, Lindsay Lee. 2002. *Soul Moon Soup.* Asheville, NC: Front Street.

Korman, Gordon and Bernice Korman. 1992. *The D- Poems of Jeremy Bloom: A Collection of Poems about School, Homework, and Life (Sort of).* New York: Scholastic.

Little, Jean. 1989. *Hey World, Here I Am!* New York: Harper & Row.

McCall, Guadalupe Garcia. 2011. *Under the Mesquite.* New York: Lee & Low.

Nikola-Lisa, W. 2006. *How We Are Smart.* Ill. by Sean Qualls.

Rosen, Michael, J.. Ed. 1992. *Home: A Collaboration of Thirty Distinguished Authors and Illustrators of Children's Books to Aid the Homeless.* New York: HarperCollins.

Rosen, Michael, J.. Ed. 1996. *Food Fight: Poets Join the Fight Against Hunger with Poems about Their Favorite Foods.* San Diego, CA: Harcourt Brace.

Sones, Sonya. 2004. *One of Those Hideous Books Where the Mother Dies.* New York: Simon & Schuster.

Stepanek, Mattie. 2002. *Heartsongs.* New York: Hyperion.

Thompson, Holly. 2011. *Orchards.* New York: Random House.

Thoms, Annie. Ed. 2002. *With Their Eyes.* New York: HarperTempest.

Turner, Ann. 2000. *Learning to Swim; A Memoir.* New York: Scholastic.

Vecchione, Patrice. Ed. 2007. *Faith and Doubt.* New York: Henry Holt.

Wardlaw, Lee. 2011. *Won Ton; A Cat Tale Told in Haiku.* Ill. by Eugene Yelchin. New York: Henry Holt.

Weatherford, Carole Boston. 2007. *Birmingham, 1963.* Honesdale, PA: Wordsong/Boyds Mills Press.

Woodson, Jacqueline. 2003. *Locomotion.* New York: Putnam.

Zimmer, Tracie Vaughn. 2007. *Reaching for Sun.* New York: Bloomsbury.

Comforting Poetry Books for Difficult Times

Here are a few collections of poetry for young people with poems that can be comforting during difficult times. Of course, one can find ANY kind of favorite poem comforting at various moments in life, but these poems, in particular, address deep emotions and difficult experiences.

Adoff, Arnold. 1997. *Love Letters*. New York: Scholastic.

Alarcón, Francisco X. 2005. *Poems to Dream Together/ Poemas para Sonar Juntos*. New York: Lee & Low.

Corcoran, Jill. Ed. 2012. *Dare to Dream… Change the World*. San Diego, CA: Kane Miller.

Engle, Margarita. 2008. *The Surrender Tree*. New York: Holt.

Fletcher, Ralph J. 2006. *Moving Day*. Honesdale, PA: Wordsong/Boyds Mills Press.

Franco, Betsy. Ed. 2001. *Things I Have to Tell You: Poems And Writing by Teenage Girls*. Cambridge, MA: Candlewick.

Franco, Betsy. Ed. 2001. *You Hear Me? Poems and Writing by Teenage Boys*. Cambridge, MA: Candlewick.

Gordon, Ruth. Ed. 1995. *Pierced by a Ray of Sun: Poems about the Times We Feel Alone*. New York: HarperCollins.

Grimes, Nikki. 1999. *Hopscotch Love: A Family Treasury of Love Poems*. New York: Lothrop, Lee & Shepard.

Grimes, Nikki. 2004. *What is Goodbye?* New York: Jump at the Sun/Hyperion.

Gunning, Monica. 2004. *A Shelter In Our Car*. San Francisco, CA: Children's Book Press.

Heard, Georgia. Ed. 2002. *This Place I Know: Poems of Comfort*. Cambridge, MA: Candlewick.

Hines, Anna Grossnickle. 2001. *Peaceful Pieces: A Year in Poems and Quilts*. New York: Greenwillow.

Ho, Minfong. 1996. *Maples in the Mist: Poems for Children from the Tang Dynasty*. New York: Lothrop, Lee, & Shepard.

Hopkins, Lee Bennett. 1995. *Been to Yesterdays: Poems of a Life*. Honesdale, PA: Wordsong, Boyds Mills Press.

Hopkins, Lee Bennett. Ed. 2008. *America at War*. New York: McElderry.

Hughes, Langston. (75th anniversary edition) 2007. *The Dream Keeper* (and seven additional poems). New York: Knopf.

Hughes, Langston. 2012. *I, Too, Am America*. Ill. by Bryan Collier. Simon & Schuster.

Levine, Gail Carson. 2012. *Forgive Me, I Meant to Do It: False Apology Poems*. Ill. by Matthew Cordell. HarperCollins.

Lyne, Sandford. Ed. 1996. *Ten-second Rainshowers: Poems by Young People*. New York: Simon & Schuster.

Lyne, Sandford. Ed. 2004. *Soft Hay Will Catch You: Poems by Young People*. New York: Simon & Schuster.

McCall, Guadalupe Garcia. 2011. *Under the Mesquite*. Lee & Low.

Mora, Pat. 2001. Ed. *Love to Mama: A Tribute to Mothers*. New York: Lee & Low.

Nye, Naomi Shihab. Ed. 1999. *What Have You Lost?* New York: Greenwillow.

Robb, Laura. Ed. 1997. *Music and Drum: Voices of War and Peace, Hope and Dreams*. New York: Philomel Books.

Rosenberg, Liz. Ed. 2000. *Light-gathering Poems*. New York: Henry Holt.

Rylant, Cynthia. 2003. *God Went to Beauty School*. New York: HarperColllins.

Sayer, Viv. Ed. 2008. *Poems of Love and Longing*. Pont Books.

Sidman, Joyce. 2007. *This is Just to Say: Poems of Apology and Forgiveness*. Ill. by Pamela Zagarenski. Boston: Houghton Mifflin.

Steptoe, Javaka. Ed. 1997. *In Daddy's Arms I Am Tall: African Americans Celebrating Fathers*. New York: Lee & Low.

Thompson, Holly. 2011. *Orchards*. New York: Random House.

Thoms, Annie. Ed. 2002. *With Their Eyes*. New York: HarperTempest.

Vecchione, Patrice. Ed. 2001. *Truth and Lies*. New York: Henry Holt.

Vecchione, Patrice. Ed. 2004. *Revenge and Forgiveness*. New York: Henry Holt.

Vecchione, Patrice. Ed. 2007. *Faith and Doubt*. New York: Henry Holt.

Willard, Nancy. Ed. 1998. *Step Lightly: Poems for the Journey*. San Diego: Harcourt.

Yolen, Jane. 1996. *Sacred Places*. San Diego, CA: Harcourt Brace.

Young, Ed. 1997. *Voices of the Heart*. New York: Scholastic.

POETRY BOOKLISTS ACROSS THE CURRICULUM

One of the most common requests I encounter is for poetry for a particular topic from the typical school curriculum. This is where poetry can add delight and dimension to the study of science, social studies, language arts, and more. What follows is a variety of lists for typical school study subjects listed in alphabetical order by topic. And this list is certainly not exhaustive—there are more poetry books available on these topics, as well as many others.

Poetry Books about Animals
Poetry Books about Baseball
Poetry Books about Birds
Poetry Books about Cats
Poetry Books about Color
Poetry Books about Dinosaurs
Poetry Books about Dogs
Poetry Books about Food
Poetry Books about Gardens and Gardening
Poetry Books about Insects and Bugs
Poetry Books about Mathematics
Poetry Books about Poetry, Books, and Reading
Poetry Books for Science
Poetry Books about Space and the Planets
Poetry Books about Sports
Poetry Books about Time
Poetry Books about Trees
Poetry Books about United States History
Poetry Books about War and Peace
Poetry Books about Weather
Poetry Books about World History

Poetry Books about Animals

*Once you start looking, you'll find that the topic of animals is a major one in children's poetry and is the focus of many poems and collections. There are even whole anthologies of animal poetry as you'll see below. Be sure and look for more poetry books about **dinosaurs, cats, dogs, birds,** and **insects** (featured in additional lists).*

Ackerman, Diane. 2003. *Animal Sense.* New York: Alfred Knopf.

Alarcón, Francisco X. 2008. *Animal Poems of the Iguazu: Poems.* San Francisco: Children's Book Press.

Bouchard, Dave. 1996. *Voices from the Wild.* San Francisco: Chronicle.

Cotner, June, comp. 2002. *Bless the Beats: Children's Prayers and Poems about Animals.* New York: SeaStar.

Curry, Jennifer. Ed. 2000. *Animal Poems.* New York: Scholastic.

Ehlert, Lois. 2008. *Oodles Of Animals.* San Diego, CA: Harcourt.

Ehlert, Lois. 2010. *Lots of Spots.* New York: Beach Lane Books.

Elliott, David. 2008. *On the Farm.* Somerville, MA: Candlewick.

Elliott, David. 2010. *In the Wild.* Somerville, MA: Candlewick.

Elliott, David. 2012. *In the Sea.* Ill. by Holly Meade. Somerville, MA: Candlewick.

Fisher, Aileen. 1989. *Animal, Animals.* New York: Scholastic.

Florian, Douglas. 1997. *In the Swim.* San Diego, CA: Harcourt Brace.

Florian, Douglas. 2000. *Mammalabilia.* San Diego, CA: Harcourt Brace.

Florian, Douglas. 2003. *Lizard, Frogs, and Polliwogs.* San Diego: Harcourt.

Florian, Douglas. 2004. *Omnibeasts.* San Diego: Harcourt.

Florian, Douglas. 2005. *Zoo's Who.* San Diego, CA: Harcourt.

Foster, John. Ed. 2001. *My First Oxford Book of Animal Poems.* Oxford: Oxford University Press.

Ghigna, Charles. 2004. *Animal Tracks: Wild Poems to Read Aloud.* New York: Abrams.

Hague, Michael. 2007. *Animal Friends: A Collection of Poems for Children.* New York: Holt.

Harley, Arvis. 2009. *African Acrostics.* Somerville, MA: Candlewick Press.

Hauth, Katherine. 2011. *What's for Dinner? Quirky, Squirmy Poems from the Animal World.* Watertown: MA: Charlesbridge.

Heard, Georgia. 1992. *Creatures of Earth, Sea, and Sky.* Honesdale, PA: Wordsong/ Boyds Mills.

Hopkins, Lee Bennett. 2002. *Hoofbeats, Claws & Rippled Fins: Creature Poems.* New York: HarperCollins.

Hubbell, Patricia. 2000. *Earthmates: Poems.* New York: Marshall Cavendish.

Hummon, David. 1999. *Animal Acrostics.* Nevada City, CA: Dawn Publications.

Jackson, Rob. 2006. *Animal Mischief: Poems.* Honesdale, PA: Boyds Mills.

Katz, Susan. 2007. *Oh, Theodore! Guinea Pig Poems.* New York: Clarion Books.

Kumin, Maxine. 2006. *Mites to Mastodons: A Book of Animal Poems.* Boston: Houghton Mifflin.

Lewis, J. Patrick. 1990. *A Hippopotamusn't and Other Animal Verses.* New York: Dial.

Lewis, J. Patrick. 1995. *Ridicholas Nicholas: More Animal Poems*. New York: Dial.

Lewis, J. Patrick. Ed. 2012. *Book of Animal Poetry*. Washington DC: National Geographic.

Maddox, Marjorie. 2008. *A Crossing of Zebras: Animal Packs in Poetry.* Honesdale, PA: Wordsong/Boyds Mills.

Mado, Michio. 1992. *The Animals: Selected Poems*. New York: McElderry.

Michelson, Rich. 2008. *Animals Anonymous: Poems*. New York: Simon & Schuster.

Pearson, Susan. 2004. *Squeal and Squawk: Barnyard Talk*. New York: Marshall Cavendish.

Prelutsky, Jack. Ed. 1997. *The Beauty of the Beast*. New York: Knopf.

Ruddell, Deborah. 2009. *A Whiff of Pine, A Hint of Skunk: Journey to the Wild Forest*. New York: McElderry.

Schwartz, David M. and Schy, Yael. 2007. *Where in the Wild? Camouflaged Creatures Concealed… and Revealed*. Berkeley, CA: Tricycle.

Schwartz, David M. and Schy, Yael. 2009. *Where Else in the Wild? MORE Camouflaged Creatures Concealed… and Revealed*. Berkeley, CA: Tricycle.

Schwartz, David M. and Schy, Yael. 2010. *What in the Wild? Mysteries of Nature Concealed… and Revealed*. Berkeley, CA: Tricycle.

Sidman, Joyce. 2000. *Just us Two: Poems about Animal Dads*. Brookfield, CT: Millbrook Press.

Singer, Marilyn. 1989. *Turtle in July*. New York: Macmillan.

Singer, Marilyn. 2012. *A Strange Place to Call Home: The World's Most Dangerous Habitats and the Animals That Call Them Home*. Ill. by Ed Young. San Francisco: Chronicle.

Spinelli, Eileen. 2007. *Polar Bear, Arctic Hare; Poems of the Frozen North*. Honesdale, PA: Wordsong/Boyds Mills.

Stockland, Patricia M. Ed. 2004. *Fur, Fangs, and Footprints: A Collection of Poems about Animals*. Minneapolis, MN: Compass.

Van Wassenhove, Sue. 2008. *The Seldom-Ever-Shady Glades*. Honesdale, PA: Wordsong/Boyds Mills.

Webster, Dennis. 2008. *Absolutely Wild*. Boston: Godine.

Whipple, Laura. Ed. 1989. *Eric Carle's Animals, Animals*. New York: Scholastic.

Wong, Janet. 2011. *Once Upon A Tiger; New Beginnings for Endangered Animals*. OnceUponaTiger.com.

Worth, Valerie. 2007. *Animal Poems*. New York: Farrar, Straus & Grioux.

Yolen, Jane. 1994. *Alphabestiary: Animal Poems from A to Z*. Honesdale, PA: Wordsong/Boyds Mills.

Yolen, Jane. 1998. *The Originals*. New York: Philomel.

Zahares, Wade. 2001. *Big, Bad, and a Little Bit Scary: Poems that Bite Back!* New York: Viking.

Zimmer, Tracie Vaughn. 2011. *Cousins of Clouds; Elephant Poems*. Houghton Mifflin.

Poetry Books about Baseball

Since there are many poetry books for young people about sports, it may be surprising that baseball alone has generated much poetry writing itself. From the classic "Casey at the Bat" to novels in verse set in the poetry world, here are poetry books that are sure to please young readers.

Burg, Ann. 2009. *All the Broken Pieces*. New York: Scholastic.

Burleigh, Robert. 2003. *Home Run*. San Diego: Voyager.

Fehler, Gene. 2008. *Beanball*. New York: Clarion.

Fehler, Gene. 2009. *Change-up; Baseball Poems*. Ill. by Donald Wu. New York: Clarion

Florian, Douglas. 2012. *Poem Runs; Baseball Poems and Paintings*. New York: Houghton Mifflin Harcourt.

Graves, Donald. 1996. *Baseball, Snakes, and Summer Squash*. Honesdale, PA: Wordsong/Boyds Mills.

Gutman, Dan. 2007. *Casey Back at Bat*. New York: HarperCollins.

Hopkins, Lee Bennett. Ed. 1993. *Extra Innings: Baseball Poems*. San Diego: Harcourt Brace Jovanovich.

Janeczko, Paul B. 1998. *That Sweet Diamond: Baseball Poems*. New York: Atheneum.

Koertge, Ron. 2006. *Shakespeare Bats Cleanup*. Somerville, MA: Candlewick.

Lewis, J. Patrick. 2007. *Tulip at the Bat*. New York: Little, Brown.

Maddox, Marjorie. 2009. *Rules of the Game: Baseball Poems*. Honesdale: Wordsong/Boyds Mills.

Morrison, Lillian. Ed. 1992. *At the Crack of the Bat: Baseball Poems*. New York: Hyperion.

Nevius, Carol. 2008. *Baseball Hour*. New York: Marshall Cavendish.

Smith, Jr., Charles R. 2004. *Diamond Life: Baseball Sights, Sounds, and Swings*. New York: Orchard.

Testa, Maria. 2002. *Becoming Joe DiMaggio*. Somerville, MA: Candlewick Press.

Thayer, Ernest Lawrence. 2006. *Casey at the Bat*. Ill. by Joe Morse. Toronto: Kids Can Press.

Thayer, Ernest. 2000. *Ernest L. Thayer's Casey at the Bat: A Ballad of the Republic Sung in the Year 1888*. Ill. by Christopher Bing. New York: Scholastic.

Poetry Books about Birds

Creatures of the sky capture our imagination as they do something we cannot—fly. Poets have shared their observations and wonderings in the following works which beg for sharing AND birdwatching.

Blackaby, Susan. 2010. *Nest, Nook & Cranny*. Watertown, MA: Charlesbridge.

Castillo, Ana. 2000. *My Daughter, My Son, the Eagle, the Dove: An Aztec Chant*. New York: Dutton.

Fleishman, Paul. 1985. *I Am Phoenix: Poems for Two Voices*. New York: Harper & Row.

Florian, Douglas. 1996. *On the Wing: Bird Poems and Paintings*. San Diego, CA: Harcourt Brace.

George, Kristine O'Connell. 2004. *Hummingbird Nest: A Journal of Poems*. New York: Harcourt.

Lear, Edward. 2007. *The Owl and the Pussycat*. Toronto: Kids Can Press.

Lewis, J. Patrick. 1995. *Black Swan White Crow*. New York: Atheneum.

Roemer, Heidi. 2009. *Whose Nest is This?* Lanham, MD: Taylor Trade.

Rosen, Michael J. 2009. *The Cuckoo's Haiku and Other Birding Poems*. Ill. by Stan Fellows. Somerville, MA: Candlewick.

Ruddell, Deborah. 2007. *Today at the Bluebird Café*. New York: McElderry.

Rylant, Cynthia. 1991. *Appalachia: The Voices of Sleeping Birds*. San Diego, CA: Harcourt Brace Jovanovich.

Wolf, Sallie. 2010. *The Robin Makes a Laughing Sound*. Charlesbridge.

Yolen, Jane. 1990. *Bird Watch*. New York: Philomel.

Yolen, Jane. 2002. *Wild Wings: Poems for Young People*. Honesdale, PA: Wordsong/Boyds Mills Press.

Yolen, Jane. 2004. *Fine Feathered Friends: Poems for Young People*. Honesdale, PA: Wordsong/Boyds Mills Press.

Yolen, Jane. 2010. *An Egret's Day*. Honesdale, PA: Wordsong/Boyds Mills Press.

Yolen, Jane. 2011. *Birds of a Feather*. Ill. by Jason Stemple. Honesdale, PA: Wordsong/Boyds Mills Press.

Poetry Books about Cats

Cats have been the subject of poetry around the world, from haiku to classics like "The Owl and the Pussycat" or "The Gingham Dog and the Calico Cat." Here is a sampling of "cat" poems of all types, including several fun concrete or shape cat poetry collections.

Crawley, Dave. 2005. *Cat Poems.* Honesdale: Wordsong/Boyds Mills Press.

Creech, Sharon. 2008. *Hate that Cat.* New York: HarperCollins.

Demi. Ed. 1994. *In the Eyes of the Cat: Japanese Poetry for All Seasons.* Translated by Tze-Si Huang. New York: Henry Holt.

Farjeon, Eleanor. 1996. *Cats Sleep Anywhere.* New York: HarperCollins.

Field, Eugene. 1990. *The Gingham Dog and the Calico Cat.* New York: Philomel.

Florian, Douglas. 2003. *Bow Wow Meow Meow: It's Rhyming Cats and Dogs.* San Diego: Harcourt Brace.

Franco, Betsy. 2009. *A Curious Collection of Cats.* Ill. by Michael Wertz. San Francisco: Tricycle Press.

Ghigna, Charles. 1992. *Good Cats/Bad Cats.* Ill. by David Catrow. New York: Hyperion.

Grimes, Nikki. 2007. *When Gorilla Goes Walking.* New York: Orchard Books.

Grindol, Diane. 2008. *Catku: Cat Haiku Poems.* CreateSpace.

Hopkins, Lee Bennett. Ed. 1981. *I am the Cat.* New York: HarperCollins.

Isaacs, Anne. 1998. *Cat up a Tree.* Ill. by Stephen Mackey. New York: Dutton.

Kirk, Daniel. 2007. *Cat Power.* New York: Hyperion Books.

Kuskin, Karla. 2005. *Toots the Cat.* New York: Henry Holt.

Lach, William. Ed. *Curious Cats: in Art and Poetry for Children.* 1999. New York: Metropolitan Museum of Art.

Lear, Edward. 2007. *The Owl and the Pussycat.* Toronto: Kids Can Press.

Leopold, Nikki Clark. 2002. *K is for Kitten.* New York: Putnam's.

Livingston, Myra Cohn. Ed. 1994. *Cat Poems.* Ill. by Trina Schart Hyman. New York: Dutton.

Phinn, Gervase. 2002. *Our Cat Cuddles.* Swindon: Child's Play.

Prelutsky, Jack. 2004. *If Not for the Cat: Haiku.* New York: Greenwillow.

Rooney, Rache. 2011. *The Language of Cat.* London: Frances Lincoln.

Shertle, Alice. 1999. *I am the Cat.* New York: Lothrop, Lee & Shepard.

Sidman, Joyce. 2006. *Meow Ruff.* Boston: Houghton Mifflin.

Tiller, Ruth. 1995. *Cats Vanish Slowly.* Atlanta: Peachtree.

Walsh, Caroline. 1996. *The Little Book of Cats.* New York: Kingfisher.

Wardlaw, Lee. 2011. *Won Ton; A Cat Tale Told in Haiku.* Ill. by Eugene Yelchin. Henry Holt.

Yolen, Jane. 1993. *Raining Cats and Dogs.* San Diego: Harcourt Brace.

Poetry Books about Color

The role of color in evoking imagery in a poem is primal. The poetry books listed here exemplify the effective and powerful place of color in poetry, whether in reflecting nature or dealing with issues of race.

Adoff, Arnold. 1982. *All the Colors of the Race.* New York: Lothrop, Lee & Shepard.

Adoff, Arnold. 1973/2004. *Black is Brown is Tan.* New York: Harper & Row/Amistad.

Brenner, Barbara. Ed. 1994. *The Earth is Painted Green: A Garden of Poems about Our Planet.* New York: Scholastic.

Graham, Joan Bransfield. 1999. *Flicker Flash.* Boston: Houghton Mifflin.

Hines, Anna Grossnickle. 2005. *Winter Lights: A Season in Poems & Quilts.* New York: Greenwillow.

Iyengar, Malathi Michelle. 2009. *Tan to Tamarind: Poems about the Color Brown.* San Francisco: Children's Book Press.

Larios, Julie. 2006. *Yellow Elephant: A Bright Bestiary.* Orlando: Harcourt.

Lewis, J. Patrick. 1995. *Black Swan White Crow.* New York: Atheneum.

Luján, Jorge. 2008. *Colors! Colores!* Ill. by Piet Grobler. Toronto: Groundwood.

Mora, Pat. 1996. *Confetti: Poems for Children.* New York: Lee & Low.

Myers, Walter Dean. 1993. *Brown Angels: An Album of Pictures and Verse.* New York: HarperCollins.

Nordine, Ken. 2000. *Colors.* San Diego: Harcourt.

O'Neill, Mary. 1989. Hailstones and Halibut Bones: Adventures in Color. New York: Doubleday.

Orozco, Jose-Luis. Ed. 1994. *De Colores and Other Latin-American Folk Songs for Children.* New York: Dutton.

Pinkney, Sandra L. 2002. *A Rainbow All Around Me.* New York: Scholastic.

Rosetti, Christina G. 2002. *What is Pink?* Oakville, Canada: Rubicon Publishers.

Salas, Laura Purdie. 2008. *Flashy, Clashy, and Oh-So-Splashy: Poems about Color.* Mankato, MN: Capstone Press.

Sidman, Joyce. 2009. *Red Sings from Treetops: A Year in Colors.* Boston, MA: Houghton Mifflin Harcourt.

Sokoloff, Carol Ann. 2000. *Colours Everywhere You Go.* Victoria, BC: Cherubim Books.

Thomas, Joyce Carol. 2008. *The Blacker the Berry.* Illus. by Floyd Cooper. New York: Amistad.

Yolen, Jane. 2000. *Color Me a Rhyme: Nature Poems for Young People.* Honesdale, PA: Wordsong/Boyds Mills.

Poetry Books about Dinosaurs

Even the popular topic of dinosaurs has been the unlikely subject of poetry. Whether presented as an exploration of their size, scale and mystery or spoofing those same qualities, these poetry books offer near-instant appeal for dinosaur fans.

Crotty, K.M. 2000. *Dinosongs: Poems to Celebrate a T-Rex Named Sue.* New York: Scholastic.

Florian, Douglas. 2009. *Dinothesaurus.* New York: Atheneum.

Fortey, Richard. 1990. *The Dinosaurs' Alphabet.* New York: Barron's.

Foster, John. 1998. *Dragons, Dinosaurs, Monster Poems.* New York: Oxford University Press.

Foster, John, comp. 2002. *Dinosaur Poems.* Oxford: Oxford University Press.

Greenfield, Eloise. 2001. *I Can Draw a Weeposaur and other Dinosaurs: Poems.* New York: Greenwillow.

Hopkins, Lee Bennett. 1995. *Dinosaurs.* New York: Random House.

Hopkins, Lee Bennett. Ed. 2011. *Dizzy Dinosaurs: An I Can Read Book.* New York: HarperCollins.

Hopkins, Lee Bennett. 1999. *Dino-Raurs.* New York: Golden Books.

McNaughton, Colin. 1993. *If Dinosaurs were Cats and Dogs.* London: Macmillan Children's.

Moses, Brian. 2002. *Dangerous Dinosaurs.* London: Macmillian Children's.

Moss, Jeff. 1997. *Bone Poems.* New York: Workman.

Most, Bernard. 1990. *Four & Twenty Dinosaurs.* New York: Harper & Row.

Prelutsky, Jack. 1992. *Tyrannosaurus was a Beast: Dinosaur Poems.* New York: Mulberry Books.

Sierra, Judy. 1996. *Good Night, Dinosaurs.* New York: Clarion.

Temperley, Howard. 2004. *In the Days of Dinosaurs: A Rhyming Romp through Dino History.* Nashville, TN: Williamson.

Weinstock, Robert. 2010. *Can You Dig It?* New York: Disney-Hyperion.

Wise, William. 2000. *Dinosaurs are Forever.* New York: Dial.

Yolen, Jane. 2000. *How Do Dinosaurs Say Good Night?* New York: Blue Sky.

Yolen, Jane. 2004. *How do Dinosaurs Get Well Soon?* London: Collins.

Yolen, Jane. 2007. *How Do Dinosaurs Go to School?* New York: Blue Sky.

Poetry Books about Dogs

Dogs may be "man's best friend," but they've also been the frequent subject of poetry for young people. Here are some of the many poetry books that feature the canine world.

Ada, Alma Flor and Campoy, F. Isabel. 2011. *Ten Little Puppies; Diez perritos.* New York: Rayo/HarperCollins.
Adoff, Arnold. 1980. *Friend Dog.* New York: HarperCollins.
Ashman, Linda. 2008. *Stella, Unleashed.* New York: Sterling.
Clements, Andrew. 2007. *Dogku.* New York: Simon & Schuster.
Crawley, Dave. 2007. *Dog Poems.* Honesdale, PA: Wordsong/Boyds Mills.
Creech, Sharon. 2001. *Love That Dog.* New York: HarperCollins.
Field, Eugene. 1990. *The Gingham Dog and the Calico Cat.* New York: Philomel.
Florian, Douglas. 2003. *Bow Wow Meow Meow.* San Diego: Harcourt.
Franco, Betsy. 2011. A *Dazzling Display of Dogs.* Ill. by Michael Wertz. Berkeley, CA: Tricycle.
George, Kristine O'Connell. 1999. *Little Dog Poems.* New York: Clarion.
George, Kristine O'Connell. 2002. *Little Dog and Duncan.* New York: Clarion.
Ghigna, Charles. 1992. *Good Dogs/Bad Dogs.* New York: Hyperion.
Gottfried, Maya. 2005. *Good Dog.* New York: Knopf.
Hopkins, Lee Bennett. Ed. 1983. *A Dog's Life.* San Diego: Harcourt.
Johnston, Tony. 2000. *It's about Dogs.* San Diego: Harcourt.
Livingston, Myra Cohn. 1990. *Dog Poems.* New York: Holiday House.
Ode, Eric. 2012. *When You're a Pirate Dog and Other Pirate Poems.* Ill. by Jim Harris. Gretna, LA: Pelican.

Prelutsky, Jack. 1999. *Dog Days: Rhymes Around the Year.* New York: Knopf.
Rosen, Michael J. 2011. *The Hound Dog's Haiku and Other Poems for Dog Lovers.* Somerville, MA: Candlewick.
Schmidt, Amy. 2009. *Loose Leashes.* Ill. by Ron Schmidt. New York: Random House.
Sidman, Joyce. 2003. *The World According to Dog: Poems and Teen Voices.* Boston: Houghton Mifflin.
Sidman, Joyce. 2006. *Meow Ruff: A Story in Concrete Poetry.* Ill. by Michelle Berg. Boston: Houghton Mifflin.
Singer, Marilyn, 2012. *Every Day's a Dog's Day: A Year in Poems.* New York: Dial.
Singer, Marilyn. 1976. *The Dog Who Insisted He Wasn't.* New York: Dutton.
Singer, Marilyn. 1993. *It's Hard to Read a Map with a Beagle on Your Lap.* New York: Holt.
Singer, Marilyn. 2000. *A Dog's Gotta Do What a Dog's Gotta Do: Dogs at Work.* New York: Holt.
Sklansky, Amy E. 2002. *From the Doghouse: Poems to Chew On.* New York: Holt.
Yolen, Jane. 1993. *Raining Cats and Dogs.* San Diego: Harcourt.

Poetry Books about Food

Food is one of the basics of day-to-day life and this has not escaped the attention of poets, particularly how food plays a part in childhood, family time, and special celebrations. Take a look at these poetry books, for example, and share them along with a cooking activity or a tasty snack.

Adoff, Arnold. 1979. *Eats*. New York: Lothrop, Lee & Shepard.
Adoff, Arnold. 1988. *Chocolate Dreams*. New York: Lothrop, Lee & Shepard.
Argueta, Jorge. 2009. *Sopa de frijoles/ Bean Soup*. Ill. by Rafael Yockteng. Toronto, ON: Groundwood.
Argueta, Jorge. 2010. *Arroz con leche; Rice Pudding*. Ill. by Fernando Vilela. Toronto, ON: Groundwood.
Argueta, Jorge. 2012. *Guacamole; Un poema para cocinar/ A Cooking Poem*. Ill. by Margarita Sada. Toronto: Groundwood.
Brown, Calef. 2008. *Soup For Breakfast*. Boston: Houghton Mifflin.
Fitzgerald, Joanne. 2007. *Yum! Yum!* Markham, Ontario. Fizhenry & Whiteside.
George, Kristine O'Connell. 2001. *Toasting Marshmallows: Camping Poems*. New York: Clarion.
Gerstein, Mordicai. 2011. *Dear Hot Dog.* New York: Abrams.
Goldstein, Bobbye S. 1992. *What's on the Menu? Food Poems.* New York: Viking.
Gunning, Monica. 1998. *Under The Breadfruit Tree: Island Poems.* Honesdale, PA: Boyds Mills Press.
Hauth, Katherine. 2011. *What's for Dinner? Quirky, Squirmy Poems from the Animal World.* Watertown: MA: Charlesbridge.
Havill, Juanita. 2006. *I Heard It from Alice Zucchini: Poems About the Garden.* San Francisco: Chronicle.
Hoberman, Mary Ann. 1997. *The Seven Silly Eaters.* San Diego, CA: Harcourt Brace.
Hopkins, Lee Bennett. Ed. 1994. *April Bubbles Chocolate.* New York: Simon & Schuster.
Hopkins, Lee Bennett. Ed. 2000. *Yummy! Eating Through a Day: Poems.* New York: Simon & Schuster.
Janeczko, Paul B. Ed. 1987. *This Delicious Day.* New York: Orchard.
Johnson, Lindsay Lee. 2002. *Soul Moon Soup.* Asheville, NC: Front Street.
Mora, Pat. 1998. *Delicious Hullabaloo/Pachanga Deliciosa.* Houston, TX: Pinata Books.
Mora, Pat. 2007. *Yum! Mmmm! Que Rico!: America's Sproutings.* New York: Lee & Low.
Morrison, Lillian, comp. 1997. *I Scream, You Scream: A Feast of Food Rhymes.* Little Rock, AR: August House.
Philip, Neil. Ed. 2004. *Hot Potato: Mealtime Rhymes.* New York: Clarion.
Rex, Adam. 2006. *Frankenstein Makes a Sandwich.* San Diego, CA: Harcourt.
Rex, Adam. 2008. *Frankenstein Takes the Cake.* New York: Harcourt Houghton Mifflin.
Rockwell, Thomas. 2010. *Emily Stew with Some Side Dishes.* New York: Roaring Brook.

Rosen, Michael, J. Ed. 1996. *Food Fight: Poets Join the Fight Against Hunger with Poems about Their Favorite Foods*. San Diego, CA: Harcourt Brace.

Salas, Laura Purdie. 2008. *Lettuce Introduce You: Poems About Food (A+ Books)*. Minneapolis, MN: Capstone.

Shields, Carol Diggory. 1995. *Lunch Money and Other Poems about School*. New York: Dutton.

Singer, Marilyn. 2008. *First Food Fight This Fall*. New York: Sterling.

Stevenson, James. 1995. *Sweet Corn: Poems*. New York: Greenwillow.

Stevenson, James. 1998. *Popcorn: Poems*. New York: Greenwillow.

Stevenson, James. 2002. *Corn-Fed: Poems*. New York: Greenwillow.

Stevenson, James. 2003. *Corn Chowder: Poems*. New York: Greenwillow.

Thomas, Joyce Carol. 1993. *Brown Honey in Broomwheat Tea: Poems*. New York: HarperCollins.

Thomas, Joyce Carol. 1995 *Gingerbread Days*. New York: HarperCollins.

Weinstock, Robert. 2009. *Food Hates You, Too*. New York: Disney-Hyperion.

Westcott, Nadine Bernard. 1987. *Peanut Butter and Jelly: A Play Rhyme*. New York: Dutton.

Westcott, Nadine Bernard. Ed. 1994. *Never Take a Pig to Lunch and Other Poems about the Fun of Eating*. New York: Orchard.

Poetry Books about Gardens and Gardening

April is "National Garden Month" in addition to be National Poetry Month. Finding poetry for children on the topic of gardens is one way to celebrate the outdoors and help kids re-connect with the earth, plants, and growing things. And of course sharing garden poetry provides an invitation to children to DO some planting. Here are a handful of poetry books on the topic of gardens and gardening.

Alarcón, Francisco X. 1997. *Laughing Tomatoes and Other Spring Poems/Jitomates Risuenos y Otros Poemas de Primavera.* San Francisco, CA: Children's Book Press.

Bosselaar, Laure-Anne. 2000. *Urban Nature: Poems about the Wildlife in the City.* Minneapolis, MN: Milkweed.

Brenner, Barbara. 1994. *The Earth is Painted Green: A Garden of Poems about Our Planet.* New York: Scholastic.

Bruchac, Joseph. 1995. *The Earth Under Sky Bear's Feet: Native American Poems of the Land.* New York: Philomel.

Harrison, David L. 2000. *Farmer's Garden: Rhymes for Two Voices.* Honesdale, PA: Wordsong/Boyds Mills.

Havill, Juanita. 2006. *I Heard it from Alice Zucchini: Poems about the Garden.* San Francisco: Chronicle.

Havill, Juanita. 2008. *Grow.* Atlanta: Peachtree.

Hubbell, Patricia. 2001. *Black Earth, Gold Sun: Poems.* New York: Marshall Cavendish.

Kemp, Moira. 1992. *Round and Round the Garden.* London: Simon & Schuster.

Lindbergh, Reeve. 1990. *Johnny Appleseed.* Boston: Joy Street Books.

Mannis, Celeste Davidson. 2002. *One Leaf Rides the Wind: Counting in a Japanese Garden.* New York: Viking.

McKay-Lawton, Toni. 2004. *In the Garden.* Watlington: Ransom.

McKay-Lawton, Toni. 2004. *In Bloom.* Watlington: Ransom.

Millen, C. M. 2010. *The Ink Garden of Brother Theophane.* Ill. by Andrea Wisnewski. Watertown, MA: Charlesbridge.

Noda, Takayo. 2006. *Song of the Flowers.* New York: Dial.

Randall, Ronne. 2001. *Bug in the Garden.* Bath, UK: Parragon.

Shannon, George. 2006. *Busy in the Garden.* New York: Greenwillow.

Spinelli, Eileen. 2004. *In our Backyard Garden: Poems.* New York: Simon & Schuster.

Yolen, Jane. 2000. *Color Me a Rhyme: Nature Poems for Young People.* Honesdale, PA: Wordsong/Boyds Mills.

Poetry Books about Insects and Bugs

To make a science connection, or enliven a summer book activity, consider sharing poetry about bugs and insects. Here are a few examples of poems focused on the insect world.

Bulion, Leslie. 2006. *Hey There, Stink Bug!* Watertown, MA: Charlesbridge.

Cyrus, Kurt. 2001. *Oddhopper Opera: A Bug's Garden of Verses.* San Diego: Harcourt Brace.

Fleishman, Paul. 1988. *Joyful Noise: Poems for Two Voices.* New York: Harper & Row.

Florian, Douglas. 1998. *Insectlopedia.* San Diego: Harcourt Brace.

Florian, Douglas. 2012. *Unbeelievables: Honeybee Poems and Paintings.* New York: Beach Lane.

Frost, Helen. 2012. *Step Gently Out.* Ill. by Rick Lieder. Somerville, MA: Candlewick.

Greenberg, David T. 2002. *Bugs!* Ill. by Lynn Munsinger. New York: Little, Brown.

Harley, Avis. 2008. *The Monarch's Progress: Poems with Wings.* Honesdale, PA: Boyds Mills/Wordsong.

Harrison, David. L. 2007. *Bugs, Poems about Creeping Things.* Honesdale, PA: Wordsong/Boyds Mills.

Hopkins, Lee Bennett. Ed. 1992. *Flit, Flutter, Fly! Poems about Bugs and Other Crawly Creatures.* New York: Doubleday.

Hopkins, Lee Bennett. Ed. 2012. *Nasty Bugs.* Ill. by Will Terry. New York: Dial.

Katz, Alan. 2011. *Mosquitoes Are Ruining My Summer! And Other Silly Dilly Camp Songs.* New York: McElderry.

Lewis, J. Patrick. 1998. *The Little Buggers: Insect & Spider Poems.* New York: Dial.

Mortensen, Lori. 2009. *In the Trees, Honey Bees!* Nevada City, CA: Dawn Publishing.

Nye, Naomi Shihab. 2008. *Honeybee.* New York: Greenwillow.

Rosen, Michael. 1992. *Itsy Bitsy Beasties: Poems from Around the World.* Minneapolis, MN: Carolrhoda Books.

Rosen, Michael. 1993. *Mini Beasties.* London: Puffin.

Ross, Michael Elsohn. 2004. *Snug as a Bug.* San Francisco: Chronicle.

Sidman, Joyce. 2005. *Song of the Water Boatman: & other Pond Poems.* Boston: Houghton Mifflin.

Sidman, Joyce. 2006. *Butterfly Eyes and Other Secrets of the Meadow.* Ill. by Beth Krommes. Boston: Houghton Mifflin.

Singer, Marilyn. 2003. *Fireflies at Midnight.* New York: Atheneum Books for Young Readers.

Walton, Rick. 1995. *What to do when a Bug Climbs in your Mouth and other Poems to Drive you Buggy.* New York: Lothrop, Lee, & Shepard.

Yolen, Jane. 2012. *Bug Off! Creepy Crawly Poems.* Ill. by Jason Stemple. Honesdale, PA: Wordsong/Boyds Mills Press.

Poetry Books about Mathematics

One might not expect to make a poetry connection in the area of mathematics, but poets sometimes use the framework of counting, sequencing, and other math processes to shape and structure a poem. These poetry books show just how it's done.

Andrew, Moira. 1993. *One in a Million: A Book of Poems Where Maths Becomes fun.* London: Puffin.

Dodds, Dayle Ann. 2005. *The Great Divide, A Mathematical Marathon.* Somerville, MA: Candlewick Press.

Dillon, Leo and Diane. 2007. *Mother Goose; Numbers on the Loose.* San Diego, CA: Harcourt.

Esbensen, Barbara Juster. 1996. *Echoes for the Eye: Poems to Celebrate Patterns in Nature.* New York: HarperCollins.

Franco, Betsy. 1999. *Counting Caterpillars and Other Math Poems.* New York: Scholastic.

Franco, Betsy. 2003. *Mathematickles!* New York: McElderry.

Franco, Betsy. 2004. *Counting Our Way to the 100th day!: 100 Poems.* New York: McElderry.

Franco, Betsy. 2008. *Bees, Snails, & Peacock Tails, Patterns and Shapes... Naturally.* New York: McElderry.

Hopkins, Lee Bennett. Ed. 1993. *It's About Time.* New York: Simon & Schuster.

Hopkins, Lee Bennett. Ed. 1997. *Marvelous Math: A Book of Poems.* New York: Simon & Schuster.

Lewis, J. Patrick. 2002. *Arithme-Tickle: An Even Number of Odd Riddle-Rhymes.* San Diego: Harcourt.

Lewis, J. Patrick. 2012. *Edgar Allan Poe's Pie; Math Puzzlers in Classic Poems.* New York: Houghton Mifflin Harcourt.

Lewis, J. Patrick and Yolen, Jane. 2012. *Take Two! A Celebration of Twins.* Ill. by Sophie Blackall. Somerville, MA: Candlewick.

Mannis, Celeste Davidson. 2005. *One Leaf Rides the Wind: Counting in a Japanese Garden.* Ill. by Susan K. Hartung. New York: Viking.

Michelson, Richard. 2000. *Ten Times Better.* New York: Marshall Cavendish.

Mora, Pat. 1996. *Uno Dos Tres, One, Two, Three.* New York: Clarion.

O'Neill, Mary. 1968. *Take a Number.* New York: Doubleday.

Pappas, Theoni. 1991. *Math Talk: Mathematical Ideas in Poems for Two Voices.* San Carlos, CA: Wide World Publishing/Tetra.

Shields, Carol Diggory. 1995. *Lunch Money and Other Poems about School.* New York: Dutton.

Siegen-Smith, Nikki. 2001. *First Morning: Poems About Time.* New York: Barefoot Books.

Yolen, Jane. 2006. *Count Me a Rhyme: Animal Poems by the Numbers.* Honesdale, PA: Wordsong/Boyds Mills.

Ziefert, Harriet. 1997. *Mother Goose Math.* New York: Viking.

Based on: Franco, Betsy. 2006. *Conversations with a Poet: Inviting Poetry into the K-12 Classroom.* Richard C. Owen Publishers.

Poetry Books about Poetry, Books, and Reading

Poets have looked inward at the topic of books and poetry itself from time to time. These poetry books lend themselves perfectly to lessons focused on the power of words and language or as the thematic center for a week-long exploration of poetry or simply to highlight for special occasions. Here is a sampling of books about poetry, books, and reading itself.

Goldstein, Bobbye S. Ed. 1992. *Inner Chimes: Poems on Poetry*. Honesdale, PA: Boyds Mills.

Hopkins, Lee Bennett. 2011. *I am the Book*. New York: Holiday House.

Hopkins, Lee Bennett. Ed. 1990. *Good Books, Good Times*. Reprinted, New York: HarperTrophy, 2000.

Hopkins, Lee Bennett. Ed. 2004. *Wonderful Words: Poems about Reading, Writing, Speaking and Listening*. New York: Simon & Schuster.

Lewis, J. Patrick. 1999. *The Bookworm's Feast: A Potluck of Poems*. New York: Dial.

Lewis, J. Patrick. 2005. *Please Bury Me In The Library*. Orlando, FL: Gulliver Books/Harcourt.

Lewis, J. Patrick. 2009. *Spot the Plot! A Riddle Book of Book Riddles*. Ill. by Lynn Munsinger. San Francisco, CA: Chronicle.

Pearson, Debora. Ed. 2001. *When I Went to the Library*. Toronto: Groundwood.

Rich, Mary Perrotta. Ed. 1998. *Book Poems: Poems from National Children's Book Week, 1959-1998*. New York: Children's Book Council.

Salas, Laura Purdie. 2011. *BookSpeak!*. Ill. by Josee Bisaillon. New York: Clarion.

Poetry Books for Science

A brief consideration of a handful of poetry books will quickly lead one to discover many poems that connect with the sciences. In fact, there are many thematic poetry collections devoted to science-related subjects such as **animals, weather, seasons, space, dinosaurs,** *and* **time,** *to name a few (and featured in additional lists). Poetry offers the special vocabulary, imagery, and conciseness that help introduce or reinforce important science concepts.*

Brenner, Barbara. Ed. 1994. *This Earth is Painted Green: A Garden of Poems About our Planet.* New York: Scholastic.

Coombs, Kate. 2012. *Water Sings Blue: Ocean Poems.* Ill. by Meilo So. San Francisco: Chronicle.

Davies, Nicola. 2012. *Outside Your Window: A First Book of Nature.* Ill. by Mark Hearld. Somerville, MA: Candlewick.

Dotlich, Rebecca. 2006. *What is Science?.* New York: Holt.

Esbensen, Barbara Juster. 1996. *Echoes for the Eye: Poems to Celebrate Patterns in Nature.* New York: HarperCollins.

Fletcher, Ralph. 1991. *Water Planet: Poems about Water.* Paramus, NJ: Arrowhead.

Florian, Douglas. 2004. *Omnibeasts.* San Diego: Harcourt.

Franco, Betsy. 2008. *Bees, Snails, & Peacock Tails, Patterns and Shapes... Naturally.* New York: McElderry.

George, Kristine O'Connell. 1998. *Old Elm Speaks: Tree Poems.* New York: Clarion.

Harley, Avis. 2008. *The Monarch's Progress: Poems with Wings.* Honesdale, PA: Boyds Mills/Wordsong.

Harley, Avis. 2006. *Sea Stars: Saltwater Poems.* Honesdale, PA: Wordsong/Boyds Mills.

Hoberman, Mary Ann and Wilson, Linda. Eds. 2009. *The Tree That Time Built: A Celebration of Nature, Science, and Imagination.* Naperville, IL: Sourcebooks.

Hopkins, Lee Bennett. Ed. 1999. *Spectacular Science: A Book of Poems.* New York: Simon & Schuster.

Hopkins, Lee Bennett. 2009. *Incredible Inventions.* New York: HarperCollins.

Hubbell, Patricia. 2000. *Earthmates: Poems.* New York: Marshall Cavendish.

Johnston, Tony. 1999. *An Old Shell: Poems of the Galapagos.* New York: Farrar, Straus & Giroux.

Katz, Bobbi. 2007. *Trailblazers; Poems of Exploration.* New York: Greenwillow.

Kennedy, Dorothy M. Ed. 1998. *Make Things Fly: Poems about the Wind.* New York: McElderry.

Koss, Amy Goldman. 1987. *Where Fish Go in Winter: And Answers to Other Great Mysteries.* Los Angeles: Price Stern Sloan.

Levy, Constance. 2002. *Splash!: Poems of Our Watery World.* New York: Orchard.

Lewis, J. Patrick. 2004. *Scien-trickery: Riddles in Science.* Orlando: Harcourt.

Lewis, J. Patrick. 2005. *Galileo's Universe.* Mankato, MN: Creative Editions.

Livingston, Myra Cohn. 1986. *Earth Songs*. New York: Holiday House.

Moss, Jeff. 1998. *Bone Poems*. New York: Scholastic.

Nicholls, Judith. 2003. *The Sun in Me: Poems about the Planet*. Somerville, MA: Barefoot Books.

Nicholls, Judith. Ed. 1993. *Earthways, Earthwise: Poems on Conservation*. Oxford, NY: Oxford University Press.

Peters, Lisa Westberg. 2003. *Earthshake: Poems from the Ground Up*. New York: HarperCollins.

Schwartz, David M. and Schy, Yael. 2010. *What in the Wild? Mysteries of Nature Concealed… and Revealed*. Berkeley, CA: Tricycle.

Scieszka, Jon. 2004. *Science Verse*. New York: Viking.

Shields, Carol Diggory. 2003. *BrainJuice: Science, Fresh Squeezed!*. Brooklyn: Handprint.

Sidman, Joyce. 2002. *Eureka! Poems about Inventors*. Ill. by K. Bennett Chavez. Brookfield, CT: Millbrook.

Sidman, Joyce. 2010. *Ubiquitous: Celebrating Nature's Survivors*. Ill. by Becky Prange. Boston: Houghton Mifflin.

Singer, Marilyn. 2002. *Footprints on the Roof: Poems about the Earth*. New York: Knopf.

Singer, Marilyn. 2012. *A Strange Place to Call Home: The World's Most Dangerous Habitats and the Animals That Call Them Home*. Ill. by Ed Young. San Francisco: Chronicle.

Sklansky, Amy E. 2012. *Out of This World: Poems and Facts About Space*. Ill. by Stacey Schuett. New York: Knopf.

Swinburne, Stephen. 2010. *Ocean Soup; Tide-Pool Poems*. Watertown, MA: Charlesbridge.

Wallace, Nancy Elizabeth. Ed. 2003. *The Sun, the Moon, and the Stars: Poems*. Boston: Houghton Mifflin.

Wolf, Allan. 2003. *The Blood-Hungry Spleen and Other Poems about Our Parts*. Somerville, MA: Candlewick.

Wong, Janet. 2011. *Once Upon A Tiger; New Beginnings for Endangered Animals*. OnceUponaTiger.com.

Yolen, Jane. 1995. *Water Music: Poems for Children*. Honesdale, PA: Boyds Mills.

Yolen, Jane. 1997. *Once Upon Ice and Other Frozen Poems*. Honesdale, PA: Boyds Mills.

Yolen, Jane. 2003. *Least Things: Poems About Small Natures*. Honesdale, PA: Boyds Mills.

Poetry Books about Space and the Planets

Although most poetry for young people focuses on the natural world, poets have also speculated about what lies beyond our world on earth. These selected works center on the planets, outer space, and even possible alien life forms.

Fisher, Aileen. 2001. *Sing of the Earth and Sky: Poems about our Planet and the Wonders Beyond.* Honesdale, PA: Wordsong/Boyds Mills.

Florian, Douglas. 2007. *Comets, Stars, the Moon, and Mars: Space Poems and Paintings.* Orlando, FL: Harcourt.

Hopkins, Lee Bennett. Ed. 1995. *Blast Off: Poems about Space.* New York: HarperCollins.

Hopkins, Lee Bennett. 2009. *Sky Magic.* Ill. by Mariusz Stawarski. New York: Dutton.

Livingston, Myra Cohn. 1998. *Space Songs.* New York: Holiday House.

Nichols, Judith. 2003. Ed. *The Sun in Me: Poems about the Planet.* Cambridge, MA: Barefoot Books.

Prelutsky, Jack. 2009. *The Swamps of Sleethe: Poems from beyond the Solar System.* New York: Knopf.

Salas, Laura Purdie. 2008. *And Then There Were Eight: Poems about Space.* Mankato, MN: Capstone.

Simon, Seymour. 1995. *Star Walk.* New York: Morrow.

Singer, Marilyn. 2012. *The Boy Who Cried Alien.* Ill. by Brian Biggs. New York: Hyperion.

Sklansky, Amy E. 2012. *Out of This World: Poems and Facts About Space.* Ill. by Stacey Schuett. New York: Knopf.

Wallace, Nancy Elizabeth. Ed. 2003. *The Sun, the Moon, and the Stars: Poems.* Boston, MA: Houghton Mifflin.

Yolen, Jane. 1993. *What Rhymes with Moon?* New York: Philomel.

Yolen, Jane. Ed. 1996. *Mother Earth, Father Sky: Poems of Our Planet.* Honesdale, PA: Wordsong/Boyds Mills.

Poetry Books about Sports

Sports and poetry may seem like an unlikely combination, but it has ancient roots with poems recited at sporting events such as victory odes at the earliest Olympics. Perhaps a poem from one of the books below can kick off an athletic competition, sporting event, or field day celebration.

Adoff, Arnold. 1986. *Sports Pages*. New York: HarperCollins.

Adoff, Arnold. 2000. *The Basket Counts*. New York: Simon & Shuster.

Brooks, Kevin and Sean Brooks. Ed. 1996. *Thru the Smoky End Boards: Canadian Poetry about Sports & Games*. Vancouver: Polestar Book Publishers.

Burleigh, Robert. 2001. *Goal*. San Diego: Harcourt Brace.

Burleigh, Robert. 1997. *Hoops*. San Diego, CA: Silver Whistle.

Dotlich, Rebecca Kai. 2004. *Over in the Pink House: New Jump Rope Rhymes*. Honesdale, PA: Wordsong/Boyds Mills.

Esbensen, Barbara Juster. 1999. *Jumping Day*. Honesdale, PA: Boyds Mills Press.

Franco, Betsy. 2009. *Messing Around the Monkey Bars and other School Poems for Two Voices*. Ill. by Jessie Hartland. Somerville, MA: Candlewick.

Glenn, Mel. 1997. *Jump Ball: a Basketball Season in Poems*. New York: Lodestar Books/ Dutton.

Greenfield, Eloise. 1997. *For the Love of the Game: Michael Jordan and Me*. New York: HarperCollins.

Hopkins, Lee Bennett. Ed. 1996. *Opening Days: Sports Poems*. San Diego, CA: Harcourt Brace.

Hopkins, Lee Bennett. Ed. 1999. *Sports! Sports! Sports!* New York: HarperCollins.

Hoyte, Carol-Ann and Roemer, Heidi Bee. Eds. 2012. *And the Crowd Goes Wild!: A Global Gathering of Sports Poems*. Ill. by Kevin Sylvester. Victoria, British Columbia: Friesens Press.

Katz, Alan. 2009. *Going, Going, Gone!: And Other Silly Dilly Sports Songs*. New York: Simon & Schuster.

Kennedy, X. J. 1999. *Elympics*. New York: Philomel.

Knudson, R. Roxanne, and May Swensen. Eds. 1988. *American Sports Poems*. New York: Orchard.

Low, Alice. 2009. *The Fastest Game on Two Feet*. New York: Holiday House.

Lowe, Ayana. 2008. *Come and Play; Children of Our World Having Fun*. New York: Bloomsbury.

Mathis, Sharon Bell. 1991. *Red Dog, Blue Fly: Football Poems*. New York: Viking.

Morrison, Lillian. Ed. 1990. *Sprints and Distances: Sports in Poetry and the Poetry in Sport*. New York: HarperCollins.

Morrison, Lillian. 2001. *Way to go! : Sports Poems*. Honesdale, Pa. : Wordsong/Boyds Mills.

Prelutsky, Jack. 2007. *Good Sports; Rhymes About Running, Jumping, Throwing, and More*. New York: Knopf.

Smith, Charles R. Jr. 1999. *Rimshots; Basketball Pix, Rolls, and Rhythms.* New York: Dutton.

Smith, Charles R. Jr. 2001. *Short Takes: Fast-Break Basketball Poetry.* New York: Dutton.

Smith, Charles R. Jr. 2003. *Hoop Queens.* Somerville, MA: Candlewick.

Smith, Charles R. Jr. 2004. *Hoop Kings.* Somerville, MA: Candlewick.

Smith, Charles R. Jr. 2007. *Twelve Rounds to Glory: The Story of Muhammad Ali.* Somerville, MA: Candlewick.

Smith, Charles R., Jr. 2010. *Black Jack; The Ballad of Jack Johnson.* New York: Roaring Brook Press.

Troupe, Quincy. 2000. *Take it to the Hoop, Magic Johnson.* New York: Hyperion.

Poetry Books about Time

As children grow up, they learn to tell time, identify the weeks and months of the year, and anticipate the calendar's changes. The passage of time is important to them, whether it's waiting for a birthday or making it through a scary night. Many poets have explored these constructs in their writing as shown in the following poetry books. A related list of poetry about the seasons may also provide poem examples on the topic of time. What a perfect tool for creating a "time for poetry" break!

Bruchac, Joseph. 1992. *Thirteen Moons on Turtle's Back: A Native American Year of Moons.* New York: Philomel Books.

Bryan, Ashley. Ed. 1994. *All Night, All Day: A Child's First Book of African-American Spirituals.* New York: Atheneum.

Farrar, Sid. 2012. *The Year Comes Round: Haiku Through the Seasons.* Ill. by Ilse Plume. Chicago: Whitman.

Foster, John. 2000. *Rhyme Time around the Day.* Oxford: Oxford Press.

Franco, Betsy. 2004. *Counting our way to the 100th day.* New York: Margaret K. McElderry Books.

Harrison, Michael and Christopher Stuart-Clark. Eds. 1999. *The Oxford Treasury of Time Poems.* Oxford: Oxford University Press.

Heide, Florence Perry. 1999. *It's about Time! Poems.* New York: Clarion Books.

Hoberman, Mary Ann and Wilson, Linda. 2009. *The Tree That Time Built: A Celebration of Nature, Science, and Imagination.* Naperville, IL: Sourcebooks.

Hopkins, Lee Bennett. Ed. 1993. *It's About Time.* New York: Simon & Schuster.

Hutchins, Hazel. 2004. *A Second is a Hiccup: A Child's Book of Time.* Markham: North Winds Press.

Katz, Bobbi. 2006. *Once Around the Sun.* Ill. by LeUyen Pham. San Diego, CA: Harcourt.

Kennedy, Dorothy M.. Ed. 1993. *I Thought I'd Take My Rat to School: Poems for September to June.* New York: Little, Brown.

Lewis, J. Patrick. 2009. *Countdown to Summer: A Poem for Every Day of the School Year.* Ill. by Ethan Long. New York: Little, Brown.

Livingston, Myra Cohn. 1959/2007. *Calendar.* New York: Holiday House.

O'Neill, Mary. 2003. *The Sound of Day; The Sound of Night.* New York: Farrar, Straus & Giroux.

Pappas, Theoni. 1991. *Math Talk: Mathematical Ideas in Poems for Two Voices.* San Carlos, CA: Wide World Publishing/Tetra.

Pierce, Terry. 2007. *Ticktock: Time Nursery Rhymes.* Minneapolis: Picture Window Books.

Prelutsky, Jack. 1999. *Dog Days: Rhymes Around the Year.* New York: Knopf.

Shields, Carol Diggory. 1995. *Lunch Money And Other Poems About School.* New York: Dutton Children's Books.

Siegen-Smith, Nikki and Giovanni Manna. 2001. *First Morning: Poems about Time.* Cambridge: Barefoot Books.

Updike, John. 2004. *A Child's Calendar.* Pine Plains, NY: Live Oak Media.

Poetry Books about Trees

Even before Joyce Kilmer penned the classic poem, "Trees," poets have found inspiration in the unique nature of the noble tree. As tree climbers, children can appreciate their enthusiasm. Share some of these tree-focused poetry books, perhaps along with a leaf collecting and tree identification activity.

Argueta, Jorge. 2003. *Trees are hanging from the sky.* Toronto: Groundwood.

Behn, Harry. 1992. *Trees: A Poem.* New York: Holt.

Brenner, Barbara. 1994. *The Earth is Painted Green: A Garden of Poems about Our Planet.* New York: Scholastic.

cummings, e. e. 2001. *Little Tree.* New York: Hyperion.

Engle, Margarita. 2008. *The Surrender Tree.* New York: Holt.

Florian, Douglas. 2010. *Poetrees.* New York: Simon & Schuster.

George, Kristine O'Connell. 1998. *Old Elm Speaks: Tree Poems.* New York: Clarion.

Gerber, Carole. 2008. *Winter Trees.* Ill. by Leslie Evans. Watertown, MA: Charlesbridge.

Greenfield, Eloise. 1988. *Under the Sunday Tree.* New York: Harper & Row.

Gunning, Monica. 1998. *Under the Breadfruit Tree: Island Poems.* Honesdale, PA: Wordsong/Boyds Mills.

Ho, Minfong. 1996. *Maples in the Mist: Children's Poems from the Tang Dynesty.* New York: Lothrop, Lee & Shepard.

Hoberman, Mary Ann and Wilson, Linda. Eds. 2009. *The Tree That Time Built: A Celebration of Nature, Science, and Imagination.* Naperville, IL: Sourcebooks.

Jones, Hettie, Ed. 1971. *The Tree Stands Shining: Poetry of the North American Indian.* New York: Dial Books.

Levy, Constance. 1994. *A Tree Place and Other Poems.* New York: McElderry.

Lindbergh, Reeve. 1990. *Johnny Appleseed.* Boston: Joy Street Books.

McCord, David. 1999. *Every Time I Climb a Tree.* New York: Little Brown.

Nye, Naomi Shihab, comp. 1995. *The Tree is Older than You Are: A Bilingual Gathering of Poems and Stories from Mexico with Paintings by Mexican Artists.* New York: Simon & Schuster.

Sidman, Joyce. 2009. *Red Sings From Treetops; A Year in Colors.* Boston: Houghton Mifflin.

Zimmer, Tracie Vaughn. 2005. *Sketches from a Spy Tree.* New York: Clarion.

Poetry Books about United States History

The stories of our country's past make for a fascinating context for many wonderful poetry books for young people. These works lend themselves to sharing in social studies and history classes as well as when commemorating important dates in American history.

Alexander, Elizabeth and Marilyn Nelson. 2007. *Miss Crandall's School for Young Ladies and Little Misses of Color.* Honesdale, PA: Wordsong/Boyds Mills.

Altman, Susan and Lechner, Susan. 1993. *Followers of the North Star: Rhymes about African American Heroes, Heroines, and Historical Times.* Chicago: Children's Press.

Bernier-Grand, Carmen T. 2004. *César: Si, se puede! Yes, We Can!* New York: Marshall Cavendish.

Clinton, Catherine. Ed. 2003. *A Poem of Her Own: Voices of American Women Yesterday and Today.* New York: Abrams.

Clinton, Catherine. Ed. 1993/1998. *I, Too, Sing America: Three Centuries of African American Poetry.* Boston: Houghton Mifflin.

Cohn, Amy L. Ed. 1993. *From Sea to Shining Sea: A Treasury of American Folklore and Folk Songs.* New York: Scholastic.

Frost, Helen. 2006. *The Braid.* New York: Farrar, Straus & Giroux.

Frost, Helen. 2009. *Crossing Stones.* New York: Farrar, Straus & Giroux.

Hemphill, Stephanie. 2010. *Wicked Girls; A Novel of the Salem Witch Trials.* New York: HarperCollins.

Hesse, Karen. 1997. *Out of the Dust.* New York: Scholastic.

Hesse, Karen. 2001. *Witness.* New York: Scholastic.

Hesse, Karen. 2003. *Aleutian Sparrow.* Simon & Schuster. Novel in verse WW2

Hopkins, Lee Bennett. Ed. 1994. *Hand in Hand: An American History through Poetry.* New York: Simon & Schuster.

Hopkins, Lee Bennett. Ed. 1999. *Lives: Poems about Famous Americans.* New York: HarperCollins.

Hopkins, Lee Bennett. 2000. *My America: A Poetry Atlas of the United States.* New York: Simon & Schuster.

Hopkins, Lee Bennett. Ed. 2002. *Home to Me: Poems Across America.* New York: Orchard.

Hopkins, Lee Bennett. Ed. 2005. *Days to Celebrate: A Full Year of Poetry, People, Holidays, History, Fascinating Facts, and More.* New York: Greenwillow.

Hopkins, Lee Bennett. Ed. 2006 *Got Geography!* New York: Greenwillow.

Hopkins, Lee Bennett. 2007. *Behind the Museum Door.* New York: Abrams.

Hopkins, Lee Bennett. 2008. *America at War.* New York: McElderry.

Hopkins, Lee Bennett. 2009. *Incredible Inventions.* Illus. by Julia Sarcone-Roach. New York: HarperCollins.

Hughes, Langston. 2012. *I, Too, Am America.* Ill. by Bryan Collier. New York: Simon & Schuster.

Izuki, Steven. 1994. *Believers in America: Poems about Americans of Asian and Pacific Islander Descent.* Chicago, IL: Children's Press.

Janeczko, Paul B. 2004. *Worlds Afire.* Somerville, MA: Candlewick.

Katz, Bobbi. 2000. *We the People.* New York: Greenwillow.

Lewis, J. Patrick. 2000. *Freedom like Sunlight: Praisesongs for Black Americans.* Mankato, MN: Creative Editions.

Lewis, J. Patrick. 2001. *A Burst of Firsts: Doers, Shakers, and Record Breakers.* New York: Dial.

Lewis, J. Patrick. 2005. *Heroes and She-roes: Poems of Amazing and Everyday Heroes.* New York: Dial.

Lewis, J. Patrick. 2005. *Vherses: A Celebration of Outstanding Women.* Mankato, MN: Creative Editions.

Lewis, J. Patrick. 2007. *The Brother's War: Civil War Voices in Verse.* Washington, DC: National Geographic.

Lewis, J. Patrick. 2008. *The World's Greatest Poems.* San Francisco: Chronicle.

Lewis, J. Patrick. 2009. *The Underwear Salesman: And Other Jobs for Better or Verse.* Ill. by Serge Bloch. New York: Simon & Schuster/Atheneum.

Lewis, J. Patrick. 2012. *When Thunder Comes: Poems for Civil Rights Leaders.* San Francisco: Chronicle.

Littlechild, George. 1993. *This Land Is My Land.* San Francisco, CA: Children's Book Press.

Livingston, Myra Cohn. 1992. *Let Freedom Ring: A Ballad of Martin Luther King Jr.* New York: Holiday House.

Livingston, Myra Cohn. 1993. *Abraham Lincoln: A Man for All the People: A Ballad.* New York: Holiday House.

Longfellow, Henry Wadsworth. 2003. *Paul Revere's Ride.* Honesdale, PA: Boyds Mills Press.

Mak, Kam. 2002. *My Chinatown: One Year in Poems.* New York: HarperCollins.

McKissack, Patricia. 2011. *Never Forgotten.* Ill. by Leo and Diane Dillon. New York: Schwartz & Wade.

Meltzer, Milton. Ed. 2003. *Hour of Freedom: American History in Poetry.* Honesdale, PA: Wordsong/Boyds Mills Press.

Myers, Walter Dean. 2004. *Here in Harlem: Poems in Many Voices.* New York: Holiday House.

Myers, Walter Dean. 2011. *We are America; A Tribute from the Heart.* Ill. by Christopher Myers. New York: HarperCollins.

Nelson, Marilyn. 2001. *Carver: A Life in Poems.* Asheville, NC: Front Street.

Nelson, Marilyn. 2004. *Fortune's Bones: The Manumission Requiem.* Asheville, NC: Front Street.

Nelson, Marilyn. 2005. *A Wreath for Emmett Till.* Boston: Houghton Mifflin.

Nelson, Marilyn. 2008. *The Freedom Business.* Asheville, NC: Front Street.

Nelson, Marilyn. 2009. *Sweethearts of Rhythm; The Story of the Greatest All-Girl Swing Band in the World.* Ill. by Jerry Pinkney. NY: Dial.

Panzer, Nora, ed. 1994. *Celebrate America in Poetry and Art.* New York: Hyperion.

Paul, Ann. W. 1999. *All by Herself: 14 Girls Who Made a Difference: Poems.* San Diego, CA: Browndeer/Harcourt Brace.

Philip, Neil. Ed. 1995. *Singing America.* New York: Viking.

Philip, Neil. Ed. 1998. *War and the Pity of War.* New York: Clarion.

Philip, Neil. Ed. 2000. *It's a Woman's World: A Century of Women's Voices in Poetry*. New York: Dutton.

Rappaport, Doreen. 2008. *Lady Liberty*. Somerville, MA: Candlewick.

Richards, Jame. 2010. *Three Rivers Rising*. New York: Knopf.

Robb, Laura. Ed. 1997. *Music and Drum: Voices of War and Peace, Hope and Dreams*. New York: Philomel Books.

Salas, Laura Purdie. 2008. *Tiny Creams, Sprouting Tall: Poems About the United States*. Minneapolis, MN: Capstone.

Shields, Carol Diggory. 2002. *American History, Fresh Squeezed*. Brooklyn, NY: Handprint Books.

Sidman, Joyce. 2002. *Eureka! Poems about Inventors*. Brookfield, CT: Millbrook.

Siebert, Diane. 1989. *Heartland*. New York: Crowell.

Siebert, Diane. 2001. *Mississippi*. Ill. by Greg Harlin. New York: HarperCollins.

Siebert, Diane. 2006. *Tour America: A Journey through Poems and Art*. San Francisco: Chronicle.

Singer, Marilyn. 2005. *Monday on the Mississippi*. New York: Henry Holt.

Smith, Charles R. Jr. 2007. *Twelve Rounds to Glory: The Story of Muhammad Ali*. Somerville, MA: Candlewick.

Smith, Charles R., Jr. 2010. *Black Jack; The Ballad of Jack Johnson*. Roaring Brook Press.

Smith, Charles R., Jr. 2012. *Stars in the Shadows: The Negro League All-Star Game of 1934*. Ill. by Frank Morrison. New York: Atheneum.

Testa, Maria. 2002. *Becoming Joe Dimaggio*. Somerville, MA: Candlewick.

Testa, Maria. 2003. *Almost Forever*. Somerville, MA: Candlewick.

Thomas, Joyce Carol. 1998. *I Have Heard of a Land*. New York: HarperCollins.

Weatherford, Carole Boston. 2002. *Remember the Bridge: Poems of a People*. New York: Philomel.

Weatherford, Carole Boston. 2006. *Dear Mr. Rosenwald*. Ill. by R. Gregory Christie. New York: Scholastic.

Weatherford, Carole Boston. 2007. *Birmingham, 1963*. Honesdale, PA: Wordsong/Boyds Mills Press.

Weatherford, Carole Boston. 2008. *Becoming Billie Holiday*. Honesdale, PA: Wordsong/Boyds Mills Press.

Whipple, Laura. Ed. 1994. *Celebrating America: A Collection of Poems and Images of the American Spirit*. New York: Philomel.

Winters, Kay. 2008. *Colonial Voices, Hear Them Speak*. New York: Dutton.

Wolf, Allan. 2004. *New Found Land; Lewis and Clark's Voyage of Discovery*. Somerville, MA: Candlewick.

Wolf, Allan. 2011. *The Watch That Ends the Night*. Somerville, MA: Candlewick.

Wong, Janet. 2012. *Declaration of Interdependence: Poems for an Election Year*. PoetrySuitcase.

Zimmer, Tracie Vaughn. 2009. *Steady Hands: Poems About Work*. New York: Clarion.

Poetry Books about War and Peace

Poets who write for adults have long tackled the topics of war and peace, but those difficult topics can be challenging for those who write for children. The sampling of poetry books below do so with great depth and sensitivity.

Applegate, Katherine. 2008. *Home of the Brave*. New York: Square Fish.

Burg, Ann. 2009. *All the Broken Pieces*. NY: Scholastic.

Crist-Evans, Craig. 1999. *Moon Over Tennessee: A Boy's Civil War Journal*. Boston: Houghton Mifflin.

Engle, Margarita. 2006. *The Poet Slave of Cuba: A Biography of Juan Francisco Manzano*. New York: Henry Holt and Co.

Engle, Margarita. 2008. *The Surrender Tree; Poems of Cuba's Struggle for Freedom*. New York: Henry Holt.

Frost, Helen. 2009. *Crossing Stones*. New York: Farrar, Straus & Giroux.

Greenfield, Eloise. 2006. *When the Horses Ride by: Children in the Times of War*. New York: Lee & Low Books.

Heard, Georgia. Ed. 2002. *This Place I Know: Poems of Comfort*. Cambridge: Candlewick Press.

Hesse, Karen. 2003. *Aleutian Sparrow*. New York: Simon & Schuster.

Hines, Anna Grossnickle. 2011. *Peaceful Pieces: A Year in Poems and Quilts*. New York: Greenwillow.

Holland, Trish and Christine Ford. 2006. *The Soldiers' Night Before Christmas*. New York: Random House.

Hopkins, Lee Bennett. Ed. 2008. *America at War*. New York: McElderry.

Hopkins, Lee Bennett. Ed. 1994. *Hand in Hand: An American History through Poetry*. New York: Simon & Schuster.

Hopkins, Lee Bennett. Ed. 2002. *Home to Me: Poems Across America*. New York: Orchard Books.

Janeczko, Paul. 2011. *Requiem; Poems of the Terezín Ghetto*. Somerville, MA: Candlewick.

Johnston, Tony. 2008. *Voice from Afar: Poems of Peace*. New York: Holiday House.

Katz, Bobbi. 2000. Ed. *We The People: Poems*. New York: Greenwillow.

Lai, Thanhha. 2011. *Inside Out and Back Again*. HarperCollins.

Levy, Debbie. 2010. *The Year of Goodbyes; A True Story of Friendship, Family and Farewells*. New York: Hyperion.

Lewis, J. Patrick. 2005. *Heroes and She-Roes: Poems of Amazing and Everyday Heroes*. New York: Dial Books.

Lewis, J. Patrick. 2007. *The Brothers' War: Civil War Voices in Verse*. Washington: National Geographic Children's Books.

Lewis, J. Patrick. 2012. *When Thunder Comes: Poems for Civil Rights Leaders*. Chronicle.

LeZotte, Ann Clare. 2008. *T4*. Boston: Houghton Mifflin.

Longfellow, Henry Wadsworth. 2001. *The Midnight Ride of Paul Revere*. New York: Handprint Books.

Meltzer, Milton. Ed. 2003. *Hour of Freedom: American History In Poetry*. Honesdale, PA: Wordsong.

Myers, Walter Dean. 2011. *We are America; A Tribute from the Heart*. Ill. by Christopher Myers. HarperCollins.

Nye, Naomi Shihab. Ed. 1992. *This Same Sky: A Collection of Poems from Around the World.* New York: Four Winds Press.

Nye, Naomi Shihab. Ed. 1998. *The Space Between out Footsteps: Poems and Paintings from the Middle East.* New York: Simon & Schuster.

Nye, Naomi Shihab. Ed. 1999. *What Have You Lost?* New York: Greenwillow.

Philip, Neil. Ed. 1998. *War and the Pity of War.* New York: Clarion.

Rappaport, Doreen. 2008. *Lady Liberty.* Cambridge: Candlewick Press.

Robb, Laura. Ed. 1997. *Music and Drum: Voices Of War and Peace, Hope and Dreams.* New York: Philomel Books.

Shange, Ntozake. 2012. *Freedom's a-Callin Me.* Ill. by Rod Brown. Amistad/Collins.

Thomas, Shelley Moore. 1998. *Somewhere Today: A Book of Peace.* Morton Grove: Albert Whitman.

Vecchione, Patrice. Ed. 2007. *Faith and Doubt; An Anthology of Poems.* New York: Henry Holt.

Volavkova, Hana. Ed. 1993. *I Never Saw Another Butterfly: Children's Drawings and Poems from Terezin Concentration Camp 1942-1944.* New York: Schocken Books.

Walker, Alice. 2007. *Why War is Never a Good Idea.* New York: HarperCollins.

Poetry Books about Weather

Poetry about the seasons offers many observations about nature, but some poets focus specifically on the weather in writing for young people. Snow, ice, rain, clouds, storms are all elements that fascinate both children and poets. Check out these examples.

Alarcón, Francisco X. 2001. *Iguanas in the Snow and Other Winter Poems/ Iguanas en la Nieve y Otros Poemas de Invierno.* San Francisco, CA: Children's Book Press.

Bauer, Caroline Feller. Ed. 1986. *Snowy Day: Poems and Stories.* New York: HarperCollins.

Cooper, Kay. 2001. *Too Many Rabbits and Other Fingerplays about Animals, Nature, Weather, and Children.* New York: Cartwheel Books.

Engle, Margarita. 2011. *Hurricane Dancers; The First Caribbean Pirate Shipwreck.* New York: Henry Holt.

Florian, Douglas. 2003. *Autumblings.* New York: Greenwillow.

Francis, Lee. 1999. *When The Rain Sings: Poems by Young Native Americans.* New York: Simon & Schuster.

Gray, Rita. Ed. 2010. *One Big Rain; Poems for Rainy Days.* Watertown, MA: Charlesbridge.

High, Linda Oatman. 2004. *City of Snow: The Great Blizzard of 1888.* New York: Walker.

Hopkins, Lee Bennett. Ed. 1994. *Weather: Poems for All Seasons.* New York: HarperTrophy.

Hubbell, Patricia. 2010. *Snow Happy!* San Francisco: Tricycle Press.

Kosaka, Fumi. 2001. *Let's Count the Raindrops.* New York: Viking.

Levy, Constance. 1998. *A Crack in the Clouds.* New York: McElderry.

Paolilli, Paul and Brewer, Dan. 2001. *Silver Seeds.* New York: Viking.

Prelutsky, Jack. 1984/2006. *It's Snowing! It's Snowing! Winter Poems.* New York: HarperCollins.

Salas, Laura Purdie. 2008. *Seed Sower, Hat Thrower: Poems About Weather.* Minneapolis, MN: Capstone.

Yolen, Jane. Ed. 1993. *Weather Report.* Honesdale, PA: Wordsong/Boyds Mills.

Yolen, Jane. 1998. *Snow, Snow: Winter Poems for Children.* Honesdale, PA: Wordsong/Boyds Mills.

Yolen, Jane. Ed. 1997. *Once Upon Ice and Other Frozen Poems.* Honesdale, PA: Wordsong/Boyds Mills.

Poetry Books about World History

The people and places of the past from around the globe have also been captured in poetry books for young people, including these examples.

Engle, Margarita. 2006. *The Poet Slave of Cuba: A Biography of Juan Francisco Manzao.* New York: Henry Holt.

Engle, Margarita. 2008. *The Surrender Tree.* New York: Holt.

Engle, Margarita. 2009. *Tropical Secrets: Holocaust Refugees in Cuba.* New York: Holt.

Engle, Margarita. 2010. *The Firefly Letters; A Suffragette's Journey to Cuba.* New York: Henry Holt.

Engle, Margarita. 2011. *Hurricane Dancers; The First Caribbean Pirate Shipwreck.* New York: Henry Holt.

Hemphill, Stephanie. 2012. *Sisters of Glass.* New York: Knopf.

Ho, Minfong. 1996. *Maples in the Mist: Poems for Children from the Tang Dynasty.* New York: Lothrop, Lee, & Shepard.

Janeczko, Paul B. 2011. *Requiem; Poems of the Terezín Ghetto.* Somerville, MA: Candlewick.

Lewis, J. Patrick and Rebecca Kai Dotlich. 2006. *Castles: Old Stone Poems.* Honesdale, PA: Wordsong/Boyds Mills.

Lewis, J. Patrick. 2002. *A World of Wonders: Geographic Travels in Verse and Rhyme.* New York: Dial Books.

Lewis, J. Patrick. 2003. *Galileo's Universe.* Mankato, MN: Creative Editions.

Lewis, J. Patrick. 2005. *Monumental Verses.* Washington, D.C.: National Geographic.

Lewis, J. Patrick. 2008. *Michelangelo's World.* Creative Editions.

Lewis, J. Patrick. 2009. *The House.* Ill. by Roberto Innocenti. Mankato, MN: Creative Editions.

LeZotte, Ann Clare. 2008. *T4.* Boston: Houghton Mifflin.

Roy, Jennifer. 2006. *Yellow Star.* New York:: Marshall Cavendish.

Serrano, Francisco. 2007. *The Poet King of Tezcoco: A Great Leader of Ancient Mexico.* Toronto: Groundwood.

Schlitz, Laura Amy. 2007. *Good Masters! Sweet Ladies!: Voices from a Medieval Village.* Somerville, MA: Candlewick.

Volavkova, Hana. Ed. 1993. *I Never Saw Another Butterfly: Children's Drawings and Poems from Terezin Concentration Camp 1942-1944.* New York: Schocken Books.

Yolen, Jane. 1996. *Sacred Places.* San Diego, CA: Harcourt Brace.

Yu, Chun. 2005. *Little Green: Growing up During the Chinese Cultural Revolution.* New York: Simon & Schuster.

BOOKLISTS HIGHLIGHTING THE FORM OF POETRY

Looking for poetry that takes different forms can lead to a amazing variety of poetry books for young people. For younger readers, you'll find lists of Mother Goose collections, single poem picture books, poetry based on folk rhymes and playground lore, songs, and more. There are lists of riddle poetry, acrostic and concrete poetry, ABC poetry, biographical poetry, limericks, parodies, memoirs, free verse, haiku, and several lists of different variants of verse novels for older readers.

Mother Goose and Nursery Rhymes
Folk Poetry Books for Children
Songs in Poetry Books for Young People
Other Sources of Poetic Language in Books for Young People
Poetry Books for Young People that Showcase Poetic Form
Single Poem Picture Books for Young People
Poetry Books that Feature the Alphabet
Poetry Books that Feature Acrostic Poetry
Riddle Poetry Books for Young People
Poetry Books with Limericks for Young People
Concrete, Visual or Shape Poetry Books for Young People
Books of Poetry Parodies for Young People
Poetry Memoirs for Young People
Point of View in Poetry for Young People
Free Verse Poetry Books for Young People
Poetry Books for Young People Featuring Haiku, Renga, Tanka, and Sijo
Verse Novels for Young Adults
Verse Novels for the Intermediate Grades (Grades 4, 5, 6)
Historical Novels in Verse for Young People
Biographical Poetry Books for Young People

Mother Goose and Nursery Rhymes

For many children, the nursery rhymes of Mother Goose (and other oral traditions) are their first exposure to poetry. They love the regular rhythm and rhyme and utter nonsense of these verses. Other children, however, completely miss hearing these rhymes which is a shame given how often we allude to them in everyday life. Either way, there are many Mother Goose collections available for sharing, including this sampling of titles.

Ada, Alma Flor and Campoy, Isabel. 2010. *Muu, Moo! Rimas de animales/Animal Nursery Rhymes*. New York: Rayo/HarperCollins.

Ada, Alma Flor, and Isabel Campoy, Eds. 2003. *Pio Peep! Traditional Spanish Nursery Rhymes*. New York: HarperCollins.

Addams, Charles. 2002. *The Charles Addams Mother Goose*. New York: Simon & Schuster.

Agard, John, and Nichols, Grace. 1995. *No Hickory, No Dickory, No Dock: Caribbean Nursery Rhymes*. Somerville, MA: Candlewick.

Baring-Gould, William and Ceil Baring-Gould. 1962. *The Annotated Mother Goose, Nursery Rhymes Old and New*. New York: C.N. Potter.

Beaton, Clare. 2000. *Mother Goose Remembers*. New York: Barefoot Books.

Benjamin, Floella, Ed. 1995. *Skip Across the Ocean: Nursery Rhymes from Around the World*. New York: Orchard.

Crews, Nina. 2004. *The Neighborhood Mother Goose*. New York: Greenwillow.

Delacre, Lulu. 2004. *Arrorró Mi Niño: Latino Lullabies and Gentle Games*. New York: Scholastic.

Dillon, Leo and Diane. 2007. *Mother Goose Numbers on the Loose*. Orlando: Harcourt.

Field, Eugene. 2008. *Wynken, Blynken, and Nod*. Illustrated by Giselle Potter. New York: Schwartz and Wade.

Fisher, Blanche. 1941. *The Real Mother Goose*. Chicago: Rand McNally.

Flor, Alma. 2003. *Pío Peep!: Traditional Spanish Nursery Rhymes*. New York: HarperCollins.

Greenberg, David T. 1999. *What Ever Happened To Humpty Dumpty? And Other Surprising Sequels to Mother Goose Rhymes*. New York: Little, Brown.

Hague, Michael. 2001. *Teddy Bears' Mother Goose*. New York: Henry Holt.

Hoberman, Mary Ann. 2005. *You Read to Me, I'll Read to You; Very Short Mother Goose Tales to Read Together*. Ill. by Michael Emberley. New York: Little, Brown.

Hopkins, Lee Bennett. Ed. 1998. *Climb Into My Lap: First Poems To Read Together*. New York: Simon & Schuster.

Hopkins, Lee Bennett. Ed. 1999. *Mother Goose and Her Animal Friends*. New York: Sadlier-Oxford.

Lobel, Arnold. 1997. *The Arnold Lobel Book of Mother Goose*. New York: Knopf.

Long, Sylvia. 1999. *Sylvia Long's Mother Goose*. San Francisco: Chronicle.

Moses, Will. 2003. *Will Moses Mother Goose*. New York: Philomel.

Most, Bernard. 1990. *Four & Twenty Dinosaurs*. New York: HarperRow.

Newcome, Zita. 2002. *Head, Shoulders, Knees, and Toes: And Other Action Rhymes*. Cambridge: Candlewick Press.

Nursery Rhyme Comics; 50 Timeless Rhymes from 50 Celebrated Cartoonists. New York: First Second.

Opie, Iona. 1996. *My Very First Mother Goose.* Somerville, MA: Candlewick.

Opie, Iona. 1999. *Here Comes Mother Goose.* Somerville, MA: Candlewick.

Opie, Iona. 2007. *Mother Goose's Little Treasures.* Somerville, MA: Candlewick.

Opie, Iona and Opie, Peter. 2000. *I Saw Esau: The Schoolchild's Pocket Book.* Ill. by Maurice Sendak. Somerville, MA: Candlewick.

Orozco, Jose-Luis. 1997. *Ten Little Fingers and Other Play Rhymes and Action Songs from Latin America* New York: Dutton.

Peck, Jan and Davis, David. (Eds.) 2011. *The Green Mother Goose; Saving the World One Rhyme at a Time.* Ill. by Carin Berger. New York: Sterling.

Penney, Ian. 1994. *Ian Penney's Book of Nursery Rhymes.* New York: Abrams.

Prelutsky, Jack. 1986. *Ride a Purple Pelican* New York: Greenwillow.

Prelutsky, Jack. 1990. *Beneath a Blue Umbrella* New York: Greenwillow.

Rosenberg, Liz. 1994. *Mama Goose: a New Mother Goose.* New York: Philomel.

Sanderson, Ruth. 2008. *Mother Goose and Friends.* New York: Little, Brown.

Scheffler, Axel. 2007. *Mother Goose's Storytime Nursery Rhymes.* New York: Scholastic.

Sierra, Judy. 2001. *Monster Goose.* San Diego: Gulliver Books.

Wheeler, Lisa. 2011. *Spinster Goose; Twisted Rhymes for Naughty Children.* New York: Atheneum.

Yaccarino, Dan. 2004. *Dan Yaccarino's Mother Goose.* New York: Random House.

Yolen, Jane. 2006. *Little Piggy: Lap Songs, Finger Plays, Clapping Games, and Pantomime Rhymes.* Somerville, MA: Candlewick.

Yolen, Jane. 1994. *Sleep Rhymes around the World.* Honesdale, PA: Boyds Mills/Wordsong.

Yolen, Jane. 2000. *Street Rhymes From Around the World.* Honesdale, PA: Boyds Mills/Wordsong.

Yolen, Jane. 1992. *Mother Goose Songbook.* Honesdale, PA: Wordsong/Boyds Mills.

Ziefert, Harriet. 1997. *Mother Goose Math.* New York: Viking.

Folk Poetry Books for Children

Many children—and adults—don't realize that the silly songs, rollicking rhymes, and nonsense games we learn in early childhood are indeed a form of literature. Folk poetry is the poetry you don't even realize is poetry. Rhymes on the playground like "Cinderella dressed in yellow" have no known author and yet are familiar to many generations of children. Books of riddles, chants, jumprope rhymes, finger plays, handclapping games, autograph sayings and often contain poetry and verse. What's more, children are often intrigued to find in print the verses they have heard and known only orally and only in the domain outside of school—at home and at play. Here are some notable collections of folk poetry that are appealing to audiences of all ages.

Ada, Alma Flor, and Isabel Campoy. Ed. 2003. *Pio Peep! Traditional Spanish Nursery Rhymes.* New York: HarperCollins.

Chambers, Veronica. 2002. *Double Dutch: A Celebration of Jump Rope, Rhyme, and Sisterhood.* New York: Hyperion.

Cole, Joanna and Calmenson, Stephanie. 1990. *Miss Mary Mack and Other Children's Street Rhymes.* New York: Morrow.

Cole, Joanna and Calmenson, Stephanie. 1991. *The Eentsy Weensy Spider: Finger Plays and Action Rhymes.* New York: Morrow.

Cole, Joanna and Calmenson, Stephanie. 1992. *Pat-a-cake and Other Play Rhymes.* New York: Morrow.

Cole, Joanna, and Stephanie Calmenson. 1995. *Yours Till Banana Splits: 201 Autograph Rhymes.* New York: HarperCollins.

Cole, Joanna. 1989. *Anna Banana: 101 Jump-Rope Rhymes.* New York: HarperCollins.

Corbett, Pie. 2000. *The Kingfisher Playtime Treasury: A Collection of Playground Rhymes, Games, and Action Songs.* New York: Kingfisher.

Delacre, Lulu. 1989. *Arroz con Leche: Popular Songs and Rhymes from Latin America.* New York: Scholastic.

Delacre, Lulu. 2004. *Arrorró Mi Niño: Latino Lullabies and Gentle Games.* New York: Lee & Low.

Delamar, Gloria. 1983. *Children's Counting-out Rhymes, Finger Plays, Jump Rope and Bounce Ball Chants and Other Rhythms.* Jefferson: McFarland.

Dotlich, Rebecca Kai. 2004. *Over In the Pink House: New Jump Rope Rhymes.* Honesdale, PA: Wordsong/Boyds Mills.

Dunn, Sonja. 1994. *Gimme a Break, Rattlesnake! Schoolyard Chants and Other Nonsense.* Toronto: Stoddart.

Factor, June and Hannan, Siobhan. 2000. *Kidspeak: A Dictionary of Australian Children's Colloquial Words, Expressions and Games.* Carlton South: Melbourne University Press.

Factor, June. 1983. *Far Out, Brussel Sprout: Australian Children's Chants and Rhymes.* New York: Oxford University Press.

Factor, June. 1989. *Captain Cook Chased a Chook: Children's Folklore in Australia.* New York: Penguin.

Foreman, Michael. 2002. *Michael Foreman's Playtime Rhymes*. Somerville, MA: Candlewick.

Harwayne, Shelley. 1995. *Jewels: Children's Play Rhymes*. New York: Mondo Publishing.

Jaramillo, Nelly Palacio. 1994. *Grandmother's Nursery Rhymes/Las Nanas De Abuelita: Lullabies, Tongue Twisters, and Riddles from South America/Canciones De Cuna, Trabalenguas Y Adivinanzas De Suramerica*. New York: Holt.

Michels, Barbara, and Bettye White. Eds. 1983. *Apples on a Stick: The Folklore of Black Children*. New York: Coward-McCann.

Morrison, Lillian. 1997. *I Scream, You Scream: A Feast of Food Rhymes*. Little Rock: August House Little Folk.

Newcombe, Zita. 2002. *Head, Shoulders, Knees, and Toes and other Action Rhymes*. Somerville, MA: Candlewick.

Opie, Iona and Peter. 1992. *I saw Esau: The Schoolchild's Pocket Book*. Cambridge, MA: Candlewick.

Orozco, José-Luis. 1997. *Diez deditos: Ten Little Fingers & Other Play Rhymes and Action Songs from Latin America*. New York: Puffin Books.

Petersham, Maud and Miska. (reissued, 1987). *The Rooster Crows*. New York: Aladdin Books.

Schwartz, Alvin. 1992. *And the Green Grass Grew all Around: Folk Poetry from Everyone*. New York: HarperCollins.

Sierra, Judy. 2005. *Schoolyard Rhymes: Kids' Own Rhymes for Rope Skipping, Hand Clapping, Ball Bouncing, and Just Plain Fun*. New York: Knopf.

Solomon. 1980. *Zickary Zan: Childhood Folklore*. Tuscaloosa, AL: University of Alabama Press.

Yolen, Jane. 1992. *Street Rhymes Around the World*. Honesdale, PA: Wordsong/Boyds Mills.

Yolen, Jane. 1994. *Sleep Rhymes Around the World*. Honesdale, PA: Wordsong/Boyds Mills.

Songs in Poetry Books for Young People

The link between songs and poetry is very close, with lyrics and poems sharing rhythm, rhyme, and emotional content. Singing songs and performing poems can also share similarities in maximizing the oral medium, incorporating musical or percussion instruments, and using gesture and movement. From lullabies to parodies, here are a few examples of songs, lyrics, and poems in book form.

Andrews, Julie and Hamilton, Emma Watson. Eds. 2009. *Julie Andrews' Collection of Poems, Songs, and Lullabies. Ill. by James McMullan.* New York: Little, Brown.

Bates, Katherine L. 1994. *O Beautiful for Spacious Skies.* San Francisco: Chronicle Books.

Bruchac, Joseph. 1996. *Four Ancestors: Stories, Songs, and Poems from Native North America.* Mahwah, NJ: BridgeWater Books.

Bryan, Ashley. 2003. *All Night, All Day: A Child's First Book of African-American Spirituals.* New York: Atheneum.

Carroll, Lewis. 1998. *"Twinkle, Twinkle Little Bat:" Poems and Songs from Alice's Adventures in Wonderland and Through the Looking- Glass.* London: Macmillan.

Cohn, Amy 1993. *From Sea to Shining Sea: A Treasury of American Folklore and Folk Songs* New York: Scholastic.

Creech, Sharon. 2005. *Who's that Baby?: New-Baby Songs.* New York: Joanna Cotler Books.

Delacre, Lulu, Ed. 1992. *Arroz con Leche: Popular Songs and Rhymes from Latin America.* New York: Scholastic.

Delacre, Lulu, Ed. 1992. *Las Navidades: Popular Christmas Songs from Latin America.* New York: Scholastic.

Delacre, Lulu. 2004. *Arrorró Mi Niño: Latino Lullabies and Gentle Games.* New York: Lee & Low.

Fox, Dan. Ed. 2003. *A Treasury of Children's Songs: Forty Favorites to Sing and Play.* New York: Henry Holt.

Hallworth, Grace, Ed. 1996. *Down by the River: Afro-Caribbean Rhymes, Games, and Songs for Children.* New York: Scholastic.

Henderson, Kathy. 2011. *Hush, Baby, Hush! Lullabies from Around the World.* Seattle: Frances Lincoln.

Hopkins, Lee Bennett. Ed. 1997. *Song and Dance: Poems.* New York: Simon & Schuster.

Hudson, Wade & Cheryl. 1995. *How Sweet the Sound: African- American Songs for Children.* New York Scholastic.

Katz, Alan. 2001. *Take Me Out of the Bathtub and Other Silly Dilly Songs.* New York: McElderry.

Katz, Alan. 2003. *I'm Still Here in the Bathtub; Brand New Silly Dilly Songs.* New York: McElderry.

Katz, Alan. 2005. *Where Did They Hide My Presents? Silly Dilly Christmas Songs.* New York: McElderry.

Katz, Alan. 2006. *Are You Quite Polite? Silly Dilly Manners Songs.* New York: McElderry.

Katz, Alan. 2008. *On Top of the Potty: And Other Get-Up-and-Go Songs.* New York: McElderry.

Katz, Alan. 2008. *Smelly Locker; Silly Dilly School Songs.* New York: Simon & Schuster.

Katz, Alan. 2009. *Going, Going, Gone!: And Other Silly Dilly Sports Songs.* New York: Simon & Schuster.

Katz, Alan. 2010. *Too Much Kissing; And Other Silly Dilly Songs About Parents.* Simon & Schuster.

Katz, Alan. 2011. *Mosquitoes Are Ruining My Summer! And Other Silly Dilly Camp Songs.* New York: McElderry.

Lessac, Frane, Ed. 2003. *Camp Granada: Sing-Along Camp Songs.* New York: Henry Holt.

Lewis, J. Patrick. 2000. *Freedom Like Sunlight: Praisesongs for Black Americans.* Mankato, MN: Creative Editions.

Morgenstern, Christian. 1995. *Lullabies, Lyrics and Gallows Songs.* New York: North-South Books.

Ode, Eric. 2007. *Tall Tales of the Wild West (and a few short ones): A Humorous Collection of Cowboy Poems and Songs.* New York: Meadowbrook Press.

Orozco, José-Luis. 1994. *De Colores and Other Latin American Folk Songs for Children.* New York: Dutton.

Orozco, José-Luis. 1997. *Diez Deditos: Ten Little Fingers and Other Play Rhymes and Action Songs from Latin America.* New York: Dutton.

Orozco, José-Luis. 2002. *Fiestas: A Year of Latin American Songs of Celebration.* New York: Dutton Children's Books.

Philip, Neil. 1995. Ed. *Songs are Thoughts: Poems of the Inuit.* New York: Orchard Books.

Pilling, Ann. 2000. Ed. *A Kingfisher Treasury of Bible Stories, Poems, and Prayers for Bedtime.* New York: Kingfisher.

Plume, Ilse. 1994. *Lullaby and Goodnight: Songs and Poems for Babies.* New York: HarperCollins.

Schwartz, Alvin. Ed. 1992. *And the Green Grass Grew All Around: Folk Poetry from Everyone.* New York: HarperCollins.

Silberg, Jackie and Pam Schiller. 2002. Ed. *The Edlete Book of Rhymes, Songs, Poems, Fingerplays, and Chants.* Beltsville: Gryphon House.

Strickland, Michael R. 1997. *My Own Song: and other Poems to Groove to.* Honesdale: Wordsong/Boyds Mills Press.

Swann, Brian. 1996. *Wearing the Morning Star: Native American Song-Poems.* New York: Random House.

Thomas, Joyce Carol. 2000. *Hush Songs: African American Lullabies.* New York: Hyperion.

Yolen, Jane. 1992. *Mother Goose Songbook.* Honesdale, PA: Wordsong/Boyds Mills Press.

Yolen, Jane. 2005. *Trot, Trot to Boston: Lap Songs, Finger Plays, Clapping Games, and Pantomime Rhymes.* Somerville, MA: Cambridge: Candlewick Press.

Zemach, Margot. 2001. *Some from the Moon, Some from the Sun: Poems and Songs for Everyone.* New York: Farrar, Straus and Giroux.

Other Sources of Poetic Language in Books for Young People

There are many types of books that are written in rhyme and might loosely be considered "poetry." They certainly hold a great deal of appeal to children who enjoy the music of the language when these books are read aloud. In fact, once you start looking you may be surprised at all the different places rhyme and poetry are appearing. Technically, many of these books might not be considered "poetry." They may be written in rhyme, but the words probably would not stand alone published as a poem. However, these books do make the point that poetry, rhyme, and verse are all around us.

1. Rhyming picture books (for example, *Move Over Rover* by Karen Beaumont; Harcourt, 2006)
2. Rhythmic picture books (for example, *Good Night Moon* by Margaret Wise Brown; Harper, 1947)
3. Predictable books (for example, *Brown Bear, Brown Bear* by Bill Martin, Jr.; Holt, 1992)
4. Alphabet books (for example, *Chicka Chicka Boom Boom* by Bill Martin, Jr. and John Archambault; Simon & Schuster, 1989)
5. Counting books (for example, *Counting Crocodiles* by Judy Sierra; Gulliver, 1997)
6. Dr. Seuss's picture books (for example, *Oh, the Places You'll Go!*; Random House, 1990)
7. Rhyming nonfiction picture books (for example, *Flush, The Scoop on Poop* by Charise Mericle Harper; Little, Brown, 2007)
8. Easy-to-read books (*"Not Now!" Said the Cow* by Joanne Oppenheim; Bantam, 1989)
9. Song-based picture books (*Mary had a Little Lamb* photo-illustrated by Bruce McMillan; Scholastic, 1992)
10. Folklore in book form (*Arroz con Leche* collected by Lulu Delacre; Scholastic, 1992)
11. Bible stories and spirituals (*Climbing Jacob's Ladder* collected by Ashley Bryan; McElderry, 1991)
12. Jump rope and ball bouncing rhymes (*Anna Banana* by Joanna Cole; HarperCollins, 1989)
13. Clapping games, chants, cheers (*Street Rhymes around the World* by Jane Yolen; Wordsong/Boyds Mills, 1992)
14. Street songs and raps (*Night on Neighborhood Street* by Eloise Greenfield; Puffin, 1996)
15. Riddles, tongue twisters, counting games, nonsense verse (*And the Green Grass Grew All Around* collected by Alvin Schwartz; HarperCollins, 1992)

Based on: Vardell, Sylvia. 2008. *Children's Literature in Action: A Librarian's Guide*. Libraries Unlimited.

Poetry Books for Young People that Showcase Poetic Form

Children enjoy discovering the different forms and shapes that poems can take, particularly unusual forms of poetry. Often they even want to try their hands at imitating the form and writing their own. Every book of poetry has elements of poetic form, of course, but the following books are specifically conceived and organized to showcase the form of poetry or variety in poetic forms.

Cleary, Brian P. 2004. *Rainbow Soup: Adventures in Poetry.* Minneapolis: Carolrhoda.

Dotlich, Rebecca. 2001. *When Riddles Come Rumbling.* Honesdale: Wordsong/Boyds Mills.

Florian, Douglas. 1994. *Bing Bang Boing: Poems and Drawings.* San Diego, CA: Harcourt Brace.

Florian, Douglas. 1999. *Laugh-eteria: Poems and Drawings.* San Diego, CA: Harcourt Brace.

Frost, Helen. 2004. *Spinning through the Universe: a Novel in Poems from Room 214.* New York: Farrar, Straus & Giroux.

Graham, Joan Bransfield. 1999. *Flicker Flash.* Boston: Houghton Mifflin.

Graham, Joan Bransfield. 1994. *Splish Splash.* Boston: Houghton Mifflin.

Grandits, John. 2004. *Technically, It's Not My Fault: Concrete Poems.* New York: Clarion.

Grandits, John. 2007. *Blue Lipstick: Concrete Poems.* New York: Clarion.

Harley, Avis. 2000. *Fly With Poetry: An ABC of Poetry* New York: Wordsong/Boyds Mills.

Harley, Avis. 2001. *Leap into Poetry: More ABC's of Poetry.* Honesdale, PA: Wordsong/Boyds Mills.

Holbrook, Sara and Allan Wolf. 2008. *More than Friends: Poems from Him and Her.* Honesdale, PA: Wordsong/Boyds Mills.

Janeczko, Paul B. 2005. *A Kick in the Head.* Somerville, MA: Candlewick.

Janeczko, Paul B. 1994. *Poetry from A to Z: A Guide for Young Writers.* Somerville, MA: Candlewick.

Janeczko, Paul B. Ed. 2002. *Seeing the Blue Between: Advice and Inspiration for Young Poets.* Somerville, MA: Candlewick.

Janeczko, Paul B.. 2006. *Wing Nuts: Screwy Haiku.* New York: Little Brown.

Kennedy, X.J and Dorothy Kennedy. Eds. 1999. *Knock at a Star: A Child's Introduction to Poetry* (Revised edition). New York: Little Brown.

Koertge, Ron. 2010. *Shakespeare Makes the Playoffs.* Somerville, MA: Candlewick.

Lewis, J. Patrick, and Janeczko, Paul B. 2008. *Birds on a Wire.* Honesdale, PA: Wordsong/Boyds Mills Press.

Lewis, J. Patrick. 2009. *Countdown to Summer: A Poem for Every Day of the School Year.* Ill. by Ethan Long. New York: Little, Brown.

Mora, Pat. 2007. *Yum! Mmmm! Que Rico!: America's Sproutings.* New York: Lee & Low.

Mora, Pat. 2010. *Dizzy in My Eyes.* New York: Knopf.

Prelutsky, Jack. 2005. *Read a Rhyme, Write a Rhyme.* New York: Random House.

Raczka, Bob. 2011. *Lemonade and Other Poems Squeezed from a Single Word*. New York: Roaring Brook.

Salas, Laura Purdie. 2008. *Flashy, Clashy, and oh-so Splashy: Poems about Color*. Mankato: Capstone Press.

Salas, Laura Purdie. 2009. *A Fuzzy-Fast Blur: Poems about Pets*. Mankato: Capstone.

Salas, Laura Purdie. 2011. *BookSpeak!*. Ill. by Josee Bisaillon. Clarion.

Salinger, Michael. 2009. *Well Defined; Vocabulary in Rhyme*. Ill. by Sam Henderson. Honesdale, PA: Wordsong/Boyds Mills Press.

Singer, Marilyn. 2010. *Mirror, Mirror*. New York: Dutton.

Vardell, Sylvia and Wong, Janet. Eds. 2011. *P*TAG*. PoetryTagTime.com.

Vardell, Sylvia and Wong, Janet. Eds. 2011. *PoetryTagTime*. PoetryTagTime.com.

Vardell, Sylvia and Wong, Janet. Eds. 2011. *Gift Tag: Holiday Poetry for Children and Young Adults*. PoetryTagTime.com.

Young, Judy. 2006. *R is for Rhyme: a Poetry Alphabet*. Chelsea: Sleeping Bear Press.

Zimmer, Tracie Vaughn. 2011. *Cousins of Clouds; Elephant Poems*. Boston: Houghton Mifflin.

Single Poem Picture Books for Young People

Many works of poetry for children are published in picture book form, but they rarely contain a single poem. That is the purview of the "poem picture book," a presentation of a single poem spread across the pages of a picture book, line by line. This format provides an excellent opportunity to re-interpret classic poems such as in the following examples.

Bates, Katharine Lee. 1994. *O Beautiful for Spacious Skies*. Ill. by Wayne Thiebaud. New York: Chronicle.

Carroll, Lewis. 2004. *Jabberwocky*. Ill. by Stephane Jorisch. Toronto: Kids Can Press.

Field, Eugene. 2008. *Wynken, Blynken, and Nod*. Ill. by Giselle Potter. New York: Schwartz and Wade.

Frost, Helen. 2012. *Step Gently Out*. Ill. by Rick Lieder. Somerville, MA: Candlewick.

Frost, Robert. 1978/2001. *Stopping by Woods on a Snowy Evening*. Ill. by Susan Jeffers. New York: Dutton.

Johnson, James Weldon. 1995. *Lift Ev'ry Voice and Sing*. Ill. by Jan Spivey Gilchrist. New York: Scholastic.

Lear, Edward. 2007. *The Owl and the Pussycat*. Ill. by Stephane Jorisch. Toronto: Kids Can Press.

Lear, Edward/Pinkwater, Daniel. 2011. *His Shoes Were Far Too Tight*. Ill. by Calef Brown. San Francisco: Chronicle.

Livingston, Myra Cohn. 2007. *Calendar*. Ill. by Will Hillenbrand. New York: Holiday House.

Longfellow, Henry Wadsworth. 1990. *Paul Revere's Ride*. Ill. by Ted Rand. New York: Dutton.

Longfellow, Henry Wadsworth. 2001. *The Midnight Ride of Paul Revere*. Ill. by Christopher Bing. New York: Handprint.

Mora, Pat. 1998. *Delicious Hullabaloo/Pachanga Deliciosa*. Houston, TX: Pinata Books.

Myers, Walter Dean. 1997. *Harlem*. Ill. by Christopher Myers. New York: Scholastic.

Noyes, Alfred. 2005. *The Highwayman*. Ill. by Murray Kimber. Toronto: Kids Can Press.

Poe, Edgar Allan. 2006. *The Raven*. Ill. by Ryan Price. Toronto: Kids Can Press.

Schertle, Alice. 2007. *We*. New York: Lee & Low.

Siebert, Diane. 2000. *Cave*. Ill. by Wayne McLoughlin. New York: HarperCollins.

Stevenson, Robert Louis. 2005. *Block City*. Ill. by Daniel Kirk. New York: Simon & Schuster.

Tennyson, Alfred Lord. 2005. *The Lady of Shalott*. Ill. by Geneviève Côté. Toronto: Kids Can Press.

Thayer, Ernest Lawrence. 2000. *Casey at the Bat*. Ill. by Christopher Bing. New York: Handprint.

Thayer, Ernest Lawrence. 2006. *Casey at the Bat*. Ill. by Joe Morse. Toronto: Kids Can Press.

Poetry Books that Feature the Alphabet

The alphabet has served as the organizing framework for poetry for generations, as far back as "in Adam's fall/ we sinned all," if not further. Below is a sampling of poetry books for children that are built around the letters of the alphabet.

Ashman, Linda. 2008. *M is for Mischief; An A to Z of Naughty Children*. New York: Dutton.

Ada, Alma Flor. 1997. *Gathering the Sun: An Alphabet in Spanish and English*. New York: Harper.

Bryan, Ashley. 1997. *Ashley Bryan's ABC of African American Poetry*. New York: Atheneum.

Curtis, Tony. 2011. *An Elephant Called Rex and A Dog Called Dumbo: An A to Z of Children's Poetry*. Ill. by Pat Mooney. London: Black Hills .

Dakos, Kalli. 1997. *Get out of the Alphabet, Number 2!: Wacky Wednesday Puzzle Poems*. New York: Simon & Schuster.

Grimes, Nikki. 1995. *C is for City*. New York: Lothrop, Lee & Shepard.

Harley, Avis. 2000. *Fly with Poetry; An ABC of Poetry*. Honesdale: Wordsong/Boyds Mills.

Harley, Avis. 2001. *Leap into Poetry: More ABCs of Poetry*. Honesdale: Wordsong/Boyds Mills.

Hopkins, Lee Bennett. 2003. *Alphathoughts*. Honesdale: Boyds Mills Press.

Hopkins, Lee Bennett. 1994. *April Bubbles Chocolate*. New York: Simon & Schuster.

Hughes, Langston. 1994. *The Sweet and Sour Animal Book*. New York : Oxford University Press.

Janeczko. Paul. Ed. 1994. *Poetry from A to Z: A Guide for Young Writers*. New York: Simon & Schuster.

MacDonald, Suse. 2005. *Edward Lear's A was Once an Apple Pie*. Orchard.

Marsalis, Wynton. 2005. *Jazz ABZ: An A to Z Collection of Jazz Portraits*. Somerville, MA: Candlewick.

Merriam, Eve. 2002. *Spooky A B C*. New York: Simon & Schuster.

Paul, A. W. 1996. *Eight Hands Round: A Patchwork Alphabet*. New York: HarperTrophy.

Schnur, Steven. 1997. *Autumn: An Alphabet Acrostic*. New York: Clarion.

Schnur, Steven. 1999. *Spring: An Alphabet Acrostic*. New York: Clarion.

Schnur, Steven. 2001. *Summer: An Alphabet Acrostic*. New York: Clarion.

Schnur, Steven. 2002. *Winter: An Alphabet Acrostic*. New York: Clarion.

Sierra, Judy. 2004. *There's a Zoo in Room 22*. San Diego: Harcourt.

Steig, Jeanne. 1992. *Alpha Beta Chowder*. New York: HarperCollins.

Updike, John. 1995. *A Helpful Alphabet of Friendly Objects: Poems*. Knopf.

Viorst, Judith. 1994. *The Alphabet from Z to A: (with much confusion on the way)* New York: Atheneum.

Wilbur, Richard. 2001. *The Disappearing Alphabet*. Orlando: Voyager.

Willard, Nancy. 1994. *An Alphabet of Angels*. New York: Scholastic.

Yolen, Jane. 1994. *Alphabestiary: Animal Poems from A to Z*. Honesdale, PA: Wordsong/Boyds Mills.

Young, Judy. 2006. *R Is for Rhyme: A Poetry Alphabet*. Chelsea: Sleeping Bear Press.

Poetry Books that Feature Acrostic Poetry

The acrostic form of poetry is very appealing to children because of its puzzle-like nature. A word, phrase, or even sentence appears vertically in a left-hand column and the lines of the poem begin with each letter of that word, phrase or sentence. Here are a few collections of poetry that include acrostic poems.

Frost, Helen. 2003. *Keesha's House*. New York: Farrar, Straus & Giroux.

Frost, Helen. 2004. *Spinning through the Universe*. New York: Farrar, Straus & Giroux.

Harley, Avis. 2009. *African Acrostics; A Word in Edgeways*. Cambridge, MA: Candlewick.

Hopkins, Lee Bennett, comp. 1988. *Side by Side: Poems to Read Together*. New York: Simon & Schuster.

Hummon, David. 1999. *Animal Acrostics*. Nevada City, CA: Dawn Publications.

Janeczko, Paul B, comp. 1994. *Poetry from A to Z: A Guide for Young Writers*. New York: Bradbury.

Janeczko, Paul B., ed. 2005. *A Kick in the Head: An Everyday Guide to Poetic Forms*. Cambridge, MA: Candlewick.

Lewis, J. Patrick. 2005. *Please Bury Me In The Library*. Orlando, FL: Gulliver Books/Harcourt.

Lewis, J. Patrick. 2009. *Countdown to Summer: A Poem for Every Day of the School Year*. New York: Little, Brown.

Mora, Pat. 2010. *Dizzy in My Eyes*. New York: Knopf.

Paolilli, Paul and Brewer, Dan. 2001. *Silver Seeds*. New York: Viking

Salas, Laura Purdie. 2011. *BookSpeak!*. Clarion.

Salas, Laura. 2009. *Stampede! Poems to Celebrate the Wild Side of School!* New York: Clarion.

Schnur, Steven. 1997. *Autumn: An Alphabet Acrostic*. New York: Clarion.

Schnur, Steven. 1999. *Spring: An Alphabet Acrostic*. New York: Clarion.

Schnur, Steven. 2001. *Summer: An Alphabet Acrostic*. New York: Clarion.

Schnur, Steven. 2002. *Winter: An Alphabet Acrostic*. New York: Clarion.

Riddle Poetry Books for Young People

The riddle is an intriguing logic puzzle that children enjoy, particularly "gifted and talented" kids. Several poets use the riddle form (with question, guess, and answer) in creating poetry, particularly in these collections.

Bloom, Valerie. 2003. *Whoop an' Shout!* London: Macmillan.
Calmenson, Stephanie. Ed. 2005. *Kindergarten Kids: Riddles, Rebuses, Wiggles, Giggles, and More!* New York: HarperCollins.
Dotlich, Rebecca Kai. 2001. *When Riddles Come Rumbling: Poems to Ponder.* Honesdale, PA: Wordsong/Boyds Mills Press.
Foster, John. 2000. *Fireworks: a Book of Wordplay Poems.* Oxford: Oxford.
Ghigna, Charles. 1995. *Riddle Rhymes.* New York: Hyperion.
Greenfield, Eloise. 2004. *In the Land of Words: New and Selected Poems.* New York: HarperCollins.
Lewis, J. Patrick. 1996. *Riddle-icious.* New York: Knopf.
Lewis, J. Patrick. 1998. *Riddle-lightful.* New York: Knopf.
Lewis, J. Patrick. 2002. *Arithmetickle.* San Diego: Harcourt.
Lewis, J. Patrick. 2004. *Scien-trickery: Riddles in Science.* Harcourt.
Lewis, J. Patrick. 2009. *Countdown To Summer: A Poem For Every Day Of The School Year.* New York: Little, Brown.
Lewis, J. Patrick. 2009. *Spot the Plot; A Riddle Book of Book Riddles.* San Francisco: Chronicle.
Livingston, Myra Cohn. 1990. *My Head is Red, and other Riddle Rhymes.* New York: Holiday House.
Morrison, Lillian. 2006. *Guess Again!: Riddle Poems.* August House.
Nims, Bonnie Larkin. 1992. *Just Beyond Reach and Other Riddle Poems.* New York: Scholastic.
Shannon, George. 2006. *Busy in the Garden.* New York: Greenwillow.
Sidman, Joyce. 2006. *Butterfly Eyes and Other Secrets of the Meadow.* Boston: Houghton Mifflin.
Sierra, Judy. 1998. *Antarctic Antics: A Book of Penguin Poems.* San Diego: Harcourt Brace.
Sneve, Virginia Driving. 1991. *Dancing Teepees: Poems of American Indian Youth.* New York: Scholastic.
Spires, Elizabeth. 1995. *With one White Wing: Puzzles in Poems and Pictures.* New York: M.K. McElderry Books.
Spires, Elizabeth. 1999. *Riddle Road: Puzzles in Poems and Pictures.* New York: M.K. McElderry Books.
Swann, Brian. 1998. *The House with no Door: African Riddle-Poems.* San Diego: Harcourt Brace.
Swann, Brian. 1998. *Touching the Distance: Native American Riddle-Poems.* San Diego: Browndeer Press.
Swann, Brian. 1998. *Touching the Distance: Native American Riddle-Poems.* San Diego: Harcourt.
Swenson, May. 1993. *The Complete Poems to Solve.* New York: Maxwell Macmillan International.
Willard, Nancy. 2001. *The Moon & Riddles Diner and the Sunnyside Cafe.* San Diego: Harcourt.

Poetry Books with Limericks for Young People

The five-line poem form of the limerick has a lot of appeal to kids with its distinctive rhyme scheme and humorous content. Several books of poetry for children include this form made popular by Edward Lear including the following.

Barron, Kathryn. 1995. *Critter Crackers: the ABC Book of Limericks.* Kansas City: Landmark Editions.

Brooks, Lou. 2009. *Twimericks; The Book of Tongue Twisting Limericks.* New York: Workman.

Ciardi, John. 1989. *The Hopeful Trout and Other Limericks.* Boston: Houghton Mifflin.

Cleary, Brian P. 2004. *Rainbow Soup: Adventures in Poetry.* Minneapolis: Carolrhoda Books.

Driscoll, Michael. 2003. *A Child's Introduction to Poetry.* New York: Black Dog & Leventhal.

Florian, Douglas. 1999. *Laugh-eteria: Poems and Drawings.* San Diego: Harcourt Brace.

Hopkins, Lee Bennett, Ed. 2005. *Days to Celebrate: A Full Year of Poetry, People, Holidays, History, Fascinating Facts, and More.* New York: Greenwillow.

Hubbell, Patricia. 1998. *Boo!: Halloween Poems and Limericks.* New York: Marshall Cavendish.

Janeczko, Paul B., Ed. 2005. *A Kick in the Head: An Everyday Guide to Poetic Forms.* Somerville, MA:Candlewick.

Kennedy, X. J. 1997. *Uncle Switch: Loony Limericks.* New York: McElderry.

Kennedy, X. J. and Dorothy M. Kennedy. 1999. *Knock at a Star: A Child's Introduction to Poetry.* New York: Little, Brown.

Krensky, Stephen. 2004. *There Once was a Very Odd School and Other Lunch-box Limericks.* New York: Dutton.

Lear, Edward. 1994. *There was an Old Man--: A Gallery of Nonsense Rhymes.* New York: Morrow.

Lewis, J. Patrick. 1998. *Boshblobberbosh; Runcible Poems for Edward Lear.* Mankato: Creative Editions.

Lewis, J. Patrick. 2009. *Countdown To Summer: A Poem For Every Day of the School Year.* New York: Little, Brown.

Livingston, Myra Cohn. 1991. *Lots of Limericks.* New York: McElderry.

Lobel, Arnold. 1983. *The Book of Pigericks.* New York: Harper.

Manley, Molly. 1994. *Talkaty Talker: Limericks.* Honesdale: Boyds Mills Press.

Pearson, Susan. 2005. *Grimericks.* New York: Marshall Cavendish.

Rovetch, Gerda. 2008. *There was a Man Who Loved a Rat and Other Terrible Little Poems.* New York: Philomel.

Smith, William Jay. 2000. *Around My Room.* New York: Farrar, Straus & Giroux.

Stockland, Patricia M. 2004. *Cobwebs, Chatters, and Chills: A Collection of Scary Poems.* Minneapolis: Edass Point Books.

Concrete, Visual or Shape Poetry Books for Young People

In concrete poetry (also known as visual poetry or shape poetry) the words of the poems are laid out on the page to suggest the subject of the poem. Children typically enjoy concrete poetry and take pleasure in the poet's creative use of the physical shape of the poem to convey meaning. It's a poetic form they like imitating and experimenting with, too. Here are a few examples of some of the poetry books that contain this fascinating form.

Adoff, Arnold. 2000. *The Basket Counts.* New York: Simon & Schuster.

Burg, Brad. 2002. *Outside the Lines: Poetry at Play.* New York: Putnam.

Douthwaite, Gina. 2002. *What Shapes an Ape? Animal Shape Poems.* London: Red Fox.

Fehler, Gene. 2009. *Change-up: Baseball Poems.* New York: Clarion.

Florian, Douglas. 2003. *Bow Wow Meow Meow: it's Rhyming Cats and Dogs.* San Diego: Harcourt.

Franco, Betsy. 2009. *A Curious Collection of Cats.* Ill. by Michael Wertz. San Francisco, CA: Tricycle.

Franco, Betsy. 2011. A *Dazzling Display of Dogs.* Ill. by Michael Wertz. San Francisco, CA: Tricycle.

Foster, John. 1998. *Word Whirls and other Shape Poems.* Oxford: Oxford University Press.

George, Kristine O'Connell. 2001. *Toasting Marshmallows: Camping Poems.* New York: Clarion.

Graham, Joan Bransfield. 1999. *Flicker Flash.* Boston: Houghton Mifflin.

Graham, Joan Bransfield.. 1994. *Splish Splash.* Boston: Houghton Mifflin.

Grandits, John. 2007. *Blue Lipstick: Concrete Poems.* New York: Clarion.

Grandits, John. 2004. *Technically, It's Not My Fault: Concrete Poems.* New York: Clarion.

Hegley, John. 2003. *My Dog is a Carrot.* Somerville, MA: Candlewick.

Heide, Florence Perry, Judith Heide Gilliland and Roxanne Heide Pierce. 1999. *It's about Time: Poems.* New York: Clarion.

Honey, Elizabeth. 2004. *Honey Sandwich.* New York: Knopf.

Hopkins, Lee Bennett. 2002. *Hoofbeats, Claws, & Rippled Fins: Creature Poems.* New York: HarperCollins.

Janeczko, Paul. 2001. *A Poke in the I.* Somerville, MA: Candlewick.

Janeczko, Paul B. Ed. 2005. *A Kick in the Head: An Everyday Guide to Poetic Forms.* Somerville, MA: Candlewick.

Lewis, J. Patrick. 1998. *Doodle Dandies: Poems that take Shape.* New York: Atheneum.

Lewis, J. Patrick. 2007. *Under the Kissletoe: Christmastime Poems.* Honesdale, PA: Wordsong/Boyds Mills.

Livingston, Myra Cohn. 1992. *I Never Told and other Poems.* New York: McElderry.

Prelutzsky, Jack. 2001. *It's Raining Pigs and Noodles.* New York: HarperCollins.

Roemer, Heidi. 2004. *Come to my Party and other Shape Poems.* New York: Henry Holt.

Sidman, Joyce. 2006. *Meow Ruff: A Story in Concrete Poetry.* Ill. by Michelle Berg. Boston: Houghton Mifflin.

Books of Poetry Parodies for Young People

In addition to being a time for celebrating poetry, April is also National Humor Month. That makes it a good time to introduce the concept of "parody" or "homage" too. This can be a particularly engaging exercise for young people in middle school and high school, in particular, offering a fun "backdoor" approach to the originals. The following titles are a few that offer a parody, riff, or twist on a classic poem, poet or other medium.

Dahl, Roald. 2005. *Vile Verses*. New York: Viking.

Katz, Alan. 2001. *Take Me Out of the Bathtub and Other Silly Dilly Songs*. New York: McElderry.

Katz, Alan. 2008. *On Top of the Potty: And Other Get-Up-and-Go Songs*. New York: McElderry.

Katz, Bobbi. 2009. *The Monsterologist; A Memoir in Rhyme*. Ill. by Adam McCauley. New York: Sterling.

Levine, Gail Carson. 2012. *Forgive Me, I Meant to Do It: False Apology Poems*. Ill. by Matthew Cordell. New York: HarperCollins.

Lewis, J. Patrick. 2007. *Tulip at the Bat*. New York: Little, Brown.

Lewis, J. Patrick and Yolen, Jane. 2012. *Last Laughs: Animal Epitaphs*. Ill. by Jeffrey Timmins. Watertown, MA: Charlesbridge.

Lewis, J. Patrick. 2006. *Once Upon a Tomb: Gravely Humorous Verses*. Somerville, MA: Candlewick.

Lewis, J. Patrick. 2012. *Edgar Allan Poe's Pie: Math Puzzlers in Classic Poems*. New York: Houghton Mifflin Harcourt.

McNaughton, Colin. 2002. *Making Friends with Frankenstein*. Somerville, MA: Candlewick.

Merriam, Eve. 1996. *The Inner City Mother Goose*. Ill. by David Diaz. New York: Simon & Schuster.

Oelschlager, Vanita. 2009. *Ivy in Bloom: The Poetry of Spring from Great Poets and Writers of the Past*. Akron, OH: VanitaBooks.

Prelutsky, Jack. 2009. *The Swamps of Sleethe; Poems From Beyond the Solar System*. New York: Knopf.

Rex, Adam. 2005. *Frankenstein Makes a Sandwich.*: Harcourt.

Rex, Adam. 2006. *Frankenstein Makes a Sandwich*. Harcourt.

Rex, Adam. 2008. *Frankenstein Takes the Cake*. New York: Harcourt Houghton Mifflin.

Scieszka, Jon. 2004. *Science Verse*. New York: Viking.

Shapiro, Karen Jo. 2007. *I Must Go Down to the Beach Again*. Watertown, MA: Charlesbridge.

Sidman, Joyce. 2007. *This is Just to Say: Poems of Apology and Forgiveness*. Ill. by Pamela Zagarenski. Boston: Houghton Mifflin.

Sierra, Judy. 2001. *Monster Goose*. San Diego: Gulliver Books.

Singer, Marilyn. 2012. *The Boy Who Cried Alien*. New York: Hyperion

Singer, Marilyn. 2004. *Creature Carnival*. New York: Hyperion.

Wheeler, Lisa. 2011. *Spinster Goose; Twisted Rhymes for Naughty Children*. Ill. by Sophie Blackall. New York: Atheneum.

Willard, Nancy. 1981. *A Visit to William Blake's Inn: Poems for Innocent and Experienced Travelers*. San Diego, CA: Harcourt.

Wilson, Karma. 2009. *What's the Weather Inside?* Simon & Schuster.

Poetry Memoirs for Young People

Poetry is one place where writers look back on their lives and share memories of significant moments and experiences. Here is a selection of poetry memoirs written specifically for young people.

Abeel, Samantha.1993. *Reach for the Moon.* Duluth, MN: Pfeifer-Hamilton.
Appelt, Kathi. 2004. *My Father's Summers: A Daughter's Memoirs.* New York: Henry Holt.
Begay, Shonto. 1995. *Navajo: Visions and Voices Across the Mesa.* New York: Scholastic.
Brown, Dale S. 1995. *I Know I Can Climb the Mountain.* Columbus, OH: Mountain Books & Music.
Corrigan, Eireann. 2002. *You Remind Me of You; A Poetry Memoir.* New York: Push/Scholastic.
Crew, Gary. 2003. *Troy Thompson's Excellent Peotry* [sic] *Book.* La Jolla, CA: Kane/Miller. (mock memoir)
Graves, Donald. 1996. *Baseball, Snakes, and Summer Squash.* Honesdale, PA: Wordsong/Boyds Mills Press.
Greenfield, Eloise. 1993. *Childtimes: A Three-Generation Memoir.* New York: HarperCollins.
Grimes, Nikki. 2004. *Tai Chi morning: Snapshots of China.* Chicago: Cricket Books.
Harrison, David L. 2004. *Connecting Dots: Poems of My Journey.* Honesdale, PA: Wordsong/Boyds Mills Press.
Herrera, Juan Felipe. 2001. *Calling The Doves/El Canto De Las Palomas.* San Francisco, CA: Children's Book Press.
Hopkins, Lee Bennett. 1995*. Been to Yesterdays: Poems of a Life.* Honesdale, PA: Wordsong, Boyds Mills Press.
Katz, Bobbi. 2009. *The Monsterologist; A Memoir in Rhyme.* Ill. by Adam McCauley. New York: Sterling. (mock memoir)
Little, Lessie Jones. 1988. *Children of Long Ago: Poems.* New York: Lee & Low. Reprinted, 2000.
Lyon, George Ella. 1999. *Where I'm From, Where Poems Come From.* Spring, TX: Absey & Co.
Mak, Kam. 2001. *My Chinatown: One Year in Poems.* New York: HarperCollins.
Rylant, Cynthia. 1991. *Appalachia: The Voices of Sleeping Birds.* San Diego, CA: Harcourt Brace Jovanovich.
Spain, Sahara Sunday. 2001. *If There Would Be No Light; Poems from My Heart.* San Francisco: HarperCollins.
Stepanek, Mattie. 2002. *Heartsongs.* New York: Hyperion.
Stevenson, James. 1995. *Sweet Corn: Poems.* New York: Greenwillow.
Stevenson, James. 1998. *Popcorn: Poems.* New York: Greenwillow.
Stevenson, James. 2002. *Corn-Fed: Poems.* New York: Greenwillow.
Stevenson, James. 2003. *Corn Chowder: Poems.* New York: Greenwillow.
Thoms, Annie. Ed. 2002. *With Their Eyes.* New York: HarperTempest.
Turner, Ann. 2000. *Learning to Swim; A Memoir.* New York: Scholastic.
Yu, Chin. 2005. *Little Green; Growing Up During the Chinese Cultural Revolution.* New York: Simon & Schuster.

Point of View in Poetry for Young People

The "voice" of the poem has been an important component of poetry for centuries. Who is "speaking" in the poem, whose perspective or point of view is expressed is often what defines and shapes the poem. Such poems are called "persona" or "mask" poems and can present the perspective of a person, object, animal, object or idea. Here are a few poetry books in which point of view is a crucial ingredient.

Alarcón, Francisco X. 2008. *Animals Poems of the Iguazú / Animalario del Iguazú*. San Francisco: Children's Book Press.

Ashman, Linda. 2008. *Stella, Unleashed*. New York: Sterling.

Beck, Carolyn. 2009. *Buttercup's Lovely Day*. Custer: Orca Books.

Engle, Margaret. 2006. *The Poet Slave of Cuba*. New York: Holt.

Engle, Margarita. 2008. *The Surrender Tree*. New York: Holt.

Engle, Margarita. 2010. *The Firefly Letters*. New York: Henry Holt.

English, Karen. 2004. *Speak to Me (And I Will Listen Between the Lines)*. New York: Farrar, Straus & Giroux.

Frost, Helen. 2003. *Keesha's House*. New York: Farrar, Straus & Giroux.

Frost, Helen. 2004. *Spinning through the Universe*. New York: Farrar, Straus & Giroux.

George, Kristine O'Connell. 1998. *Old Elm Speaks: Tree Poems*. New York: Clarion.

Glenn, Mel. 2000. *Split Image*. New York: HarperCollins.

Grimes, Nikki. 2002. *Bronx Masquerade*. New York: Dial.

Grimes, Nikki. 2005. *Dark Sons*. New York: Hyperion.

Grimes, Nikki. 2004. *What is Goodbye?* New York: Jump at the Sun/Hyperion.

Harrison, David L. *Pirates*. Honesdale, PA: Wordsong/Boyds Mills Press.

Harrison, David. 2012. *Cowboys*. Honesdale, PA: Wordsong/Boyds Mills Press.

Hesse, Karen. 2001. *Witness*. New York: Scholastic.

Holbrook, Sara and Wolf, Allan. 2008. *More Than Friends; Poems from Him and Her*. Honesdale, PA: Wordsong/Boyds Mills.

Hopkins, Lee Bennett. Ed. 1996. *School Supplies: A Book of Poems*. New York: Simon & Schuster.

Hopkins, Lee Bennett. Ed. 2010. *Amazing Faces*. Ill. By Chris Soentpiet. Lee and Low.

Hughes, Langston. 2012. *I, Too, Am America*. Ill. by Bryan Collier. New York: Simon & Schuster.

Janecczko, Paul. Ed. 2001. *Dirty Laundry Pile. Poems in Different Voices*. New York: HarperCollins.

Janeczko, Paul. Ed. 2007. *Hey, You! Poems to Skyscrapers, Mosquitoes, and Other Fun Things*. New York: HarperCollins.

Larios, Julie. 2008. *Imaginary Menagerie: A Book of Curious Creatures*. New York: Houghton Mifflin Harcourt.

Lewis, J. Patrick. 2005. *Please Bury Me In The Library*. Orlando, FL: Gulliver Books/Harcourt.

Mora, Pat. 1994. *The Desert is My Mother/El Desierto es Mi Madre*. Houston, TX: Pinata Books.

Myers, Walter Dean. 2011. *We are America; A Tribute from the Heart*. Ill. by Christopher Myers. New York: HarperCollins.

Nelson, Marilyn. 2009. *Sweethearts of Rhythm; The Story of the Greatest All-Girl Swing Band in the World*. Ill. by Jerry Pinkney. New York: Dial.

Nye, Naomi Shihab. Ed. 1999. *What Have You Lost?* New York: Greenwillow.

Rosenthal, Betsy R. 2004. *My House is Singing*. New York: Harcourt.

Schertle, Alice. 1999. *I am the Cat*. New York: Lothrop, Lee & Shepard.

Schertle, Alice. 2009. *Button Up! Wrinkled Rhymes*. Ill. by Petra Mathers. New York: Harcourt.

Schlitz, Laura Amy. 2007. *Good Masters! Sweet Ladies!: Voices from a Medieval Village*. Somerville, MA: Candlewick.

Sidman, Joyce. 2003. *The World According to Dog: Poems and Teen Voices*. Ill. by Doug Mindell. Boston: Houghton Mifflin.

Sidman, Joyce. 2007. *This is Just to Say: Poems of Apology and Forgiveness*. Ill. by Pamela Zagarenski. Boston: Houghton Mifflin.

Singer, Marilyn. 1989. *Turtle in July*. New York: Macmillan.

Singer, Marilyn. 1996. *All We Needed to Say: Poems about School from Tanya and Sophie*. New York: Atheneum.

Singer, Marilyn. 2004. *Creature Carnival*. New York: Hyperion.

Singer, Marilyn. 2010. *Mirror, Mirror*. New York: Dutton.

Smith, Charles R. Jr. 2003. *I am America*. New York: Scholastic.

Soto, Gary. 2008. *Partly Cloudy; Poems of Love and Longing*. Boston: Houghton Mifflin Harcourt.

Weatherford, Carole Boston. 2007. *Birmingham, 1963*. Honesdale, PA: Wordsong/Boyds Mills Press.

Weinstock, Robert. 2009. *Food Hates You, Too*. New York: Disney-Hyperion.

Whipple, Laura. 2002. *If the Shoe Fits; Voices from Cinderella*. New York: Margaret McElderry.

Wolf, Allan. 2003. *The Blood-Hungry Spleen and Other Poems about Our Parts*. Somerville, MA: Candlewick

Wolf, Allan. 2011. *The Watch That Ends the Night*. Somerville, MA: Candlewick.

Zimmer, Tracie Vaughn. 2009. *Steady Hands: Poems About Work*. New York: Clarion

Free Verse Poetry Books for Young People

Although much of the poetry published for young people is full of rhyme, most contemporary poets also write plenty of free verse or non-rhyming poetry. And although this form does not rhyme, it often has a rhythm and structure that is quite metrical and musical. Young readers and listeners enjoy both forms and should experience a wide variety of each. Here are just a handful of examples of poetry books containing free verse by some of our biggest names in poetry for youth.

Adoff, Arnold. 2000. *Touch the Poem.* New York: Blue Sky Press.
Alarcón, Francisco X. 2005. *Poems to Dream Together/ Poemas para Sonar Juntos.* New York: Lee & Low.
Creech, Sharon. 2001. *Love That Dog.* New York: HarperCollins.
Lewis, J. Patrick and Rebecca Kai Dotlich. 2006. *Castles: Old Stone Poems.* Honesdale, PA: Wordsong/Boyds Mills.
Fletcher, Ralph J. 2006. *Moving Day.* Honesdale, PA: Wordsong/Boyds Mills.
George, Kristine O'Connell. 2009. *Emma Dilemma: Big Sister Poems.* Il. by Nancy Carpenter. New York: Clarion.
Greenfield, Eloise. 1978. *Honey, I Love and Other Love Poems.* New York: HarperCollins.
Grimes, Nikki. 2006. *Thanks a Million.* New York: Amistad.
Harrison, David. 2009. *Vacation, We're Going to the Ocean!* Ill. by Rob Shepperson. Honesdale, PA: Wordsong/Boyds Mills Press.
Hopkins, Lee Bennett. 1995. Good Rhymes, Good Times: Original Poems. *New York: HarperCollins.*
Hopkins, Lee Bennett. 2009. *City I Love.* Ill. by Marcellus Hall. Abrams.
Lewis, J. Patrick. 2008. *The World's Greatest Poems.* Chronicle.
Mora, Pat. 1996. *Confetti: Poems for Children.* New York: Lee & Low.
Mordhorst, Heidi. 2009. *Pumpkin Butterfly; Poems from the Other Side of Nature.* Honesdale PA: Wordsong/Boyds Mills Press.
Myers, Walter Dean. 1997. *Harlem: A Poem.* New York: Scholastic.
Nye, Naomi Shihab. 2005. *A Maze Me: Poems for Girls.* New York: Greenwillow.
Sidman, Joyce. 2009. *Red Sings From Treetops; A Year in Colors.* Ill. by Pamela Zagarenski. Boston: Houghton Mifflin.
Singer, Marilyn. 2012. *A Stick Is an Excellent Thing.* Ill. by LeUyen Pham. Clarion.
Soto, Gary. 1990. *A Fire in My Hands.* New York: Scholastic.
Thomas, Joyce Carol. 2008. *The Blacker the Berry.* Illus. by Floyd Cooper. New York: Amistad.
Weatherford, Carole Boston. 2002. *Remember the Bridge: Poems of a People.* New York: Philomel.
Wong, Janet S. 2000. *Night Garden: Poems from the World of Dreams.* New York: Margaret K. McElderry.
Worth, Valerie. 2002. *Peacock and Other Poems.* New York: Farrar, Straus & Giroux.
Yolen, Jane. 2007. *Shape Me a Rhyme.* Honesdale, PA: Wordsong.
Zimmer, Tracie Vaughn. 2009. *Steady Hands: Poems About Work.* New York: Clarion.

Poetry Books for Young People Featuring Haiku, Renga, Tanka, and Sijo

Haiku is a Japanese form of poetry that has long been popular in schools and classrooms. The three line, 17-syllable structure seems deceptively simple, but can offer a sophisticated synthesis of language and ideas. The books listed below are some of the titles that feature this unique form, as well as the tanka, renga, and sijo, other poetic forms grounded in ancient Asian literary traditions.

Asch, Frank. 1998. *Cactus Poems.* San Diego: Harcourt.

Chaikin, Miriam. 2002. *Don't Step on the Sky: A Handful of Haiku.* New York: Henry Holt.

Clements, Andrew. 2007. *Dogku.* New York: Simon & Schuster.

Demi. 1992. *In the Eyes of the Cat: Japanese Poetry for all Seasons.* New York: Henry Holt.

Farrar, Sid. 2012. *The Year Comes Round: Haiku Through the Seasons.* Ill. by Ilse Plume. Whitman.

Frost, Helen. 2004. *Spinning through the Universe: A Novel in Poems from Room 214.* New York: Farrar, Straus & Giroux.

George, Kristine O'Connell. 2005. *Fold me a Poem.* Orlando, FL: Harcourt.

Gollub, Matthew. 1998. *Cool Melons Turn to Frogs: The Life and Poems of Issa.* New York: Lee & Low.

Grimes, Nikki. 2001. *A Pocketful of Poems.* New York: Clarion.

Haas, Robert. Ed. 1994. *The Essential Haiku.* Hopewell, NJ: Ecco Press.

Holbrook, Sara and Allan Wolf. 2008. *More than Friends: Poems from Him and Her.* Honesdale, PA: Wordsong/Boyds Mills.

Janeczko, Paul B. Ed. 2005. *A Kick in the Head: An Everyday Guide to Poetic Forms.* Somerville, MA: Candlewick.

Janeczko, Paul B. & J. Patrick Lewis. 2008. *Birds on a Wire.* Honesdale, PA: Wordsong/Boyds Mills.

Janeczko, Paul B. 2000. *Stone Bench in an Empty Park.* New York: Orchard Books.

Kobayahsi, Issa. 2007. *Today and Today.* New York: Scholastic.

Lewis, J. Patrick. 1995. *Black Swan/ White Crow.* New York: Atheneum.

Lewis, J. Patrick and Janeczko, Paul B. 2006. *Wing Nuts: Screwy Haiku.* New York: Little, Brown.

Livingston, Myra Cohn. 1997. *Cricket Never Does: A Collection of Haiku and Tanka.* New York: McElderry.

Mannis, Celeste Davidson. 2002. *One Leaf Rides the Wind: Counting in a Japanese Garden.* New York: Viking.

Mecum, Ryan. 2008. *Zombie Haiku.* Cincinnati, OH: How Books.

Mecum, Ryan. 2009. *Vampire Haiku.* Cincinnati, OH: How Books.

Mora, Pat. 2007. *Yum! Mmm! Que Rico! Americas' Sproutings.* New York: Lee & Low.

Park, Linda Sue. 2007. *Tap Dancing on the Roof: Sijo Poems.* New York: Clarion.

Prelutsky, Jack. 2004. *If not for the Cat: Haiku.* New York: Greenwillow.

Raczka, Bob. 2010. *Guyku: A Year of Haiku for Boys.* Ill. by Peter Reynolds. Boston: Houghton Mifflin.

Reibstein, Mark. 2008. *Wabi Sabi*. Ill. by Ed Young. New York: Little, Brown.

Rosen, Michael J. 2009. *The Cuckoo's Haiku and Other Birding Poems*. Ill. by Stan Fellows. Somerville, MA: Candlewick.

Rosen, Michael J. 2011. *The Hound Dog's Haiku and Other Poems for Dog Lovers*. Cambridge, MA: Candlewick.

Shannon, George. 1996. *Spring: a Haiku Story*. New York: Greenwillow.

Spivak, Dawine. 2009. *Grass Sandals: The Travels of Basho*. New York: Atheneum.

Venokur, Ross. 2001. *Haiku! Gesundheit: an Illustrated Collection of Ridiculous Haiku Poetry*. New York: Simon & Schuster.

Wardlaw, Lee. 2011. *Won Ton; A Cat Tale Told in Haiku*. Ill. by Eugene Yelchin. Henry Holt.

Whipple, Laura. Ed. 1989. *Eric Carle's Animals, Animals*. New York: Scholastic.

Yolen, Jane. 2003. *Least Things: Poems about Small Natures*. Honesdale, PA: Wordsong/Boyds Mills.

Verse Novels for Young Adults

A relatively new poetic form with roots in ancient epic poetry, the verse novel or novel in verse is a form that is growing in popularity, particularly with tweens and teens. The best verse novels are built on poems that are often lovely "stand alone" works of art. A narrative unfolds poem by poem, often with multiple points of view and in colloquial, conversational language. It can also be very engaging to read these works out loud in parts, with different readers voicing different characters in readers theater style. Here are some of the best of the recent novels in verse for young adults.

Adoff, Jaime. 2005. *Jimi & Me*. New York: Hyperion.
Adoff, Jaime. 2008. *The Death of Jayson Porter*. New York: Jump at the Sun/Hyperion.
Applegate, Katherine. 2008. *Home of the Brave*. New York: Square Fish.
Atkins, Jeannine. 2010. *Borrowed Names; Poems About Laura Ingalls Wilder, Madam C. J. Walker, Marie Curie, and Their Daughters*. New York: Holt.
Bryant, Jen. 2004. *The Trial*. New York: Knopf.
Bryant, Jen. 2008. *Ringside 1925; Views From the Scopes Trial*. New York: Knopf.
Bryant, Jen. 2009. *Kaleidoscope Eyes*. New York: Knopf.
Burg, Ann. 2009. *All the Broken Pieces*. NY: Scholastic.
Carvell, Marlene. 2004. *Who Will Tell My Brother?* New York: Hyperion.
Carvell, Marlene. 2005. *Sweetgrass Basket*. New York: Dutton.
Chaltas, Thalia. 2009. *Because I Am Furniture*. New York: Viking.
Chaltas, Thalia. 2011. *Displacement*. New York: Viking.
Cormier, Robert. 1999. *Frenchtown Summer*. New York: Delacorte.
Corrigan, Eireann. 2002. *You Remind Me of You; A Poetry Memoir*. New York: Push/Scholastic.
Crisler, Curtis. 2007. *Tough Boy Sonatas*. Honesdale, PA: Wordsong/Boyds Mills.
Engle, Margaret. 2006. *The Poet Slave of Cuba: A Biography of Juan Francisco Manzano*. New York: Holt.
Engle, Margarita. 2008. *The Surrender Tree*. New York: Holt.
Engle, Margarita. 2009. *Tropical Secrets: Holocaust Refugees in Cuba*. New York: Holt.
Engle, Margarita. 2010. *The Firefly Letters; A Suffragette's Journey to Cuba*. Henry Holt.
Engle, Margarita. 2011. *Hurricane Dancers; The First Caribbean Pirate Shipwreck*. Henry Holt.
Fields, Terri. 2002. *After the Death of Anna Gonzales*. New York: Holt.
Ford, Christine. 2006. *Scout*. New York: Delacorte.
Franco, Betsy. 2009. *Metamorphosis, Junior Year*. Somerville, MA: Candlewick.
Frost, Helen. 2003. *Keesha's House*. New York: Farrar, Straus & Giroux.
Frost, Helen. 2006. *The Braid*. New York: Farrar, Straus & Giroux.
Frost, Helen. 2009. *Crossing Stones*. New York: Farrar, Straus & Giroux.
Frost, Helen. 2011. *Hidden*. Farrar, Straus & Giroux.
Glenn, Mel. 1982. Class Dismissed! High School Poems. New York: Clarion.

Glenn, Mel. 1991. My Friend's Got This Problem, Mr. Candler: High School Poems. New York: Clarion.

Glenn, Mel. 1996. *Who Killed Mr. Chippendale?* New York: Lodestar Books/Dutton.

Glenn, Mel. 1997. *Jump Ball: A Basketball Season in Poems.* New York: Lodestar Books/Dutton.

Glenn, Mel. 1997. *The Taking of Room 114: A Hostage Drama in Poems.* New York: Lodestar Books/Dutton.

Glenn, Mel. 1999. *Foreign Exchange: A Mystery in Poems.* New York: Morrow Junior Books.

Glenn, Mel. 2000. *Split Image.* New York: HarperCollins.

Grimes, Nikki. 2002. *Bronx Masquerade.* New York: Dial.

Grimes, Nikki. 2005. *Dark Sons.* New York: Hyperion.

Grover, Lorie Ann. 2005. *Hold Me Tight.* Simon & Schuster.

Havill, Juanita. 2008. *Grow.* Atlanta, GA: Peachtree.

Hemphill, Stephanie. 2005. *Things Left Unsaid.* New York: Hyperion.

Hemphill, Stephanie. 2007. *Your Own, Sylvia.* New York: Knopf.

Hemphill, Stephanie. 2010. *Wicked Girls; A Novel of the Salem Witch Trials.* New York: HarperCollins.

Hemphill, Stephanie. 2012. *Sisters of Glass.* Knopf.

Herrera, Juan Felipe. 1999. *Crashboomlove.* Albuquerque: University of New Mexico Press.

Herrera, Juan Felipe. 2011. *Skate Fate.* New York: HarperCollins.

Herrick, Steven. 2004. *By the River.* Asheville, NC: Front Street.

Herrick, Steven. 2004. *The Simple Gift.* New York: Simon & Schuster.

Herrick, Steven. 2006. *The Wolf.* Asheville, NC: Front Street.

Herrick, Steven. 2009. *Cold Skin.* Asheville, NC: Front Street.

Hesse, Karen. 2001. *Witness.* New York: Scholastic.

High, Linda Oatman. 2008. *Planet Pregnancy.* Asheville, NC: Front Street.

Hopkins, Ellen. 2006. *Burned.* New York: McElderry.

Hopkins, Ellen. 2007. *glass.* New York: McElderry.

Hopkins, Ellen. 2008. *Identical.* New York: McElderry.

Hopkins, Ellen. 2011. *Perfect.* New York: McElderry.

Hopkins, Ellen. 2010. *Crank.* New York: McElderry.

Janeczko, Paul B. 2004. *Worlds Afire.* Somerville, MA: Candlewick.

Janeczko, Paul B. 2011. *Requiem; Poems of the Terezín Ghetto.* Candlewick.

Koertge, Ron, 2003. *Shakespeare Bats Clean-up.* Somerville, MA: Candlewick.

Koertge, Ron. 2001. *The Brimstone Journals.* Somerville, MA: Candlewick.

Koertge, Ron. 2010. *Shakespeare Makes the Playoffs.* Somerville, MA: Candlewick.

Koertge, Ron. 2012. *Lies, Knives, and Girls in Red Dresses.* Ill. by Andrea Dezsö. Somerville, MA: Candlewick.

Levithan, David. 2004. *The Realm of Possibility.* New York: Knopf.

Marcus, Kimberly. 2011. *exposed.* Random House.

McCall, Guadalupe Garcia. 2011. *Under the Mesquite.* Lee & Low.

McCormick, Patricia. 2008. *Sold.* New York: Hyperion.

Montgomery, Hugh. 2002. *The Voyage of the Arctic Tern.* Somerville, MA: Candlewick.

Mora, Pat. 2010. *Dizzy in My Eyes*. New York: Knopf.

Myers, Walter Dean. 2004. *Here in Harlem: Poems in Many Voices*. New York: Holiday House.

Nelson, Marilyn. 2001. *Carver: A Life in Poems*. Asheville, NC: Front Street.

Nelson, Marilyn. 2004. *Fortune's Bones: The Manumission Requiem*. Asheville, NC: Front Street.

Nelson, Marilyn. 2005. *A Wreath for Emmett Till*. Boston: Houghton Mifflin.

Nelson, Marilyn. 2008. *The Freedom Business*. Asheville, NC: Front Street.

Newman, Leslea. 2012. *October Mourning: A Song for Matthew Shepard*. Somerville, MA: Candlewick.

Ostlere, Cathy. 2011. *Karma*. New York: Razorbill.

Peters, Andrew Fusek and Peters, Polly. 2004. *Crash*. London: Hodder Children's Books.

Richards, Jame. 2010. *Three Rivers Rising*. Knopf.

Rylant, Cynthia. 1990. *Soda Jerk*. New York: Orchard.

Rylant, Cynthia. 2003. *God Went to Beauty School*. New York: HarperColllins.

Sandell, Lisa Ann. 2007. *Song of the Sparrow*. New York: Scholastic.

Smith, Hope Anita. 2003. *The Way a Door Closes*. New York: Henry Holt.

Smith, Hope Anita. 2008. *Keeping the Night Watch*. New York: Henry Holt.

Sones, Sonya. 1999. *Stop Pretending: What Happened When My Big Sister Went Crazy*. New York: HarperCollins.

Sones, Sonya. 2001. *What My Mother Doesn't Know*. New York: Simon & Schuster.

Sones, Sonya. 2004. *One of Those Hideous Books Where the Mother Dies*. New York: Simon & Schuster.

Sones, Sonya. 2007. *What My Girlfriend Doesn't Know*. New York: Simon & Schuster.

Thompson, Holly. 2011. *Orchards*. New York: Random House.

Turner, Ann Warren. 2003. *Learning to Swim*. New York: Scholastic.

Turner, Ann Warren. 2006. *Hard Hit*. New York: Scholastic.

Wolf, Allan. 2004. *New Found Land; Lewis and Clark's Voyage of Discovery*. Somerville, MA: Candlewick.

Wolf, Allan. 2011. *The Watch That Ends the Night; Voices from the Titanic*. Cambridge, MA: Candlewick.

Wolff, Virginia Euwer. 1993. *Make Lemonade*. New York: Scholastic.

Wolff, Virginia Euwer. 2001. *True Believer*. New York: Atheneum.

Wolff, Virginia Euwer. 2009. *This Full House*. New York: Harper Teen/The Bowen Press.

Yu, Chin. 2005. *Little Green; Growing Up During the Chinese Cultural Revolution*. NY: Simon & Schuster.

Verse Novels for the Intermediate Grades (Grades 4, 5, 6)

The novel in verse form offers the generous white space, short lines, and conversational tone that young readers who are still developing their comprehension expertise find helpful. For kids in the intermediate grades (grades 4, 5, 6), these sample verse novels offer younger protagonists and problems and issues that are relevant and interesting.

Applegate, Katherine. 2012. *The One and Only Ivan*. New York: Harper.

Bryant, Jen. 2004. *The Trial*. New York: Knopf.

Bryant, Jen. 2006. *Pieces of Georgia*. New York: Knopf.

Cheng, Andrea. 2008. *Where the Steps Were*. Honesdale, PA: Boyds Mills/Wordsong.

Creech, Sharon. 2001. *Love That Dog*. New York: HarperCollins.

Creech, Sharon. 2004. *Heartbeat*. New York: HarperCollins.

Creech, Sharon. 2008. *Hate that Cat*. New York: HarperCollins.

Crist-Evans, Craig. 1999. *Moon Over Tennessee: A Boy's Civil War Journal*. Boston: Houghton Mifflin.

Crist-Evans, Craig. 2004. *North of Everything*. Somerville, MA: Candlewick.

Durango, Julia. 2011. *Under the Mambo Moon*. Watertown, MA: Charlesbridge.

Engle, Margarita. 2012. *The Wild Book*. Boston: Houghton Mifflin.

Frost, Helen. 2004. *Spinning through the Universe*. New York: Farrar, Straus & Giroux.

Frost, Helen. 2008. *Diamond Willow*. New York: Farrar, Straus & Giroux.

Grimes, Nikki. 1998. *Jazmin's Notebook*. New York: Dial.

Grimes, Nikki. 2004. *What is Goodbye?* New York: Jump at the Sun/Hyperion.

Grimes, Nikki. 2011. *Planet Middle School*. New York: Bloomsbury.

Herrick, Steven. 2008. *Naked Bunyip Dancing*. Honesdale, PA: Boyds Mills/Wordsong.

Hesse, Karen. 1997. *Out of the Dust*. New York: Scholastic.

Hesse, Karen. 2003. *Aleutian Sparrow*. New York: Simon & Schuster.

Hopkins, Lee Bennett. 1995. *Been to Yesterdays: Poems of a Life*. Honesdale, PA: Wordsong, Boyds Mills Press.

Lai, Thanhha. 2011. *Inside Out and Back Again*. New York: HarperCollins.

Levy, Debbie. 2010. *The Year of Goodbyes; A True Story of Friendship, Family and Farewells*. New York: Hyperion.

Smith, Hope Anita. 2009. *Mother; Poems*. New York: Henry Holt.

Soto, Gary. 2002. *Fearless Fernie: Hanging Out with Fernie & Me*. New York: Putnam.

Soto, Gary. 2005. *Worlds Apart: Fernie and Me*. New York: Putnam.

Spinelli, Eileen. 2007. *Summerhouse Time*. New York: Knopf.

Spinelli, Eileen. 2007. *Where I Live*. New York: Dial.

Spinelli, Eileen. 2010. *The Dancing Pancake*. New York: Knopf.

Testa, Maria. 2002. *Becoming Joe Dimaggio*. Somerville, MA: Candlewick.

Testa, Maria. 2003. *Almost Forever*. Somerville, MA: Candlewick.

Testa, Maria. 2005. *Something about America*. Somerville, MA: Candlewick.

Wayland, April Halprin. 2002. *Girl Coming in for a Landing: A Novel in Poems*. New York: Knopf.

Weston, Robert Paul. 2008. *Zorgamazoo*. New York: Razorbill/Penguin.

Weston, Robert Paul. 2012. *Prince Pugly*. New York: Razorbill.

Williams, Vera B. 2001. *Amber Was Brave, Essie Was Smart.* New York: Greenwillow.

Wong, Janet S. 2003. *Minn and Jake*. New York: Farrar, Straus & Giroux.

Wong, Janet. 2008. *Minn and Jake's Almost Terrible Summer.* New York: Farrar, Straus & Giroux.

Woodson, Jacqueline. 2003. *Locomotion*. New York: Putnam.

Zimmer, Tracie Vaughn. 2007. *Reaching for Sun.* New York: Bloomsbury.

Zimmer, Tracie Vaughn. 2008. *42 Miles*. New York: Clarion.

Historical Novels in Verse for Young People

The novel in verse format offers an engaging story told through entries, vignettes, and dialogue in poem form and the addition of an historical context can add another layer of interest. Many verse novels use a setting in the past very effectively for both factual (biographical) and fictional stories. Such works can lend themselves to the study of history or social studies as well as be meaningful reading on their own.

Atkins, Jeannine. 2010. *Borrowed Names; Poems About Laura Ingalls Wilder, Madam C. J. Walker, Marie Curie, and Their Daughters.* New York: Holt.

Bernier-Grand, Carmen T. 2006. *César; ¡Sí, Se Puede! Yes, We can!* New York: Marshall Cavendish.

Bernier-Grand, Carmen T. 2007. *Frida: ¡Viva la vida! Long Live Life!* New York: Marshall Cavendish.

Bernier-Grand, Carmen T. 2009. *Diego; Bigger Than Life.* Ill. by David Diaz. New York: Marshall Cavendish.

Bryant, Jen. 2004. *The Trial.* New York: Knopf.

Bryant, Jen. 2008. *Ringside 1925; Views From the Scopes Trial.* New York: Knopf.

Bryant, Jen. 2009. *Kaleidoscope Eyes.* New York: Knopf.

Burg, Ann. 2009. *All the Broken Pieces.* New York: Scholastic.

Cormier, Robert. 1999. *Frenchtown Summer.* New York: Delacorte.

Crist-Evans, Craig. 1999. *Moon Over Tennessee: A Boy's Civil War Journal.* Boston: Houghton Mifflin.

Engle, Margaret. 2006. *The Poet Slave of Cuba: A Biography of Juan Francisco Manzano.* New York: Holt.

Engle, Margarita. 2008. *The Surrender Tree.* New York: Holt.

Engle, Margarita. 2009. *Tropical Secrets: Holocaust Refugees in Cuba.* New York: Holt.

Engle, Margarita. 2010. *The Firefly Letters; A Suffragette's Journey to Cuba.* New York: Holt.

Engle, Margarita. 2011. *Hurricane Dancers; The First Caribbean Pirate Shipwreck.* New York: Holt.

Engle, Margarita. 2012. *The Wild Book.* Boston: Houghton Mifflin.

Frost, Helen. 2006. *The Braid.* New York: Farrar, Straus & Giroux.

Frost, Helen. 2009. *Crossing Stones.* New York: Farrar, Straus & Giroux.

Grimes, Nikki. 2005. *Dark Sons.* New York: Hyperion.

Hemphill, Stephanie. 2007. *Your Own, Sylvia.* New York: Knopf.

Hemphill, Stephanie. 2010. *Wicked Girls; A Novel of the Salem Witch Trials.* New York: HarperCollins.

Hemphill, Stephanie. 2012. *Sisters of Glass.* New York: Knopf.

Hesse, Karen. 2003. *Aleutian Sparrow.* New York: McElderry.

Hesse, Karen. 2000. *Out Of the Dust.* New York: Scholastic.

Hesse, Karen. 2001. *Witness.* New York: Scholastic.

Janeczko, Paul B. 2004. *Worlds Afire.* Somerville, MA: Candlewick.

Janeczko, Paul B. 2011. *Requiem; Poems of the Terezín Ghetto.* Somerville, MA: Candlewick.

Lai, Thanhha. 2011. *Inside Out and Back Again.* New York: HarperCollins.

Levy, Debbie. 2010. *The Year of Goodbyes; A True Story of Friendship, Family and Farewells.* New York: Hyperion.

LeZotte, Ann Clare. 2008. *T4.* Boston: Houghton Mifflin.

Montgomery, Hugh. 2002. *The Voyage of the Arctic Tern.* Somerville, MA: Candlewick.

Nelson, Marilyn. 2001. *Carver: A Life in Poems.* Asheville, NC: Front Street.

Nelson, Marilyn. 2004. *Fortune's Bones: The Manumission Requiem.* Asheville, NC: Front Street.

Nelson, Marilyn. 2005. *A Wreath for Emmett Till.* Boston: Houghton Mifflin.

Nelson, Marilyn. 2008. *The Freedom Business.* Asheville, NC: Front Street.

Richards, Jame. 2010. *Three Rivers Rising.* New York: Knopf.

Shahan, Sherry. 2011. *Purple Daze.* Running Press Kids.

Testa, Maria. 2002. *Becoming Joe Dimaggio.* Somerville, MA: Candlewick.

Testa, Maria. 2003. *Almost Forever.* Somerville, MA: Candlewick.

Wolf, Allan. 2004. New Found Land; Lewis and Clark's Voyage of Discovery. Somerville, MA: Candlewick.

Wolf, Allan. 2011. The Watch That Ends the Night; Voices from the Titanic. Somerville, MA: Candlewick.

Biographical Poetry Books for Young People

A big trend in recent years is to tell the true story of real people in history through the vehicle of poetry. The following books are based on the life stories of famous people as well as not-so-well known individuals—both fascinating sources for poetry for young people.

Bernier-Grand, Carmen T. 2004. *César; ¡Sí, Se Puede! Yes, We can!* New York: Marshall Cavendish.

Bernier-Grand, Carmen T. 2007. *Frida: ¡Viva la vida! Long Live Life!* New York: Marshall Cavendish.

Bernier-Grand, Carmen T. 2009. *Diego; Bigger Than Life.* Ill. by David Diaz. New York: Marshall Cavendish.

Engle, Margarita. 2006. *The Poet Slave of Cuba: A Biography of Juan Francisco Manzano.* New York: Henry Holt.

Engle, Margarita. 2008. *The Surrender Tree.* New York: Holt.

Engle, Margarita. 2010. *The Firefly Letters; A Suffragette's Journey to Cuba.* New York: Henry Holt.

Giovanni, Nikki. 2005. *Rosa.* New York: Henry Holt.

Gollub, Matthew. 1998. *Cool Melons Turn to Frogs: The Life and Poems of Issa.* New York: Lee & Low.

Hemphill, Stephanie. 2007. *Your Own, Sylvia.* New York: Knopf.

Hopkins, Lee Bennett. 1999. *Lives: Poems about Famous Americans.* New York: HarperCollins.

Izuki, Steven. 1994. *Believers in America: Poems about Americans of Asian and Pacific Islander Descent.* Chicago, IL: Children's Press.

Katz, Susan. 2011. The *President's Stuck in the Bathtub: Poems About U.S. Presidents.* New York: Clarion.

Lewis, J. Patrick. 2006. *Black Cat Bone.* North Mankato: Creative Editions.

Lewis, J. Patrick. 2000. *Freedom Like Sunlight: Praisesongs for Black Americans.* Mankato: Creative Editions.

Lewis, J. Patrick. 2005. *Heroes and She-roes : Poems of Amazing and Everyday Heroes.* New York: Dial.

Lewis, J. Patrick. 2005. *Vherses: A Celebration of Outstanding Women.* Mankato: Creative Editions.

Lewis, J. Patrick. 2006. *Black Cat Bone: The Life of Blues Legend Robert Johnson.* Creative Editions.

Lewis, J. Patrick. 2006. *Blackbeard, the Pirate King.* Washington, D.C.: National Geographic.

Lewis, J. Patrick. 2008. *Michelangelo's World.* Mankato, MN: Creative Editions.

Lewis, J. Patrick and Yolen, Jane. 2011. *Self Portrait with Seven Fingers: A Life of Marc Chagall in Verse.* Creative Editions.

Lewis, J. Patrick. 2012. *When Thunder Comes: Poems for Civil Rights Leaders.* San Francisco: Chronicle.

Livingston, Myra Cohn. 1992. *Let Freedom Ring: A Ballad of Martin Luther King Jr.* New York: Holiday House.

Livingston, Myra Cohn. 1993. *Abraham Lincoln: A Man for All the People: A Ballad.* New York: Holiday House.

Marsalis, Wynton. 2005. *Jazz ABZ: An A to Z Collection of Jazz Portraits.* Somerville, MA: Candlewick.

Nelson, Marilyn. 2001. *Carver: A Life in Poems.* Asheville: Front Street.

Nelson, Marilyn. 2008. *The Freedom Business.* Asheville, NC: Front Street.

Paul, Ann Whitford. 1999. *All by Herself: 14 Girls Who Made a Difference.* San Diego: Harcourt Brace.

Sidman, Joyce. 2002. *Eureka! Poems about Inventors.* Ill. by K. Bennett Chavez. Brookfield, CT: Millbrook.

Smith, Charles R. Jr. 2007. *Twelve Rounds to Glory: The Story of Muhammad Ali.* Somerville, MA: Candlewick.

Smith, Charles R., Jr. 2010. *Black Jack; The Ballad of Jack Johnson.* Roaring Brook Press.

Smith, Charles R., Jr. 2012. *Stars in the Shadows: The Negro League All-Star Game of 1934.* Ill. by Frank Morrison. New York: Atheneum.

Weatherford, Carole Boston. 2008. *Becoming Billie Holiday.* Honesdale, PA: Wordsong/Boyds Mills Press.

Weatherford, Carole Boston. 2008. *I, Matthew Henson: Polar Explorer.* Ill. by Eric Velasquez.

CREATING A POETRY-FRIENDLY ENVIRONMENT

In this section, the focus shifts from lists of poetry books to lists of tips and strategies for sharing poetry with young people. You'll find lists that showcase a rationale, preparation and presentation tips, display ideas, poetry quotes, lesson plan tips, two sample day-to-day approaches for April (an "almanac" and a game of poetry "tag"), and a scavenger hunt and treasure hunt for kids. There are also lists of poet birthdays and celebration occasions, including National Poetry Month tips. These should all help jumpstart your poetry approach and keep it energized and fresh all year long.

Twenty Reasons to Share Poetry with Young People
How to Begin Sharing Poetry with Young People
Checklist for Creating a Positive Poetry Environment
Poetry Preparation Tips
Tips for Presenting Poetry to Young People
A Poetry Almanac for April
Poetry Tag: Connecting Poems for Young People
Poetry Scavenger Hunt
Treasure Hunt for Poem Parts
Calendar of Poet Birthdays
Poetry Celebration Occasions
Poetry Display Ideas
Poetry Quotes
Poems about Libraries, Books, and Reading
Silverstein and Prelutsky Poetry Book Read-Alikes
Tips for Featuring Poets for Young People
Tips for Celebrating National Poetry Month with Young People
Tips for Planning Poetry Lessons
Choosing Poetry for English Language Learners (ELL/ESL)

Twenty Reasons to Share Poetry with Young People

Poetry does so much for young people as they develop their language and literacy skills. It offers a bridge from children's earliest oral language development to their first steps in reading and writing language. In fact, author and literacy expert Mem Fox has noted, "Rhymers will be readers; it's that simple. Experts in literacy and child development have discovered that if children know eight nursery rhymes by heart by the time they're four years old, they're usually among the best readers by the time they're eight" (2001, p. 85). Here are 20 major benefits of sharing poetry with young people.

1. Poetry introduces new vocabulary and figurative language.
2. Poetry reinforces word sounds, rimes, rhymes and patterns (think phonics!).
3. Poetry provides practice for word recognition and word pronunciation.
4. Poetry provides examples of synonyms, antonyms, puns, word play, and coining of new words and expressions.
5. Poetry is rich in imagery and in stimulating the imagination.
6. Poetry can provide sensory experiences giving children the sense of touching, feeling, smelling, and seeing.
7. Poetry is an important part of our literary and cultural heritage. Remember Beowulf? The Psalms? Twinkle Twinkle Little Star? "Hold fast to dreams?"
8. Poetry is meant to be heard and shared, and provides practice for oral language development, listening, oral fluency, and choral reading and performing.
9. Poetry has many teaching and pedagogical uses across the curriculum, for building science concepts, reinforcing historical themes, adding motivation to math lessons, as a "sponge" activity in transition times, etc.
10. Poetry is one of the earliest forms of literature children experience, albeit often in oral rather than print form. Consider the importance of Mother Goose nursery rhymes, for example.
11. Poetry offers an emotional connection and can reflect and elicit powerful and deeply felt moments.
12. The brevity, focus, and conciseness of poetry lends itself to sharing in short periods of time (as little as 3 minutes) and can be readily integrated with other lessons and activities.
13. Poetry's conceptual focus and rich vocabulary make it a natural teaching tool for connecting with nonfiction.
14. Poetry can heighten the awareness of the use of mechanical conventions in print, from spacing and margins to commas and quotation marks.
15. Poetry is accessible to a wide range of reading abilities and language learning skill levels.
16. Poetry has a long shelf-life and poems can be revisited again and again prompting different responses at different ages and stages.
17. Poetry can make a topic memorable (and memorizable) because of the use of highly charged words and/or vivid images.

18. Poetry has an honored tradition of being shared at special occasions and historic events like graduations, weddings, funerals, inaugurations, etc.
19. Poetry is part of childhood in the lullabies, jumprope rhymes, skipping songs, rhyming riddles, and playground verses that cross cultures and generations.
20. Poetry is primal, speaking to a basic human need for expression, made from the basic building blocks of language.

How to Begin Sharing Poetry with Young People

How do we begin sharing poetry with young people, especially if we're new to poetry? We can learn from motivated readers about what is important in encouraging reading in any genre. Typically we are fairly diligent about using these strategies for promoting fiction reading, by reading aloud, displaying books, sharing booklists, and developing activities and programs. How often do we apply this same "full court press" to promoting poetry for children? What would happen if we gave poetry this same "royal" treatment?

1. Be an adult who reads poetry for young people.

2. Make poems and poetry books accessible (at arm's length, if possible).

3. Put poetry books and poems on the agenda every day.

4. Model joy and enthusiasm for poems and poetry.

5. Begin where the children are, with their interests, concerns, and experiences.

6. Provide opportunities for choral reading and active participation.

7. Feature notable poets and access to quality poetry books.

8. Focus on meaning, cross-curricular connections, and children's responses.

Based on: *Children's Literature, Briefly,* Jacobs and Tunnell (2004).

Checklist for Creating a Positive Poetry Environment

Creating an environment that values poetry depends partly on the physical arrangement of space and materials and partly on the emotional climate that is established. Consider these questions as you assess the poetry books in your classroom, school, or public library, as well as these common poetry practices:

1. Check the children's poetry shelves for ease of access and appeal. Are the poetry books as easy to find as the fiction and nonfiction? Is the area well labeled and welcoming?
2. Do poetry posters and poetry book displays invite children to browse through poetry even if they're not immediately seeking it out? Are some poetry books displayed face out?
3. Is there room on the poetry shelves for browsing and expansion?
4. Are there plenty of poetry books to choose from? Are there currently published poetry books available?
5. Is there a balance of poetry anthologies and collections by individual poets?
6. Are the poetry award winners represented and highlighted?
7. Are there multiple copies of the most current and popular poetry titles?
8. Have you familiarized yourself with some of children's favorite poetry books? Do you know 10 poetry titles you can recommend depending on reader interests?
9. Do you highlight new poetry books, overlooked poetry book gems, books by featured poets, and children's favorite poetry books on a shelf, table, desk, chalk rail, pup tent, red wagon, etc.?
10. Do you mention children's poetry choices when general subject requests come up?
11. Do you include children's poetry books on your recommended reading lists and bibliographies?
12. Do you actively seek out poetry books from diverse perspectives?
13. Do you take advantage of opportunities to link poems with picture books, novels, and nonfiction?
14. Do you inject children's poetry when possible into instruction in language arts, social studies, science, and mathematics?
15. Do you feature individual children's poets in displays, promotional materials and booktalks?
16. Do you incorporate poems for children in your lessons, storytimes, read alouds, openings, transitions, and closings?
17. Do you provide opportunities for children to participate actively in the choral reading performance of poetry?
18. Do you have a designated area to feature kids' reviews of their favorite poetry books or their own original poems—such as a door or hallway?
19. Have you tried poetry celebration activities such as a morning poem reading or coffeehouse-style "Poetry Friday" readings at the end of the week?
20. Do you have special plans to acknowledge and celebrate National Poetry Month in April?

Poetry Preparation Tips

In our role as adults, we set the stage and take the lead in creating a poetry-friendly environment. Here are tips for preparing yourself to be an effective poetry advocate and poetry practitioner.

1. Search for poetry—starting today. Look for anything that appeals to you.
2. Collect poems, posters, poetry books related to upcoming activities. Keep them close at hand and display them.
3. Watch for opportunities to use poetry related to any topic on any occasion.
4. Memorize some of your favorite poems—even just a line or two that grabs you. "Keep a poem in your pocket" for special moments.
5. Create displays, including poem and poetry book collections (or bibliographies) for topics that are often the subject of study.
6. Collect specialized anthologies—poems by several poets on one subject.
7. Collect generalized anthologies—by many poets on many subjects.
8. Collect individualized anthologies—books containing the works of one poet.
9. Copy special poems on large poster paper to share with large groups. Place poem posters in library corners, classroom displays, block cities, housekeeping corners, play stores, etc.
10. Keep a variety of types of poetry on topics that appeal to the young people you work with, remembering that tastes can vary.
11. Alert young people to an upcoming event or topic of study by asking THEM to find poems on the topic. They can share what they find and post their poems in a display.
12. Keep poetry alive by seeking out new voices as well as cherishing the old. Collaborate with others (bookstores, libraries, teachers) to keep posted on new poetry books as they become available. If possible, take students to the poetry section of the library to browse through the poetry.
13. Read professional journals, blogs, listservs, and web sites that list and annotate the latest in poetry books for children.
14. Acquaint young people with the works of award-winning poets, particularly winners of the National Council of Teachers of English Award for Excellence in Poetry for Children, the Lee Bennett Hopkins Poetry Award, the Claudia Lewis Award, and the Lion and the Unicorn Award.
15. Consult your own friends and family members, colleagues and even students about their favorite poems.

Based on: Cullinan, Bernice E. Cullinan; Scala, Marilyn C., and Schroder, Virginia C. 1995. *Three Voices: An Invitation to Poetry Across the Curriculum.* York, ME: Stenhouse, p. 6-8.

Tips for Presenting Poetry to Young People

In their book, Poetry Everywhere, *Collom and Noethe (2005) provide many strategies and tips for guiding young people in their poetry writing. To set the stage, they offer these practical suggestions for taking a "hands-on approach" to leading poetry sessions.*

1. Be yourself. You needn't and shouldn't show reverence for poetry by means of an artificially dignified atmosphere.
2. Walking around while teaching, sharing, and especially reading orally grabs ALL the students' attention, involves them as a community" (Chris Casterson, 3rd grade teacher). It also helps lend a physical sense to the poetry.
3. Energy is the key—but it shouldn't be forced. It can be "quiet" energy.
4. In some ways, you can be less "in charge." Much of the learning in poetry comes from the inside out.
5. It's probably best not to "push" your beliefs about the beauties of poetry, but to let them emerge through examples and practice.
6. Don't over-explain.
7. Avoid abstractions. When you speak in concrete terms, it helps bring out better poems.
8. Read poetry aloud with energy, expressiveness, and rhythm (this can be the variable rhythm of everyday speech). For example, read or tell the Greek myths as if they happened this morning.
9. Make a conscious choice as to whether to read with pauses at the ends of lines (which tends to emphasize the breath, the connection of poetry to the body) or not (which can emphasize the flow of sound and ideas).
10. It's helpful to admit your own errors, blank-outs, and ignorance. This helps create an open mood.
11. A brisk pace is good and energizing, as long as you're willing to be flexible and slow down when the situation needs it.
12. Don't worry. Decide thoughtfully what you're going to do, go for it. Relax and concentrate. Have fun. Freely intersperse humor and seriousness.
13. Be open to children's visions-- they really have them.

Based on: Collom, Jack and Noethe, Sheryl. 2005. *Poetry Everywhere; Teaching Poetry Writing in School and in the Community.* New York: Teachers and Writers Collaborative, p. 5-7.

A Poetry Almanac for April

To celebrate "National Poetry Month," here are 100 recent poetry books for young people connected to a significant event or happening for each day of the month of April—a kind of almanac of children's poetry. Depending on your time constraints, you can feature just one poem to celebrate the day, connect any of the recommended poetry selections with a related book of fiction or nonfiction for storytime, or even lead a compare/contrast discussion of multiple approaches to the same topic (in poetry, fiction, or and/nonfiction). Any of these approaches will help anchor the notion that poetry is indeed for every day.

April 1: Humor
Event: In addition to being "National Poetry Month," April is also designated as "National Humor Month," beginning with April Fool's Day, of course.
Poetry: Humorous poetry often ranks as children's favorite type and luckily there are many collections of poetry to share and laugh about.
Katz, Alan. 2011. *Poems I Wrote When No One Was Looking.* New York: McElderry/Simon & Schuster.
Lewis, J. Patrick and Yolen, Jane. 2012. *Last Laughs: Animal Epitaphs.* Ill. by Jeffrey Timmins. Charlesbridge.
Nesbitt, Kenn. 2009. *My Hippo Has the Hiccups with CD: And Other Poems I Totally Made Up.* Naperville, IL: Sourcebooks.
Silverstein, Shel. 2011. *Every Thing On It.* New York: HarperCollins.

April 2: Internationalism
Event: Today is "International Children's Book Day" in honor of the birthday of Hans Christian Andersen, the Danish collector of many classic fairy tales.
Poetry: Poets beyond our U.S. borders offer wonderful works for young readers.
Rasmussen, Halfdan. 2011. *A Little Bitty Man and Other Poems for the Very Young.* Translated by Marilyn Nelson and Pamela Espeland. Somerville, MA: Candlewick.
Greenberg, Jan. Ed. 2008. *Side by Side: New Poems Inspired by Art from Around the World.* New York: Abrams.
Luján, Jorge. 2008. *Colors! Colores!* Toronto: Groundwood.

April 3: Dogs
Event: April has also been set aside as "Dog Appreciation Month."
Poetry: These poetry books showcase the unique qualities of the canine world.
Franco, Betsy. 2011. A *Dazzling Display of Dogs.* Berkley, CA: Tricycle.
Rosen, Michael J. 2011. *The Hound Dog's Haiku and Other Poems for Dog Lovers.* Somerville, MA: Candlewick.
Singer, Marilyn, 2012. *Every Day's a Dog's Day: A Year in Poems.* New York: Dial.

April 4: Baseball
Event: Baseball season begins in the spring with "Opening Day" scheduled for many pro teams this week.

Poetry: These titles about baseball offer poetry in motion.

Florian, Douglas. 2012. *Poem Runs; Baseball Poems and Paintings.* New York: Houghton Mifflin Harcourt.

Fehler, Gene. 2009. *Change-up: Baseball Poems.* New York: Clarion.

Maddox, Marjorie. 2009. *Rules of the Game: Baseball Poems.* Honesdale: Wordsong/Boyds Mills Press.

April 5: Breakthroughs

Event: On this day in 1887, Anne Sullivan made a breakthrough in communicating with her deaf and blind student, Helen Keller, showing her that the word "water," spelled with the Manual Alphabet, corresponded to the cool water running over her hand.

Poetry: Here are several poetry works that experiment with new and different poetic forms.

Heard, Georgia. Ed. 2012. *The Arrow Finds its Mark; A Book of Found Poems.* New York: Macmillan.

Jensen, Dana. 2012. *A Meal of the Stars; Poems Up and Down.* Boston: Houghton Mifflin.

Raczka, Bob. 2011. *Lemonade and Other Poems Squeezed from a Single Word.* New York: Roaring Brook.

April 6: Math

Event: April is also "Mathematics Awareness Month" to "promote awareness of mathematics-- its applications and beauty."

Poetry: Mathematics plus poetry may seem to be an unlikely pair, these titles prove otherwise.

Dillon, Leo and Diane. 2007. *Mother Goose; Numbers on the Loose.* San Diego, CA: Harcourt.

Franco, Betsy. 2003. *Mathematickles!* New York: McElderry.

Lewis, J. Patrick. 2012. *Edgar Allan Poe's Pie; Math Puzzlers in Classic Poems.* New York: Houghton Mifflin Harcourt.

April 7: Health

Event: Today is "World Health Day" sponsored by the World Health Organization (WHO) to draw attention to the importance of global health.

Poetry: Are there poetry books about body parts and body movement? Yes!

Wesiburd, Stefi. 2008. *Barefoot: Poems for Naked Feet.* Honesdale, PA: Boyds Mills/Wordsong.

Wolf, Allan. 2003. *The Blood-Hungry Spleen and Other Poems about Our Parts.* Somerville, MA: Candlewick.

Wong, Janet. 2007. *Twist: Yoga Poems.* New York: McElderry.

April 8: Spring

Event: Spring is on its way and today, in particular, many people celebrate Easter.

Poetry: The season of spring is a primary focus of these fresh poetry collections.

Florian, Douglas. 2006. *Handsprings.* New York: Greenwillow.

Hopkins, Lee. Bennett. Ed. 2010. *Sharing the Seasons.* New York: Margaret McElderry.

Thomas, Patricia. 2008. *Nature's Paintbox: A Seasonal Gallery of Art and Verse*. Minneapolis, MN: Millbrook Press, Inc.

April 9: Books
Event: On this day the first U. S. public library opened in 1833, in Peterborough, NH. It's time for "National Library Week," April 8-14, 2012, an opportunity to celebrate the contributions of our nation's libraries and librarians and to promote library use and support.
Poetry: Several playful poetry picture books spotlight books, reading, and libraries.
Hopkins, Lee Bennett. Ed. 2004. *Wonderful Words: Poems about Reading, Writing, Speaking and Listening*. New York: Simon & Schuster.
Hopkins, Lee Bennett. Ed. 2011. *I am the Book*. New York: Holiday House.
Lewis, J. Patrick. 2005. *Please Bury Me In The Library*. Orlando, FL: Gulliver Books/Harcourt.
Salas, Laura Purdie. 2011. *BookSpeak!*. New York: Clarion.

April 10: Siblings
Event: Today is "National Sibling Day," a day to honor and enjoy brothers and sisters.
Poetry: Siblings are the center of attention in these poetry books.
George, Kristine O'Connell. 2011. *Emma Dilemma: Big Sister Poems*. New York: Clarion.
Greenfield, Eloise. 2009. *Brother & Sisters: Family Poems*. New York: HarperCollins.
Lewis, J. Patrick and Yolen, Jane. 2012. *Take Two! A Celebration of Twins*. Somerville, MA: Candlewick.

April 11: African American History
Event: On this day in 1947, Jackie Robinson became the first African American to play major-league baseball. Interestingly, it also marks the date that the U. S. Civil Rights Act became law.
Poetry: Several excellent poetry books celebrate African American history including these.
Adoff, Arnold. 2011. *Roots and Blues; A Celebration*. New York: Clarion.
Greenfield, Eloise. 2011. *The Great Migration: Journey to the North*. New York: Amistad/HarperCollins.
Myers, Walter Dean. 2004. *Here in Harlem: Poems in Many Voices*. New York: Holiday House.
Weatherford, Carole Boston. 2007. *Birmingham, 1963*. Honesdale, PA: Wordsong/Boyds Mills Press.

April 12: Teens
Event: Today is "Teen Literature Day," celebrated every Thursday of National Library Week to raise awareness of the value of Young Adult (YA) literature.
Poetry: Look for these poetry titles that specifically target the edgy teen audience.
Mecum, Ryan. 2008. *Zombie Haiku*. Cincinnati, OH: How Books.
Mora, Pat. 2010. *Dizzy in Your Eyes*. New York: Knopf.

Paschen, Elise and Raccah, Dominique, Eds. 2010. *Poetry Speaks; Who I Am*. Naperville, IL: Sourcebooks.

Vardell, Sylvia and Wong, Janet. Eds. 2011. *P*TAG*. PoetryTagTime.com.

April 13: Hopkins Birthday

Event: Poet and anthologist Lee Bennett Hopkins celebrates his birthday today, the Guinness World Record holder for publishing more poetry anthologies for young people than any other person in history.

Poetry: Here are three recent poetry publications from the prolific Hopkins.

Hopkins, Lee Bennett. Ed. 2012. *Nasty Bugs*. New York: Dial.

Hopkins, Lee Bennett. Ed. 2011. *Dizzy Dinosaurs; An I Can Read Book*. New York: HarperCollins.

Hopkins, Lee Bennett, Ed. 2010. *Amazing Faces*. New York: Lee and Low.

April 14: Ships

Event: Shortly before midnight on April 14, the Titanic collided with an iceberg causing the ship to sink early the following morning, at 2:20 am on April 15.

Poetry: These novels in verse capture multiple points of view of impending disaster and mystery and the aftermath.

Engle, Margarita. 2011. *Hurricane Dancers; The First Caribbean Pirate Shipwreck*. New York: Henry Holt.

Montgomery, Hugh. 2002. *The Voyage of the Arctic Tern*. Somerville, MA: Candlewick.

Wolf, Allan. 2011. *The Watch That Ends the Night; Voices from the Titanic*. Somerville, MA: Candlewick.

April 15: Dreamers

Event: Today is Leonardo Da Vinci's birthday, born this day in 1452.

Poetry: Seek out poetry that inspires young readers and reveals the inspiration behind the creative or inventive mind.

Corcoran, Jill. Ed. 2012. *Dare to Dream… Change the World*. La Jolla, CA: Kane Miller.

Hopkins, Lee Bennett. Ed. 2009. *Incredible Inventions*. New York: HarperCollins.

Lewis, J. Patrick. 2001. *A Burst of Firsts: Doers, Shakers, and Record Breakers*. New York: Dial.

Sidman, Joyce. 2002. *Eureka! Poems about Inventors*. Brookfield, CT: Millbrook.

April 16: Flight

Event: Wilbur Wright, born this day in 1867, and his brother, Orville, were the first American aviators to fly in Kitty Hawk, North Carolina in 1903.

Poetry: Poetry about flight begins with birds and goes beyond.

George, Kristine O'Connell. 2004. *Hummingbird Nest: A Journal of Poems*. New York: Harcourt.

Hopkins, Lee Bennett. Ed. 2010. *Give Me Wings*. New York: Holiday House.

Yolen, Jane. 2011. *Birds of a Feather*. Honesdale, PA: Wordsong/Boyds Mills Press.

April 17: Space
Event: On April 17, 1970 Apollo 13 made it safely back to earth after the spacecraft suffered serious malfunctions ("Houston, we have a problem.").
Poetry: These poetry books offer a look at the world beyond our planet.
Florian, Douglas. 2007. *Comets, Stars, the Moon, and Mars*. Orlando, FL: Harcourt.
Salas, Laura Purdie. 2008. *And Then There Were Eight: Poems about Space*. Mankato, MN: Capstone.
Sklansky, Amy E. 2012. *Out of This World; Poems and Facts About Space*. New York: Knopf.

April 18: Patriotism
Event: On this day in 1775, the American patriot, Paul Revere, rode from Lexington to Concord, Massachusetts, to warn that the British were coming to attack.
Poetry: Patriotic poetry offers a perspective on what our homeland means to us.
Gunning, Monica. 2004. *America, My New Home*. San Francisco, CA: Children's Book Press.
Myers, Walter Dean. 2011. *We are America; A Tribute from the Heart*. New York: HarperCollins.
Smith, Charles R. Jr. 2003. *I am America*. New York: Scholastic.

April 19: The Holocaust
Event: Today is "Holocaust Remembrance Day," marking the anniversary of the Warsaw ghetto uprising during World War II.
Poetry: These novels in verse offer compelling Holocaust stories.
Janeczko, Paul B. 2011. *Requiem; Poems of the Terezín Ghetto*. Somerville, MA: Candlewick.
Levy, Debbie. 2010. *The Year of Goodbyes; A True Story of Friendship, Family and Farewells*. New York: Hyperion.
Roy, Jennifer. 2006. *Yellow Star*. Tarrytown, NY: Marshall Cavendish.

April 20: Gardens
Event: April has been designated "National Garden Month."
Poetry: Planting and poetry go together in these lovely books.
Havill, Juanita. 2006. *I Heard from Alice Zucchini: Poems about the Garden*. San Francisco, CA: Chronicle Books.
Shannon, George. 2006. *Busy in the Garden*. New York: Greenwillow.
Spinelli, Eileen. 2004. *In our Backyard Garden: Poems*. New York: Simon & Schuster.

April 21: Kindergarten
Event: Today is Kindergarten Day commemorating the birth of Friedrich Froebel who founded the first kindergarten in Blankenburg, Germany, in 1837. Appropriately, April 22–28, 2012 has also been designated as the Week of the Young Child (WOYC) by the National Association for Education of Young Children.
Poetry: These poetry collections are especially appropriate for very young children.

Calmenson, Stephanie. 2005. *Kindergarten Kids: Riddles, Rebuses, Wiggles, Giggles, and More*! New York: HarperCollins.

Schertle, Alice. 2009. *Button Up! Wrinkled Rhymes*. New York: Harcourt.

Yolen, Jane and Peters, Andrew Fusek. Eds. 2007. *Here's a Little Poem; A Very First Book of Poetry*. Somerville, MA: Candlewick.

Yolen, Jane and Peters, Andrew Fusek. Eds. 2010. *Switching on the Moon; A Very First Book of Bedtime Poems*. Somerville, MA: Candlewick.

April 22: Earth

Event: Since 1970 "Earth Day" has been celebrated worldwide on April 22 as a day for promoting recycling and other ways of conserving the Earth's natural resources.

Poetry: Here are several poetry collections that feature an earth-friendly focus.

Peck, Jan and Davis, David. Eds. 2011. *The Green Mother Goose; Saving the World One Rhyme at a Time*. New York: Sterling.

Peters, Lisa Westberg. 2003. *Earthshake: Poems from the Ground Up*. Ill. by Cathie Felstead. New York: HarperCollins.

Singer, Marilyn. 2002. *Footprints on the Roof: Poems about the Earth*. New York: Knopf.

Wassenhove, Sue Van. 2008. *The Seldom-Ever-Shady Glades*. Honesdale, PA: Boyds Mills/Wordsong.

April 23: Shakespeare

Event: William Shakespeare, one of the greatest poets and playwrights in history, was (probably) born on this day in 1564 in Stratford-upon-Avon. In honor of the bard, April 23 has been designated "Talk Like Shakespeare Day."

Poetry: These poetic collections and dramatic monologues are ideal for the aspiring performer or poet.

Ashman, Linda. 2009. *Come to the Castle*. Ill. by S. D. Schindler. New York: Roaring Brook Press.

Franco, Betsy. 2011. *21 Monologues for Teen Actors*. CreateSpace.

Schlitz, Laura Amy. 2007. *Good Masters! Sweet Ladies!: Voices from a Medieval Village*. Somerville, MA: Candlewick.

April 24: Geography

Event: In 1800 President John Adams approves $5000 to purchase "such books as many be necessary for the use of Congress," thus establishing what we now call the Library of Congress. The first collection arrives from London and includes 740 books and 3 maps.

Poetry: Geography is the focus of these poetry gems.

Hopkins, Lee Bennett. Ed. 2006. *Got Geography! Poems*. New York: Greenwillow.

Lewis, J. Patrick. 2002. *A World of Wonders: Geographic Travels in Verse and Rhyme*. New York: Dial.

Siebert, Diane. 2006. *Tour America: A Journey through Poems and Art*. San Francisco: Chronicle.

April 25: Riddles
Event: Alvin Schwartz's birthday, a collector of folklore, ghost stories, superstitions, jokes, tongue twisters, and riddles—with more than 50 books for children.
Poetry: Kids will enjoy sharing these riddle poems and guessing at the answers.
Dotlich, Rebecca Kai. 2001. *When Riddles Come Rumbling: Poems to Ponder.* Honesdale, PA: Wordsong/Boyds Mills Press.
Lewis, J. Patrick. 2004. *Scien-trickery: Riddles in Science.* Orlando: Silver Whistle.
Lewis, J. Patrick. 2009. *Spot the Plot; A Riddle Book of Book Riddles.* San Francisco: Chronicle.

April 26: Wings
Event: On April 26, 1795, John James Audubon, naturalist and artist, was born on a plantation in Haiti. He would become famous in his adopted country, the new United States, for painting and cataloging its winged creatures.
Poetry: Introduce birds, bees, and butterflies in these poetry collections.
Florian, Douglas. 2012. *Unbeelievables: Honeybee Poems and Paintings.*
Frost, Helen. 2012. *Step Gently Out.* Somerville, MA: Candlewick.
Harley, Avis. 2008. *The Monarch's Progress: Poems with Wings.* Honesdale, PA: Wordsong/Boyds Mills Press.
Nye, Naomi Shihab. 2008. *Honeybee.* New York: Greenwillow.

April 27: Trees
Event: On the last Friday of April most states celebrate "Arbor Day," a time to plant and care for trees.
Share: It's the perfect time to share these poet-tree books.
Florian, Douglas. 2010. *Poetrees.* Simon & Schuster.
Hoberman, Mary Ann and Wilson, Linda. Eds. 2009. *The Tree That Time Built: A Celebration of Nature, Science, and Imagination.* Naperville, IL: Sourcebooks.
Sidman, Joyce. 2009. *Red Sings From Treetops; A Year in Colors.* Boston: Houghton Mifflin.

April 28: School
Event: April is also national "School Library Month," a time to "celebrate the essential role that strong school library programs play in a student's educational career."
Poetry: Poetry about school is a favorite topic of many young people, capturing both the humor and the pathos of classroom life.
Dakos, Kalli. 2011. *A Funeral in the Bathroom and Other School Bathroom Poems.* New York: Albert Whitman.
Franco, Betsy. 2009. *Messing Around the Monkey Bars and other School Poems for Two Voices.* Somerville, MA: Candlewick.
Frost, Helen. 2004. *Spinning Through the Universe.* New York: Farrar, Straus & Giroux.
Salas, Laura. 2009. *Stampede! Poems to Celebrate the Wild Side of School!* New York: Clarion.

April 29: Writing

Event: As you come to the end of a month of poetry reading, students will often naturally turn to writing too, experimenting with creating their own original poetry.

Poetry: Offer these books full of poetry writing by young people themselves.

Franco, Betsy. 2008. Ed. *Falling Hard: Teenagers on Love.* Somerville, MA: Candlewick.

Lowe, Ayana. Ed. 2008. *Come and Play; Children of Our World Having Fun.* New York: Bloomsbury.

McLaughlin, Timothy. Ed. 2012. *Walking on Earth and Touching the Sky; Poetry and Prose by Lakota Youth at Red Cloud Indian School.* New York: Abrams.

Michael, Pamela, Ed. 2008. *River of Words.* Minneapolis, MN: Milkweed.

April 30: Día

Event: Today is "Children's Day/Book Day," also known as El día de los niños/El día de los libros (Día, for short), a celebration of children, families, and reading culminating on an annual celebration on April 30. Día emphasizes the importance of advocating literacy for every child regardless of linguistic and cultural background.

Poetry: Share these novels in verse that feature characters for whom learning to read is an empowering activity.

Engle, Margarita. 2006. *The Poet Slave of Cuba: A Biography of Juan Francisco Manzano.* New York: Henry Holt.

Engle, Margarita. 2012. *The Wild Book.* New York: Houghton Mifflin Harcourt.

Rose, Caroline Starr. 2012. *May B.* New York: Random House.

Based on: Vardell, Sylvia. 2012. 30 Days, 100 Poems. *Book Links.* March, pp. 12-19.

NOTE: For more literature-focused "almanac" resources, look for Anita Silvey's web site, the Children's Book Almanac http://childrensbookalmanac.com/archive/date/ and Susan Ohanian's resource book, *Books Day by Day; Anniversaries, Anecdotes & Activities* (Heinemann, 2001).

Poetry Tag: Connecting Poems for Young People

To celebrate National Poetry Month (in April or any other month), try this game of Poetry Tag. Choose a poem to begin. Find another poem to link to it based on some connection between the two poems: a word, an image, a topic, the form, or a poetic device, etc. Then find a third poem linked to the second one in some way. Then a fourth linked to the third. And so on. The connections may be different each time, taking the game of tag in new and unexpected directions. There is no "right" answer and the possibilities and permutations at each point are nearly endless. The key is to have fun finding, sharing, and linking poems. Here is one example of a "chain" of 30 poems beginning with Heidi Mordhorst's poem, "April Gale," from Pumpkin Butterfly. *Invite children to take the game find their own poems and make their own connections.*

1. Begin with "April Gale" by Heidi Mordhorst
From: Mordhorst, Heidi. 2009. *Pumpkin Butterfly; Poems from the Other Side of Nature.* Wordsong/Boyds Mills Press.

2. Then look for "Spring" by Lee Bennett Hopkins
From: Hopkins, Lee. Bennett. Comp. 2010. *Sharing the Seasons.* Margaret McElderry.
Connection to previous poem: The image of spring blossoms

3. Next, find "Grass" by Joyce Sidman
From: Sidman, Joyce. 2010. *Ubiquitous; Celebrating Nature's Survivors.* Houghton Mifflin.
Connection to previous poem: What is sprouting?

4. Link with "Spring Welcome" by Deborah Ruddell
From: Ruddell, Deborah. 2009. *A Whiff of Pine, A Hint of Skunk.* Simon & Schuster.
Connection to previous poem: Personification of grass/trees

5. Seek out "Giant Sequoias" by Douglas Florian
From: Florian, Douglas. 2010. *Poetrees.* Beach Lane Books.
Connection to previous poem: The topic of trees

6. Find "Can You Dig It?" by Robert Weinstock
From: Weinstock, Robert. 2010. *Can You Dig It?* Hyperion.
Connection to previous poem: What is ancient?

7. Share "Clay" by Marilyn Singer
From: Hopkins, Lee Bennett. Comp. 2007. *Behind the Museum Door Poems to Celebrate the Wonders of Museums*. Abrams.
Connection to previous poem: The earth

8. Link with "Before" by Avis Harley
From: Harley, Avis. 2008. *The Monarch's Progress; Poems with Wings*. Wordsong/Boyds Mills Press.
Connection to previous poem: Looking back

9. Connect with "Swarm" by Laura Purdie Salas
From: Salas, Laura Purdie. 2009. *Stampede! Poems to Celebrate the Wild Side of School!* Clarion.
Connection to previous poem: From butterflies to bumblebees

10. Tie to "Watch Your Step" by Leslie Bulion
From: Bulion, Lesley. 2006. *Hey, There, Stink Bug!* Charlesbridge.
Connection to previous poem: From bumblebees to bugs

11. Look for "Dear Orangutan" by David Elliott
From: Elliott, David. 2010. *In the Wild*. Candlewick.
Connection to previous poem: What was here "before us"?

12. Share "Brothers and Sisters" by Eloise Greenfield
From: Greenfield, Eloise. 2009. *Brothers and Sisters: Family Poems*. Amistad/HarperCollins.
Connection to previous poem: From cousins to family

13. Read aloud "Q and A" by Hope Anita Smith
From: Smith, Hope Anita. 2009. *Mother; Poems*. Henry HoltMacmillan.
Connection to previous poem: From siblings to parents

14. Tie to "When Dad Is Away" by Gene Fehler
From: Fehler, Gene. 2009. *Change-up; Baseball Poems*. Clarion.
Connection to previous poem: From mothers to fathers

15. Find and share "Songs" by Pat Mora
From: Mora, Pat. 2010. *Dizzy in Your Eyes: Poems About Love*. Knopf
Connection to previous poem: From fathers to grandfathers

16. Link with "Birthday Lights" by Calef Brown
From: Brown, Calef. 2006. *Flamingos on the Roof: Poems and Paintings*.
Houghton Mifflin.
Connection to previous poem: Grandfather's wisdom

17. Follow up with "Put the World in Your Pocket" by Bobbi Katz
From: Katz, Bobbi. 2009. *More Pocket Poems*. Dutton.
Connection to previous poem: Look for magic; "carry a sunset"

18. Now hunt for "Old Coin" by John Frank
From: Frank, John. 2008. *Keepers: Treasure-Hunt Poems*. Roaring Brook.
Connection to previous poem: "Holding a quarter," finding a dime

19. Share "Are We There Yet?" by David L. Harrison
From Harrison, David L. 2009. *Vacation; We're Going to the Ocean*.
Wordsong/Boyds Mills Press.
Connection to previous poem: Century, years, hours

20. Seek out "Anatomy Class" by Betsy Franco
From: Franco, Betsy. 2009. *Messing Around the Monkey Bars and other
School Poems for Two Voices*. Candlewick.
Connection to previous poem: Hours, clocks, and watches

21. Search for "A School of Fish" by Marjorie Maddox
From: Maddox, Marjorie. 2008. *A Crossing of Zebras; Animal Packs in
Poetry*. Wordsong/Boyds Mills Press.
Connection to previous poem: Another kind of school

22. Read and share "Dreams" by Tracie Vaughn Zimmer
From: Zimmer, Tracie Vaughn. 2007. *Reaching for Sun*. Bloomsbury.
Connection to previous poem: What to know, what to be

23. Tie to "Ode to Blue Jeans" by Rebecca Kai Dotlich
 From: Hopkins, Lee Bennett. Comp. 2009. *Incredible Inventions*.
HarperCollins.
Connection to previous poem: All kinds of jobs

24. Follow up with "Someone for Each of Us" by Linda Ashman
From: Ashman, Linda. 2008. *Stella, Unleashed; Notes from the Doghouse*.
Sterling.
Connection to previous poem: All kinds of people

25. Have fun with "The Hippopotabus" by J. Patrick Lewis
From: Lewis, J. Patrick. 2009. *Countdown to Summer: A Poem for Every Day of the School Year*. Little Brown.
Connection to previous poem: All kinds of books

26. Now look for "The Library" by Monica Gunning
From: Gunning, Monica. 2004. *America, My New Home*. Wordsong/Boyds Mills Press.
Connection to previous poem: All kinds of libraries

27. Link with "Juan" by Margarita Engle
From: Engle, Margarita. 2006. *The Poet Slave of Cuba: A Biography of Juan Francisco Manzano*. Henry Holt.
Connection to previous poem: The power of books

28. Connect with "My Needs" by JonArno Lawson
From: Lawson, JonArno. 2010. *Think Again*. Toronto: Kids Can Press.
Connection to previous poem: A place to wander

29. Tie with "Wish" by Linda Sue Park
From: Park, Linda Sue. 2007. *Tap Dancing on the Roof; Sijo Poems*. Clarion.
Connection to previous poem: A poem to ponder

30. Conclude with "Breath" by Janet Wong
From: Wong, Janet. 2007. *Twist; Yoga Poems*. Simon & Schuster.
Connection to previous poem: The heart

Based on: Vardell, Sylvia M. (2011). Everyday poetry: Poetry tag. *Book Links*. 20, (3), 14-15.

For more examples of poetry tag, see:
Vardell, Sylvia and Wong, Janet. Eds. 2011. *P*TAG*. PoetryTagTime.com.
Vardell, Sylvia and Wong, Janet. Eds. 2011. *PoetryTagTime*. PoetryTagTime.com.
Vardell, Sylvia and Wong, Janet. Eds. 2011. *Gift Tag*. PoetryTagTime.com.

Poetry Scavenger Hunt

As we begin sharing poetry with young people, we need to introduce them to what the library shelves can offer. One way of doing that is using a "scavenger hunt" kind of game to challenge them to take the books off the shelf and thumb through them. They can work in pairs or small groups to see who can find the most items first. Perhaps they'll want to share a new-found favorite poem, too.

1. Find a book of rhyming poetry

2. Find a collection of Mother Goose poetry or nursery rhymes

3. Find a book containing non-rhyming poetry (free verse)

4. Find a poem picture book (containing a single poem) or a novel in verse

5. Find a book of bilingual poetry

6. Find a book of poetry by an African American poet

7. Find a book of concrete or shape poetry or haiku poetry

8. Find a book of poetry by Jack Prelutsky or Shel Silverstein

9. Find a book of poetry published before 2000

10. Find a thematic collection of poetry (linked by subject, like "Halloween" poems)

Treasure Hunt for Poem Parts

Challenge kids to work with a poetry buddy to put their developing poetry knowledge to use in searching for the following poetic parts in one single poetry book. By the end, they may also have found a fun poem to share, too.

1. Find a line of poetry that mentions an animal or color

2. Find a line of poetry that mentions the name of a person or place

3. Find two lines of poetry that rhyme

4. Find three pairs of rhyming words

5. Find a line of poetry with alliteration (repeated first letter)

6. Find a line of poetry that is four words long

7. Find a line of poetry that has ten syllables or more

8. Find the title (or page number) of the shortest poem in the collection

9. Find the title of the last poem in the collection

10. Find the first line of the first poem in the collection

Based on: Fitch, Sheree and Swartz, Larry. 2008. *The Poetry Experience; Choosing and Using Poetry in the Classroom.* Markham, ON: Pembroke, p. 16.

Calendar of Poet Birthdays

As we look for a "hook" for promoting poetry, celebrating poet birthdays is one way to make a personal connection—one that children particularly enjoy.

January
2 Jean Little
5 Monica Gunning
6 Carl Sandburg
7 Minfong Ho
6 Carl Sandburg
18 A. A. Milne; Grace Nichols
19 Pat Mora; Edgar Allan Poe; Effie Lee Newsom
25 Robert Burns
27 Lewis Carroll
29 Tony Johnston

February
1 Langston Hughes
2 Judith Viorst
3 Liz Rosenberg
11 Jane Yolen
15 Sonya Sones
20 Kenn Nesbitt
21 Francisco X. Alarcón
26 Allan Wolf
27 Laura E. Richards

March
1 Alan Katz
4 Craig Crist-Evans
9 Robert Pottle
12 Naomi Shihab Nye
13 David Harrison
17 Lilian Moore; Ralph Fletcher
18 Douglas Florian
26 Robert Frost

April
7 Alice Schertle
12 Gary Soto
13 Lee Bennett Hopkins
20 April Halprin Wayland
22 William Jay Smith; Ron Koertge
25 George Ella Lyon
26 Marilyn Nelson
28 Barbara Juster Esbensen

May

2 Bobbi Katz
5 J. Patrick Lewis
6 Kristine O'Connell George; José-Luis Orozco
7 Michael Rosen
8 Constance Levy
10 Mel Glenn
12 Edward Lear, Limerick Day
17 Eloise Greenfield
25 Joyce Carol Thomas

June

1 Bruce Lansky
6 Cynthia Rylant
7 Nikki Giovanni
8 Judy Sierra
16 Kalli Dakos
20 Nancy Wood
24 John Ciardi
26 Nancy Willard

July

6 Kathi Appelt
10 Rebecca Kai Dotlich; Patricia Hubbell
13 Anna Grossnickle Hines
16 Arnold Adoff
17 Karla Kuskin
19 Eve Merriam
27 Paul B. Janeczko

August

12 Mary Ann Hoberman; Walter Dean Myers
15 Betsy Franco
17 Myra Cohn Livingston
19 Ogden Nash
21 X.J. Kennedy
29 Karen Hesse; Sylvia Cassedy
31 Dennis Lee

September

5 Paul Fleischman
8 Jack Prelutsky
9 Aileen Fisher
15 Sara Holbrook
25 Harry Behn; Shel Silverstein
30 Janet S. Wong

October
3 Marilyn Singer
20 Nikki Grimes
27 Lillian Morrison
29 Valerie Worth
31 Joan Bransfield Graham

November
2 Ted Scheu
13 Robert Louis Stevenson
15 David McCord
18 Robin Hirsch
22 Brod Bagert

December
1 Carol Diggory Shields
5 Christina Rossetti
10 Emily Dickinson
13 Georgia Heard
21 Susan Pearson
27 Juan Felipe Herrera
30 Rudyard Kipling

Poetry Celebration Occasions

As we build an environment where enthusiasm for poetry will flourish, we can consider what poet Georgia Heard calls "poetry rituals." These are poetry traditions that provide a natural way to incorporate poetry into pre-existing routines and special occasions. They give children something to look forward to and in many cases provide opportunities for child participation. One excellent resource for finding "occasional" poetry is Lee Bennett Hopkins' new book, Days to Celebrate: A Full Year of Poetry, People, Holidays, History, Fascinating Facts, and More *(Greenwillow, 2005). As Maria Brountas (1995) has said, "Poetry is a lovely gift we give to children that appreciates in value and lasts throughout their lifetime." Here is a list of possible poetry celebration occasions and ideas.*

1. Invite children to perform their own poem readings on the last Friday of the month (or other set day) as a Poetry Friday event, popular in the children's literature world. Create a coffee house setting with tablecloths, bongos, and a microphone for fun. Record some of the readings for a homemade listening center.

2. If audio or public address announcements are made on a regular basis, include the oral reading of a poem (by a child or other volunteer) on a daily or weekly basis. Challenge children to work with a partner to prepare a performance reading with multiple voices, sound effects, or musical instruments.

3. Read aloud individually selected poems for children's birthdays (e.g., birthday poems or favorite poems of the birthday child). Invite families to donate a new poetry book in honor of the birthday child.

4. Research poet biographies and celebrate poet birthdays by sharing some of their poems on the poet's birthday. Create a Hall of Poets where poems and poet info can be displayed in the hallway.

5. Look for a poem to share that is tied to current news or historical events of the day or week such as a weather disaster news story or the opening of the first U.S. public library on April 9, 1833, or "Children's Day/Book Day," also known as El día de los niños/El día de los libros on April 30. Tie this in with social activism, letter writing, or other awareness building activity.

6. Share holiday poems from varied perspectives to celebrate special holidays such as Labor Day, Thanksgiving, Chinese (Lunar) New Year, etc. Over the course of the year, collect the poems to build a homemade holiday anthology.
`
7. Combine poems with food sharing a poem about food while children enjoy a snack at lunch, snack time, parent meetings, Mother's Day Tea, or Open House. Choose poems from an e-book (such as PoetryTagTime) and project the poem for all to see during the event.

8. Open with a poem for the first day of school, last day of school, or graduation or commencement celebration to add dignity to the occasion. If radio or cable television time is available, record the reading and use to begin or end the segment.

9. Prepare a poem recitation in honor of a visiting guest—a speaker, a local celebrity, a sports figure, an author, etc. Post quoted excerpts from his/her writings or speeches to accompany the poem(s).

10. Consider hosting a poet-in-residence as a culminating poetry event or to promote poetry reading and writing. Be sure the kids are prepared and have read the poet's work. If an actual on-site visit is difficult, consider a virtual visit via Skype, FaceTime, or other phone conferencing tool.

Poetry Display Ideas

We all know that a good visual display can generate extra interest. When was the last time poetry for children was the priority? Highlighting new poetry books, low-circulating poetry book gems, books by featured poets, and children's favorite poetry books are all possibilities for inviting displays. This can be through traditional shelf, table top, and showcase book displays or in other creative ways. Here are 5 key ways to make poems and poetry a part of the physical and virtual environment that kids experience.

1. PROPS: Poet Janet Wong talks fondly of her "poetry suitcase." She has gathered an assortment of objects and realia that connect with some of her poems (e.g., a toy turtle, shoe, play telephone). She asks children to choose an object, and then shares the poem that "corresponds" with that object and explains the connection. She encourages children to do the same—choose favorite poems, find related objects, and use them as props when sharing the poem. For kids who are kinesthetic learners, sharing props means "touching" the poem! These physical objects can also then be displayed with the poem.

2. POSTERS: Favorite poems can be made into poem posters (please follow fair use practice) and displayed on doors, lockers, in hallways, at entrances, etc. One enterprising teacher displays poems on the wall over the pencil sharpener or the water fountain where children often wait (and read idly). This is similar to the initiative launched by the Poetry Society of America, the "Poetry in Motion" project which put poems in public transportation systems around the country. Make poems an incidental part of their everyday world.

3. MOBILES: New or favorite poems can also be displayed via mobiles and other three-dimensional displays. One librarian created a "poet-tree" by using rolled up brown paper to create a tree trunk and branches and invited children to write their favorite poems on green paper cut into leaf shapes which were attached to the "tree limbs"—the more leaves and poems, the better.

4. MASCOTS: If you want a poetry "mascot," consider using Danitra Brown (in the poetry of Nikki Grimes) or Everett Anderson (in the poem picture books of Lucille Clifton) or Fearless Fernie (in the poetry of Gary Soto). These characters appear in multiple poetry collections and thus have several attributes to explore. But other distinctive personalities emerge from children's poetry as well, such as Mother Goose characters, Anna Banana or Miss Mary Mack, the owl and the pussycat, Casey (at the bat), and others.

6. WEB SITES: If you have access to a school or library web site, blog site, Facebook page, etc., consider adding a poetry presence to that display. A poetry quote can easily be featured on a rotating basis. If more space is available, showcase children's original poems (with their permission), information about new poetry books, lists of children's favorite poems or poetry books, or a featured poet of local or national stature. Children themselves can assist you with taking your poetry display efforts online.

Poetry Quotes

Sharing a timely quote can be an inspiring way to remind young people of the power of poetry across the ages. Here are just a few of the most well known.

Poetry and Hums aren't things which you get, they're things which get YOU. And all you can do is to go where they can find you.
A. A. Milne, *The House At Pooh Corner*

Only the rarest kind of best in anything can be good enough for the young.
Walter de la Mare

Poets are the unacknowledged legislators of the world.
Percy Bysshe Shelley

A poem begins with a lump in the throat.
Robert Frost

Poetry-- the best words in their best order.
Samuel Taylor Coleridge

For what is a poem but a hazardous attempt at self-understanding: it is the deepest part of autobiography.
Robert Penn Warren

Genuine poetry can communicate before it is understood.
T.S. Eliot

A child's first encounter with poetry happens only once.
Brod Bagert

Poetry begins in delight and ends in wisdom.
Robert Frost

Kids need to become friends with poetry as well. They need to know that poems can comfort them, make them laugh, help them remember, nurture them to know and understand themselves more completely.
Georgia Heard

Poems for children are like toys, that are made of words, and these words give wings to their imagination. Children want to sing them, to dance with them, and to play with them. Therefore, the poems have to be musical, colorful and easy for children to be used as toys.
Mahmud Kianush

If... it makes my whole body so cold no fire can warm me, I know that is poetry
Emily Dickinson

Poetry needs to be read out loud. Even though reading alone, the words sound better when spoken out loud to yourself. It's easier to savor the flavor of the words as they roll around in your mouth for your ears to enjoy.
Eve Merriam

It is difficult to get the news from poems yet men die miserably every day for lack of what is found there.
William Carlos Williams

Ordering a man to write a poem is like commanding a pregnant woman to give birth to a red-headed child.
Carl Sandburg

Immature poets imitate; mature poets steal.
T.S. Eliot

Out of a quarrel with others we make rhetoric, out of a quarrel with ourselves we make poetry.
W. B. Yeats

Every poet is a big child. And every child is a little poet. Childhood is the poetry of life. Poetry is the childhood of the world.
Boris Novak

Poetry is the renewal of words forever and ever. Poetry is that by which we live forever and ever unjaded. Poetry is that by which the world is never old.
Robert Frost

The language of the poem gives it its shape, as does its mood. The story shapes the verse.
Karla Kuskin

Poetry is simply the most beautiful way of saying things.
Matthew Arnold

Poetry is when an emotion has found its thought and the thought has found words.
Robert Frost

Poetry is all that is worth remembering in life.
William Hazlitt

Like the onion, poetry is a constant discovery. Peel the onion, layer after layer, until its very heart is reached...it adds taste, zest, and a sharp but sweet quality that enriches our lives.
Ruth Gordon

Poetry is most poetry when it makes noise.
Donald Hall

Next to being a great poet, is the power of understanding one.
Henry Wadsworth Longfellow

At the touch of love everyone becomes a poet.
Plato

Poetry is what gets lost in translation.
Robert Frost

Listen, real poetry doesn't say anything, it just ticks off the possibilities.
Jim Morrison (of *The Doors*)

You don't have to suffer to be a poet. Adolescence is enough suffering for anyone.
John Ciardi

Tell all the truth but tell it slant.
Emily Dickinson

A poem is never finished, only abandoned.
Paul Valery

Poetry is truth in its Sunday clothes.
Joseph Roux

There's no money in poetry, but there's no poetry in money either.
Robert Graves

Poetry is the spontaneous overflow of powerful feelings recollected in tranquillity.
William Wordsworth

Don't just make poetry available, make it unavoidable.
Bernice Cullinan

My parents and my teachers were my best audience.
Karla Kuskin

Part of being a reader of poetry is getting to know poets and their poetry intimately.
Georgia Heard

Instead of building a fence of formality around poetry, I want to emphasize its accessibility, the sound, rhythm, humor, the inherent simplicity. Poetry can be as natural and effective a form of self-expression as singing or shouting.
Karla Kuskin

Poetry teaches us the power of a few words.
Ralph Waldo Emerson

You will not find poetry anywhere unless you bring some of it with you.
Joseph Joubert

With me poetry has not been a purpose, but a passion.
Edgar Allan Poe

Poetry comes nearer to vital truth than history.
Plato

When power leads man towards arrogance, poetry reminds him of his limitations. When power narrows the areas of man's concern, poetry reminds him of the richness and diversity of his existence. When power corrupts, poetry cleanses.
John F. Kennedy

Between what I see and what I say,
Between what I say and what I keep silent,
Between what I keep silent and what I dream,
Between what I dream and what I forget,
Poetry.
Octavio Paz

Poetry always remembers that it was an oral art before it was a written art. It remembers that it was first song.
Jorge Luis Borges

Poetry is the music of the soul; and, above all, of great and feeling souls.
Voltaire

Poetry is the synthesis of hyacinths and biscuits.
Carl Sandburg

Poems about Libraries, Books, and Reading

Poets have been writing about the power of reading, libraries, and books for generations. With a focus on books and reading, these poems are the perfect way to open up a storytime, lesson, or read aloud session. In fact, a favorite book-related poem can become the ritual that gathers the children together, brings a lesson to closure, or welcomes parents and adults. Here is just a sampling of selections.

1. Alarcón, Francisco X. 1999. "Books" from *Angels Ride Bikes: And Other Fall Poems/ Los Angeles Andan en Bicicleta: Y Otros Poemas de Otoño*. San Francisco, CA: Children's Book Press.

2. Appelt, Kathi. 1997. "Javier" from *Just People and Paper/Pen/Poem: A Young Writer's Way to Begin*. Spring, TX: Absey & Co.

3. Bagert, Brod. 1999. "Library-Gold" from *Rainbows, Head Lice and Pea-Green Tile; Poems in the Voice of the Classroom Teacher*. Gainesville, FL: Maupin House.

4. Dakos, Kalli. 2003. "When the Librarian Reads to Us" from *Put Your Eyes Up Here: And Other School Poems*. New York: Simon & Schuster.

5. Frost, Helen. 2003. "Do Not Leave Children Unattended" from *Keesha's House*. New York: Farrar, Straus & Giroux.

6. George, Kristine O'Connell. 2002. "School Librarian" from *Swimming Upstream: Middle School Poems*. New York: Clarion Books.

7. Giovanni, Nikki. 1971. "ten years old" from *Spin a Soft Black Song*. New York: Hill & Wang.

8. Glenn, Mel. 2000. "Eddie Sabinsky" from *Split Image*. New York: HarperCollins.

9. Greenfield. Eloise. 2006. "At the Library" from *The Friendly Four*. New York: HarperCollins.

10. Grimes, Nikki. 1997. "At the Library" from *It's Raining Laughter*. New York: Dial.

11. Grimes, Nikki. 1998. "42nd Street Library" form *Jazmin's Notebook*. New York: Dial.

12. Gunning, Monica. 2004. "The Library" from *America, My New Home*. Honesdale, PA: Wordsong/Boyds Mills Press.

13. Herrick, Steven. 2004. "Lord of the Lounge" from *The Simple Gift.* New York: Simon & Schuster.

14. Hopkins, Ellen. 2006. "See, the Library" from *burned.* New York: McElderry.

15. Hopkins, Lee Bennett. Ed. 2000. "Good Books, Good Times" from *Good Books, Good Times!* New York: HarperTrophy.

16. Katz, Alan. 2001. "Give Me a Break" from *Take Me Out of the Bathtub and Other Silly Dilly Songs.* New York: Scholastic.

17. Lewis, J. Patrick. 2005. "Please Bury Me in the Library" and "Necessary Gardens" from *Please Bury Me in the Library.* San Diego, Harcourt.

18. Lewis, J. Patrick. 1999. "Read... Think... Dream" from: *The Bookworm's Feast: A Potluck of Poems.* New York: Dial.

19. Lewis, J. Patrick. 2009. "#66 The Hippopotabus," "*#174 The Librarian,*" "*#116 Library Fine,*" and "*#89 New York Public Library*" from *Countdown to Summer: A Poem for Every Day of the School Year.* New York: Little, Brown.

20. Lewis, J. Patrick. 2009. "Librarian" from *The Underwear Salesman: And Other Jobs for Better or Verse.* New York: Simon & Schuster/Atheneum.

21. Livingston, Myra Cohn. 1994. "Quiet" in Hopkins, Lee Bennett. Ed. *April Bubbles Chocolate; An ABC of Poetry.* New York: Simon & Schuster.

22. Lottridge, Celia Barker. 2002. "Anna Marie's Library Book and What Happened' in Pearson, Deborah. Ed. *When I Went to the Library.* Toronto: Groundwood Books.

23. McLoughland, Beverly. 1990. "Surprise" in Hopkins, Lee Bennett. Ed. 1990. *Good Books, Good Times!* New York: HarperTrophy.

24. Medina, Jane. 1999. "The Library Card" from *My Name is Jorge on Both Sides of the River: Poems.* Honesdale, PA: Boyds Mills Press.

25. Merriam, Eve. 1998. "Reach for a Book" in Rich, Mary Perrotta, Ed. 1998. *Book Poems: Poems from National Children's Book Week, 1959-1998.* New York: Children's Book Council.

26. Nye, Naomi Shihab. 1998. "Because of Libraries We Can Say These Things" from *Fuel.* Rochester, NY: BOA Editions.

27. Nye, Naomi Shihab. 2005. "The List" from *A Maze Me; Poems for Girls*. New York: Greenwillow.

28. Prelutsky, Jack. 2006. "It's Library Time" from *What a Day It Was at School!* New York: Greenwillow.

29. Sidman, Joyce. "This Book" from:
http://www.joycesidman.com/bookmark.html

30. Silverstein, Shel. 1981. "Overdues" from *A Light in the Attic*. New York: HarperCollins.

31. Soto, Gary. 1992. "Ode To My Library" from *Neighborhood Odes*. San Diego: Harcourt.

32. Worth, Valerie. 1994. "Library" from *All the Small Poems and Fourteen More*. New York: Farrar, Straus & Giroux.

33. Zimmer, Tracie Vaughn. 2009. "Librarian" from *Steady Hands: Poems About Work*. New York: Clarion.

Based on: Vardell, Sylvia M. (2006). A place for poetry: Celebrating the library in poetry. *Children and Libraries*. 4, (2), 35-41 and Vardell, S. M. (2007). Everyday poetry: Celebrating Children's Book Week with book-themed poetry. *Book Links*. 17, (2), 14-15.

Also look for the following poetry books:
Rich, Mary Perrotta. Ed. 1998. *Book Poems: Poems from National Children's Book Week, 1959-1998*. New York: Children's Book Council.
Hopkins, Lee Bennett. Ed. 2004. *Wonderful Words: Poems about Reading, Writing, Speaking and Listening*. New York: Simon & Schuster.
Hopkins, Lee Bennett. Ed. 2011. *I am the Book*. Holiday House.
Salas, Laura Purdie. 2011. *BookSpeak!*. Ill. by Josee Bisaillon. Clarion.

Silverstein and Prelutsky Poetry Book Read-Alikes

In survey after survey, we find many libraries hold multiple copies of Shel Silverstein's poetry collections. His work is a staple of children's poetry for several decades now. Jack Prelutsky follows in being represented in most library collections with his zany humor and musical rhythms. Here are additional poets to recommend when young readers ask for "more like this" with one sample title suggested for each poet. These poets each have their own unique and distinctive style, of course, but they offer some of the same qualities in humor, wordplay, topic, or style that young readers appreciate about Silverstein's and Prelutsky's poetry.

If you like Shel Silverstein… try:
John Ciardi
Douglas Florian
Sara Holbrook
Alan Katz
X. J. Kennedy
Karla Kuskin

Ciardi, John. 1962/1987. *You Read to Me, I'll Read to You.* Philadelphia: Lippincott. Reprinted. New York: HarperTrophy, 1987.

Florian, Douglas. 1999. *Laugh-eteria: Poems and Drawings.* San Diego, CA: Harcourt Brace.

Holbrook, Sara. 2011. *Weird? (Me, Too!) Let's Be Friends.* Honesdale, PA: Wordsong/Boyds Mills Press.

Katz, Alan. 2011. *Poems I Wrote When No One Was Looking.* Ill. by Ed Koren. New York: Simon & Schuster.

Kennedy, X.J. 2002. *Exploding Gravy, Poems to Make You Laugh.* New York: Little, Brown.

Kuskin, Karla. 2003. *Moon, Have You Met My Mother? The Collected Poems of Karla Kuskin.* New York: HarperCollins.

If you like Jack Prelutsky… try:
Calef Brown
Kalli Dakos
J. Patrick Lewis
David McCord
Judy Sierra
Marilyn Singer

Brown, Calef. 2006. *Flamingos on the Roof.* Boston: Houghton Mifflin.

Dakos, Kalli. 2003. *Put Your Eyes Up Here: And Other School Poems.* New York: Simon & Schuster.

Lewis, J. Patrick. 2009. *The Underwear Salesman: And Other Jobs for Better or Verse.* Ill. by Serge Bloch. New York: Simon & Schuster.

McCord, David. 1999. *Every Time I Climb a Tree.* New York: Little, Brown.

Sierra, Judy. 2005. *Gruesome Guide to World Monsters.* Somerville, MA: Candlewick.

Singer, Marilyn. 2001. *Monster Museum.* New York: Hyperion.

Tips for Featuring Poets for Young People

We typically feature popular fiction writers with booktalks and displays in our book promotion activities, but have we considered giving poets the same publicity and close study? Creating time and space for featured poets helps introduce their work and encourage children to read more poetry. In addition, it can be inspiring for young would-be poets to see that there are successful adults who have made poetry writing their career. Here are guidelines for showcasing a "featured poet."

1. Consider featuring a "poet of the month." Choosing a variety of poets to highlight on a rotating basis to provide children with more in-depth exposure to the poems and poetry writing of each poet.
2. Start with the award-winning poets and other contemporary poets whose works children enjoy (e.g., NCTE Poetry Award, Lee Bennett Hopkins Award, Claudia Lewis Award, Lion and Unicorn Award).
3. Look for poets who may live and work in your immediate vicinity. Check with the local branch of the Society of Children's Book Writers and Illustrators.
4. Research poet birthdays and consider using a poet birthday as the "hook" for featuring a given poet.
5. Research biographical information about the poet and share with children.
6. Look for autobiographies, biographies, video/audio interviews, and poet Web sites to share.
7. Create a bulletin board, poster, mobile, or physical display featuring the poet (include a photo, a print out of her/his web site home page, feature "five fun facts" about her/him).
8. Collect the poet's works, display them as a set, make them prominent and available.
9. Read the poets' works aloud often throughout the month (at openings, closings, transitions, storytimes, etc.).
10. Investigate setting up an online chat, Skype visit, or even a guest appearance by the poet; be sure to prepare the children beforehand with extensive reading.
11. If funds allow, see about setting up a Poet-in-Residence program inviting a poet to work with children on an ongoing basis for a short period of time.
12. Create a Hall of Poets to collect and feature highlights of ALL the featured poets over time.
13. Involve children in choosing poets to study and in developing featured poet centers or displays.

Based on: Vardell, Sylvia. 2007. *Poetry People: A Practical Guide to Children's Poets.* Libraries Unlimited.

Tips for Celebrating National Poetry Month with Young People

Probably the biggest celebration of poetry occurs during April, designated as National Poetry Month across the U.S since 1996. There are a variety of ways to make poetry special in April, however, don't wait until April to share good poems with children. April is simply a good time to reach out to parents, families, care-givers, and the community at large to share poetry in all kinds of creative ways. Here are a few ideas.

1. Start each day with a poem read aloud by someone different (invite guest readers); strive for 30 poems for 30 days.
2. Set up a coffeehouse-style poetry reading in a classroom or library. (Don't forget the refreshments.)
3. Contact local banks and businesses to ask them to consider displaying student poetry on their walls.
4. Write poems on postcards or letters and mail them to friends and neighbors.
5. Contact radio stations about hosting a live on-air poetry reading either at a school, library, or radio station.
6. Leave a poem on the answering machine at home or school or as a cell phone message.
7. Make a National Poetry Month Time Capsule. Students can submit favorite poems or their own original writing. Put them in the Time Capsule and have a ceremonial sealing, not to be opened until National Poetry Month next year or in five years or other designated interval.
8. Send a poem to a state or local representative or other government official.
9. Make National Poetry Month buttons. Inscribe them with haiku poems, short poems, or favorite lines of poetry. Wear them the whole month of April.
10. Pen-pal with another classroom or student group, locally or nationally, and pass favorite and original poems back and forth throughout the month. Make a book of the correspondence.
11. Plan a poetry reading for a senior center, hospital, or local business.
12. Experiment with developing a poetry blog or other web resource where students can share favorite poems or respond to posted poems.

Based on: Potato Hill Poetry web site (*http://www.potatohill.com/npm.html* accessed March, 2005; March 21, 2012).

Tips for Planning Poetry Lessons

There are many ways to prepare a lesson focused on poetry. In the field of reading instruction, there are generally a "pre," "during," and "post" components of lesson planning. Here are some tips for each of these parts.

Before reading the poem
Build background, set a purpose, create interest, and/or make predictions.
- Introduce the poem by title and the poet by name.
- Connect the subject of the poem to other things read previously.
- Highlight any vocabulary that may be difficult beforehand.

Over time, try these pre-reading strategies, but only one at a time.
- Guess what the poem might be about based on the poem's title.
- Preview the poem's structure noting anything unusual.
- Preview the poem's content noting anything unusual.

During the poem reading
Read the poem aloud to the group. If possible, provide the poem text (via book, poster, or projection) so students can follow along.

Have students read the poem along orally in a second reading.

Over time, try various choral reading and poetry performance strategies.

Monitor student fluency and understanding. Incorporate one of the following strategies. Vary over time.
- Discuss and verify their earlier predictions.
- Discuss key vocabulary.
- Highlight favorite lines or key lines and stanzas and discuss.
- Repeat reading, chorally or individually a third (or more) time(s).

After reading the poem
Plan follow-up instruction based on your observations. Mini lessons can focus on content, structure, skills or additional poetry background building.
Content Focus:
- Discuss responses to the poem.
- Invite students to paraphrase the poem in prose.

Structure Focus:
- Discuss the stanzas, lines, line breaks, and/or spacing of the poem.
- Work together to decide on how the various stanzas/lines of the poem could best be read aloud or performed.

Skills Focus:
- Practice oral fluency by choral reading. Record the reading.
- Develop vocabulary by highlighting key words for chanting, pantomiming, etc..

Background Focus:
- Discuss how this poem compares with others they've read or heard.
- Seek out other poems by the same poet or on the same topic.

Based on: Stanley, Nile. 2004. *Creating Readers with Poetry*. Gainesville, FL: Maupin House, p. 82-83.

Choosing Poetry for English Language Learners (ELL/ESL)

When we think about sharing poetry with young people, we might assume that children who are learning English as a new language are not "ready" for poetry. Nothing could be further from the truth. For young people adding English to their linguistic repertoire, poetry offers a connection that can help them learn the words and concepts of their new language, stay motivated and interested in learning, and even participate as equals. Here are helpful guidelines to keep in mind.

1. RELEVANCE: What questions should we ask as we ponder potential poetry book selections for young people who are learning English as a new language? The "typical" grade level suitability may not apply. The maturity, backgrounds (family, cultural, language, knowledge), and interests of English language learners vary tremendously. Choose poems that have some relevance to the children's lives and experiences. Topics such as school, seasons, weather, numbers and counting, days of the week and months of the year, food, family, and home have some degree of familiarity and practical utility. Poetry that is deep in symbolism and divorced in time and space from their lives may be too abstract for beginning English language learners.

2. SOUNDS: Students learning English especially enjoy the sound of poetry, the rhyme, the rhythm, the music of this new language. Start with poems that rhyme and have a strong rhythm. This enables students to use their developing language knowledge to "guess" at how words and phrases should sound. Also, read poetry aloud and invite (don't assign) children to join in on reading out loud. Poetry needs to be heard and spoken, especially if English is not one's native language. Choral reading can provide wonderful, welcoming ways of practicing English and improving one's oral fluency-- for all students.

3. CULTURE: Look for books that are also culturally relevant to the lives of students. Invite them to search for and share poems that mean something to them. Depending on whether they are foreign born, U.S. born, or new immigrants, their connection with their cultural heritage may vary. Incorporating poetry that represents the immigrant or acculturation experience across cultures or the roots and traditions of the home culture can be a source of validation and identification.

4. HUMOR: Unlike previous research findings on children's poetry preferences, young people for whom English is not their native tongue may not enjoy the same hilarious, slapstick, tongue-in-cheek poems that native English speakers do. Why? Humor is culturally specific, and they may not have experienced humor in that way before in their home cultures. Puns, parodies, irony, and sarcasm are communicated differently in different languages. Don't be surprised if you share a funny poem, and they don't laugh. Beginning

English speakers are not going to get the humor even with an explanation. It might be best to share poetry for the words, sounds, rhythm, and meaning first.

5. RESPONSE: Provide opportunities for students learning English to respond to poetry. They may be uncomfortable sharing their thoughts in front of a large group (as are most people). Instead, allow small group or dyad partners, or better yet provide materials for artistic response. They can enjoy working in pairs and small groups to illustrate a poem, create a collage, develop a mural, or even make a poem picture book as a way of responding to and interpreting a poem. Encourage a native language response to a poem, too. Some students may even be brave enough to try writing poetry, often by imitating the formats of their favorite poems (bilingual list poems, for example.) Encourage their self-expression, even with a sometimes limited vocabulary; it may be surprising how poetic their developing grasp of English can be.

Based on: Hadaway, N., Vardell, S. M., and Young, T. (2002). Literature-based instruction with English language learners. Boston, MA: Allyn and Bacon Longman and Hanauer, David Ian. 2004. *Poetry and the Meaning of Life; Reading and Writing Poetry in Language Arts Classrooms*. Toronto, Canada: Pippin, pp. 67-70.

SHARING AND RESPONDING TO POETRY OUT LOUD

My favorite approach for sharing poetry with young people is out loud and often. In this section you'll find more tips and strategies, this time focused on sharing poetry orally, leading poetry performance, and helping young people assess themselves as performers or audience members. There are also multiple lists of question prompts to help guide meaningful discussions after sharing poetry.

Poetry Performance Practices
Poetry Break Pointers
Ten Strategies For Sharing Poetry Out Loud
Song Tunes for Matching with Poems
Audio Poetry for Young People
Creative Alternatives for Performing Poetry
Oral Reading/Poetry Performance Rubric
Audience Guidelines for Listening to Poetry Read Aloud
Discussion Questions for Responding to a Poem
Discussion Questions about How We Connect with the Poem
Discussion Questions about How a Poem Works
Prompts for Arguing about Poetry

Poetry Performance Practices

As we plan activities that prepare young people to perform poems in front of an audience—even an informal audience of peers—here are guidelines based on the work of Nile Stanley that can be very helpful in establishing comfortable parameters for all.

Children should experience poetry of all kinds on a daily basis. Include rhymed and free verse, serious poems, and silly slapstick to help make poetic language both familiar and provocative.

Choose simple, active, conversational poems that lend themselves easily to performance. Notice which poems your students ask to hear again and again.

Keep performances brief (15-30 minute blocks)

Molding versus unfolding your students' performances. Encourage your students to perform spontaneously, using their imaginations and self-expression.... Know when to lead, follow, or get out of the way. Strike a balance between performing FOR and performing WITH the children.

Respect learning style differences. Do not pressure a child to perform.... Be sensitive to language differences and learning delays.

Model good audience manners. The audience is an important part of a performance—teach your students the proper way to behave when watching others perform. Discuss some ground rules with them. Tell them at times they may laugh and even participate, but at other times, they have to remain silent.... Always show respect when someone is performing.

Be willing to get out of your comfort zone. Many teachers are afraid to use poetry during anything but "language arts" time.... Use poetry across the curriculum.

Guide children to appreciate more sophisticated poetry. Mother Goose rhymes and silly slapstick poems are great for introducing children to performance. However, children can develop an appreciation for more sophisticated poetry under the guidance of a skillful teacher.

Based on: Stanley, Nile. 2004. *Creating Readers with Poetry*. Gainesville, FL: Maupin House, p. 94-95.

Poetry Break Pointers

Caroline Feller Bauer proposes a wandering poetry presenter who drops in to share a poem throughout the day in her book, The Poetry Break *(1995). The "poetry break" is a way to infuse poems throughout a school or library program. Whether it's a poem for beginning the day, starting off the hour, transitioning to lunch or a break, or for wrapping things up, the idea of "breaking" for poetry seems very practical. Of course, that doesn't mean that a more in-depth study of poetry is not a good idea. It is. But for the average teacher, librarian, day care provider or parent, sharing a three-minute poem break is a good way to begin. Here are some pointers:*

1. The poetry break can begin with a sign, bell, and/or chime announcing "Poetry Break"
2. Be sure to give the title and author of the poem
3. If possible, show the book the poem comes from
4. Feel free to re-read the poem immediately
5. Be sure to enunciate each word distinctly (and check uncertain pronunciations and meanings beforehand)
6. Avoid sing-song delivery of rhyming verses
7. Use commas and periods as signals to pause in the read aloud
8. Read mini-conversations in poems with dramatic voices and vocal changes
9. Glance at the audience occasionally
10. Consider sharing the poem read by the poet if available on audio
11. Add variety in setting the stage with a flashlight or music
12. Invite a guest presenter to share a poem (including in multiple languages)
13. A favorite puppet can present the poem
14. A portable microphone can add to the effect

To add variety, poem introductions can include:
1. Information about the poet
2. Information about the topic of the poem
3. How you felt when you first read the poem or how it affected you
4. Why you chose that poem (or for that particular day)
5. A prop that fits the poem
6. "This reminds me of" connection to another poem, book, song, etc.

Based on: Bauer, Caroline Feller. 1995) *The Poetry Break: An Annotated Anthology with Ideas for Introducing Children to Poetry.* New York: H W Wilson and O'Connor, John S. 2004. *Wordplaygrounds; Reading, Writing & Performing Poetry in the English Classroom.* Urbana, IL: National Council of Teachers of English, p. 115.

Ten Strategies For Sharing Poetry Out Loud

As you experiment with using each of these ten strategies for sharing poems with young people, it will quickly become obvious that the strategies can be combined and overlapped. For example, there are many poems that have BOTH a repeated line or refrain suited to whole group participation as well as a linear list format that invites individual volunteers. Many poems offer similar combinations of whole group, small group, individual, and other read aloud configurations. Often the poem itself will "show" you how to perform it if you study the lines and their arrangement on the page. Once you begin inviting children's participation in poem performance, you will find that they themselves will have ideas about how to try a poem this way or that way. Follow their lead!

1. ADULT READ ALOUD
The adult reads the poem aloud to the class. Choose poems *you* like and read them slowly, but expressively. Show the poem via a projector or on a poster while you read it so the children can follow along with the words.

2. UNISON
The adult still reads the poem out loud first. But then, everyone joins in on repeated reading to read the poem in unison. Once the children have heard this poem read aloud, they usually enjoy joining in. You can adapt this approach with "echo" reading of some poems, in which children repeat lines after you read each one, echoing your reading.

3. CHORUS
The adult leads the poem reading, but children participate in a word or phrase or refrain that is reoccurring, much like the classic Greek chorus joining in for repeated lines.

4. MOVEMENT
Fingerplays and rhymes with motions and movement are a staple of early introductions to poetry for many young children. It can still be inviting and engaging to use participatory rhymes with older children, particularly when you have multiage groups or book buddies with older children paired with younger ones. Use unison reading or leader reading of a poem with action words and phrases and invite listeners to join in with designated motions or gestures.

5. CALL AND RESPONSE
The whole group is divided into two smaller groups to take turns reading lines in a "back and forth" kind of way.

6. GROUPS
The class or large group is divided into multiple groups for multiple stanzas. This takes some practice with timing, but creates a "wave" effect with the poem flowing across the room.

7. SOLOS

Individual children volunteer for individual solo lines. "Volunteer" is the key word. Do not put children on the spot. If you continue sharing poetry orally every day, eventually nearly everyone will want a turn to shine. Many "list" poems work well in the line-around read aloud format.

8. TWO VOICES

This is the most complex form of choral reading. It takes a bit of practice, but is very powerful. Two individuals volunteer to practice and perform poems for two voices (often with overlapping lines). It can be effective with two groups, rather than with two individuals, but it does take practice. (Underline the lines that are spoken simultaneously to help cue the children. Be aware that they may be saying different words at the same time.) Paul Fleischman's *Joyful Noise* is the perfect example of poems written specifically for this strategy.

9. CANON

Reading poems in a canon in two alternating groups with staggered beginnings is one other strategy that involves timing and overlapping lines and can be a fun challenge. In addition, not many poems lend themselves to reading in a round. They must have a very regular beat or meter and some repetition. But when you find a suitable poem and try this technique with children, you will find it is fun and challenging, just like singing "Row, row, row, your boat" in a canon. This usually takes practice, but it can be very appealing, like chanting or cheering at a sports event. Physically clapping the rhythm of the poem together can also help with reading a poem canon-style.

10. SINGING POEMS

Perhaps the silliest form of choral reading is singing poems. It's not especially difficult, but it is irresistible fun and does require a bold adult (or child) to get it started. You simply sing poems by adapting those that have a strong, rhythmic beat to familiar tunes that have the same beat or meter, such as: Mary Had a Little Lamb, Row, Row, Row Your Boat, 99 Bottles of Pop, On Top of Old Smoky, etc.

BONUS EXTRAS

These spoken word events allow children to participate with the support of a partner or group and help them gain confidence as they share poetry with an audience. Other ideas include:

*inviting guests to read poetry aloud, particularly professional actors in your area who can offer a polished delivery of poetry

*welcoming bilingual members of your community who can read poems in languages other than English

*inviting a traveling poetry troupe from the national organization, Poetry Alive! (http://www.poetryalive.com)

Based on: *Poetry Aloud Here* by Sylvia Vardell (ALA, 2006) and *Children's Literature in Action: A Librarian's Guide* also by Sylvia Vardell (Libraries Unlimited, 2008).

Song Tunes for Matching with Poems

Putting poems to music is a popular strategy with kids. Basically, you match poems to song tunes that contain the same meter in their first lines, often with an equal number of strong stresses in a line. Count the beats in the first line or two of the poem, then count the beats in the first line or two of the song to match them. It is most effective with nonsensical or humorous poems and with tunes that have a strong, rhythmic beat such as "Row, Row, Row Your Boat" or "Mary Had a Little Lamb." It may be surprising how many poems have a strong enough rhythm and structure to be effective when sung. Many of Jack Prelutsky's poems, in particular, match song tunes, for example. Alan Katz uses this approach to hilarious effect in his series of "Silly Dilly" picture books full of song/poem parodies such as *Take Me Out of the Bathtub and Other Silly Dilly Songs* (Simon & Schuster, 2001. Below is a list of popular childhood song tunes (among many, many others) to offer a starting point.

1. Battle hymn of the republic (14 = number of beats in first line)
2. She'll be coming 'round the mountain (12)
3. If you're happy and you know it (11)
4. 99 bottles of pop (10)
5. When Johnny comes marching home (9)
6. Are you sleeping (8)
7. I've been working on the railroad (8)
8. Oh Tannenbaum (8)
9. Bingo (8)
10. Clementine (8)
11. Twinkle twinkle little star (7)
12. Mary had a little lamb (7)
13. Old MacDonald (7)
14. Yankee doodle (7)
15. London bridge (7)
16. On top of old smoky (6)
17. Ring around the rosy (6)
18. Three blind mice (6)
19. The farmer in the dell (6)
20. Hot cross buns (6)
21. Home on the range (5)
22. Row, row, row your boat (5)
23. Turkey in the straw (5)
24. Etc.

Audio Poetry for Young People

There are several places to find audio adaptations of poetry for young people. Many are available as CDs (formerly cassettes) accompanying print books or as downloadable audio files. If you want to hear how poetry should sound, there is no better resource than hearing the poets themselves read their poems aloud or professional narrators bring poetry to life. And we're fortunate to have more and more access to recorded poetry through iTunes, audioclips, CDs and tapes, downloadable audio from web sites, audio stores, and more.

Select poets whose Web sites feature audio recordings of their poetry:
Kristine O'Connell George: http://www.kristinegeorge.com/poetry_aloud.html
Janet S. Wong: http://www.janetwong.com/
Nikki Grimes: http://www.nikkigrimes.com/
Joyce Sidman: http://www.joycesidman.com/

Select poetry-related Web sites with audio files among their links:
The Academy of American Poets http://www.poets.org/
PoetryMagazine.com http://www.poetrymagazine.com/
Poets and Writers http://www.pw.org/
LibriVox http://librivox.org/
Favorite Poem Project http://www.favoritepoem.org/

Select children's poetry in audiobook form:
Andrews, Julie and Hamilton, Emma Walton. *Julie Andrews' Collection of Poems, Songs, and Lullabies* (Hachette Audio, 2009)
Brown, Calef. *Flamingos on the Roof* (Recorded Books, 2009)
Creech, Sharon. *Hate that Cat* (Harper Children's Audio, 2008)
Creech, Sharon. *Heartbeat* (Recorded Books, 2004)
Creech, Sharon. *Love that Dog* (Harper Children's Audio, 2002)
Dakos, Kalli. *If You're Not Here, Please Raise Your Hand* (Recorded Books, 2009)
Engle, Margarita. *The Poet Slave of Cuba* (Listening Library, 2009)
Engle, Margarita. *The Surrender Tree* (Listening Library, 2009)
Engle, Margarita. *Tropical Secrets* (Listening Library, 2009)
Fleischman, Paul. *Joyful Noise/I Am Phoenix* (Audio Bookshelf, 2001)
Franco, Betsy. *Metamorphosis: Junior Year* (Brilliance, 2010)
Frost, Helen. *Crossing Stones* (Recorded Books, 2010)
Frost, Helen. *Keesha's House* (Recorded Books, 2004)
Frost, Helen. *Diamond Willow* (Recorded Books, 2009)
Giovanni, Nikki. *Hip Hop Speaks to Children* (Sourcebooks, 2008)
Grimes, Nikki. *Bronx Masquerade* (Recorded Books, 2006)
Grimes, Nikki. *Dark Sons* (Zondervan, 2010)
Grimes, Nikki. *Jazmin's Notebook* (Penguin, 2008)
Hemphill, Stephanie. *Your Own, Sylvia* (Listening Library, 2009)
Hesse, Karen. *Aleutian Sparrow* (Listening Library, 2003)
Hesse, Karen. *Out of the Dust* (Listening Library, 2006)
Hesse, Karen. *Witness* (Listening Library, 2006)

Hoberman, Mary Ann and Wilson, Linda. *The Tree That Time Built: A Celebration of Nature, Science, and Imagination* (Sourcebooks, 2009)

Lewis, J. Patrick. *The Brothers' War: Civil War Voices in Verse* (Recorded Books, 2007)

Lithgow, John. *The Poets' Corner: The One-and-Only Poetry Book for the Whole Family* (Hachette, 2007)

Milne, A.A. *When We Were Very Young* and *Now We Are Six* (Harper Children's Audio, 2004)

Myers, Walter Dean. *Blues Journey* (Live Oak Media, 2003)

Myers, Walter Dean. *Harlem: A Poem* (Spoken Arts, 1998)

Myers, Walter Dean. *Here in Harlem* (Live Oak Media, 2010)

Myers, Walter Dean. *Jazz* (Live Oak Media, 2007)

Myers, Walter Dean. *Looking Like Me* (Live Oak Media, 2010)

Nesbitt, Kenn. *My Hippo Has the Hiccups and Other Poems I Totally Made Up* (Sourcebooks, 2009)

Paschen, Elise and Raccah, Dominque. *Poetry Speaks to Children* (Sourcebooks, 2005)

Paschen, Elise and Raccah, Dominque. *Poetry Speaks; Who I Am* (Sourcebooks, 2010)

Prelutsky, Jac. *A Pizza the Size of the Sun* (Harper Audio, 2007)

Prelutsky, Jack. *Be Glad Your Nose Is on Your Face: And Other Poems: Some of the Best of Jack Prelutsky* (Greenwillow, 2008)

Prelutsky, Jack. *Behold the Bold Umbrellaphant* (Harper Audio, 2006)

Prelutsky, Jack. *In Aunt Giraffe's Green Garden* (Harper Audio, 2007)

Prelutsky, Jack. *It's Raining Pigs and Noodles* (Harper Audio, 2008)

Prelutsky, Jack. *Monday's Troll* (Listening Library, 1996)

Prelutsky, Jack. *My Dog May Be a Genius* (Harper Audio, 2008)

Prelutsky, Jack. *Scranimals* (Harper Audio, 2007)

Prelutsky, Jack. *Something Big Has Been Here* (Harper Audio, 2007)

Prelutsky, Jack. *The Frogs Wore Red Suspenders* (Harper Audio, 2005)

Prelutsky, Jack. *The Jack Prelutsky Holiday CD Audio Collection* (Greenwillow, 2005)

Prelutsky, Jack. *The New Kid on the Block* (Harper Audio, 2007)

Raschka, Chris. *Charlie Parker Played Be Bop* (Live Oak Media, 2003)

Sidman, Joyce. *Dark Emperor.* (Recorded Books, 2010)

Silverstein, Shel. *A Light in the Attic* (20th Anniversary Edition) (HarperCollins, 2001)

Silverstein, Shel. *Where the Sidewalk Ends* (25th Anniversary Edition) (HarperCollins, 2000)

Singer, Marilyn. *Mirror, Mirror: A Book of Reversible Verse* (Live Oak Media, 2011)

Sones, Sonya. *What My Mother Doesn't Know* (Brilliance, 2008)

Steptoe, Javaka. *In Daddy's Arms I am Tall* (Live Oak Media, 2003)

The Caedmon Poetry Collection: A Century of Poets Reading their Work (Caedmon, 2000)

Thomas, Joyce Carol. *Brown Honey in Broomwheat Tea* (Spoken Arts, 1998)

Updike, John. *A Child's Calendar* (Live Oak Media, 2004)

Weatherford, Carole Boston. *Birmingham 1963* (Recorded Books, 2007)

Williams, Vera B. *Amber was Brave, Essie was Smart* (Live Oak Media, 2003)

Wolf, Allan. *The Watch that Ends the Night: Voices from the Titanic* (Candlewick, 2011)

Woodson, Jacqueline. *Locomotion* (Recorded Books, 2012)

Yolen, Jane. *How Do Dinosaurs Say Good Night* (Weston Woods, 2005)

Also look for many, many audiobook collections of Mother Goose nursery rhymes and of poetry by classic poets of the past, such as The Voice of the Poet series

Creative Alternatives for Performing Poetry

Once young people join in on poetry performance, they may enjoy experimenting with other creative ways to make poetry come alive. Here are a few suggestions.

1. Employ props and physical objects referenced in the poem
2. Try puppetry for poem character voices
3. Find or create simple masks to suggest poem persona
4. Make or find simple shadow puppets for poem characters
5. Manipulate a strand of string to help tell the poem-story
6. Cut out relevant paper shapes while reading/reciting the poem
7. Fold paper into origami shapes related to the poem
8. Draw a simple picture (ala Pictionary) while reading the poem
9. Cook, mix, bake along with the poem reading ala a cooking show
10. Perform poem using signing (American Sign Language)
11. Choose poems with monologues or dialogues for solo and duet performances
12. Try role playing (with hats or simple costumes) to convey the character in a poem that has a strong persona or point of view
13. Select excerpts from a novel in verse to perform with multiple narrators in readers theater style.
14. Act out movements or emotions in the poem through pantomime
15. Add simple dance moves to a well-suited poem
16. Use simple movements like a hop or bounce for poems with a regular rhythm
17. Try chanting, hand claps, and/or jumping rope for strong rhythmic rhymes
18. Create simple sound effects as the background for a poem reading
19. Add a musical soundtrack as the background for a poem performance
20. Use PowerPoint slides or video images to showcase key words (and images) in poem
21. Flash a digital banner of key poem lines like a refrain
22. Stage a "tableaux," a frozen moment of a poem posed as a "scene," for a poem that suggests a scene. Photograph and/or film the tableaux to share it more widely.
23. Orchestrate a "flash mob" reading of a favorite poem
24. Invite young people to suggest their own poetry performance techniques combining any of these above or offering additional new ideas.

Oral Reading/Poetry Performance Rubric

As young people gain experience in reading or performing poems out loud, providing feedback can help them learn and grow in confidence and skill. Here's on example based on the work of Nile Stanley in Creating Readers with Poetry (Maupin House, 2004). *You can simply provide feedback using the following list or assess each criterion using the usual scale of excellent, satisfactory, or needs improvement.*

Volume
The reader projects in an audible, but not distorted voice, that can be heard by all.

Fluency
The reader pronounces words without hesitation, with accuracy, ease, and appropriate rhythm.

Pronunciation
The reader says each word clearly and articulates each sound of each word clearly, including word endings.

Expression
The reader shows clear understanding of the poem using appropriate tone, emotion, facial expressions, and body language.

Movement
The reader uses gestures and big motions to convey meaning when appropriate.

Polish
The reader introduces the poem title, poet, and (book) source, and displays a confident stance.

Audience Guidelines for Listening to Poetry Read Aloud

As we provide opportunities for young people to experience poetry "live," they often need guidance in how to be a good audience. Introduce these guidelines and discuss appropriate examples and perhaps non-examples to help them prepare for a guest poet visit or poetry performance of any kind.

PREPARATION: If possible, involve young people in developing prior knowledge about the visiting poet or poetry performer(s) beforehand. They can participate in advance preparation for the event such as creating and displaying welcome signs, creating book displays, arranging prepared seating, setting the stage, etc.

1. The audience shows interest, enthusiasm, and appropriate body language.

2. The audience has an appropriate level of attention for age and developmental level.

3. The audience is respectful, quiet, and well-behaved.

4. The audience displays open-mindedness and respect for the performer(s)'s race, language, accent, mannerisms, style, and content of performance.

5. The audience reacts appropriately (e.g., applauds, laughs, interacts, or listens).

FOLLOW UP: After the performance, the audience can recall, discuss, and make personal connections to the content presented.

Based on: Stanley, Nile. 2004. *Creating Readers with Poetry*. Gainesville, FL: Maupin House, p. 116.

Discussion Questions for Responding to a Poem

How do we help young people articulate their responses to poetry after hearing it read aloud or sharing it orally? It's an art that takes a bit of practice since we don't want to overwhelm their thoughtful processing of their feelings and observations with our own expectations and insights. This set of 10 questions based on the work of Fitch and Swartz (2008) offers a helpful starting point. Just choose 2 or 3 of these question prompts and vary which questions you use for each discussion.

1. Can you describe what this poem is about in one sentence?

2. What is it about the poem that you particularly liked? Or disliked?

3. What did this poem remind you of?

4. What things did you "see" in the poem? Hear? Feel? Taste?

5. Did this poem give you any special feeling(s)? How did this happen?

6. How did the poet use words or groups of words effectively?

7. How is the poem different from or the same as other poems you have read?

8. Did this poem surprise you in any way? How?

9. What would you tell or ask the poet about the poem?

10. How is this a poem? How it like or unlike a story?

Based on: Fitch, Sheree and Swartz, Larry. 2008. *The Poetry Experience; Choosing and Using Poetry in the Classroom*. Markham, Canada: Pembroke, p. 27 and O'Connor, John S. 2004. *Wordplaygrounds; Reading, Writing & Performing Poetry in the English Classroom*. Urbana, IL: National Council of Teachers of English.

Discussion Questions about How We Connect with the Poem

Some poems particularly lend themselves to making personal connections with our own lives and stories. Here are question prompts that invite young people to think about the poem in relation to their own life experiences. Again, only 2-3 questions (don't use ALL at once please) can prompt a lively and thoughtful discussion after reading and sharing a poem, particularly narrative poems.

1. What does the poet say to you in this poem? Why do you think the poet said that?

2. Does this poem remind you of anything you know about?

3. How are the people in this poem like people you know? Or not like people you know?

4. Would you like to go to the place described in this poem? Why or why not?

5. Did the things in this poem ever happen to you? Where or when?

6. What things are there in this poem to see? Have you seen them before? Where?

7. Is this poem honest or true? Do you believe what it says? Why or why not?

8. What things happen in this poem that you would like to happen to you? Or not happen to you?

9. What do you think made the poet write this poem?

10. Is this a head, heart, or belly poem? (Make you think, feel, laugh, groan?)

Based on: Patrick Groff's "poetry talk" questions (cited in Booth, David and Moore, Bill. 2003. *Poems Please! Sharing Poetry with Children*. 2nd edition. Markham, Ontario, CA: Pembroke Publishers, pp. 64-65); Amy McClure's facilitating questions (*Sunrises and Songs; Reading and Writing Poetry in the Elementary Classroom*, Heinemann, 1990), and Aaren Perry's "Poetry Critique Guide Sheet" (*Poetry Across the Curriculum; An Action Guide for Elementary Teachers*, Allyn & Bacon, 1997, p. 182).

Discussion Questions about How a Poem Works

Once young people become comfortable with hearing and sharing poems and discussing and conversing about them, they may be ready to consider how the poem works and the writer creates. These questions lead them to discuss some of the "nuts and bolts" of the poem and its construction and effect. Choose 2-3 questions to start and vary which questions regularly. Consider letting students choose which questions they want to tackle.

1. What does the poet do to make the poem more inviting?

2. Can you state the main idea of the poem in one sentence?

3. Do all the lines end in strong words? Where are line breaks most effective, most surprising?

4. What are the most pleasing and most interesting sounds in the poem?

5. Why does the poem have the number of stanzas it has? Why is the poem shaped the way it is?

6. Are there any places where the poet uses repetition effectively?

7. How does the title of the poem prepare you for what follows?

8. What elements give the poem its own rhythm or pacing?

9. What are some questions or puzzles that you have about this poem?

10. What would you like to ask the poet about the poem if you could?

Based on: O'Connor, John S. 2004. *Wordplaygrounds; Reading, Writing & Performing Poetry in the English Classroom.* Urbana, IL: National Council of Teachers of English, p. 104-105; Burkhardt, Ross. M. 2006. *Using Poetry in the Classroom: Engaging Students in Learning.* Lanham, MD: Rowman & Littlefield Education; Fitch, Sheree and Swartz, Larry. 2008. *The Poetry Experience; Choosing and Using Poetry in the Classroom.* Markham, Canada: Pembroke.

Prompts for Arguing about Poetry

With poetry, there is rarely one right answer. Try these discussion prompts to get kids thinking about poetry. Be open to a variety of opinions. Encourage them to defend their responses with example poems drawn from their favorite poetry books. Challenge older kids to take BOTH sides of the question in a debate.

1. The best poems rhyme.
2. Serious poetry is more interesting than funny poetry.
3. Poetry is never about underwear.
4. You can't have just one poem in a poetry book.
5. Some poems mix facts and poetry.
6. Songs are never considered poetry.
7. Zombies and poetry don't mix.
8. The pictures can be just as important as the poems in a book.
9. All the best poets are in the past.
10. Novels in verse are not really poetry.
11. "Real" poetry books don't include poetry written by children and teens.
12. Poems can't be rhythmic without rhyme.
13. The most frequently occurring topics in poetry for young people focus on animals and nature.
14. Audio adaptations of poetry books are even better than print versions.
15. History is best told through poetry.
16. Teens should skip YA poetry and go straight to poetry for adults.
17. The best poets for children are Shel Silverstein and Jack Prelutsky.
18. There is no topic that is off limits in poetry for young people.
19. Poets of color are writing some of the most distinctive poetry for young people.
20. Poetry is more fun in print book form than in e-book form.

TEACHING POETRY WRITING

Once you have immersed young people in reading, listening to, performing, and discussing poetry, they often naturally turn to writing poetry. There are many books for adults detailing the teaching of writing poetry and a resource list of these titles is provided. A rationale with the benefits of writing poetry can help make a case to administrators and young people themselves may find the advice from poets helpful in the list of books about writing poetry. The poetry books that feature poet commentary alongside the poetry may also provide insight for young readers, as may books of published poetry containing the original poems of children and teens. Those who lean more toward the artistic side will find helpful examples in the list of poets who are also artists and in the list of books of poetry inspired by art. Finally, several teacher tools may assist with the process including a glossary of poetry terms, a list of poem forms (including the popular biopoem example), a list of rhyming phonemes, and some survival vocabulary to jump-start the writing process. Two checklists for aspiring poets and a list of places to consider publishing the work of young writers round out this section.

> The Benefits of Writing Poetry with Young People
> Books for Kids about Writing Poetry
> Poetry Books with Commentary by Poets
> Poet Artists
> Poetry Books that Feature Fine Art
> Poetry Books with Poetry Written by Children
> Poetry Books with Poetry Written by Teens
> Glossary of Poetry Terminology
> Phonograms, Rimes and Rhymes
> Survival Vocabulary
> Possible Poetic Forms
> The Biopoem Formula
> Poetry Writing Checklist and Guidelines
> Places to Publish Children's Poetry Writing
> Resource Books for Teaching Poetry Writing to Children

The Benefits of Writing Poetry with Young People

Children who are immersed in poetry, hear poems read aloud every day, participate in reading poetry aloud, experience poetry across the curriculum, and talk about and share their responses to poetry will quite naturally want to try their hand at creating and writing poetry, too. Not every child will be a poet, of course, but all children should have the opportunity to express themselves through poetry. Poet Sara Holbrook offers these sound reasons for encouraging children's poetry writing efforts.

Writing poetry jogs the memory.
"Working my memory over, I prioritize, make order out of chaos, rediscover details, and put events in sequence."

Writing poetry demands keen observation.
"We want students to do more than watch—we want them to see."

Writing poetry requires precise language.
"Poetry asks the important questions and forces us to define ourselves in concrete visual terms."

Writing poetry stimulates good communication skills.
"What good is knowing something if we can't communicate our ideas to others?"

Writing poetry encourages reading fluency.
"Poems want to be read again and again."

Writing poetry helps us learn about ourselves and our world.
"Reading is trickle-down learning; writing is building our own learning curve."

Poetry—written, spoken, or read—is powerful language.
"Poetry has been a jungle gym in my life, a place to stretch and flip, climb to the top for a look-see, and occasionally fall and skin my nose."

Based on: Holbrook, Sara. 2005. *Practical Poetry; A Nonstandard Approach to Meeting Content-Area Standards.* Portsmouth, NH: Heinemann, p. 4-7.

Books for Kids about Writing Poetry

Several poets have written books for young people ABOUT poetry writing, as well as writing poetry itself. Here are a few of those resources that young readers and aspiring poets may find helpful and enjoyable.

Fletcher, Ralph J. 2001. *A Writer's Notebook*. New York: HarperTrophy.

Fletcher, Ralph J. 2002. *Poetry Matters: Writing a Poem from the Inside Out*. New York:

Fletcher, Ralph J. 2005. *A Writing Kind of Day: Poems for Young Poets*. Honesdale, PA: Wordsong/Boyds Mills Press.

Fletcher, Ralph J. 2006. *Boy Writers; Reclaiming Their Voices*. York, ME.: Stenhouse Publishers.

Janeczko, Paul B. 1983. *Poetspeak: In Their Work, About Their Work: A Selection*. New York: Atheneum.

Janeczko, Paul B, comp. 1990. *The Place My Words are Looking for*. New York: Bradbury.

Janeczko, Paul B, comp. 1994. *Poetry from A to Z: A Guide for Young Writers*. New York: Bradbury.

Janeczko, Paul B, comp. 2002. *Seeing the Blue Between: Advice and Inspiration for Young Poets*. Cambridge, MA: Candlewick.

Lawson, JonArno. 2008. *Inside Out: Children's Poets Discuss Their Work*. London: Walker.

Loewen, Nancy. 2009. *Words, Wit, and Wonder: Writing Your own Poem*. Picture Window Books.

Prelutsky, Jack. 2008. *Pizza, Pigs, and Poetry; How to Write a Poem*. New York: Greenwillow.

Salas, Laura Purdie. 2008. *Write Your Own Poetry*. Minneapolis, MN: Compass Point Books.

Salas, Laura Purdie. 2011. *Picture Yourself Writing Poetry: Using Photos to Inspire Writing*. Minneapolis, MN: Capstone.

Wolf, Allan. 2006. *Immersed in Verse: An Informative, Slightly Irreverent & Totally Tremendous Guide to Living the Poet's Life*. New York: Sterling.

Poetry Books with Commentary by Poets

In these books the poets provide a few lines of explanations about where the ideas for the poem comes from—fascinating and insightful, especially for aspiring poets.

Brenner, Barbara. 2000. *Voices: Poetry and Art From Around the World*. Washington D.C.: National Geographic Society.

Clinton, Catherine. 1998. *I, Too, Sing America: Three Centuries of African-American Poetry*. Boston: Houghton Mifflin.

Cullinan, Bernice E. 1996. *A Jar of Tiny Stars: Poems By NCTE Award Winning Poets*. Honesdale, PA: Wordsong, Boyds Mills.

Cullinan, Bernice and Wooten, Deborah, eds. 2009. *Another Jar of Tiny Stars.; Poems by NCTE Award-winning Poets*. Honesdale, PA: Wordsong/Boyds Mills.

Fisher, Aileen and Bruce E. Cullinan, ed. 2002. *I Heard a Bluebird Sing: Children Select Their Favorite Poems*. Honesdale, PA: Wordsong/Boyds Mills.

Janeczko, Paul B. 1983. *Poetspeak: In Their Work, About Their Work: A Selection*. New York: Bradbury.

Janeczko, Paul B., selector. 1990. *The Place My Words Are Looking For: What Poets Say About and Through Their Work*. New York: Bradbury.

Janeczko, Paul. 2002. *Seeing The Blue Between: Advice and Inspiration For Young Poets*. Somerville, MA: Candlewick.

Kennedy, X.J. and Kennedy, D. 1982. *Knock at a Star*. New York: Little Brown.

Kuskin, Karla. 1980. *Dogs & Dragons, Trees & Dreams: A Collection of Poems*. New York: Harper & Row.

Lawson, JonArno. 2008. *Inside Out: Children's Poets Discuss Their Work*. London: Walker.

Lyon, George Ella. 1999. *Where I'm From: Where Poems Come From*. New York: Absey & Co.

Soto, Gary. 1990. *A Fire in My Hands: A Book of Poems*. New York: Scholastic.

Vardell, Sylvia and Wong, Janet. Eds. 2011. *P*TAG: Poetry for Teens*. PoetryTagTime.com.

Vardell, Sylvia and Wong, Janet. Eds. 2011. *PoetryTagTime: Poetry for Children*. PoetryTagTime.com.

Vardell, Sylvia and Wong, Janet. Eds. 2011. *Gift Tag: Holiday Poetry for Young People*. PoetryTagTime.com.

Wong, Janet S. 1996. *A Suitcase of Seaweed, and Other Poems*. New York: McElderry.

Poet Artists

There are many poets who also produce the illustrations for their own poetry collections. They are known for their art, as well as their writing, including Douglas Florian's distinctive paintings+collages, the outrageous cartoon monsters of Adam Rex, the iconic photography of Charles R. Smith, Jr., the textured quilts of Anna Grossnickle Hines, the irreverent pen and ink sketches of Shel Silverstein, and more. Here are a few titles by each of a dozen poet-artists and artist-poets. Encourage young people to collaborate with a partner, one as illustrator and one as writer, in creating their own poem and art.

Agee, Jon. 2009. *Orangutan Tongs; Poems to Tangle Your Tongue*. New York: Disney-Hyperion.

Brown, Calef. 2006. *Flamingos on the Roof*. Boston: Houghton Mifflin.

Brown, Calef. 2010. *Hallowilloween: Nefarious Silliness*. Houghton Mifflin.

Cyrus, Kurt. 2001. *Oddhopper Opera: A Bug's Garden Of Verses*. San Diego, CA: Harcourt.

Cyrus, Kurt. 2005. *Hotel Deep: Light Verse from Dark Water*. Harcourt.

Ehlert, Lois. 2008. *Oodles Of Animals*. New York: Harcourt.

Ehlert, Lois. 2010. *Lots of Spots*. New York: Beach Lane Books.

Florian, Douglas. 1999. *Winter Eyes: Poems and Paintings*. New York: Greenwillow.

Florian, Douglas. 2005. *Zoo's Who*. San Diego, CA: Harcourt.

Florian, Douglas. 2007. *Comets, stars, the moon, and mars*. Harcourt:

Florian, Douglas. 2009. *Dinothesaurus*. New York: Simon & Schuster.

Florian, Douglas. 2012. *Unbeelievables: Honeybee Poems and Paintings*. New York: Beach Lane.

Grandits, John. 2004. *Technically, It's Not My Fault: Concrete Poems*. New York: Clarion.

Grandits, John. 2007. *Blue Lipstick: Concrete Poems*. New York: Clarion.

Hines, Anna Grossnickle. 2011. *Peaceful Pieces: A Year in Poems and Quilts*. New York: Greenwillow.

Hines, Anna Grossnickle. 2005. *Winter Lights: A Season in Poems & Quilts*. New York: Greenwillow.

Rex, Adam. 2005. *Frankenstein Makes a Sandwich*. San Diego: Harcourt.

Rex, Adam. 2008. *Frankenstein Takes the Cake*. New York: Harcourt Houghton Mifflin.

Silverstein, Shel. 1974. *Where the Sidewalk Ends*. New York: Harper and Row.

Silverstein, Shel. 1981. *A Light in the Attic*. New York: Harper & Row.

Silverstein, Shel. 1996. *Falling Up*. New York: HarperCollins.

Silverstein, Shel. 2011. *Every Thing On It*. New York: HarperCollins.

Smith, Charles R. Jr. 2003. *Hoop Queens*. Somerville, MA: Candlewick.

Smith, Charles R. Jr. 2004. *Hoop Kings*. Somerville, MA: Candlewick.

Smith, Hope Anita. 2009. *Mother; Poems*. New York: Henry Holt.

Wassenhove, Sue Van. 2008. *The Seldom-Ever-Shady Glades*. Honesdale, PA: Boyds Mills/Wordsong.

Weinstock, Robert. 2009. *Food Hates You, Too*. New York: Disney-Hyperion.

Weinstock, Robert. 2010. *Can You Dig It?* New York: Disney-Hyperion.

Poetry Books that Feature Fine Art

Since poetry is full of imagery and emotion, it may not be surprising that it has often been paired with fine art from around the world. Books such as these can provide an introduction to art, as well as an opportunity to discuss the sources of artistic and poetic inspiration. Consider these examples. Several of these feature poetry written in response to the art, called "ekphrastic" poetry. Encourage aspiring writers to choose a piece of art that "speaks" to them and then try writing a poem in response to it.

Brenner, Barbara. Ed. 2000. *Voices: Poetry and Art from Around the World.* Washington, DC: National Geographic Society.

Greenberg, Jan. 2001. *Heart to Heart: New Poems Inspired by Twentieth-Century American Art.* New York: Abrams.

Greenberg, Jan. 2008. *Side by Side: New Poems Inspired by Art from Around the World.* New York: Abrams.

Heard, Georgia. Ed. 2000. *Songs of Myself: An Anthology of Poems and Art.* New York: Mondo.

Koch, Kenneth, and Kate Farrell. Eds. 1985. *Talking to the Sun; An Illustrated Anthology of Poems for Young People.* New York: Henry Holt.

Lach, William. Ed. 1999. *Curious Cats in Art and Poetry for Children.* New York: Atheneum.

Lewis, J. Patrick. 2008. *Michelangelo's World.* Mankato, MN: Creative Editions.

Lewis, J. Patrick and Yolen, Jane. 2011. *Self Portrait with Seven Fingers: A Life of Marc Chagall in Verse.* Mankato, MN: Creative Editions.

Nye, Naomi Shihab. Ed. 1998. *The Space Between Our Footsteps: Poems and Paintings From the Middle East.* New York: Simon & Schuster.

Nye, Naomi Shihab. Ed. 1995. *The Tree is Older than You Are: A Bilingual Gathering of Poems and Stories from Mexico with Paintings by Mexican Artists.* New York: Simon & Schuster.

Panzer, Nora. Ed. 1994. *Celebrate America in Poetry and Art.* New York: Hyperion.

Rochelle, Belinda. Ed. 2001. *Words with Wings: A Treasury of African-American Poetry and Art.* New York: HarperCollins.

Siebert, Diane. 2006. *Tour America: A Journey through Poems and Art.* San Francisco: Chronicle.

Sullivan, Charles. Ed. 1994. *Here is My Kingdom: Hispanic-American Literature and Art for Young People.* New York: Abrams.

Sullivan, Charles. Ed. 1989. *Imaginary Gardens; American Poetry and Art for Young People.* New York: Abrams.

Whipple, Laura. Ed. 1994. *Celebrating America: A Collection of Poems and Images of the American Spirit.* New York: Philomel.

Poetry Books with Poetry Written by Children

Children are not only consumers of poetry, but they can be creators of it too. And children who are interested in becoming poets or trying to write poetry themselves can benefit from seeing published poetry by other young writers. But even if they're not aspiring poets, young readers are often empowered by experiencing the published words of their peers. Here are examples of published books that feature poetry written by children.

Abeel, Samantha.1993. *Reach for the Moon.* Duluth, MN: Pfeifer-Hamilton.

Adedjouma, D. Ed. 1996. *The Palm of My Heart: Poetry by African American Children.* New York: Lee & Low.

Akaza, Norihisa. Ed. 1994. *Smell of the Rain, Voices of the Stars.* Orlando, FL: Harcourt.

Francis, Lee. Ed. 1999. *When The Rain Sings: Poems by Young Native Americans.* New York: Simon & Schuster.

Lowe, Ayana. Ed. 2008. *Come and Play: Children of Our World Having Fun.* New York: Bloomsbury.

Lyne, Sandford. Ed. 1996. *Ten-second Rainshowers: Poems by Young People.* New York: Simon & Schuster.

Lyne, Sanford. Ed. 2004. *Soft Hay Will Catch You: Poems by Young People.* New York: Simon & Schuster.

McLaughlin, Timothy. Ed. 2012. *Walking on Earth and Touching the Sky; Poetry and Prose by Lakota Youth at Red Cloud Indian School.* New York: Abrams.

Michael, Pamela. Ed. 2008. *River of Words.* Minneapolis, MN: Milkweed.

Navasky, Bruno. Trans. 1993. *Festival in my Heart: Poems by Japanese Children.* New York: Abrams.

Nye, Naomi Shihab. Ed. 2000. *Salting the Ocean: 100 Poems by Young Poets.* New York: Greenwillow.

Simon, John O. Ed. 2011. *Cyclops Wearing Flip-Flops.* San Francisco: Center for the Art of Translation.

Spain, Sahara Sunday. 2001. *If There Would Be No Light; Poems from My Heart.* San Francisco: HarperCollins.

Stepanek, Mattie. 2002. *Heartsongs.* New York: Hyperion.

Volavkova, Hana. Ed. 1993. *I Never Saw Another Butterfly: Children's Drawings and Poems from Terezin Concentration Camp 1942-1944.* New York: Schocken Books.

Poetry Books with Poetry Written by Teens

There are many examples of published poetry by teens, including volumes from the WritersCorps, pocket-sized graphic poetry collections, and culminations from writing competitions. Poets like Naomi Shihab Nye, Sanford Lyne, Joyce Sidman, and Betsy Franco, to name a few, have assembled several notable collections of poetry written by young people-- all books full of unsentimental and authentic young voices. These can be particularly inspiring for young people who want to become poets—to see their peers pave the way before them.

Aguado, Bill, ed. 2003. *Paint Me Like I Am*. New York: Harper.

Francis, Lee. 1999. *When The Rain Sings: Poems by Young Native Americans*. New York: Simon & Schuster.

Franco, Betsy. 2001. *Things I Have to Tell You: Poems And Writing by Teenage Girls*. Cambridge, MA: Candlewick.

Franco, Betsy. 2001. *You Hear Me? Poems and Writing by Teenage Boys*. Cambridge, MA: Candlewick.

Franco, Betsy. 2008. Comp. *Falling Hard: 100 Love Poems by Teenagers*. Cambridge, MA: Candlewick.

Hirschfelder, Arlene B., and Beverly Singer, comp. 1992. *Rising Voices: Writings of Young Native Americans*. New York: Scribner's.

Johnson, Dave, ed. 2000. *Movin': Teen Poets Take Voice*. Orchard.

Lyne, Sandford, comp. 1996. *Ten-second Rainshowers: Poems by Young People*. New York: Simon & Schuster.

Lyne, Sandford, comp. 2004. *Soft Hay Will Catch You*. Simon & Schuster.

McLaughlin, Timothy. Ed. 2012. *Walking on Earth and Touching the Sky; Poetry and Prose by Lakota Youth at Red Cloud Indian School*. Abrams.

Michael, Pamela, ed. 2008. *River of Words*. Milkweed.

Nye, Naomi Shihab, comp. 2000. Salting the Ocean: 100 Poems by Young Poets. New York: Greenwillow.

Ochoa, Annette Piña, Betsy Franco, and Traci L. Gourdine, Eds. 2003. Night is Gone, Day is Still Coming; Stories and Poems by American Indian Teens and Young Adults. Cambridge, MA: Candlewick.

Okutoro, Lydia Omolola, comp. 1999. *Quiet Storm: Voices of Young Black Poets*. New York: Hyperion.

Sidman, Joyce. 2003. *The World According to Dog: Poems and Teen Voices*. Ill. by Doug Mindell. Boston: Houghton Mifflin.

Simon, John O. 2011. *Cyclops Wearing Flip-Flops*. San Francisco: Center for the Art of Translation.

Thoms, Annie. Ed. 2002. *With Their Eyes*. New York: HarperTempest.

Tom, Karen, and Kiki. 2001. *Angst! Teen Verses from the Edge*. New York: Workman Publishing.

WritersCorps. 2008. *Tell the World*. New York: HarperCollins.

Glossary of Poetry Terminology

When digging deep into poetry, it can be helpful to have a vocabulary for discussing the differing aspects of how language is used to create a poem and give it its impact. Young people can enjoy learning these "big words" as they are learning more and more about poetry, too. But please don't let this aspect dominate poetry study or get in the way of enjoying the poems WITHOUT discussing these aspects as well. That said, this list of a handful of key terms may provide a helpful starting point. It is based on a reference guide created for students by Paul Williams and used with permission.

Alliteration: The repetition of consonants for effect, particularly as the initial sound in a string of words

Ballad: A short narrative poem, originally a song and with strong links to the oral tradition

Couplet: Paired lines of verses, often rhyming

Epic: A long, serious narrative poem, typically historical or mythological

Foot: A regular, repeated unit of stress in a line giving a poem its meter; a pattern of stressed (/) and unstressed (x) syllables. These are some of the most common metrical feet:
anapaest x x /
choriamb / x x /
cretic (or amphimacer) / x /
dactyl / x x
dibrach (or pyrrhic) x x
iamb x /
spondee / /
trochee / x

Free verse: Poetry that does not follow a set metrical pattern and is usually irregular in line length

Haiku: A three-line poem derived from the Japanese tradition generally featuring a focus on the natural world. The first and third lines have five syllables and the second line has seven. The senyru uses the same pattern but focuses on the human world. A tanka has five lines with a five, seven, five, seven, seven-syllable pattern.

Image: A word or words usually used figuratively to invoke sensory perceptions; imagery is the collective term for images, usually in the single poem.

Internal rhyme: The rhyming words within the line of poetry

Limerick: A verse made up of five lines with the aabba rhyme scheme usually humorous, often lewd in content

Lyric: Literally meaning to be sung accompanied by the lyre; lyric has come to mean a short poem usually expressive of the poet's emotions

Metaphor: A figure of speech in which one thing or idea is represented by implicit comparison with another.

Meter: The pattern of stressed and unstressed syllables in verse creating a distinctive rhythm

Narrative poem: A poem that tells a story (includes the ballad, epic)

Ode: A thoughtful lyric poem often commemorative or ceremonial in nature

Prose poem: A poem that may appear as a paragraph, but employs poetic elements such as imagery, metaphor and other devices that give it a poetic effect

Quatrain: A four-line stanza

Rhyme: The matching of sounds of syllables at the ends of lines of verse

Rhyme scheme: A way of representing the pattern of rhyme in a poem or stanza

Rhythm: The pattern of beats or stresses in a line of poetry, conveying a sense of movement or sound

Simile: An explicit comparison between two things or ideas, usually using "as" or "like"

Sonnet: Literally "little song," a poem of fourteen lines with various rhyme schemes

Stanza: A group of poetic lines often repeated according to a fixed pattern throughout a poem

Stress: The emphasis placed on a particular syllable or syllables in a word

Symbol: An image that represents itself and or one or more other things or concepts

Phonograms, Rimes and Rhymes

A phonogram or word rime is a part of a word that contains the vowel and following consonant sound. They are often used in teaching phonics because substituting the initial consonant sound is a way of teaching words by blending letters and word parts. Word rimes can also be helpful prompts for playing with rhyme in creating poems. Here is just a sampling of common phonograms and example words.

Phonogram;	Example words
-ay	jay, say, day
-ill	hill, will, spill
-ip	ship, dip, tip
-at	cat, sat, fat
-am	ham, jam, ram
-ag	bag, rag, sag
-ack	back, sack, track
-ank	bank, blank, thank
-ick	sick, pick, quick
-ell	bell, sell, yell
-ot	pot, not, trot
-ing	ring, sing, thing
-ap	cap, map, clap
-unk	junk, bunk, flunk
-ail	pail, jail, tail
-ain	rain, main, plain
-eed	feed, seed, week
-y	my, dry, try
-out	pout, scout, shout
-ug	rug, bug, tug
-op	mop, cop, hop
-in	pin, chin, thin
-an	pan, man, tan
-est	best, nest, test
-ink	pink, link, drink
-ow	low, grow, show
-ew	new, chew, grew
-ore	more, sore, store
-ed	bed, red, fed
-ab	cab, lab, crab
-ock	sock, block, clock
-ake	cake, lake, brake
-ine	line, nine, shine
-ight	light, right, knight
-im	swim, him, brim
-uck	duck, luck, truck
-um	gum, drum, plum

From: "Phonics- Phonograms" in Fry, Edward. 2004. *The Vocabulary Teacher's Book of Lists*. San Francisco, CA: Jossey-Bass, p. 152.

Survival Vocabulary

The following 100 words are part of what is sometimes called "survival vocabulary" for daily life in the U.S. Young people who are learning English as a new language need to become familiar with these terms. But even fluent English speakers will find it interesting and challenging to create poetry using these unique and essential building blocks. Involve students in making your own set of homemade magnetic poetry with these key "survival" words.

1. admission
2. ambulance
3. apartment
4. bank
5. breakfast
6. bus
7. cancel
8. car
9. cash
10. caution
11. charge
12. cleaners
13. closed
14. cold
15. collect
16. danger
17. delivery
18. dentist
19. deposit
20. dinner
21. directions
22. doctor
23. down
24. driver
25. due
26. east
27. electric
28. elevator
29. emergency
30. entrance
31. exit
32. food
33. fragile
34. free
35. garage
36. gas
37. glass
38. grocery
39. help
40. hospital
41. hot

42. hotel
43. information
44. job
45. laundry
46. license
47. lights
48. local
49. lost
50. lunch
51. manager
52. map
53. medicine
54. money
55. north
56. notice
57. nurse
58. open
59. operator
60. order
61. out
62. oxygen
63. parking
64. pedestrians
65. perishable
66. phone
67. poison
68. police
69. price
70. private
71. pull
72. push
73. quiet
74. receipt
75. refund
76. rent
77. repair
78. reserved
79. restroom
80. restaurant
81. sale
82. schedule
83. school
84. sick
85. size
86. skills
87. smoking
88. south
89. stairs
90. stop
91. store

92. taxi
93. toll
94. total
95. train
96. walk
97. warning
98. wash
99. water
100. work

Based on: "Daily Living Words" in Fry, Edward, Kress, Jacqueline, and Fountoukidis. 1993. *The Reading Teacher's Book of Lists*, Third Edition. Englewood Cliffs, NJ: Prentice Hall, pp. 38-39.

Possible Poetic Forms

Once children are immersed in poetry, they often begin to notice poems can take many different forms. They enjoy seeing the innovative ways the poets have crafted poems. Poems can rhyme or not, be completely free-flowing, or follow a specific form. Adults can introduce children to the various forms and techniques in context, by using interesting examples from excellent poetry. Here are some of those forms.

1. Acrostic poem (first letter of each line adds up to spell a word)
2. Autograph rhyme (e.g., U R 2 sweet 2 B 4 got 10)
3. Biopoem (11 line auto/biographical poem)
4. Blessing/prayer poem (list poem beginning with "May" or "Let")
5. Beat poetry (poetry that is experimental, informal, spontaneous)
6. Cheer/chant/yell (e.g., come on fans, clap your hands)
7. Cinquain (5 line poem with unrhymed lines of 2, 4, 6, 8, and 2 syllables)
8. Clerihew (funny poem of 2 rhyming couplets, 1 rhyme containing a name)
9. Concrete/picture/shape poetry (lines arranged to suggest poem subject visually)
10. Curse poem (rhythmic poem of exaggeration, many lines begin with "May")
11. Dada poetry (nonsense, semi-random words)
12. Diamante (seven-line diamond-shape poem based on two contrasting ideas)
13. Direct address (a poem that talks directly to another person or thing)
14. Dredging song (rhyming, rhythmic song designed to make work easier)
15. Epitaph and elegy poems (commemorating the passing or loss of someone or something)
16. "Found" poetry (rearranging words of exposition or prose to create a poem)
17. Ghazal (Persian form with unrhymed couplets that are re-arrangeable)
18. Graffiti poem (building a poem from found text and images in the environment)
19. Haiku (Japanese poem of 17 syllables with three lines of 5, 7, and 5)
20. Haikuestion (same format as the haiku, only with a question as a fourth line)
21. How-to poem (serious or silly directions with strong sequence words)
22. Letter/note/diary poem (poem of address, apology, argument, explanation or thanks to someone or something)
23. Limerick (humorous poem with five lines with the a/a/b/b/a rhyme scheme)
24. List/litany poem (an organized list usually in free verse)
25. Pantoum (second and fourth line of first quatrain repeated as the first and third lines of the following quatrain)
26. Persona or mask poem (writing as if you are someone or something else)

27. Question poem (the poem asks a question or each line is a question)
28. Rap (musical form featuring chanted rhyming lyrics with a strong rhythm)
29. Rebus poem (pictures substitute for key words)
30. Recipe poem (poem incorporating recipe ingredients, directions, and occasion)
31. Riddle poem (a descriptive poem that requires one to guess at the subject)
32. Sijo (Korean form with three lines averaging 14-16 syllables for a total of 44-46)
33. Sonnet (Italian, Elizabethan, etc. 14-line verse form)
34. Tanka (a Japanese poem with 31 syllables in 5 lines)
35. "Take off" poem (imitating or copying a known poem in form, style, rhythm)
36. Terse verse (hink pinks; rhyming word pairs)
37. Tongue twister (use of various devices to make poem lines difficult to pronounce)
38. Triangular triplet (3 lines read in any order)

The Biopoem Formula

The biopoem is a popular form of poetry writing with young people. It's an easy way to begin writing poetry, to break the ice in helping young writers introduce themselves to one another, to help jumpstart autobiographical or biographical writing, or to be adapted for simple character sketches. There are many variations, but the most prevalent is probably this 11-line form.

Line 1: First name
Line 2: Three traits or adjectives that describe the person
Line 3: Relative status ("Brother," "sister," " husband," "wife," "son," "daughter," etc.) of _____
Line 4: Who loves _____ (list three things or people that person loves)
Line 5: Who feels _____ (three items)
Line 6: Who needs _____ (three items)
Line 7: Who fears _____ (three items)
Line 8: Who gives _____ (one item fully explained)
Line 9: Who would like to see _____ (one item)
Line 10: Who lives _____ (place identified or described)
Line 11: Last name

Poetry Writing Checklist and Guidelines

Poets of all ages often need guidance in looking at their own work critically. A checklist or guidelines can be helpful in developing skill in revising one's own writing. No single list is perfect, nor is each step necessary every time, but such checklists can be a good tool. Here are two examples designed especially for developing young writers.

Holbrook's Self-Edit Checklist

1. Have I written from one point of view?
2. Have I narrowed the focus?
3. Have I defined all of my opinion words?
4. Have I double-checked the basics (like subject-verb agreement, verb tense, spelling)?
5. Have I worked to get the trite out (of over-used words and phrases)?
6. Have I practiced cutting out excess words (like articles)?
7. Have I read the poem aloud to see if it flows and makes sense?
8. Does the poem contain any fake rhymes (a rhyme used for the rhyme's sake, rather than for the sake of the message)?
9. Have I used action verbs to clarify images?
10. Was I consistent with the pattern I chose?
11. Did I maintain a clear and consistent image?
12. Have I shared my poem with another person? (It shouldn't need explaining.)

Based on: Holbrook, Sara. 2005. *Practical Poetry; A Nonstandard Approach to Meeting Content-Area Standards.* Portsmouth, NH: Heinemann, p. 54-56.

Perry's Self-Questioning Guidelines

1. What can I put in my poem?
   *Who, what, when, where, why, how?
   *Sight, sound, smell, feel, taste?
2. Are there things I would like to fix?
   *Line breaks, compound words, spelling?
   *Title, beginning, middle, end?
3. Maybe I could add more…
4. Maybe I don't need that one word.
5. How does this look on the page?
6. How will this sound when I read it out loud?
   *Rhythm, movement, and emphases.
   *Loud? Quiet? Both?
7. What tools could I use to help me?

Based on: Perry, Aaren Yeatts. 1997. *Poetry Across the Curriculum; An Action Guide for Elementary Teachers.* Boston: Allyn & Bacon, p. 183.

Places to Publish Children's Poetry Writing

Nearly all children who hear and read a lot of poetry will naturally try writing poetry, too. A few children will even love writing poetry enough to want to try share their work in some public venue. Here are a variety of print and online sources that include writing by children and teens. One note: be sure to guide young writers through the submission process and prepare them for possible rejection. Be encouraging and have fun with poetry!

Creative Kids
P O Box 8813
Waco, TX 76144
http://www.prufrock.com/client/client_pages/prufrock_jm_createkids.cfm

New Moon: The Magazine for Girls and Their Dreams
34 E. Superior St. Suite 200
Duluth, MNL 55802
http://www.newmoon.com/

Skipping Stones
P O Box 3939
Eugene OR 97403
http://www.skippingstones.org

Stone Soup Magazine
Box 83
Santa Cruz, CA 950636
http://www.stonesoup.com

Merlyn's Pen
11 South Angell St., Suite 301
Providence, RI 02906
http://www.merlynspen.com

Teen Ink
P O Box 30
Newton, MA 02461
http://www.teenink.com

OWL and *Chickadee* magazine
56 The Esplanade, Suite 304
Toronto, Ontario M5E 1A7, Canada
http://www.owlkids.com/

Kidsworld Magazine
345 Danforth Ave.
Toronto Ontario M4K 1N7, Canada
http://www.kidsworld-online.com/

Highlights for Children ("Our Own Pages")
803 Church St.
Honesdale PA 18431
http://www.highlights.com/

Carus Publishing (*Appleseeds, Calliope, Cicada, Cobblestone, Odyssey* magazines, etc.)
http://www.cobblestonepub.com/index.html

Poetry Hill Poetry
http://www.potatohill.com

Cyberkids
http://www.cyberkids.com

Cyberteens
http://www.cyberteens.com

KidLit
http://mgfx.com/kidlit/

KidPub
http://www.kidpub.org

Scholastic Writing Contests
http://www.scholastic.com/artandwritingawards/enter.htm

Resource Books for Teaching Poetry Writing to Children

These professional resources specifically address the teaching of poetry writing with children and young adults. They provide a variety of strategies and perspectives on guiding and evaluating young people's poetry writing efforts.

Ambrosini, Michelle and Morretta, Teresa. 2003. *Poetry Workshop for Middle School.* Newark, DE: International Reading Association.

Burkhardt, Ross. M. 2006. *Using Poetry in the Classroom: Engaging Students in Learning.* Lanham, MD: Rowman & Littlefield Education.

Collom, Jack and Noethe, Sheryl. 2005. *Poetry Everywhere; Teaching Poetry Writing in School and in the Community.* Teachers & Writers.

Esbensen, Barbara J. 1995. *A Celebration of Bees; Helping Children to Write Poetry.* New York: Henry Holt.

Franco, Betsy. 2005. *Conversations With a Poet: Inviting Poetry into K-12 Classrooms.* Richard C. Owen.

Frost, Helen. 2001. *When I Whisper, Nobody Listens: Helping Young People Write About Difficult Issues.* Heinemann.

Glover, M. K. 1999. *A Garden of Poets; Poetry Writing in the Elementary Classroom.* Urbana, IL: NCTE.

Hanauer, David Ian. 2004. *Poetry and the Meaning of Life; Reading and Writing Poetry in Language Arts Classrooms.* Toronto: Pippin.

Heard, Georgia. 1994. *For the Good of the Earth and Sun.* Portsmouth,

Heard, Georgia. 1999. *Awakening the Heart.* Portsmouth, NH: Heinemann.

Holbrook, Sara. 2005. *Practical Poetry; A Nonstandard Approach to Meeting Content-Area Standards.* Portsmouth, NH: Heinemann.

Holbrook, Sara and Salinger, Michael. 2006. *Outspoken: How to Improve Writing and Speaking Through Poetry Performance.* Heinemann.

Janeczko, Paul B. 1999. *Scholastic Guides: How to Write Poetry.* Scholastic.

Lipson, S. L. 2006. *Writing Success through Poetry: Create a Writers' Workshop.* Prufrock Press.

Livingston, Myra Cohn. 1991. *Poem-making: Ways to Begin Writing Poetry.* HarperCollins, New York.

McClure, A. 1990. *Sunrises and Songs: Reading and Writing Poetry in the Classroom.* Portsmouth, NH: Heinemann.

O'Connor, John S. 2004. *Wordplaygrounds; Reading, Writing, and Performing Poetry in the English Classroom.* Urbana, IL: NCTE.

Routman, Regie. 2000. *Kids' Poems: Teaching First Graders to Love Writing Poetry.* New York: Scholastic.

Ruurs, Margriet. 2001. *The Power of Poems; Teaching the Joy of Writing Poetry.* Gainesville, FL: Maupin House.

Sloan, Glenna. 2003. *Give Them Poetry; A Guide for Sharing Poetry with Children K-8.* New York: Teachers College Press.

Tiedt, Iris McClellan. 2002. *Tiger Lilies, Toadstools, And Thunderbolts: Engaging K-8 Students With Poetry.* International Reading Association.

Wood, Jaime R. 2007. *Living Voices: Multicultural Poetry in the Middle School Classroom.* Urbana, IL: NCTE.

GENERAL POETRY TEACHING RESOURCES

Here you'll find a variety of lists geared primarily to the adult who selects and shares poetry for kids. There are web sites and blogs for poets and poetry and a long list of "text sets" for close study—featuring multiple books by individual poets chosen for their similarity in topic or approach. There is also a list of biographical and autobiographical works if you want to share information about the lives of the poets who have written for young people. You'll find step-by-step guidelines for evaluating and critiquing poetry books as you seek out the very best and a long list of books for adults about poetry for young people. Finally, a timeline of the history of poetry for children shows where we've come from and a list of the works of Peter and Iona Opie adds another layer to our understanding of that history.

Poet Web Sites for Young People
Biographies and Autobiographies of Poets for Young People
Poet Text Sets for Young People
Popular Poetry Web Sites for Young People
Blogs About Poetry for Young People
Guidelines for Evaluating Poetry Books for Young People
Timeline of the History of Children's Poetry
The Opie Collection: The Works of Peter and Iona Opie
Professional Resource Books about Poetry for Young People

Poet Web Sites for Young People

One of the wonderful aspects of the Internet is having access to "inside" perspectives from poets themselves. Many poets writing for young people maintain rich and lively web sites that offer interesting biographical information, current booklists, and ideas and strategies for connecting kids with poetry. Plus, they have an appealing look that engages kids. Some even offer opportunities for interaction and communication with the poet. These sites help budding poets see how poets live and work. They can also help the poetry-phobic teacher or librarian feel less intimidated about poetry. For starters, check these out.

Arnold Adoff/ http://www.arnoldadoff.com/
Jaime Adoff/ http://www.jaimeadoff.com/
Kathi Appelt/ http://www.kathiappelt.com/
Jorge Argueta/ http://jorgeargueta.com
Linda Ashman/ http://www.lindaashman.com/
Jeannine Atkins/ http://www.jeannineatkins.com/
Brod Bagert/ http://brodbagert.com/
Carmen T. Bernier-Grand/ http://www.carmenberniergrand.com
Calef Brown/ http://www.polkabats.com/
Jen Bryant/ http://www.jenbryant.com/
Leslie Bulion/ http://www.lesliebulion.com/
Stephanie Calmenson/ http://www.stephaniecalmenson.com/
Thalia Chaltas/ http://www.thaliachaltas.com/
Sherryl Clark/ http://www.poetry4kids.net/index.html
Jill Corcoran/ http://jillcorcoran.com
Kalli Dakos/ http://www.kalllidakos.com
Rebecca Kai Dotlich/ http://www.rebeccakaidotlich.com
Margarita Engle/ http://margaritaengle.com/
Carole Gerber/ http://www.carolegerber.com/
Paul Fleischman/ http://www.paulfleischman.net/
Ralph Fletcher/ http://www.ralphfletcher.com
Douglas Florian/ http://floriancafe.blogspot.com/
Betsy Franco/ http://www.betsyfranco.com/
Helen Frost/ http://www.helenfrost.net/
Kristine O'Connell George/ http://www.kristinegeorge.com
Charles Ghigna/ http://charlesghigna.com/
Joan Bransfield Graham/ http://www.joangraham.com/
John Grandits/ http://johngrandits.com/
Nikki Grimes/ http://www.nikkigrimes.com
Lorie Ann Grover/ http://www.lorieanngrover.com/
David L. Harrison/ http://www.davidlharrison.com/
Georgia Heard/ http://georgiaheard.com/
Juan Felipe Herrera/ http://www.juanfelipe.org/pageone.html
Steven Herrick/ http://www.stevenherrick.com.au/
Anna Grossnickle Hines/ http://www.aghines.com/
Mary Ann Hoberman/ http://maryannhoberman.com/
Sara Holbrook/ http://www.saraholbrook.com/
Ellen Hopkins/ http://www.ellenhopkins.com/

Lee Bennett Hopkins/ http://www.leebennetthopkins.com/
Patricia Hubbell/ http://www.kidspoet.com/main.html
Paul B. Janeczko/ http://www.paulbjaneczko.com/
Alan Katz/ http://www.alankatzbooks.com/
Bobbi Katz/ http://www.bobbikatz.com/
X.J. and Dorothy Kennedy/ http://xjanddorothymkennedy.com/
Bruce Lansky/ http://www.gigglepoetry.com
Julie Larios/ http://julielarios.blogspot.com/
Constance Levy/ http://www.constancelevy.com/
Debbie Levy/ http://www.debbielevybooks.com/
J. Patrick Lewis/ http://www.jpatricklewis.com/
George Ella Lyon/ http://www.georgeellalyon.com/
Guadalupe Garcia McCall/ http://guadalupegarciamccall.com/
Pat Mora/ http://www.patmora.com
Heidi Mordhorst/ http://www.heidimordhorst.com/
Kenn Nesbitt/ http://www.poetry4kids.com/
Jose Luis Orozco/ http://www.joseluisorozco.com/
Ann Whitford Paul/ http://www.annwhitfordpaul.net/
Andrew Fusek Peters/ http://www.twopeters.com/
Jack Prelutsky/ http://jackprelutsky.com/
Mary Quattlebaum/ http://www.maryquattlebaum.com/
Jame Richards/ http://www.jamerichards.com/
Heidi Bee Roemer/ http://heidibroemer.com
Michael J. Rosen/ http://www.fidosopher.com/
Michael Rosen/ http://www.michaelrosen.co.uk/
Deborah Ruddell/ http://www.deborahruddell.com/index.htm
Laura Purdie Salas/ http://laurasalas.com/
Michael Salinger/ http://www.michaelsalinger.com/
Joyce Sidman/ http://www.joycesidman.com/
Shel Silverstein/ http://www.shelsilverstein.com
Marilyn Singer/ http://marilynsinger.net/
Charles R. Smith, Jr./ http://www.charlesrsmithjr.com/index.htm
Hope Anita Smith/ http://hopeanitasmith.com/
Sonya Sones/ http://www.sonyasones.com
Gary Soto/ http://www.garysoto.com/
Eileen Spinelli/ http://www.eileenspinelli.com
Joyce Carol Thomas/ http://www.joycecarolthomas.com
Amy Ludwig VanDerwater/ http://www.amylv.com/
Lee Wardlaw/ http://www.leewardlaw.com/
Charles Waters/ http://www.charleswaters.net/
April Halprin Wayland/ http://www.aprilwayland.com/
Carole Boston Weatherford/ http://www.caroleweatherford.com/
Robert Weinstock/ http://www.callmebob.com/
Robert Paul Weston/ http://www.robertpaulweston.com/
Steven Withrow/ http://cracklesofspeech.blogspot.com/
Allan Wolf/ http://www.allanwolf.com/
Janet S. Wong/ http://www.janetwong.com
Joyce Lee Wong/ http://joyceleewong.com/
Jane Yolen/ http://www.janeyolen.com
Tracie Vaughn Zimmer/ http://www.tracievaughnzimmer.com

Biographies and Autobiographies of Poets for Young People

Sharing books about the lives of poets and how they came to write poetry can be interesting and inspiring to young readers, particularly those who want to write poetry themselves. The Academy of American Poets also offers a massive web site with a comprehensive directory of American poets and there are several resource books contain biographical sketches about a variety of poets who write for young people including: Pauses: Autobiographical Reflections of 101 Creators of Children's Books *by Lee Bennett Hopkins (HarperCollins, 1995), Jeffrey and Vicky Copeland's* Speaking of Poets I and II: Interviews with Poets Who Write for Children and Young Adults *(Urbana, IL: National Council of Teachers of English, 1993; 1995), and my own* Poetry People; A Practical Guide to Children's Poets *(Vardell, Libraries Unlimited, 2007). In addition, the list below includes more titles of poet autobiographical and biographical works in a variety of formats.*

Anaya, Rudolfo. 2000. *Elegy on the Death of Cesar Chavez*. Ill. by Gaspar Enriquez. El Paso, Texas: Cinco Puntos Press.

Bober, Natalie S. 1991. *A Restless Spirit: The Story of Robert Frost*. New York: Henry Holt.

Brown, Monica. 2005. *My Name is Gabriela: The Life of Gabriela Mistral*. Ill. by John Parra. Flagstaff, Arizona: Luna Rising Books.

Brown, Monica. 2011. *Pablo Neruda*. Ill. by Julie Paschkis. New York: Henry Holt.

Bryant, Jen. 2008. *A River of Words: The Story of William Carlos Williams*. New York: Eerdmans.

Burleigh, Robert. 2004. *Langston's Train Ride*. Ill. by Leonard Jenkins. New York: Scholastic.

Christensen, Bonnie. 2001. *Woody Guthrie: Poet of the People*. New York: Knopf.

Cooper, Floyd. 1994. *Coming Home: From the Life of Langston Hughes*. New York: Philomel.

Delano, Poli. 2006. *When I Was a Boy Neruda Called Me Policarpo*. Ill. by Manuel Monroy. Toronto/Berkeley: Groundwood Press.

Florian, Douglas. 2006. *See for Your Self*. Katonah, NY: Richard C. Owen Publishers.

Gherman, Beverly. 1996. *Robert Louis Stevenson, Teller of Tales*. New York: Atheneum.

Gollub, Matthew. 1998. *Cool Melons Turn to Frogs: The Life and Poems of Issa*. New York: Lee & Low.

Hemphill, Stephanie. 2007. *Your Own, Sylvia*. New York: Knopf.

Hopkins, Lee Bennett. 1993. *The Writing Bug*. Katonah, NY: Richard C. Owen Publishers.

Izuki, Steven. 1994. *Believers in America: Poems about Americans of Asian and Pacific Islander Descent*. Chicago, IL: Children's Press.

Josephson, Judith Pinkerton. 2000. *Nikki Giovanni, Poet of the People*. New York: Enslow.

Kerley, Barbara. 2004. *Walt Whitman: Words for America*. Ill. by Brian Selznick. New York: Scholastic Press.

Kuskin, Karla. 1995. *Thoughts, Pictures, and Words*. Photographs by Nicholas Kuskin. Katonah, NY: Richard C. Owen Publishers.

Lasky, Kathryn. 2003. *A Voice of Her Own: The Story of Phillis Wheatley, Slave Poet*. Ill. by Paul Lee. Cambridge, MA: Candlewick.

Lewis, J. Patrick. 1998. *Boshblobberbosh; Runcible Poems for Edward Lear*. Mankato: Creative Editions; San Diego: Harcourt.

McKissack, Patricia C. 1984. *Paul Laurence Dunbar, A Poet to Remember*. Chicago, IL: Children's Press.

Meltzer, Milton. 1997. *Langston Hughes: A Biography*. Ill. by Stephen Alcorn. Minneapolis, MN: Millbrook.

Meltzer, Milton. 1999. *Carl Sandburg: A Biography*. Breckenridge, CO: Twenty-First Century Books.

Meltzer, Milton. 2002. *Walt Whitman: A Biography*. Breckenridge, CO: Twenty-First Century Books.

Meltzer, Milton. 2004. *Emily Dickinson: A Biography*. Breckenridge, CO: Twenty-first Century Books.

Murphy, Jim. 1993. *Across America On An Emigrant Train*. New York: Clarion.

Niven, Penelope. 2003. *Carl Sandburg: Adventures of a Poet*. Ill. by Marc Nadel. San Diego: Harcourt Brace.

Osofsky, Audrey. 1996. *Free to Dream: The Making of a Poet: Langston Hughes*. Lothrop, Lee & Shepard.

Perdomo, Willie. 2002. *Visiting Langston*. Ill. by Bryan Collier. Henry Holt.

Ray, Deborah Kogan. 2006. *To Go Singing Through the World: the Childhood of Pablo Neruda*. New York: Farrar, Straus and Giroux.

Reef, Catherine. 2000. *Paul Laurence Dunbar: Portrait Of A Poet*. New York: Enslow.

Reef, Catherine. 1995. *Walt Whitman*. New York: Clarion.

Ryan, Pam Munoz. 2010. *The Dreamer*. New York: Scholastic.

Strickland, Michael R. 1996. *African-American Poets*. New York: Enslow.

Strong, Amy. 2003. *Lee Bennett Hopkins: A Children's Poet*. New York: Franklin Watts.

Winter, Jeanette. 2002. *Emily Dickinson's Letters to the World*. New York: Frances Foster Books/FSG.

Wong, Janet S. 2006. *Before It Wriggles Away*. Katonah, NY: Richard C. Owen Publishers.

Yolen, Jane. 1992. *A Letter from Phoenix Farm*. Katonah, NY: Richard C. Owen Publishers.

Yolen, Jane. 2009. *My Uncle Emily*. New York: Philomel.

Poet Text Sets for Young People

Once we get comfortable sharing poetry with young people, it can be especially meaningful to share SETS of poetry gathered around similarities. Such "text sets" can prompt lessons of compare/contrast and discussion of poetic voice, stylistic choices, etc. The following text sets are presented in four categories: for very young children (ages 0-5), for elementary aged children (ages 5-12), for middle school (ages 11-14), and for young adults (ages 13 and up). However, these are general recommendations based on overall readability and appeal. These poetry selections are certainly suitable for a much wider age range. Each mini set includes 3 or more poetry books authored by one poet, focused on a single topic or theme, and formatted to be very similar in design and appearance. This aids in guiding discussion, comparison, and analysis.

FOR VERY YOUNG CHILDREN (ages 0-5)
Folk-based rhymes (bilingual Spanish/English)
Ada, Alma Flor and Campoy, Isabel. 2010. *Muu, Moo! Rimas de animales/Animal Nursery Rhymes.* Rayo/HarperCollins.
Ada, Alma Flor, and Isabel Campoy. Ed. 2003. *Pio Peep! Traditional Spanish Nursery Rhymes.* New York: HarperCollins.
Ada, Alma Flor and Campoy, F. Isabel. 2011. *Ten Little Puppies; Diez perritos.* Rayo/HarperCollins.

Song-based rhymes (bilingual Spanish/English)
Delacre, Lulu. Ed. 1992. *Arroz con Leche: Popular Songs and Rhymes from Latin America.* New York: Scholastic.
Delacre, Lulu. Ed. 1992. *Las Navidades: Popular Christmas Songs from Latin America.* New York: Scholastic.
Delacre, Lulu. 2004. *Arrorró Mi Niño: Latino Lullabies and Gentle Games.* New York: Scholastic.

Folk songs and fingerplays (bilingual Spanish/English)
Orozco, José Luis. 2002. Diez Deditos: *Ten Little Fingers and Other Play Rhymes and Action Songs from Latin America.* New York: Dutton.
Orozco, José Luis.1994. *Fiestas: A Year of Latin American Songs of Celebration.* New York: Dutton.
Orozco, Jose-Luis. 1994. *De Colores and Other Latin-American Folk Songs for Children.* New York: Dutton.

Animal rhymes
Elliott, David. 2008. *On the Farm.* Somerville, MA: Candlewick.
Elliott, David. 2010. *In the Wild.* Somerville, MA: Candlewick.
Elliott, David. 2012. *In the Sea.* Somerville, MA: Candlewick.

Poems to read aloud with a parent/adult
Hoberman, Mary Ann. 2001. *You Read to Me, I'll Read to You; Very Short Stories to Read Together.* Ill. by Michael Emberley. Boston: Little, Brown.

Hoberman, Mary Ann. 2004. *You Read to Me, I'll Read to You; Very Short Fairy Tales to Read Together*. Ill. by Michael Emberley. Boston: Little, Brown.

Hoberman, Mary Ann. 2005. *You Read to Me, I'll Read to You; Very Short Mother Goose Tales to Read Together*. Ill. by Michael Emberley. Boston: Little, Brown.

Hoberman, Mary Ann. 2007. *You Read to Me, I'll Read to You; Very Short Scary Tales to Read Together*. Ill. by featMichael Emberley. Boston: Little, Brown.

FOR ELEMENTARY SCHOOL AGE CHILDREN (ages 5-12)
The Shel Silverstein set
Silverstein, Shel. 1974. *Where the Sidewalk Ends*. New York: Harper and Row.

Silverstein, Shel. 1981. *A Light in the Attic*. New York: Harper & Row.

Silverstein, Shel. 1996. *Falling Up*. New York: HarperCollins.

Silverstein, Shel. 2011. *Every Thing On It*. HarperCollins.

The Jack Prelutsky set
Prelutsky, Jack. 1984. *The New Kid on the Block*. New York: Greenwillow.

Prelutsky, Jack. 1990. *Something Big Has Been Here*. New York: Scholastic.

Prelutsky, Jack. 1996. *A Pizza the Size of the Sun*. New York: Greenwillow.

Prelutsky, Jack. 2000. *It's Raining Pigs & Noodles*. New York: Greenwillow.

Prelutsky, Jack. 2008. *My Dog May Be a Genius*. New York: Greenwillow.

School poetry
Dakos, Kalli. 1990. *If You're Not Here, Please Raise Your Hand: Poems about School*. New York: Four Winds Press.

Dakos, Kalli. 1993. *Don't Read This Book Whatever You Do!: More Poems about School*. New York: Trumpet Club.

Dakos, Kalli. 1995. *Mrs. Cole on an Onion Roll and Other School Poems*. New York: Simon & Schuster.

Dakos, Kalli. 1996. *The Goof Who Invented Homework and Other School Poems*. New York: Dial.

Dakos, Kalli. 1999. *The Bug in Teacher's Coffee*. New York: HarperCollins.

Dakos, Kalli. 2003. *Put Your Eyes Up Here: And Other School Poems*. New York: Simon & Schuster.

Dakos, Kalli. 2011. *A Funeral in the Bathroom and Other School Bathroom Poems*. Albert Whitman.

Humor and nonsense
Brown, Calef. 1998. *Polkabats and Octopus Slacks: 14 Stories*. Boston: Houghton Mifflin.

Brown, Calef. 2000. *Dutch Sneakers and Flea Keepers: 14 More Stories*. Boston: Houghton Mifflin.

Brown, Calef. 2006. *Flamingos on the Roof*. Boston: Houghton Mifflin.

Brown, Calef. 2008. *Soup For Breakfast*. Boston: Houghton Mifflin.

Identity and friendship
Grimes, Nikki. 1994. *Meet Danitra Brown*. New York: Lothrop, Lee & Shepard.
Grimes, Nikki. 2002. *Danitra Brown Leaves Town*. New York: HarperCollins.
Grimes, Nikki. 2005. *Danitra Brown, Class Clown*. New York: Lothrop, Lee & Shepard.

Poems and quilts
Hines, Anna Grossnickle. 2005. *Winter Lights: A Season in Poems & Quilts*. New York: Greenwillow.
Hines, Anna Grossnickle. 2011. *Peaceful Pieces: A Year in Poems and Quilts*. New York: Greenwillow.
Hines, Anna Grossnicle. 2001. *Pieces: A Year in Poems and Quilts*. New York: Greenwillow.

The seasons (bilingual Spanish/English)
Alarcón, Francisco X. 1997. *Laughing Tomatoes and Other Spring Poems/Jitomates Risuenos y Otros Poemas de Primavera*. San Francisco, CA: Children's Book Press.
Alarcón, Francisco X. 1998. *From the Bellybutton of the Moon and Other Summer Poems/Del Ombligo de la Luna y Otros Poemas de Verano*. San Francisco: Children's Book Press.
Alarcón, Francisco X. 1999. *Angels Ride Bikes and Other Fall Poems*. San Francisco, CA: Children's Book Press.
Alarcón, Francisco X. 2001. *Iguanas in the Snow and Other Winter Poems/ Iguanas en la Nieve y Otros Poemas de Invierno*. San Francisco, CA: Children's Book Press.

More seasonal poems
Schnur, Steven. 1997. *Autumn: An Alphabet Acrostic*. New York: Clarion.
Schnur, Steven. 1999. *Spring: An Alphabet Acrostic*. New York: Clarion.
Schnur, Steven. 2001. *Summer: An Alphabet Acrostic*. New York: Clarion.
Schnur, Steven. 2002. *Winter: An Alphabet Acrostic*. New York: Clarion.

Holiday poems
Livingston, Myra Cohn. Ed. 1985. *Easter Poems*. New York: Holiday House.
Livingston, Myra Cohn. Ed. 1985. *Thanksgiving Poems*. New York: Holiday House.
Livingston, Myra Cohn. Ed. 1986. *Poems for the Jewish Holidays*. New York: Holiday House.
Livingston, Myra Cohn. Ed. 1987. *Valentine Poems*. New York: Holiday House.
Livingston, Myra Cohn. Ed. 1988. *Poems for Mothers*. New York: Holiday House.
Livingston, Myra Cohn. Ed. 1989. *Halloween Poems*. New York: Holiday House.
Livingston, Myra Cohn. 1985. *Celebrations*. New York: Holiday House.
Livingston, Myra Cohn. 1989. *Birthday Poems*. New York: Holiday House.

Food poetry (bilingual Spanish/English)

Argueta, Jorge. 2009. *Sopa de frijoles/ Bean Soup*. Ill. by Rafael Yockteng. Toronto, ON: Groundwood.

Argueta, Jorge. 2010. *Arroz con leche; Rice Pudding*. Ill. by Fernando Vilela. Toronto, ON: Groundwood.

Argueta, Jorge. 2012. *Guacamole; Un poema para cocinar/ A Cooking Poem*. Ill. by Margarita Sada. Groundwood.

Animals

Florian, Douglas. 1996. *On the Wing: Bird Poems and Paintings*. San Diego, CA: Harcourt Brace.

Florian, Douglas. 1997. *In the Swim: Poems and Paintings*. San Diego, CA: Harcourt Brace.

Florian, Douglas. 1998. *Insectlopedia: Poems and Paintings*. San Diego, CA: Harcourt Brace.

Florian, Douglas. 2000. *Mammalabilia: Poems and Paintings*. San Diego, CA: Harcourt Brace.

Florian, Douglas. 2001. *Bow Wow Meow Meow*. San Diego: Harcourt.

Florian, Douglas. 2003. *Lizard, Frogs, and Polliwogs*. San Diego: Harcourt.

Florian, Douglas. 2004. *Omnibeasts*. San Diego: Harcourt.

Florian, Douglas. 2005. *Zoo's Who*. San Diego, CA: Harcourt.

Florian, Douglas. 2009. *Dinothesaurus*. New York: Simon & Schuster.

Birds

Yolen, Jane. 2002. *Wild Wings: Poems for Young People*. Honesdale, PA: Wordsong/Boyds Mills Press.

Yolen, Jane. 2004. *Fine Feathered Friends: Poems for Young People*. Honesdale, PA: Wordsong/Boyds Mills Press.

Yolen, Jane. 2010. *An Egret's Day*. Honesdale, PA: Wordsong/Boyds Mills Press.

Yolen, Jane. 2011. *Birds of a Feather*. Ill. by Jason Stemple. Boyds Mills Press.

Ecosystem poems

Sidman, Joyce. 2005. *Song of the Water Boatman and Other Pond Poems*. Ill. By Beckie Prange. Boston: Houghton Mifflin.

Sidman, Joyce. 2006. *Butterfly Eyes and Other Secrets of the Meadow*. Ill. by Beth Krommes. Boston: Houghton Mifflin.

Sidman, Joyce. 2010. *Dark Emperor and Other Poems of the Night*. Ill. by Rick Allen. Boston: Houghton Mifflin.

U.S. history and poetry

Hopkins, Lee Bennett. Ed. 1994. *Hand in Hand: An American History through Poetry*. New York: Simon & Schuster.

Hopkins, Lee Bennett. Ed. 1999. *Lives: Poems about Famous Americans*. New York: HarperCollins.

Hopkins, Lee Bennett. 2000. *My America: A Poetry Atlas of the United States*. New York: Simon & Schuster.

Hopkins, Lee Bennett. 2008. *America at War*. New York: McElderry.

Famous historical figures

Lewis, J. Patrick. 2005. *Vherses: A Celebration of Outstanding Women*. Mankato, MN: Creative Editions.

Lewis, J. Patrick. 2005. *Heroes and She-Roes: Poems of Amazing and Everyday Heroes*. New York: Dial.

Lewis, J. Patrick. 2000. *Freedom Like Sunlight: Praisesongs for Black Americans*. Mankato, MN: Creative Editions.

Lewis, J. Patrick. 2012. *When Thunder Comes: Poems for Civil Rights Leaders*. Chronicle.

Poems of place

Siebert, Diane. 1988. *Mojave*. New York: Crowell.

Siebert, Diane. 1989. *Heartland*. New York: Crowell.

Siebert, Diane. 1991. *Sierra*. New York: HarperCollins.

Siebert, Diane. 2000. *Cave*. New York: HarperCollins.

Native American perspectives

Bruchac, Joseph. 1992. *Thirteen Moons on Turtle's Back: A Native American Year of Moons*. New York: Philomel Books.

Bruchac, Joseph. 1995. *The Earth under Sky Bear's Feet: Native American Poems of the Land*. New York: Philomel Books.

Bruchac, Joseph. 1996. *Between Earth and Sky: Legends of Native American Sacred Places*. San Diego, CA: Harcourt Brace.

Poems and music

Myers, Walter Dean. 1997. *Harlem: A Poem*. New York: Scholastic.

Myers, Walter Dean. 2003. *Blues Journey*. New York: Holiday House.

Myers, Walter Dean. 2006. *Jazz*. Ill. by Christopher Myers. New York: Holiday House.

Poem riddles

Lewis, J. Patrick. 1996. *Riddle-icious*. New York: Scholastic.

Lewis, J. Patrick. 1998. *Riddle-Lightful: Oodles of Little Riddle-Poems*. Knopf.

Lewis, J. Patrick. 2004. *Scientrickery: Riddles in Science*. San Diego: Harcourt.

Lewis, J. Patrick. 2009. *Spot the Plot! A Riddle Book of Book Riddles*. Ill. by Lynn Munsinger. San Francisco, CA: Chronicle.

Poem forms

Janeczko, Paul B. Ed. 2001. *A Poke in the I: A Collection of Concrete Poems*. Somerville, MA: Candlewick.

Janeczko, Paul B.. Ed. 2005. *A Kick in the Head: An Everyday Guide to Poetic Forms*. Somerville, MA: Candlewick.

Janeczko, Paul. 2009. *A Foot in the Mouth; Poems to Speak, Sing, and Shout*. Ill. by Chris Raschka. Somerville, MA: Candlewick.

Poetry e-books

Vardell, Sylvia and Wong, Janet. Eds. 2011. *P*TAG*. PoetryTagTime.

Vardell, Sylvia and Wong, Janet. Eds. 2011. *PoetryTagTime*. PoetryTagTime

Vardell, Sylvia and Wong, Janet. Eds. 2011. *Gift Tag*. PoetryTagTime.

Poems with audio CDs of poets reading

Giovanni, Nikki. Coll. 2008. *Hip Hop Speaks to Children*. Naperville, IL: Sourcebooks.

Paschen, Elise and Raccah, Dominique. Ed. 2005. *Poetry Speaks to Children*. Naperville, IL: Sourcebooks.

Paschen, Elise and Raccah, Dominique. Ed. 2010. *Poetry Speaks; Who I Am*. Naperville, IL: Sourcebooks.

FOR MIDDLE SCHOOL (ages 11-14)
Historical novels in verse set in Cuba

Engle, Margarita. 2006. *The Poet Slave of Cuba: A Biography of Juan Francisco Manzano*. New York: Holt.

Engle, Margarita. 2008. *The Surrender Tree*. New York: Holt.

Engle, Margarita. 2009. *Tropical Secrets: Holocaust Refugees in Cuba*. New York: Holt.

Engle, Margarita. 2010. *The Firefly Letters; A Suffragette's Journey to Cuba*. Henry Holt.

Engle, Margarita. 2011. *Hurricane Dancers; The First Caribbean Pirate Shipwreck*. Henry Holt.

Earth, water, and fire

Singer, Marilyn. 2002. *Footprints on the Roof: Poems about the Earth*. New York: Knopf.

Singer, Marilyn. 2003. *How to Cross a Pond: Poems about Water*. New York: Knopf.

Singer, Marilyn. 2005. *Central Heating: Poems about Fire and Warmth*. New York: Knopf.

For reading aloud with multiple voices

Fleishman, Paul. 1985. *I Am Phoenix: Poems for Two Voices*. New York: Harper & Row.

Fleishman, Paul. 1988. *Joyful Noise: Poems for Two Voices*. New York: Harper & Row.

Fleishman, Paul. 2000. *Big Talk: Poems for Four Voices*. Somerville, MA: Candlewick.

Basketball

Smith, Charles R. Jr. 1999. *Rimshots; Basketball Pix, Rolls, and Rhythms*. New York: Dutton.

Smith, Charles R. Jr. 2001. *Short Takes: Fast-Break Basketball Poetry*. New York: Dutton.

Smith, Charles R. Jr. 2003. *Hoop Queens*. Somerville, MA: Candlewick.

Smith, Charles R. Jr. 2004. *Hoop Kings*. Somerville, MA: Candlewick.

About middle school angst

Holbrook, Sara. 1996. *Am I Naturally This Crazy?* Honesdale, PA: Boyds Mills Press.

Holbrook, Sara. 1996. *I Never Said I Wasn't Difficult.* Honesdale, PA: Boyds Mills Press.

Holbrook, Sara. 1996. *The Dog Ate My Homework.* Honesdale, PA: Boyds Mills Press.

Holbrook, Sara. 1996. *Which Way to the Dragon! Poems for the Coming-on-strong.* Honesdale, PA: Boyds Mills Press.

Free verse poem collections
Worth, Valerie. 1972. *Small Poems.* New York: Farrar, Straus & Giroux.
Worth, Valerie. 1976. *More Small Poems.* New York: Farrar, Straus & Giroux.
Worth, Valerie. 1978. *Still More Small Poems.* New York: Farrar, Straus & Giroux.
Worth, Valerie. 1985. *Small Poems Again.* New York: Farrar, Straus & Giroux.
Worth, Valerie. 1994. *All the Small Poems and Fourteen More.* New York: Farrar,

Poetic memoirs
Stevenson, James. 1995. *Sweet Corn: Poems.* New York: Greenwillow.
Stevenson, James. 1998. *Popcorn: Poems.* New York: Greenwillow.
Stevenson, James. 2002. *Corn-Fed: Poems.* New York: Greenwillow.
Stevenson, James. 2003. *Corn Chowder: Poems.* New York: Greenwillow.

Biographical poetry
Bernier-Grand, Carmen T. 2006. *César; ¡Sí, Se Puede! Yes, We can!* New York: Marshall Cavendish.
Bernier-Grand, Carmen T. 2007. *Frida: ¡Viva la vida! Long Live Life!* New York: Marshall Cavendish.
Bernier-Grand, Carmen T. 2009. *Diego; Bigger Than Life.* Ill. by David Diaz. New York: Marshall Cavendish.

FOR YOUNG ADULTS (ages 13 and up)
Global poetry
Nye, Naomi Shihab. Ed. 1992. *This Same Sky: A Collection of Poems from Around the World.* New York: Four Winds Press.
Nye, Naomi Shihab. Ed. 1995. *The Tree is Older than You Are: A Bilingual Gathering of Poems and Stories from Mexico with Paintings by Mexican Artists.* New York: Simon & Schuster.
Nye, Naomi Shihab. Ed. 1998. *The Space Between Our Footsteps: Poems and Paintings From the Middle East.* New York: Simon & Schuster.

African American History
Nelson, Marilyn. 2001. *Carver: A Life in Poems.* Asheville, NC: Front Street.
Nelson, Marilyn. 2004. *Fortune's Bones: The Manumission Requiem.* Asheville, NC: Front Street.
Nelson, Marilyn. 2005. *A Wreath for Emmett Till.* Boston: Houghton Mifflin.
Nelson, Marilyn. 2008. *The Freedom Business.* Asheville, NC: Front Street.

Poetry paradoxes
Vecchione, Patrice. Ed. 2001. *Truth and Lies.* New York: Henry Holt.
Vecchione, Patrice. Ed. 2004. *Revenge and Forgiveness.* New York: Henry Holt.

Vecchione, Patrice. Ed. 2007. *Faith and Doubt*. New York: Henry Holt.

Poetry anthologies
Rosenberg, Liz. Ed. 1996. *The Invisible Ladder*. New York: Henry Holt.
Rosenberg, Liz. Ed. 1998. *Earth-shattering Poems*. New York: Henry Holt.
Rosenberg, Liz. Ed. 2000. *Light-gathering Poems*. New York: Henry Holt.
Rosenberg, Liz. Ed. 2001. *Roots & Flowers' Poets and Poems on Family*. New York: Henry Holt.

Poetry, people & history
Philip, Neil. Ed. 1995. *Singing America*. New York: Viking.
Philip, Neil. Ed. 1996. *Earth Always Endures: Native American Poems*. New York: Viking.
Philip, Neil. Ed. 1998. *War and the Pity of War*. New York: Clarion.
Philip, Neil. Ed. 2000. *It's a Woman's World: A Century of Women's Voices in Poetry*. New York: Dutton.

Poetry by teens
Franco, Betsy. Ed. 2001. *Things I Have to Tell You: Poems And Writing by Teenage Girls*. Somerville, MA: Candlewick.
Franco, Betsy. Ed. 2001. *You Hear Me? Poems and Writing by Teenage Boys*. Somerville, MA: Candlewick.
Franco, Betsy. 2008. Ed. *Falling Hard: 100 Love Poems by Teenagers*. Somerville, MA: Candlewick.

Novel in verse trilogies
Wolff, Virginia Euwer. 1993. *Make Lemonade*. New York: Scholastic.
Wolff, Virginia Euwer. 2001. *True Believer*. New York: Atheneum.
Wolff, Virginia Euwer. 2009. *This Full House*. New York: Harper Teen/The Bowen Press.

Popular Poetry Web Sites for Young People

As we look for new places for poetry to pop up, you can be sure that includes the Internet. Many web sites make available actual poems, often including audio recordings of the poems and/or biographical information about poets, too. Some include teaching activities and even welcome child participation. Each site also offers links to additional poetry resources on the web. Here is a select list of sites that are particularly helpful in sharing poetry with young people.

Poetry Foundation
http://www.poetryfoundation.org/children/

Poetry Out Loud
http://www.poetryoutloud.org/

The Academy of American Poets
http://www.poets.org

Poet's Corner
http://www.theotherpages.org/poems/

Poetry 180
http://www.loc.gov/poetry/180/

Poetry Daily
http://www.poems.com/

The Library of Congress Poetry and Literature Center
http://www.loc.gov/poetry/

Favorite Poem Project
http://www.favoritepoem.org/

Magnetic Poetry
http://www.magneticpoetry.com/

Semantic Rhyming Dictionary
http://www.rhymezone.com/

Columbia Granger's World of Poetry
http://www.columbiagrangers.org/

How to Read a Poem
http://www.shmoop.com/poetry/how-to-read-poem/how-to-read.html

Poetry Slams, Inc.
http://www.poetryslam.com

Poetry Speaks
https://www.poetryspeaks.com/

PoetryMagazine
http://www.poetrymagazine.com/

Poets and Writers
http://www.pw.org/

Voice Thread
http://voicethread.com/

LibriVox
http://librivox.org/

It's a Small World: International Nursery Rhymes
http://itsasmallworld.co.nz/index.php

Giggle Poetry
http://www.gigglepoetry.com/

Teen Ink magazine
http://www.teenink.com/

Poetry Hill Poetry
http://www.potatohill.com

Poetry Alive
http://poetryalive.com/

Poetry Tag Time
http://poetrytagtime.com

No Water River
http://www.nowaterriver.com/

Blogs About Poetry for Young People

There are a surprising number of blogs that feature poetry for young people on a regular basis. Blogs offer another resource for timely, chatty, and varied information. Several are written by poets themselves. Many more participate in the regular "Poetry Friday" celebration posting a poem or poetry-related items on Fridays. Here are some of the best, most consistent blogs featuring poetry for children and young adults.

Poetry for Children by Sylvia Vardell
http://www.poetryforchildren.blogspot.com

Chicken Spaghetti by Susan Thomsen
http://www.chickenspaghetti.typepad.com

Wild Rose Reader by Elaine Magliaro
http://wildrosereader.blogspot.com/

The Miss Rumphius Effect by Tricia Stohr-Hunt
http://missrumphiuseffect.blogspot.com/

The Poem Farm by Amy Ludwig VanDerwater
http://poemfarm.blogspot.com/

Wordswimmer by Bruce Black
http://wordswimmer.blogspot.com/

Writing the World for Kids by Laura Purdie Salas
http://laurasalas.livejournal.com/

Writing and Ruminating by Kelly Fineman
http://kellyrfineman.livejournal.com/

GottaBook by Greg Pincus
http://gottabook.blogspot.com/

Liz in Ink by Liz Garton Scanlon
http://liz-scanlon.livejournal.com/

Read Write Believe by Sara Lewis Holmes
http://www.saralewisholmes.blogspot.com/

A Wrung Sponge by Andromeda Jazmon
http://awrungsponge.blogspot.com/

Seven Impossible Things Before Breakfast by Eisha Prather
http://blaine.org/sevenimpossiblethings/

Author Amok by Laura Shovan
http://authoramok.blogspot.com/

Karen Edmisten's blog
http://karenedmisten.blogspot.com/

A Year of Reading by Franki Sibberson and Mary Lee Hahn
http://readingyear.blogspot.com/

Alphabet Soup by Jama Rattigan
http://jamarattigan.livejournal.com

David L. Harrison's blog
http://davidlharrison.wordpress.com/

Father Goose by Charles Ghigna
http://charlesghigna.blogspot.com

Bookjoy by Pat Mora
http://sharebookjoy.blogspot.com/

Florian Café by Douglas Florian
http://floriancafe.blogspot.com/

Polkabats by Calef Brown
http://polkabats.blogspot.com/

Jill Corcoran Books by Jill Corcoran
http://jillcorcoran.blogspot.com/

The Drift Record by Julie Larios
http://julielarios.blogspot.com/

Nikki Sounds Off by Nikki Grimes
http://www.nikkigrimes.com/blog/

Poetry at Play; Poetry Advocates for Children and YA
http://poetryatplay.org/

Lee Bennett Hopkins Poetry Award Teaching Toolbox
http://leebennetthopkinsaward.blogspot.com/

Guidelines for Evaluating Poetry Books for Young People

How do we evaluate poetry? Clearly poetry is different from prose in its form and structure. But poetry has poetic elements that give it distinctiveness: rhythm, sound, language, imagery, and emotion. As you read poems, you can probably say whether you like them or not. Saying WHY you like them can be more challenging.

To begin:
Begin by identifying and describing the poetry.
*What is it? Humorous? Abstract? Familiar? Fresh?
*How does it work? Through rhyming? Free verse? Shape?
*Is the use of language distinctive? Which words stick with you?
*Can you visualize the image or feel the experience? Why?

Overall
Then consider the book as a whole. Use the following guidelines based on questions developed by Goforth (1998) which provide assistance in evaluating individual poetry books.
*Are the poems appropriate for young people?
*Is there a balance and variety of poems?
*Is the book well organized and designed?
*Do the illustrations complement or overpower the poems?
*Does the book make you want to read more poems by this poet (or anthologist)?

Language
Determine the quality of the poetry by considering questions such as:
*Does the poetry have the potential to evoke sensory images?
*Does the poetry have a cadence, a beat, a definite rhythm?
*If the poetry is written in a rhyming format, are the rhymes natural?
*Are the sounds of the poetry appealing?
*Does the poet use language in unique, impressive ways to succinctly present ideas, descriptions, and emotions?
*Does the poet present fresh, imaginative ideas and feeling?

Organization
Consider the overall organization of a book by asking questions such as:
*Which poets are represented? Are they generally familiar or unfamiliar to young readers?
*How current are the poem selections? Does that make a difference?
*How are the poems grouped or organized? Is the overall length of the collection appropriate? Of each section?
*Is there evidence of different styles and modes of expression across the collection?
*Do the poems stimulate a variety of thoughts and emotions?
*Is background information on the poets or poems provided?
*Is there a table of contents? Subject index? First line index? Are they helpful?

Layout

Review the layout of the book by considering questions such as:
*Are the poems arranged according to a particular theme?
*Are appropriate illustrations or visuals used to enhance and supplement the poetry?
*Are the poems and illustrations arranged in a suitable visual design?
*Is there a distinctive use of spacing, line breaks and poem formatting?

Appeal

In matching poems and children appropriately, these questions might also help:
*Does the poet use poetic types and forms that are naturally appealing to young people and retain their attention?
*Are familiar childhood experiences or interesting topics presented in the poem?
*Does the poem extend and enrich a person's insight or knowledge?
*Will the poem's language be understood by the audience, yet expand their linguistic abilities?
*Does the poem stimulate the emotions and imagination of the intended audience?

Based on: Goforth, F.S. 1998. *Literature and the Learner.* Belmont, CA: Wadsworth.

Timeline of the History of Children's Poetry

As we seek to share poetry with children, it can be interesting to revisit the roots of the genre and appreciate the milestones from the last 200 years of creating poetry for young people. The following timeline focuses on poetry publishing in English; obviously the oral tradition and the global perspective offers even more examples of poetry for young people.

c1765
John Newbery published a collection of English rhymes, *Mother Goose's Melody, or, Sonnets for the Cradle* in London.

1789
Songs of Innocence, an illustrated collection of 19 poems by William Blake followed by *Songs of Experience* (26 poems) published in 1794, including the well-known poem, "The Tyger"

1804
Original Poems for Infant Minds by Ann and Jane Taylor was first issued in two volumes and includes the classic, "Twinkle, Twinkle, Little Star."

1823
"A Visit from St. Nicholas" also known as "The Night Before Christmas" first published anonymously and generally attributed to Clement Clark Moore and widely considered the best-known American poem.

1846
Edward Lear published *A Book of Nonsense*, a volume of limericks followed by the compilation, *Nonsense Songs, Stories, Botany and Alphabets* (1870) which included "The Owl and the Pussycat."

1872
"Jabberwocky" by Lewis Carroll featured as part of his novel *Through the Looking-Glass and What Alice Found There*

Also in 1872, Christina Rossetti published *Sing-Song; A Nursery Rhyme Book* which includes the poems "Hurt No Living Thing" and "Who Has Seen the Wind?" among others.

1885
A Child's Garden of Verses by Robert Louis Stevenson is published, first under the title, *Penny Whistles* and includes "The Swing" and "My Shadow," among others.

1910
Rudyard Kipling published the poem "If" considered the "UK's favorite poem" in *Rewards and Fairies.*

1924
A.A. Milne published *When We Were Very Young* illustrated by E. H. Shepard, followed by *Now We Are Six* (1927).

1932
Langston Hughes published *The Dream Keeper and Other Poems*, his only collection of poetry specifically for young people.

1951
Iona and Peter Opie, a husband-and-wife team of folklorists applied modern technique to the analysis of children's literature culminating in *The Oxford Dictionary of Nursery Rhymes* (1951) and *The Lore and Language of Schoolchildren* (1959).

1956
Gwendolyn Brooks published *Bronzeville Boys and Girls*, a groundbreaking work of poetry about children growing up in an urban neighborhood.

1959
Louis Untermeyer compiled and published the landmark comprehensive anthology for children, *The Golden Treasury of Poetry* with Golden Press.

1966
Stephen Dunning, Edward Luders, and Hugh Smith published a milestone anthology of contemporary poetry for young people, *Reflections on a Gift of Watermelon Pickle.*

1968
Arnold Adoff gathered and published several anthologies of important African American poetry for young people beginning with *I am the Darker Brother: An Anthology of Modern Poems by Negro Americans (1968),* as well as his own poetry and goes on to receive the National Council of Teachers of English Award for Excellence in Poetry for Children in 1988.

1971
Two pioneering works by poets of color appeared: Nikki Giovanni's *Spin a Soft Black Song* and Hettie Jones's anthology, *The Tree Stands Shining: Poetry of the North American Indian.*

1972
Poet and anthologist Lee Bennett Hopkins published *Pass the Poetry, Please!,* the first major work on sharing poetry with children followed by Kenneth Koch's *Rose, Where Did You Get That Red? Teaching Great Poetry to Children* (1973).

1974
Shel Silverstein published his first of several irreverent works, *Where the Sidewalk Ends;* what would become the bestselling children's poetry book ever.

>Scholar Ann Terry conducted a touchstone study of the poetry preferences of elementary school students finding a predilection for rhyme, narrative, and humor.

1977
National Council of Teachers of English established the first award for poetry for young people with the NCTE Award for Excellence in Poetry for Children to honor a living American poet for his or her lifetime achievement in works for children ages 3–13. It was awarded to David McCord (*Far and Few: Rhymes of the Never Was and Always Is*, 1952) creator of "The Pickety Fence" and many other beloved poems.
>English teacher, poet, and anthologist Paul B. Janeczko published his first anthology of poems for young readers with *The Crystal Image*, with many more to follow (e.g., *A Kick in the Head*, 2005).

1978
Aileen Fisher, nature poet (*I Heard a Bluebird Sing: Children Select Their Favorite Poems by Aileen Fisher*, 2002), received the National Council of Teachers of English Award for Excellence in Poetry for Children.

1979
Karla Kuskin author of *Dogs and Dragons, Trees and Dreams* (1980) and *Moon, Have You Met My Mother?* received the National Council of Teachers of English Award for Excellence in Poetry for Children (and designed the medallion for this award).

1980
Myra Cohn Livingston, poet, anthologist, and poetry scholar and mentor, received the National Council of Teachers of English Award for Excellence in Poetry for Children.

1981
Eve Merriam (*There is no Rhyme for Silver,* 1962) received the National Council of Teachers of English Award for Excellence in Poetry for Children.
>Nancy Willard's *A Visit to William Blake's Inn: Poems for Innocent and Experienced Travelers* was the first work of poetry for children to receive the Newbery medal from the American Library Association.

1982
John Ciardi received the National Council of Teachers of English Award for Excellence in Poetry for Children and was the creator of one of the most beloved contemporary children's poems, "Mummy Slept Late and Daddy Fixed Breakfast."
>Mel Glenn published the groundbreaking young adult poetry book featuring multiple voices, *Class Dismissed! High School Poems*.

1983
Jack Prelutsky, himself a notable poet, published one of the most popular and bestselling contemporary anthologies, *The Random House Book of*

Poetry for Children followed by many extremely popular books of his own poetry beginning with *The New Kid on the Block* (1984).

1985
Lilian Moore (*Mural on Second Avenue, and Other City Poems,* 2004) received the National Council of Teachers of English Award for Excellence in Poetry for Children.

1987
Poet and author Georgia Heard published her seminal work about the teaching of poetry with young people, *For the Good of the Earth and Sun: Teaching Poetry.*

1988
Paul Fleishman's unique poetry book for two voices, *Joyful Noise,* received the Newbery medal.

1990
Gary Soto published *A Fire in My Hands*, the first major Latino poetry collection for teens.

1991
Valerie Worth, author of the "Small Poems" collections of free verse, received the National Council of Teachers of English Award for Excellence in Poetry for Children.

1992
More significant collections of poetry by poets of color in the U.S. and beyond were published including: Michio Mado's *The Animals: Selected Poems* from Japan, Joseph Bruchac's *Thirteen Moons on Turtle's Back,* a milestone work of Native American poetry for children, and Naomi Shihab Nye's *This Same Sky: A Collection of Poems from Around the World*, the first of several compilations of world poetry for young people.

1993
Lee Bennett Hopkins established the Lee Bennett Hopkins Poetry Award (in association with Pennsylvania State University) for an American poet or anthologist for the most outstanding new book of children's poetry, The first recipient was Ashley Bryan for *Sing to the Sun.*
>Several new poets published their first works for young people including Douglas Florian with *Monster Motel,* Walter Dean Myers's (already an established author of fiction and nonfiction) with *Brown Angels: An Album of Pictures and Verse*, and Joyce Carol Thomas and *Brown Honey in Broomwheat Tea.*

1994
Barbara Esbensen received the National Council of Teachers of English Award for Excellence in Poetry for Children.
>The first mainstream Asian American poet for young people, Janet S. Wong published *Good Luck Gold and Other Poems.*

1995
Lee Bennett Hopkins established the Promising Poet award in collaboration with the International Reading Association to encourage new poets in their writing beginning with Deborah Chandra (*Rich Lizard and Other Poems*, 1993).

1996
The first mainstream Latina poet for young people, Pat Mora, published *Confetti: Poems for Children.*
>Professor and scholar Bernice Cullinan compiled and published the first collection of poetry by NCTE Poetry Award recipients and voted on by children in *A Jar of Tiny Stars: Poems by NCTE Award-winning Poets*.

1997
Eloise Greenfield, author of *Honey, I Love* (1978), *Nathaniel Talking* (1988), and *Night on Neighborhood Street* (1991) and others, received the National Council of Teachers of English Award for Excellence in Poetry for Children.
>A landmark collection of bilingual poetry in Spanish and English was published, Francisco Alarcón's *Laughing Tomatoes and Other Spring Poems/Jitomates Risuenos y Otros Poemas de Primavera.*
>Karen Hesse's novel in verse, *Out of the Dust* was awarded the Newbery medal.

1998
Bank Street College established the Claudia Lewis Poetry Award for the best poetry book of the year in honor of the late Claudia Lewis, a distinguished children's book expert and longtime member of the Bank Street College faculty. The first recipient was *The Invisible Ladder; An Anthology of Contemporary American Poems for Young Readers* compiled by Liz Rosenberg.

1999
Poet Donald Hall compiled and published the comprehensive *The Oxford Illustrated Book of American Children's Poems*.

2000
X. J. Kennedy (creator of the landmark work with wife Dorothy Kennedy, *Knock at a Star: A Child's Introduction to Poetry*, 1982) received the National Council of Teachers of English Award for Excellence in Poetry for Children.

2003
Mary Ann Hoberman (*The Llama Who Had No Pajama: 100 Favorite Poems*; *You Read to Me, I'll Read to You* series) was awarded the National Council of Teachers of English Award for Excellence in Poetry for Children.
>*Keesha's House,* a novel in verse for teens by Helen Frost wins an honor distinction for the Michael L. Printz Award for Young Adult Literature.

2004
ALSC began featuring the Poetry Blast with poets reading from their works at the annual conference of the American Library Association.

2005
Elise Paschen and Dominque Raccah compile and publish the anthology, *Poetry Speaks to Children,* which included a CD (compact disc) of many of the poets included in the book reading their poems aloud.

2006
The Children's Poet Laureate was established by the Poetry Foundation to raise awareness of the fact that children have a natural receptivity to poetry and are its most appreciative audience, especially when poems are written specifically for them. The first Children's Poet Laureate was Jack Prelutsky.
>Nikki Grimes, creator of the "Danitra Brown" books and *Bronx Masquerade,* among others, received the National Council of Teachers of English Award for Excellence in Poetry for Children.
>The audiobook adaptation of *Jazz* by Walter Dean Myers created by Live Oak Media won the first ever Odyssey Award for audiobooks given by the American Library Association.
>The National Council of Teachers of English initiated the annual "Poetry Notables for Children" list.

2007
Laura Amy Schlitz received the Newbery medal for *Good Masters! Sweet Ladies!: Voices from a Medieval Village,* a work of poetry in multiple voices.

2008
Mary Ann Hoberman was selected as the second Children's Poet Laureate.

2009
Lee Bennett Hopkins, poet and creator of more than 200 poetry books and anthologies, received the National Council of Teachers of English Award for Excellence in Poetry for Children.

2011
J. Patrick Lewis (first poetry book: *A Hippopotamusn't and Other Animal Verse,* 1990) was selected as Children's Poet Laureate and also received the National Council of Teachers of English Award for Excellence in Poetry for Children.

The first digital anthologies of original poetry for young people were published in e-book (only) form: the Poetry Tag Time series compiled by Sylvia Vardell and Janet Wong (*PoetryTagTime, P*TAG, Gift Tag*).

The Opie Collection: The Works of Peter and Iona Opie

Peter and Iona Opie were a husband and wife team who had extensive careers as folklorists and authors, known for establishing a world class collection of some 20,000 works written or published for children ranging from the 16th to the 20th century (mainly British) as a private research resource. The Opie Collection has been microfiche formatted by University Microfiche International and subsequently distributed by them. Several individual items are also available in book form as listed below.

By Iona Opie

Opie, Iona, ed. 1954. *Ditties for the Nursery*. London: Oxford University Press.

Opie, Iona and Moira Tatem, ed. 1989. *A Diary of Superstitions*. London: Oxford University Press.

Opie, Iona, Robert Opie, and Brian Alderson. 1989. *The Treasures of Childhood: Books, Toys, and Games from the Opie Collection*. New York: Little, Brown.

Opie, Iona. 1993. *The People in the Playground*. New York: Oxford University.

Opie, Iona, ed. 1996. *My Very First Mother Goose*. Cambridge, MA: Candlewick.

Opie, Iona, ed. 1997. *Humpty Dumpty and Other Rhymes*. Cambridge, MA: Candlewick.

Opie, Iona, ed. 1997. *Little Boy Blue and Other Rhymes*. Cambridge, MA: Candlewick.

Opie, Iona, ed. 1997. *Pussycat Pussycat and Other Rhymes*. Candlewick.

Opie, Iona, ed. 1997. *Wee Willie Winkie and Other Rhymes*. Candlewick.

Opie, Iona, ed. 1999. *Here Comes Mother Goose*. Cambridge, MA: Candlewick.

Collaborative Work of Iona and Peter Opie:

Opie, Peter and Iona Opie, ed. 1947. *I saw Esau*. London: Williams and Norgate.

Opie, Peter and Iona Opie, ed. 1951. *The Oxford dictionary of nursery rhymes*. New York: Oxford University Press.

Opie, Peter and Iona Opie, ed. 1955. *The Oxford nursery rhyme* book. New York: Oxford University Press.

Opie, Peter and Iona Opie. 1959. *The lore and language of schoolchildren*. New York: Oxford University Press.

Opie, Peter and Iona Opie, ed. 1963. *The Puffin Book of Nursery Rhymes*. Baltimore, MD: Penguin Books.

Opie, Peter and Iona Opie, ed. 1964. *A Family Book of Nursery Rhymes*. New York: Oxford University Press.

Opie, Peter and Iona Opie. 1969. *Children's Games in Street and Playground: Chasing, Catching, Seeking, Hunting, Racing, Dueling, Exerting, Daring, Guessing, Acting, Pretending*. Oxford: Clarendon Publishing.

Opie, Peter and Iona Opie, ed. 1973. *The Oxford Book of Children's Verse.* New York: Oxford University Press.

Opie, Peter and Iona Opie, ed. 1973. *Three Centuries of Nursery Rhymes and Poetry for Children.* London: Oxford University Press.

Opie, Peter and Iona Opie, ed. 1980. *A Nursery Companion.* Oxford University Press.

Opie, Peter and Iona Opie, ed. 1983. *The Oxford Book of Narrative Verse.* New York: Oxford University Press.

Opie, Peter and Iona Opie. 1985. *The Singing Game.* Oxford University Press.

Opie, Peter and Iona Opie. 1988. *Tail Feathers of Mother Goose: The Opie Rhyme Book.* Boston: Little, Brown.

Opie, Peter and Iona Opie. 1989. *The Treasures of Childhood: Books, Toys, and Games from the Opie Collection.* New York: Arcade.

Professional Resource Books about Poetry for Young People

These professional reference sources will provide additional background you'll find helpful in selecting and sharing poetry with young people, including guiding them through the poetry writing process.

Ada, Alma Flor; Harris, Violet, and Hopkins, Lee Bennett. 1993. *A Chorus of Cultures; Developing Literacy through Multicultural Poetry*. Carmel, CA: Hampton-Brown Books.

Ambrosini, Michelle and Morretta, Teresa. 2003. *Poetry Workshop for Middle School; Activities That Inspire Meaningful Language Learning*. Newark, DE: International Reading Association.

Barton, Bob and David Booth. 2004. *Poetry Goes to School: From Mother Goose to Shel Silverstein*. Markham, Ontario, CA: Pembroke Publishers.

Bauer, Caroline Feller. 1995. *The Poetry Break: An Annotated Anthology with Ideas for Introducing Children to Poetry*. New York: H W Wilson.

Booth, David and Moore, Bill. 2003. *Poems Please! Sharing Poetry with Children*. 2nd edition. Markham, Ontario, CA: Pembroke Publishers.

Burkhardt, Ross. M. 2006. *Using Poetry in the Classroom: Engaging Students in Learning*. Lanham, MD: Rowman & Littlefield Education.

Chatton, Barbara. 2010. *Using Poetry Across the Curriculum* (second edition). Santa Barbara, CA: ABC-CLIO.

Collom, Jack and Noethe, Sheryl. 2005. *Poetry Everywhere; Teaching Poetry Writing in School and in the Community*. New York: Teachers & Writers Collaborative.

Cullinan, Bernice E. Cullinan; Scala, Marilyn C., and Schroder, Virginia C. 1995. *Three Voices: An Invitation to Poetry Across the Curriculum*. York, ME: Stenhouse.

Durica, Karen Morrow. 2007. *How We "Do" School; Poems to Encourage Teacher Reflection*. Newark, DE: International Reading Association.

Fisher, Maisha T. 2007. *Writing in Rhythm: Spoken Word Poetry in Urban Classrooms*. New York: Teachers College Press.

Fitch, Sheree and Swartz, Larry. 2008. *The Poetry Experience; Choosing and Using Poetry in the Classroom*. Markham, Canada: Pembroke.

Franco, Betsy. 2005. *Conversations With a Poet: Inviting Poetry into K-12 Classrooms*. Richard C. Owen.

Glover, M. K. 1999. *A Garden of Poets*. Urbana, IL: National Council of Teachers of English.

Hanauer, David Ian. 2004. *Poetry and the Meaning of Life; Reading and Writing Poetry in Language Arts Classrooms*. Toronto, Canada: Pippin.

Hatcher, Margaret, Ed. 2002. *Bearing Witness: Poetry by Teachers about Teaching*. Tucson, AZ: Zephyr Press.

Heard, Georgia. 1994. *For the Good of the Earth and Sun; Teaching Poetry*. Portsmouth, NH: Heinemann.

Heard, Georgia. 1999. *Awakening the Heart: Exploring Poetry in Elementary and Middle School*. Portsmouth, NH: Heinemann.

Heitman, Jane. 2003. *Rhymes and Reasons; Librarians and Teachers Using Poetry to Foster Literacy, Grades K-6*.

Holbrook, Sara. 2002. *Wham! It's a Poetry Jam; Discovering Performance Poetry*. Honesdale, PA: Wordsong/Boyds Mills Press.

Holbrook, Sara. 2005. *Practical Poetry; A Nonstandard Approach to Meeting Content-Area Standards*. Portsmouth, NH: Heinemann.

Holbrook, Sara and Salinger, Michael. 2006. *Outspoken: How to Improve Writing and Speaking Through Poetry Performance*. Portsmouth, NH: Heinemann.

Hopkins, L. B. 1972/1986. *Pass the Poetry Please.* 3rd edition. New York: HarperCollins.

Hopkins, Lee Bennett. 1995. *Pauses; Autobiographical Reflections of 101 Creators of Children's Books*. New York: HarperCollins.

Intrator, Sam M. and Scribner, Megan, Eds. 2003. *Teaching With Fire: Poetry That Sustains the Courage to Teach*. San Francisco, CA: Jossey-Bass.

Israel, Susan E. ed. 2006. *Poetic Possibilities; Using Poetry to Enhance Literacy Learning*. Newark, DE: International Reading Association.

Janeczko, Paul B. 2011. *Reading Poetry in the Middle Grades: 20 Poems and Activities that Meet the Common Core Standards and Cultivate a Passion for Poetry*. Portsmouth, NH: Heinemann.

Kennedy, X. J. and Kennedy, D. (revised) 1999. *Knock at a Star*. New York: Little Brown.

Koch, Kenneth. 1973. *Rose, Where Did You Get That Red? Teaching Great Poetry to Children.* New York: Random House.

Koch, Kenneth. 1970. *Wishes, Lies, and Dreams; Teaching Children to Write Poetry.* New York: Chelsea House.

Lipson, S. L. 2006. *Writing Success through Poetry: Create a Writers' Workshop*. Prufrock Press.

Livingston, Myra Cohn. 1991. *Poem-making: Ways to Begin Writing Poetry*. HarperCollins, New York.

Livingston, Myra Cohn. 1984. *The Child as Poet: Myth or Reality?* Boston: Horn Book.

Livingston, Myra Cohn. 1990. *Climb into the Bell Tower: Essays on Poetry*. New York: HarperCollins.

McElmeel, Sharron. 1993. *The Poet Tree*. Englewood, CO: Teacher Ideas Press.

McClure, Amy. 1990. *Sunrises and Songs; Reading and Writing Poetry in the Elementary Classroom*. Portsmouth, NH: Heinemann.

Mora, Pat. 2010. *Zing! Seven Creativity Practices for Educators and Students.* Corwin.

Morice, Dace. 2002. *Poetry Comics; An Animated Anthology*. New York: Teachers & Writers Collaborative.

Morice, Dave. 2007. *The Adventures of Dr. Alphabet: 104 Ways to Write Poetry*. New York: Teachers and Writers Collaborative.

O'Connor, John S. 2004. *Wordplaygrounds; Reading, Writing, and Performing Poetry in the English Classroom*. Urbana, IL: National Council of Teachers of English.

Opitz, Michael F. 2000. *Rhymes and Reasons; Literature & Language Play for Phonological Awareness*. Portsmouth, NH: Heinemann.

Partington, Richie. 2009. *I Second that Emotion: Sharing Children's and Young Adult Poetry: A 21st Century Guide for Teachers and Librarians*. Hi Willow Research & Pub.

Perry, Aaren Yeatts. 1997. *Poetry Across the Curriculum; An Action Guide for Elementary Teachers*. Boston: Allyn & Bacon.

Ruurs, Margriet. 2001. *The Power of Poems; Teaching the Joy of Writing Poetry*. Gainesville, FL: Maupin House.

Sloan, Glenna. 2003. *Give Them Poetry; A Guide for Sharing Poetry with Children K-8*. New York: Teachers College Press.

Stanley, Nile. 2004. *Creating Readers with Poetry*. Gainesville, FL: Maupin House.

Statman, Mark. 2000. *Listener In The Snow: The Practice And Teaching Of Poetry*. New York: Teachers & Writers Collaborative.

Thomas, Joseph T., Jr. 2007. *Poetry's Playground: The Culture of Contemporary American Children's Poetry*. Detroit, MI: Wayne State University Press.

Tiedt, Iris McClellan. 2002. *Tiger Lilies, Toadstools, And Thunderbolts: Engaging K-8 Students With Poetry*. Newark, DE: International Reading Association.

Treviño, Rose Z. 2009. *Read Me a Rhyme in Spanish and English*. Chicago, IL: American Library Association.

Vardell, Sylvia M. 2006. *Poetry Aloud Here: Sharing Poetry with Children in the Library*. Chicago, IL: American Library Association.

Vardell, Sylvia M. 2007. *Poetry People; A Practical Guide to Children's Poets*. Englewood, CO: Libraries Unlimited.

Wood, Jaime R. 2007. *Living Voices: Multicultural Poetry in the Middle School Classroom*. Urbana, IL: National Council of Teachers of English.

About the Author

Sylvia M. Vardell is Professor in the School of Library and Information Studies at Texas Woman's University and has taught graduate courses in children's and young adult literature at various universities since 1981. Vardell has published extensively, including ten books on literature for children, as well as over 20 book chapters and 75 journal articles. Her current work focuses on poetry for children, including her collaborations with poet Janet Wong, *The Poetry Friday Anthologies* (for K-5 and grades 6-8). She maintains a regular blog, *PoetryforChildren* since 2006. She is also the author of *Poetry Aloud Here*, with a second edition in 2012, as well as *Poetry People, A Practical Guide to Children's Poets* and *Children's Literature in Action*. She is also the regular "Everyday Poetry" columnist for ALA's *Book Links* magazine.

Vardell has served on several national award committees including the NCTE Award for Poetry, the NCTE Notables committee, the Cybils Poetry Award committee, the ALA Odyssey Award for audiobooks, the ALA Sibert Award for informational literature, and the NCTE Orbis Pictus Award for nonfiction, among others. She has conducted over 100 presentations at state, regional, national, and international conferences, and has received grants from the Young Adult Library Service Association, Ezra Jack Keats Foundation, NCTE, the ALAN Foundation, the Texas Library Association, and the National Endowment for the Humanities. She taught at the University of Zimbabwe in Africa as a Fulbright scholar in 1989.

Other books by Sylvia Vardell
Poetry Aloud Here (Second edition, in press, 2012)
Children's Literature in Action: A Librarian's Guide (2008)
Poetry People: A Practical Guide to Children's Poets (2007)
Literature-based Instruction with English Language Learners (2002)
    (with Nancy Hadaway and Terrell Young)

Poetry anthologies edited and compiled with Janet Wong
The Poetry Friday Anthology (K-5) (2012)
The Poetry Friday Anthology (6-8) (2013)

Blog about poetry teaching
    http://PoetryforChildren.blogspot.com

E-books of poetry for young readers
PoetryTagTime: 30 Poems by 30 Poets (2011) (Edited with Janet Wong)
*P*TAG: Poetry for Teens* (2011) (Edited with Janet Wong)
Gift Tag: Holiday Poems for Young People (2011) (Edited with Janet Wong)

The Poetry Teacher's Book of Lists Blog
Remember to check out the supplemental blog for this book for suggestions, recommendations, and updates: PoetryTeachersBookofLists.blogspot.com

Made in the USA
San Bernardino, CA
16 March 2013